International Technica

MW01252282

SOA Solutions Using IBM Information Server

July 2007

SG24-7402-00

Note: Before using this information and the product it supports, read the information in "Notices" on page xxi.

First Edition (July 2007)

This edition applies to Version 8, Release 0 of IBM Information Server (product number 5724-Q36).

Contents

Figures

Examples

Notices

This information was developed for products and services offered in the U.S.A.

IBM may not offer the products, services, or features discussed in this document in other countries. Consult your local IBM representative for information on the products and services currently available in your area. Any reference to an IBM product, program, or service is not intended to state or imply that only that IBM product, program, or service may be used. Any functionally equivalent product, program, or service that does not infringe any IBM intellectual property right may be used instead. However, it is the user's responsibility to evaluate and verify the operation of any non-IBM product, program, or service.

IBM may have patents or pending patent applications covering subject matter described in this document. The furnishing of this document does not give you any license to these patents. You can send license inquiries, in writing, to:
IBM Director of Licensing, IBM Corporation, North Castle Drive, Armonk, NY 10504-1785 U.S.A.

The following paragraph does not apply to the United Kingdom or any other country where such provisions are inconsistent with local law: INTERNATIONAL BUSINESS MACHINES CORPORATION PROVIDES THIS PUBLICATION "AS IS" WITHOUT WARRANTY OF ANY KIND, EITHER EXPRESS OR IMPLIED, INCLUDING, BUT NOT LIMITED TO, THE IMPLIED WARRANTIES OF NON-INFRINGEMENT, MERCHANTABILITY OR FITNESS FOR A PARTICULAR PURPOSE. Some states do not allow disclaimer of express or implied warranties in certain transactions, therefore, this statement may not apply to you.

This information could include technical inaccuracies or typographical errors. Changes are periodically made to the information herein; these changes will be incorporated in new editions of the publication. IBM may make improvements and/or changes in the product(s) and/or the program(s) described in this publication at any time without notice.

Any references in this information to non-IBM Web sites are provided for convenience only and do not in any manner serve as an endorsement of those Web sites. The materials at those Web sites are not part of the materials for this IBM product and use of those Web sites is at your own risk.

IBM may use or distribute any of the information you supply in any way it believes appropriate without incurring any obligation to you.

Information concerning non-IBM products was obtained from the suppliers of those products, their published announcements or other publicly available sources. IBM has not tested those products and cannot confirm the accuracy of performance, compatibility or any other claims related to non-IBM products. Questions on the capabilities of non-IBM products should be addressed to the suppliers of those products.

This information contains examples of data and reports used in daily business operations. To illustrate them as completely as possible, the examples include the names of individuals, companies, brands, and products. All of these names are fictitious and any similarity to the names and addresses used by an actual business enterprise is entirely coincidental.

COPYRIGHT LICENSE:

This information contains sample application programs in source language, which illustrate programming techniques on various operating platforms. You may copy, modify, and distribute these sample programs in any form without payment to IBM, for the purposes of developing, using, marketing or distributing application programs conforming to the application programming interface for the operating platform for which the sample programs are written. These examples have not been thoroughly tested under all conditions. IBM, therefore, cannot guarantee or imply reliability, serviceability, or function of these programs.

Trademarks

The following terms are trademarks of the International Business Machines Corporation in the United States, other countries, or both:

AIX®	IBM®	Redbooks®
AIX 5L™	IMS™	Redbooks (logo) ®
CICS®	MQSeries®	System p™
DB2®	MVS™	WebSphere®
DRDA®	Rational®	

The following terms are trademarks of other companies:

SAP, and SAP logos are trademarks or registered trademarks of SAP AG in Germany and in several other countries.

Oracle, JD Edwards, PeopleSoft, Siebel, and TopLink are registered trademarks of Oracle Corporation and/or its affiliates.

DataStage, are trademarks or registered trademarks of Ascential Software Corporation in the United States, other countries, or both.

EJB, Java, JDBC, JSP, J2EE, and all Java-based trademarks are trademarks of Sun Microsystems, Inc. in the United States, other countries, or both.

Active Directory, Microsoft, Visual Basic, Visual Studio, Windows Server, Windows, and the Windows logo are trademarks of Microsoft Corporation in the United States, other countries, or both.

UNIX is a registered trademark of The Open Group in the United States and other countries.

Linux is a trademark of Linus Torvalds in the United States, other countries, or both.

Other company, product, or service names may be trademarks or service marks of others.

Preface

This IBM® Redbooks® publication documents the procedures for implementing IBM Information Server and related technologies using a typical financial services business scenario.

It is aimed at IT architects, Information Management specialists, and Information Integration specialists responsible for developing IBM Information Server on a Microsoft® Windows® 2003 platform.

We offer a step-by-step approach to implementing IBM Information Server on a Microsoft Windows Server® 2003 platform accessing information stored on IBM AIX® and Microsoft Windows platforms. WebSphere® Integration Developer and WebSphere Portal Server are used in the scenario.

This book is organized as follows:

► Chapter 1, "IBM Information Server architecture" on page 1 provides a detailed description of IBM Information Server, its architecture, configuration flow, and runtime flow.

► Chapter 2, "Financial services business scenario" on page 31 describes a step-by-step approach to implementing IBM Information Server on a Windows 2003 platform using a typical financial services business scenario.

► Appendix A, "Service Oriented Architecture (SOA) overview" on page 435 provides an overview of Service Oriented Architecture for an audience of Information Management specialists.

► Appendix B, "WebSphere Integration Developer overview" on page 459 provides an overview of WebSphere Integration Developer for an audience of Information Management specialists.

► Appendix C, "Code and scripts used in the business scenario" on page 475 documents some of the code and scripts used in the development of A2Z Financial Services' self service scenario.

The team that wrote this Redbooks publication

This Redbooks publication was produced by a team of specialists from around the world working at the International Technical Support Organization, San Jose Center.

Nagraj Alur is a Project Leader with the IBM ITSO, San Jose Center. He holds a Master's degree in Computer Science from the Indian Institute of Technology (IIT), Mumbai, India. He has more than 30 years of experience in database management systems (DBMSs), and has been a programmer, systems analyst, project leader, independent consultant, and researcher. His areas of expertise include DBMSs, data warehousing, distributed systems management, database performance, information integration, and client/server and Internet computing. He has written extensively on these subjects and has taught classes and presented at conferences all around the world. Before joining the ITSO in November 2001, he was on a two-year assignment from the Software Group to the IBM Almaden Research Center, where he worked on Data Links solutions and an eSourcing prototype.

Zhebin Cong is an IT/Specialist with IBM Global Delivery Center in Dalian, Liaoning province of China. He has 13 years of experience as an electrical engineer and software engineer. He is a IBM certified AIX system administrator, SUN certified Java programmer and Microsoft certified solution developer and system administrator. His areas of expertise include J2EE and Dot Net. Since joining IBM in 2005, he has provided high-quality services to three IBM customers. One of his products has been approved to apply for an American patent by IBM Intellectual Property Law Department.

Maciej Mlynski is an IBM Certified Advanced Technical Expert - IBM System p™ and AIX 5L™. He works for ASpartner Sp. z o.o., an IBM Premier Business Partner. He holds a Master's Degree in Computer Science from the Silesian University of Technology, Gliwice, Poland. He has more than 10 years experience in information technology including banking, insurance, and telecommunication area. His areas of expertise include autonomic problem determination, continuous integration, automatic performance tuning, Java-based application servers, very large databases, and highly-loaded and mission-critical computer systems. He also holds many professional certifications including WebSphere, DB2®, and SAN. He is a frequent speaker at scientific conferences and technical events. He is presently involved in Ph.D. research. His topics of interest are dynamic resources allocation and virtual execution environments.

Sivaram Balakrishnan is a Senior Software Engineer at Object Edge Inc with more than 10 years of experience in building frameworks and distributed application systems. He specializes in software patterns, frameworks, object-oriented design, service oriented architecture, and J2EE programming. He has extensive experience with WebSphere products and has developed tooling on eclipse/RAD platforms. His current interests are SOA, Enterprise Service Bus, and open source frameworks.

Oliver Suhre is a Senior Software Engineer at the IBM development lab in Boeblingen, Germany. Since joining IBM in 2000 he has worked on a number of projects in the area of Text Analysis and Information Integration. Currently, he is working both as an architect and a developer on a project related to the integration of IBM Information Server with other products across the IBM software portfolio, such as WebSphere Process Server. His areas of expertise include Services Oriented Architectures (SOA), Information Integration, Eclipse, and Java/J2EE™-based application development. Oliver is the author of several patents and publications and holds an MSc from the University of Tübingen, Germany.

We also acknowledge the inclusion of the chapter on SOA overview from the IBM Redbooks® publication *Patterns: Service-Oriented Architecture and Web Services*, SG24-6303.

Thanks to the following people for their contributions to this project:

Aakash Bordia
Martin Breining
Dimple Bhatia
Atul Chadha
Sreejith Kurup
Robin Noble-Thomas
Lorri Paulsen
Paul Wilms
IBM Silicon Valley Laboratory, San Jose, USA

Ernie Ostic
Guenter Sauter
Ian Schmidt
Brian Tinnel
IBM USA

David McCarty
IBM France

Bernhard Jakob
IBM Germany

Yvonne Lyon
International Technical Support Organization, San Jose Center

Become a published author

Join us for a two- to six-week residency program! Help write an IBM Redbooks publication dealing with specific products or solutions, while getting hands-on experience with leading-edge technologies. You will have the opportunity to team with IBM technical professionals, Business Partners, and Clients.

Your efforts will help increase product acceptance and customer satisfaction. As a bonus, you will develop a network of contacts in IBM development labs, and increase your productivity and marketability.

Find out more about the residency program, browse the residency index, and apply online at:

`ibm.com`/redbooks/residencies.html

Comments welcome

Your comments are important to us!

We want our Redbooks to be as helpful as possible. Send us your comments about this or other Redbooks in one of the following ways:

► Use the online **Contact us** review Redbooks publication form found at:

`ibm.com`/redbooks

► Send your comments in an e-mail to:

redbooks@us.ibm.com

► Mail your comments to:

IBM Corporation, International Technical Support Organization
Dept. HYTD Mail Station P099
2455 South Road
Poughkeepsie, NY 12601-5400

IBM Information Server architecture

In this chapter we provide an overview of IBM Information Server architecture and processing flow.

The topics covered are:

► IBM Information Server architecture
► Configuration flow
► Runtime flow

1.1 Introduction

Over the years, most organizations have made significant investments in enterprise resource planning, customer relationship management, and supply chain management packages in addition to their home grown applications. This has resulted in larger amounts of data being captured about their businesses. To turn all this data into consistent, timely, and accurate information for decision-making requires an effective means of integrating information. Statutory compliance requirements such as Basel II and Sarbanes-Oxley place additional demands for consistent, complete, and trustworthy information.

IBM Information Server addresses these critical information integration requirements of consistent, complete, and trustworthy information with a comprehensive, unified foundation for enterprise information architectures, capable of scaling to meet any information volume requirement so that companies can deliver business results faster and with higher quality results for all the following initiatives:

► Business intelligence:

   IBM Information Server makes it easier to develop a unified view of the business for better decisions. It helps you understand existing data sources, cleanse, correct, and standardize information, and load analytical views that can be reused throughout the enterprise.

► Master data management:

   IBM Information Server simplifies the development of authoritative master data by showing where and how information is stored across source systems. It also consolidates disparate data into a single, reliable record, cleanses and standardizes information, removes duplicates, and links records together across systems. This master record can be loaded into operational data stores, data warehouses, or master data applications such as WebSphere Customer Center and WebSphere Product Center. The record can also be assembled, completely or partially, on demand.

► Infrastructure rationalization:

   IBM Information Server aids in reducing operating costs by showing relationships between systems and by defining migration rules to consolidate instances or move data from obsolete systems. Data cleansing and matching ensure high-quality data in the new system.

► Business transformation:

   IBM Information Server can speed development and increase business agility by providing reusable information services that can be plugged into applications, business processes, and portals. These standards-based information services are maintained centrally by information specialists but are widely accessible throughout the enterprise.

► Risk and compliance:

IBM Information Server helps improve visibility and data governance by enabling complete, authoritative views of information with proof of lineage and quality. These views can be made widely available and reusable as shared services, while the rules inherent in them are maintained centrally.

IBM Information Server combines the technologies of key information integration functions within the IBM Information Integration Solutions portfolio into a single unified platform that enables companies to understand, cleanse, transform, move, and deliver trustworthy and context-rich information as shown in Figure 1-1 on page 5.

IBM Information Server includes the following product modules:

► IBM WebSphere DataStage™:

This enables organizations to design data flows that extract information from multiple source systems, transform it in ways that make it more valuable, and then deliver it to one or more target databases or applications.

► IBM WebSphere QualityStage:

This is designed to help organizations understand and improve the overall quality of their data assets, WebSphere QualityStage provides advanced features to help investigate, repair, consolidate, and validate heterogeneous data within an integration workflow.

► IBM WebSphere Federation Server:

This enables applications to access and integrate diverse data and content sources as if they were a single resource — regardless of where the information resides — while retaining the autonomy and integrity of the heterogeneous data and content sources. This enabling technology is transparent, heterogeneous, and extensible, and provides high function and high performance.

► IBM WebSphere Information Services Director:

IBM Information Server provides a unified mechanism for publishing and managing shared Service Oriented Architecture (SOA) services across data quality, data transformation, and federation functions, allowing information specialists to easily deploy services for any information integration task and consistently manage them. This enables developers to take data integration logic built using IBM Information Server and publish it as an "always on" service — in minutes. The common services also include the metadata services, which provide standard service-oriented access and analysis of metadata across the platform.

► IBM WebSphere Information Analyzer:

IBM WebSphere Information Analyzer profiles and analyzes data so that you can deliver trusted information to your users. It can automatically scan samples of your data to determine their quality and structure. This analysis aids you in understanding the inputs to your integration process, ranging from individual fields to high-level data entities. Information analysis also enables you to correct problems with structure or validity before they affect your project. While analysis of source data is a critical first step in any integration project, you must continually monitor the quality of the data. IBM WebSphere Information Analyzer enables you to treat profiling and analysis as an ongoing process and create business metrics that you can run and track over time.

► IBM WebSphere Business Glossary:

IBM Information Server provides a Web-based tool that enables business analysts and subject-matter experts to create, manage, and share a common enterprise vocabulary and classification system. WebSphere Business Glossary functionality is powered by and actively connected to WebSphere Metadata Server. This enables users to link business terms to more technical artifacts managed by WebSphere Metadata Server. The Metadata Server also enables sharing of the business terms by IBM Rational® Data Architect and WebSphere Information Analyzer, creating a common set of semantic tags for reuse by data modelers, data analysts, business analysts, and end users.

► IBM WebSphere Metadata Server:

IBM Information Server provides the next-generation metadata repository that is fully integrated and common across all product modules, including WebSphere Information Analyzer, WebSphere QualityStage, WebSphere DataStage, and WebSphere Business Glossary. The metadata services infrastructure of IBM Information Server is designed to allow metadata to be more easily managed, accessed by those who need it, and shared across heterogeneous technologies through an SOA.

► IBM WebSphere DataStage MVS™ Edition:

IBM Information Server brings data transformation capabilities to the mainframe with its WebSphere DataStage MVS Edition product module. WebSphere DataStage MVS Edition consolidates, collects, and centralizes information from various systems and mainframes using native execution, from a single design environment.

> **Note:** For complete details on these product modules, refer to the documentation in the following Web site:
>
> `http://www.ibm.com/software/data/integration/info_server/`

A number of companion products support IBM Information Server, such as
Rational Data Architect and WebSphere Replication Server Event Publisher.

1.2 IBM Information Server architecture

IBM Information Server provides a unified architecture that works with all types of
information integration, as shown in Figure 1-1. A unified user interface, common
services, key integration functions (understand, cleanse, transform and move,
and deliver), unified parallel processing, and unified metadata are at the core of
the architecture.

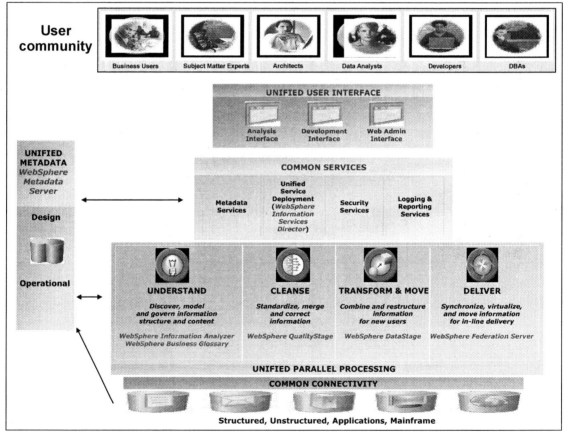

Figure 1-1   IBM Information Server architecture

The architecture is service oriented, enabling IBM Information Server to work
within an organization's evolving enterprise service-oriented architectures. A
service-oriented architecture also connects the individual product modules of

IBM Information Server. By eliminating duplication of functions, the architecture efficiently uses resources and reduces the amount of development and administrative effort that are required to deploy an integration solution.

In the following sections we briefly describe each of these components:

- ▶ Unified user interface
- ▶ Common services
- ▶ Key integration functions (understand, cleanse, transform and move, deliver)
- ▶ Unified parallel processing
- ▶ Unified metadata
- ▶ Common connectivity

1.2.1 Unified user interface

The unified user interface enables an organization's entire user community of business users, subject matter experts, architects, data analysts, developers, and database administrators (DBAs) to collaborate, administer, and query information within the enterprise. A security infrastructure ensures that users are permitted to access information and perform tasks for which they are authorized.

The face of IBM Information Server is a common graphical interface and tool framework. Shared interfaces such as the IBM Information Server console and Web console provide a common look and feel, visual controls, and user experience across products. Common functions such as catalog browsing, metadata import, query, and data browsing all expose underlying common services in a uniform way. IBM Information Center provides rich client interfaces for highly detailed development work and thin clients that run in Web browsers for administration. Application programming interfaces (APIs) support a variety of interface styles that include standard request-reply, service-oriented, event-driven, and scheduled task invocation.

The three broad user interface categories are the analysis interface, development interface, and Web Admin interface as shown in Figure 1-1 on page 5.

1.2.2 Common services

IBM Information Server is built entirely on a set of shared services that centralize core tasks across the platform. These include administrative tasks such as unified service deployment, security, user administration, logging, and reporting. The common services provides flexible, configurable interconnections among the many parts of the architecture.

Shared services allow these tasks to be managed and controlled in one place, regardless of which product module is being used. The common services also include the metadata services, which provide standard service-oriented access and analysis of metadata across the platform. In addition, the common services layer manages how services are deployed from any of the product functions, allowing cleansing and transformation rules or federated queries to be published as shared services within an SOA, using a consistent and easy-to-use mechanism.

The common services layer is deployed on J2EE-compliant application servers such as IBM WebSphere Application Server.

> **Attention:** Today, common services are consumed exclusively by the various components of IBM Information Server. These common services are currently *not* exposed as public SOA services, and therefore cannot be invoked by applications or tools.

IBM Information Server products can access four general categories of service: design, execution, metadata, and unified service deployment, which we discuss in the following sections.

Design services

Design services help developers create function-specific services that can also be shared. For example, WebSphere Information Analyzer calls a column analyzer service that was created for enterprise data analysis but can be integrated with other parts of IBM Information Server because it exhibits common SOA characteristics.

Execution services

Execution services include logging, scheduling, monitoring, reporting, security, and Web framework:

> ► Logging services help you manage logs across all of the IBM Information Server suite components. The Web console shown in Figure 1-2 provides a central place to view logs and resolve problems. Logs are stored in the common repository, and each IBM Information Server suite component defines relevant logging categories.
>
> You can configure which categories of logging messages are saved in the repository. Log views are saved queries that an administrator can create to help with common tasks. For example, you might want to display all of the errors in DataStage jobs that ran in the past 24 hours. Logging is organized by server components. The Web console displays default and active configurations for each component.

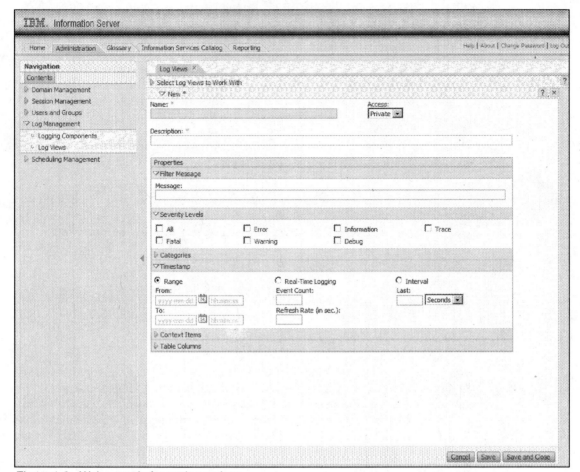

Figure 1-2   Web console for setting up logs

► Scheduling services help plan and track activities such as logging and reporting, and suite component tasks such data monitoring and trending. Schedules are maintained using the IBM Information Server console shown in Figure 1-3, which helps you define schedules, view their status, history, and forecast, and purge them from the system.

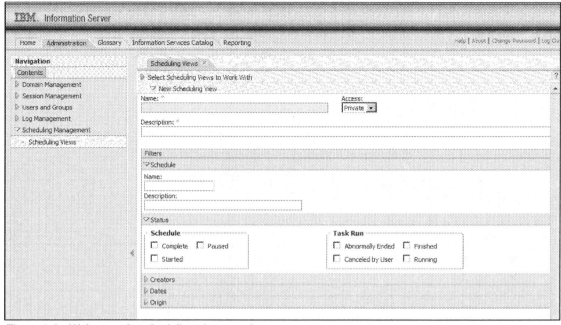

Figure 1-3   Web console scheduling view creation

► Reporting services manage run time and administrative aspects of reporting for IBM Information Server. You can create product-specific reports for WebSphere DataStage, WebSphere QualityStage, and WebSphere Information Analyzer, and cross-product reports for logging, monitoring, scheduling, and security services. All reporting tasks are set up and run from a single interface, the IBM Information Server Web console. You can retrieve and view reports and schedule reports to run at a specific time and frequency.

You define reports by choosing from a set of predefined parameters and templates as shown in Figure 1-4. You can specify a history policy that determines how the report will be archived and when it expires. Reports can be formatted as HTML, PDF or Microsoft Word documents.

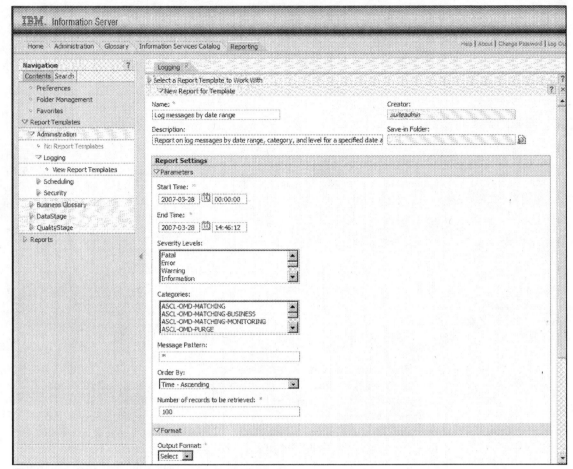

Figure 1-4   Web console logging report creation

► Security services support role-based authentication of users, access-control services, and encryption that complies with many privacy and security regulations. The Web console shown in Figure 1-5 helps administrators add users, groups, and roles and lets administrators browse, create, delete, and update operations within Information Server.

Directory services act as a central authority that can authenticate resources and manage identities and relationships among identities. You can base directories on IBM Information Server's own internal directory or on external directories that are based on LDAP, Microsoft's Active Directory®, or UNIX®. Users only use one credential to access all the components of Information Server. A set of credentials is stored for each user to provide single sign-on to the products registered with the domain.

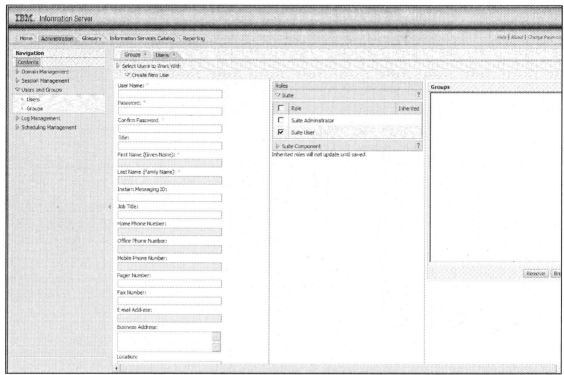

Figure 1-5 Web console to administer users and groups

Metadata services

Metadata services enable metadata to be shared "live" across tools so that changes made in one IBM Information Server product are instantly visible across all of the product modules. Metadata services are tightly integrated with the common repository and are packaged in WebSphere Metadata Server. You can also exchange metadata with external tools by using metadata services.

The major metadata services components of IBM Information Server are WebSphere Business Glossary, WebSphere Metadata Server, and WebSphere MetaBrokers and bridges.

- WebSphere Business Glossary is a Web-based application that provides a business-oriented view into the data integration environment. By using WebSphere Business Glossary, you can view and update business descriptions and access technical metadata. Metadata is best managed by business analysts who understand the meaning and importance of the information assets to the business. Designed for collaborative authoring, WebSphere Business Glossary gives users the ability to share insights and experiences about data. It provides users with the following information about data resources:
  - Business meaning and descriptions of data
  - Stewardship of data and processes
  - Standard business hierarchies
  - Approved terms

  WebSphere Business Glossary is organized and searchable according to the semantics that are defined by a controlled vocabulary, which you can create by using the Web console.

- WebSphere Metadata Server provides a variety of services to other components of IBM Information Server:
  - Metadata access
  - Metadata integration
  - Metadata import and export
  - Impact analysis
  - Search and query

  WebSphere Metadata Server provides a common repository with facilities that are capable of sourcing, sharing, storing, and reconciling a comprehensive spectrum of metadata including business metadata and technical metadata as follows:
  - Business metadata provides business context for information technology assets and adds business meaning to the artifacts that are created and managed by other IT applications. Business metadata includes controlled vocabularies, taxonomies, stewardship, examples, and business definitions.
  - Technical metadata provides details about source and target systems, their table and field structures, attributes, derivations, and dependencies. Technical metadata also includes details about profiling, quality, and ETL processes, projects, and users.

- WebSphere MetaBrokers and bridges provide semantic model mapping technology that allows metadata to be shared among applications for all products that are used in the data integration lifecycle:
  - Data modeling or case tools
  - Business intelligence applications

- Data marts and data warehouses
- Enterprise applications
- Data integration tools

These components can be used to establish common data definitions across business and IT functions:

▶ Drive consistency throughout the data integration lifecycle
▶ Deliver business-oriented and IT-oriented reporting
▶ Provide enterprise visibility for change management
▶ Easily extend to new, existing, and homegrown metadata sources

Unified service deployment

IBM Information Server provides an SOA infrastructure that exposes data transformation processes[1], federated queries[2], and database stored procedures as a set of shared services and operations. This is performed by using a consistent and intuitive graphical interface, and managed after publication using the same user interface.

IBM Information Server provides standard service-oriented interfaces for enterprise data integration. The built-in integration logic of IBM Information Server can easily be encapsulated as service objects that are embedded in user applications. These service objects have the following characteristics:

▶ Always on:

By definition, the services are always running and waiting for requests. This ability removes the overhead of batch startup and shutdown and enables services to respond instantaneously to requests.

▶ Scalable:

The services distribute request processing and stop and start jobs across multiple WebSphere DataStage servers, enabling high performance with large, unpredictable volumes of requests.

▶ Standards-based:

The services are based on open standards and can easily be invoked by standards-based technologies including Web Services Description Language (WSDL), enterprise application integration (EAI) and enterprise service bus (ESB) platforms, applications, and portals.

▶ Manageable:

Monitoring services coordinate timely reporting of system performance data.

---

[1] Created from new or existing WebSphere DataStage or WebSphere QualityStage jobs
[2] Created by WebSphere Federation Server

- ▶ Flexible:

  You can invoke the services by using multiple mechanisms (bindings) and choose from many options for using the services.

- ▶ Reliable and highly available:

  If any WebSphere DataStage server becomes unavailable, it routes service requests to a different server in the pool.

- ▶ Reusable:

  The services publish their own metadata, enabling them to be found and called across any network.

- ▶ High performance:

  Load balancing and the underlying parallel processing capabilities of IBM Information Server create high performance for any type of data payload.

A data integration service is created by designing the data integration process logic in IBM Information Server and publishing it as a service. These services can then be accessed by external projects and technologies.

WebSphere Information Services Director provides a foundation for information services by allowing you to leverage the other components of IBM Information Server for understanding, cleansing, and transforming information and deploying those integration tasks as consistent and reusable information services.

WebSphere Information Services Director provides an integrated environment for designing services that enables you to rapidly deploy integration logic as services without assuming extensive development skills. With a simple, wizard-driven interface, in a few minutes you can attach a specific binding and deploy a reusable integration service. WebSphere Information Services Director also provides these features:

- ▶ Administrator services for cataloging and registering services.
- ▶ Shared reporting and security services.
- ▶ A metadata services layer that promotes reuse of the information services by actually defining what the service does and what information it delivers.

1.2.3 Key integration functions

The four key integration functions shown in Figure 1-1 on page 5 are briefly described here:

- ▶ Understand your data:

  IBM Information Server helps you to automatically discover, define, and model information content and structure, and to understand and analyze the meaning, relationships, and lineage of information. By automating data profiling and data-quality auditing within systems, organizations can achieve the following goals:

- Understand data sources and relationships
- Eliminate the risk of using or proliferating bad data
- Improve productivity through automation
- Leverage existing IT investments

IBM Information Server makes it easier for businesses to collaborate across roles. Data analysts can use analysis and reporting functionality, generating integration specifications and business rules that they can monitor over time. Subject matter experts can use Web-based tools to define, annotate, and report on fields of business data. A common metadata foundation makes it easier for different types of users to create and manage metadata by using tools that are optimized for their roles.

The upcoming WebSphere Information Analyzer product module will provide this functionality.

► Cleanse your information:

IBM Information Server supports information quality and consistency by standardizing, validating, matching, and merging data. It can certify and enrich common data elements, use trusted data such as postal records for name and address information, and match records across or within data sources. IBM Information Server allows a single record to survive from the best information across sources for each unique entity, helping you to create a single, comprehensive, and accurate view of information across source systems.

The WebSphere QualityStage product module currently provides this functionality.

► Transform your data into information and move:

IBM Information Server transforms and enriches information to ensure that it is in the proper context for new uses. Hundreds of prebuilt transformation functions combine, restructure, and aggregate information.

Transformation functionality is broad and flexible, to meet the requirements of varied integration scenarios. For example, IBM Information Server provides inline validation and transformation of complex data types such as U.S. Health Insurance Portability and Accountability Act (HIPAA), along with high-speed joins and sorts of heterogeneous data. IBM Information Server also provides high-volume, complex data transformation and movement functionality that can be used for standalone extract/transform/load (ETL) scenarios, or as a real-time data processing engine for applications or processes.

The WebSphere DataStage product modules currently provide this functionality.

▶ Deliver your information:

IBM Information Server provides the ability to virtualize, synchronize, or move information to the people, processes, or applications that need it. Information can be delivered through federation or time-based or event-based processing, moved in large bulk volumes from location to location, or accessed in place when it cannot be consolidated.

IBM Information Server provides direct, native access to a wide variety of information sources, both mainframe and distributed. It provides access to databases, files, services and packaged applications, and to content repositories and collaboration systems. Companion products allow high-speed replication, synchronization and distribution across databases, change data capture, and event-based publishing of information.

The WebSphere Federation Server product module currently provides this functionality.

1.2.4 Unified parallel processing

Much of the work that IBM Information Server does takes place within the parallel processing engine. The engine handles data processing needs as diverse as performing analysis of large databases for WebSphere Information Analyzer, data cleansing for WebSphere QualityStage, and complex transformations for WebSphere DataStage. This parallel processing engine is designed to deliver:

▶ Parallelism and pipelining to complete increasing volumes of work in decreasing time windows:

– Data partitioning is an approach to parallelism that involves breaking the record set into partitions, or subsets of records. Data partitioning generally provides linear increases in application performance.

IBM Information Server automatically partitions data based on the type of partition that the stage requires. In a well-designed, scalable architecture, the developer does not need to be concerned about the number of partitions that will run, the ability to increase the number of partitions, or re-partitioning data.

– Data pipelining is the process of pulling records from the source system and moving them through the sequence of processing functions that are defined in the data-flow (the job). Because records are flowing through the pipeline, they can be processed without writing the records to disk,

▶ Scalability by adding hardware (for example, processors or nodes in a grid) with no changes to the data integration design.

▶ Optimized database, file, and queue processing to handle large files that cannot fit in memory all at once or with large numbers of small files.

Note: The dynamic parallelization of all potential service implementations is an objective of this architecture.

1.2.5 Unified metadata

IBM Information Server is built on a unified metadata infrastructure that enables shared understanding between business and technical domains. This infrastructure reduces development time and provides a persistent record that can improve confidence in information.

All functions of IBM Information Server share the same metamodel, making it easier for different roles and functions to collaborate. A common metadata repository provides persistent storage for all IBM Information Server product modules. All of the products depend on the repository to navigate, query, and update metadata.

The repository contains two kinds of metadata:

▸ Dynamic metadata that includes design-time information.

▸ Operational metadata that includes performance monitoring, audit and log data, and data profiling sample data.

Because the repository is shared by all product modules, profiling information that is created by WebSphere Information Analyzer is instantly available to users of WebSphere DataStage and QualityStage, for example.The repository is a J2EE application that uses a standard relational database such as IBM DB2, Oracle®, or SQL Server for persistence (DB2 is provided with IBM Information Server). These databases provide backup, administration, scalability, parallel access, transactions, and concurrent access.

1.2.6 Common connectivity

IBM Information Server connects to information sources whether they are structured, unstructured, on the mainframe, or applications.

Metadata-driven connectivity is shared across the product modules, and connection objects are reusable across functions. Connectors provide design-time importing of metadata, data browsing and sampling, run-time dynamic metadata access, error handling, and high functionality and high performance run-time data access.

Prebuilt interfaces for packaged applications called Packs provide adapters to SAP®, Siebel®, Oracle, and others, enabling integration with enterprise applications and associated reporting and analytical systems.

1.2.7 Client application access to services

After an information service is enabled by IBM Information Server, any enterprise application, .Net, or Java™ developer, Microsoft Office or integration software can invoke the service by using a binding protocol such as SOAP over HTTP or EJB™.

Figure 1-6 shows how IBM Information Server information services participate in the SOA Reference Architecture — refer to Appendix A.1, "Service-oriented architecture overview" on page 436 for an overview of SOA. Briefly:

► An information service (blue dots) may access content systems and data systems, while other (non IBM Information Server) services (pink dots) may access applications and registry services. Applications will most likely access data or content using "proprietary" APIs.

► Information services may be invoked by other (non IBM Information Server) services.

► Business processes may invoke information services and other (non IBM Information Server) services.

► Service consumers may invoke information services, business processes, or other (non IBM Information Server) services directly or indirectly.

The Enterprise Service Bus (ESB) layer enables the integration of services through the introduction of a reliable set of capabilities such as intelligent routing, protocol mediation, and other transformation mechanisms. An ESB provides a location independent mechanism for integration.

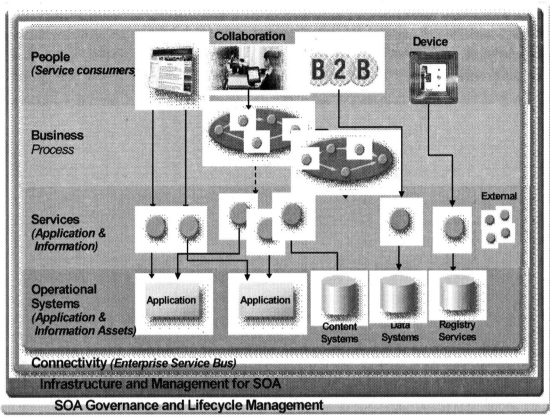

Figure 1-6   Information Services in the SOA Reference Architecture

A service-ready data integration job accepts requests from client applications:

- ► Mapping request data to input rows, and passing them to the underlying jobs in the case of DataStage and QualityStage jobs
- ► Mapping request data to input parameters, which are executed against a federated database in the case of a federated query or stored procedure

A job instance can include database access (federated queries), transformations (DataStage jobs), data standardization and matching (QualityStage jobs), and other data integration tasks (database stored procedures) that are supplied by IBM Information Server.

The design of a real-time job determines whether it is always running or runs once to completion. All jobs that are exposed as services process requests on a 24-hour basis.

The SOA infrastructure supports three job topologies for different load and work style requirements — this relates specifically to DataStage and QualityStage jobs, and not to federated queries or stored procedures:

► Batch jobs:

This topology uses new or existing batch jobs that are exposed as services. A batch job starts on demand. Each service request starts one instance of the job that runs to completion. This job typically initiates a batch process from a real-time process that does not need direct feedback on the results. This topology is tailored for processing bulk data sets and is capable of accepting job parameters as input arguments.

► Batch jobs with a Service Output stage:

This topology uses an existing batch job and adds an output stage. The Service Output stage is the exit point from the job, returning one or more rows to the client application as a service response. These jobs typically initiate a batch process from a real-time process that requires feedback or data from the results. This topology is designed to process large data sets and can accept job parameters as input arguments.

► Jobs with a Service Input stage and a Service Output stage:

This topology uses both a Service Input stage and a Service Output stage. The Service Input stage is the entry point to a job, accepting one or more rows during a service request. These jobs are always running. This topology is typically used to process high volumes of smaller transactions where response time is important. It is tailored to process many small requests rather than a few large requests.

Current restriction: Client applications can only access IBM Information Server services in synchronous mode, where the model requires feedback to be received for any request made before the client application can proceed to its next course of action. IBM Information Server services that are long running tasks (batch jobs and batch jobs with service output stage topologies) or tasks where no feedback is returned to the requestor (batch jobs topology) need special handling if the client application is to avoid "waiting". Such topology jobs must be redesigned to return feedback to the requestor as soon as the request has been processed, and the client application will have to be designed to check on the status of the job at some later point in time. An upcoming release will provide async support with JMS binding.

1.3 Configuration flow

This section describes the processing flow involved when configuring a service.

Multiple steps are involved in configuring a service before it can become the target of a client application invocation.

There is a hierarchy of containers when defining an information service — **Project** → **Application** → **Service** → **Operation**. This is reflected in the main steps in creating an SOA service using IBM Information Server shown in Figure 1-7. These are described in more detail in the following sections.

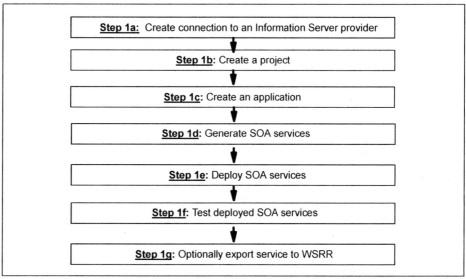

Figure 1-7   Steps in creating SOA services

1.3.1 Step 1a: Create a connection to an Information Server provider

An information provider is both the server that contains functions that you can expose as services, and the functions themselves, such as WebSphere DataStage and WebSphere QualityStage jobs, database stored procedures, or federated SQL queries.

Before an SOA service can be generated for a function, the information provider must be enabled using WebSphere Information Services Director.

There are two types of Information Server providers — a "DataStage or QualityStage" type for DataStage and QualityStage jobs, and a "DB2 or Federation Server" type for database stored procedures and federated queries.

"Step 3a: Create connection to an Information Provider" on page 63 describes the main steps in enabling an Information Server provider.

1.3.2 Step 1b: Create a project

A project is a collaborative environment that you use to design applications, services, and operations. All project information that you create is saved in the common metadata repository so that it can easily be shared among other IBM Information Server components. You can export a project to back up your work or share work with other IBM Information Server users. The export file includes applications, services, operations, and binding information.

Therefore, you must create a project first.

"Step 3b: Create a project" on page 72 describes the steps in creating a project.

1.3.3 Step 1c: Create an application

An application is a container for a set of services and operations. An application contains one or more services that you want to deploy together as an Enterprise Archive (EAR) file on an application server.

All design-time activity occurs in the context of applications:

► Creating services and operations
► Describing how message payloads and transport protocols are used to expose a service
► Attaching a reference provider, such as a WebSphere DataStage job or an SQL query, to an operation

You can also export services from an application before it is deployed and import the services into another application.

Therefore, you must create an application in the project created.

"Step 3c: Create an application" on page 75 describes the steps in creating an application in the project created earlier.

1.3.4 Step 1d: Generate SOA services

An information service exposes results from processing by information providers such as DataStage servers and federated servers. A deployed service runs on an application server and processes requests from service client applications.

An information service is a collection of operations that are selected from jobs, federated queries, or other information providers. You can group operations in the same information service or design them in separate services. You create an information service for a set of operations that you want to deploy together. You also specify the bindings (SOAP over HTTP and/or EJB) for the service.

As mentioned earlier, an information service is associated with a particular application.

"Generate a stored procedure service" on page 79 describes the main steps in generating a stored procedure based information service.

1.3.5 Step 1e: Deploy SOA services

After the information service is generated, it must be deployed. You deploy an application on WebSphere Application Server to enable the information services that are contained in the application to receive service requests. You can exclude one or more services, bindings, and operations from the deployment, change runtime properties such as minimum number of job instances, or, for WebSphere DataStage jobs, set constant values for job parameters. WebSphere Information Services Director deploys the Enterprise Archive (EAR) file on the application server.

"Deploy the stored procedure service" on page 91 describes the main steps in deploying the generated stored procedure based information service.

1.3.6 Step 1f: Test deployed SOA services

After deployment, we strongly recommend that you test the deployed information service before making it available to client applications.

"Test the stored procedure service (SOAP binding)" on page 95 and "Test the stored procedure service (EJB binding)" on page 106 describe the main steps in testing the deployed stored procedure based information service with SOAP over HTTP and EJB bindings respectively.

1.3.7 Step 1g: Optionally export service to WSRR

> **Note:** WebSphere Service Registry and Repository (WSRR) is not a prerequisite for IBM Information Server, nor is it mandatory for SOA. If your organization has implemented a WebSphere Server Registry and Repository (WSRR), you can choose to export the IBM Information Server service you generated to it.

The WSRR is a separate entity from IBM Information Server that can serve as the master metadata repository (not related in any way to the IBM Information

Server metadata repository mentioned earlier) for service descriptions. As the integration point for service metadata, WSRR establishes a central point for finding and managing service metadata acquired from a number of sources, including service application deployments and other service metadata and endpoint registries and repositories, such as UDDI. It is where service metadata that is scattered across an enterprise is brought together to provide a single, comprehensive description of a service. Once that happens, visibility is controlled, versions are managed, proposed changes are analyzed and communicated, usage is monitored and other parts of the SOA foundation can access service metadata, confident that they have found the copy of record.

In this context, WSRR handles the metadata management aspects of operational services and provides the system of record of these metadata artifacts — the place where anybody looking for a catalog of all services deployed in or used by the enterprise would go first. The WSRR provides registry functions supporting publication of metadata about services, their capabilities, requirements, and semantics of services that enable service consumers to find services or to analyze their relationships.

"Step 3e: Optionally export service to WSRR" on page 138 describes the main steps in exporting the IBM Information Server service to the WSRR.

1.4 Runtime flow

This section provides an overview of the runtime flow associated with processing an invocation of an IBM Information Server service by a client application.

A brief overview of the service artifacts is covered before describing the flow of a request through the system.

1.4.1 Service artifacts

Every IBM Information Server service generated by WISD is generated as an EJB session bean (Service Session Bean in Figure 1-8) regardless of whether the function is a DataStage job, QualityStage job, database stored procedure, or federated query. After the service session bean has been generated, additional artifacts get created depending upon whether SOAP over HTTP or EJB binding is requested for the service.

▶ With SOAP over HTTP binding, a router servlet and facade session bean is generated. The servlet invokes the facade session bean that in turn invokes the service session bean.

▶ With EJB binding, a facade session bean is generated that invokes the service session bean.

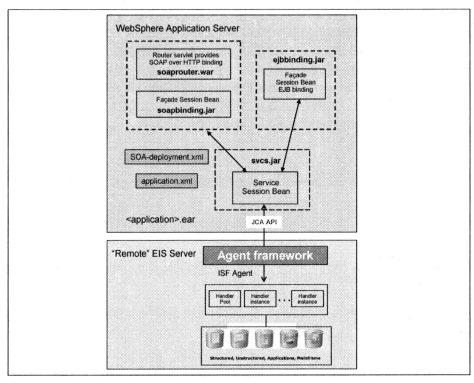

Figure 1-8   Partial contents of IBM Information Server application EAR file

Note: The jar and war files shown in Example 1-1 through Example 1-4 relate to the creation of an information service named AccountService with SOAP over HTTP and EJB bindings in the BrokerageApp application within the A2ZProject.

The service session bean is packaged into an svcs.jar file along with other files as shown in Example 1-1.

Example 1-1   svcs.jar file contents

```
AccountService.class
AccountServiceBean.class
AccountServiceForWSDL.class
AccountServiceHome.class
AccountServiceRemote.class
ejb-jar.xml
ibm-ejb-jar-bnd.xmi
Manifest.mf
```

```
Response.class
RTIServiceEJBBase.class
```

The router servlet is packaged into a soaprouter.war file along with other files as shown in Example 1-2.

Example 1-2   soaprouter.war file contents

```
ibm-web-bnd.xml
ibm-web-ext.xml
Manifest.mf
web.xml
```

The facade session bean is packaged into a soapbinding.jar file along with other files as shown in Example 1-3.

Example 1-3   soapbinding.jar file contents

```
AccountService.wsdl
AccountService_mapping.xml
AccountServiceSOAPBindingBean.class
ejb-jar.xml
ibm-ejb-jar-bnd.xmi
ibm-webservices-bnd.xmi
ibm-webservices-ext.xmi
Manifest.mf
webservices.xml
```

The facade session bean is packaged into an ejbbinding.jar file along with other files as shown in Example 1-4.

Example 1-4   ejbbinding.jar file contents

```
AccountServiceBean.class
ejb-jar.xml
ibm-ejb-jar-bnd.xmi
Manifest.mf
```

All these jar files along with a soa-deployment.xml descriptor (shown in Example 1-5 on page 27 as including both SOAP over HTTP and EJB bindings), and application.xml (Example 1-7 on page 28) descriptor are packaged into A2ZBrokerageApp.ear file (shown in Example 1-6 on page 28) that eventually gets deployed on the WebSphere Application Server (associated with IBM Information Server) by WISD.

Important: We strongly recommend that you do *not* modify the various descriptors in the IBM Information Server <application>.ear file generated by WISD and attempt to deploy it in WAS using other tools. The results may be unpredictable.

Example 1-5   soa-deployment.xml descriptor

```
<?xml version="1.0" ?>
- <soa-descriptor name="A2ZBrokerageApp">
- <service-descriptor name="AccountService" type="value">
- <description>
- <![CDATA[ Service for opening accounts
  ]]>
  </description>
- <entry-point>
  <home>com.ibm.isd.A2ZBrokerageApp.AccountService.server.AccountServiceHome</home>

<remote>com.ibm.isd.A2ZBrokerageApp.AccountService.server.AccountServiceRemote</remot
e>

<ejb-class>com.ibm.isd.A2ZBrokerageApp.AccountService.server.impl.AccountServiceBean<
/ejb-class>
  <business>com.ibm.isd.A2ZBrokerageApp.AccountService.AccountService</business>
  </entry-point>
- <j2ee-descriptor reference="true">
  <jndi-name>ascential/rti/A2ZBrokerageApp/AccountService</jndi-name>
  <ejb-name>com.ibm.isd.A2ZBrokerageApp.AccountService.AccountService</ejb-name>
  <bean-type value="stateless" />
  </j2ee-descriptor>
  <category>/RTI</category>
  <initialization jndiName="" priority="1" />
  <allowable-binding>EJB</allowable-binding>
- <binding name="EJB">
  <property name="BeanDescription" value="" />
  <property name="JNDIName" value="ejb/A2ZBrokerageApp/AccountService" />
  <property name="Package" value="com.ibm.isd.A2ZBrokerageApp.AccountService.ejb" />
  </binding>
  <allowable-binding>SOAPHttp</allowable-binding>
- <binding name="SOAPHttp">
  <property name="Package" value="com.ibm.isd.A2ZBrokerageApp.AccountService" />
  <property name="TargetNameSpace"
value="http://AccountService.A2ZBrokerageApp.isd.ibm.com/soapoverhttp/" />
  <property name="UriRoot" value="wisd" />
```

```
  <property name="WSDLClass"
value="com.ibm.isd.A2ZBrokerageApp.AccountService.AccountServiceForWSDL" />
  <property name="SOAPStyle" value="DOCLIT" />
  <property name="SOAPAction" value="NONE" />
  </binding>
  </service-descriptor>
  </soa-descriptor>
```

Example 1-6   BrokerageApp.ear file

```
A2ZBrokerageApp_client.jar
application.xml
ejbbinding.jar
Manifest.mf
soa-deployment.xml
soapbinding.jar
soaprouter.war
svcs.jar
```

Example 1-7   Information Server application.xml

```
<?xml version="1.0" encoding="UTF-8" ?>
- <application xmlns="http://java.sun.com/xml/ns/j2ee"
xmlns:xsi="http://www.w3.org/2001/XMLSchema-instance" id="Application_ID"
version="1.4" xsi:schemaLocation="http://java.sun.com/xml/ns/j2ee
http://java.sun.com/xml/ns/j2ee/application_1_4.xsd">
  <display-name>A2ZBrokerageApp</display-name>
- <module>
  <ejb>svcs.jar</ejb>
  </module>
- <module>
- <web>
  <web-uri>soaprouter.war</web-uri>
  <context-root>/wisd/A2ZBrokerageApp</context-root>
  </web>
  </module>
- <module>
  <ejb>soapbinding.jar</ejb>
  </module>
- <module>
  <ejb>ejbbinding.jar</ejb>
  </module>
  </application>
```

1.4.2 Flow of a request

A request for an IBM Information Server service can be invoked using SOAP over HTTP binding or EJB binding.

With SOAP over HTTP binding, an incoming request from a remote client is de-serialized by the WAS SOAP stack (associated with IBM Information Server) and passed to the IBM Information Server and Information Services Framework as follows:

1. Invokes the router servlet with the interface parameters.

2. The router servlet then invokes the facade session bean

3. Facade session bean invokes the service session bean using EJB binding.

4. The service session bean connects to the Information Services Framework (ISF) Agent[3] via the Agent framework using a J2EE Connector Architecture[4] (JCA) API to send a request to the back-end and obtain a response.

> **Note:** As shown in Figure 1-8 on page 25, the Agent Framework, ISF Agent and back-end data sources reside on a logically "remote" EIS server, which means that these components may be physically located on a separate server, or co-located on the same server as the IBM Information Server.

---

[3] There is one ISF Agent associated with a DataStage server or Federation Server. If both DataStage server and Federation Server are installed on a server, only a single ISF Agent is installed on that server. An ISF Agent can be configured to access only one IBM Information Server. This architecture allows DataStage and Federation servers to be installed on servers distinct from where IBM Information Server is installed. A discussion of configuring IBM Information Server with multiple ISF Agents is beyond the scope of this publication.

[4] The J2EE Connector Architecture specifies a standard architecture for accessing resources in diverse Enterprise Information Systems (EIS) such as ERP systems, mainframe transaction processing systems, legacy applications and non-relational database systems. The Connector Architecture defines a common interface (using the JCA API) between application servers and EIS systems, implemented in EIS specific resource adapters. A resource adapter is a system library specific to an EIS system such as SAP, and provides connectivity to that EIS via the JCA API. It is somewhat similar to a JDBC™ driver. The interface between the resource adapter and the EIS is typically specific to the underlying EIS. A Connector Architecture compliant resource adapter works with any J2EE server. A single resource adapter is provided with IBM Information Server that handles both the DataStage/QualityStage data source, and database stored procedure/federated query.

The ISF Agent provides a framework for sending requests from the IBM Information Server to remote (ISF) clients (where the ISF Agent is located) without the need for a full J2EE Application Server at each client location. The ISF Agent utilizes a plug-in architecture to allow different types of requests to be passed from the IBM Information Server. The ISF Agent framework also provides load balancing and pooling of resources.

The code that processes a request in the ISF Agent is called a Handler. Each ISF Agent can be configured to support multiple different Handlers at the same time. Currently, there are two handlers — a DataStage/QualityStage handler, and a database stored procedure/federated query handler.

The ISF Agent framework takes care of routing requests and returning any responses. The clients (service session bean in our case) of the ISF Agent use the Java Connection Architecture (JCA) to send data. This consists of obtaining a Connection in much the same way that a JDBC Connection is obtained.

5. As each request arrives, the ISF Agent framework selects an instance of the requested Handler to process it. It does that by requesting a Handler instance from the handler pool. The handler pool in turn can decide to create a new instance or reuse an existing instance.

6. The Handler instance then processes the request and returns a response.

With EJB binding, an application such as a servlet or JSP™ invokes the facade session bean directly, which invokes the service session bean. Thereafter, the processing is identical to that of SOAP over HTTP.

Financial services business scenario

In this chapter, we describe a typical financial services company in the mid-1990s transitioning to the opportunities of the Internet era to improve customer service, reduce costs, and expand business opportunities.

The topics covered include:

- ► Business requirements
- ► Environment configuration
- ► Step-by-step approach

2.1 Introduction

In the mid 1990s, A2Z Financial Services Inc. was a technically progressive and growing financial services company offering brokerage and credit card services the traditional way primarily to residents in California and neighboring states. It grew from a small brokerage business by acquiring another financial services company offering credit services. It incorporated the early 1990s emerging technologies of data warehousing and business intelligence to integrate its two heterogeneous and stovepipe systems, to develop applications that identified high value customers and to cross sell and up sell its portfolio of services to its customer base in the brokerage and credit card businesses.

However, given the technology of the day, its customers interacted with the company via mail, fax and telephone to have services performed. The company for its part used the same channels to communicate with customers — from delivering monthly statements and promotional material via mail, to the occasional telemarketing campaign. An unsolicited call to the customer service representative (CSR) from a customer was seen as an opportunity to cross sell and up sell the company's product offerings.

The configuration of this environment is shown in Figure 2-1, which also indicates that the CSR applications used "proprietary" APIs to access the brokerage, credit card, operational data store (ODS)[1] and enterprise data warehouse (EDW)[2] systems. Details of the data models of the applications, and DB2 stored procedures are described in Appendix C, "Code and scripts used in the business scenario" on page 475.

---

[1] The ODS contains integrated information from the two stovepipe systems (brokerage and credit card) and has a latency of one day. It only has current information (no history information).

[2] The EDW differs from the ODS in that it contains history information and some additional attributes in some of the individual tables.

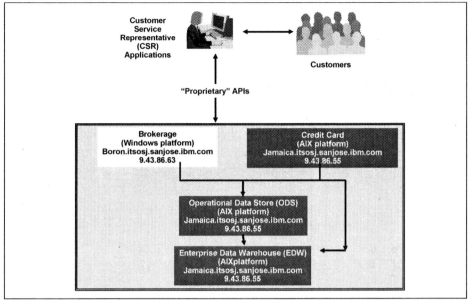

Figure 2-1   A2Z Financial Services' pre-Internet configuration

The emergence of Internet technologies in the latter half of the 1990s was seen as a huge opportunity to leverage this new channel to expand A2Z Financial Services' customer base, while providing superior customer service and reducing operational costs.

2.2 Business requirement

In the latter half of the 1990s, Internet technologies were seen by one and all as having the potential to completely transform the way companies conducted their business, by breaking down barriers of geography (both domestic and international), time zones and accessibility. Beginning with a self service concept that provided sales and marketing information, to allowing customers to bypass the CSR to perform common business transactions, to providing the company opportunities to actively market to customers and prospects during Web site visits and via e-mail, the Internet seemed to open up limitless opportunities for businesses to expand and reach new markets.

A2Z Financial Services determined that their survival as well as growth depended upon embracing Internet and other emerging technologies (such as data mining) with an agile infrastructure capable of assimilating future business opportunities and technologies.

Important: Had Service-Oriented Architecture (SOA) concepts, and IBM Information Server and WebSphere Process Server technologies, existed in the latter half of the 1990s, A2Z Financial Services would have chosen to implement them to address their goals of an agile infrastructure to address immediate and emerging business requirements. In this section, we showcase "what could have been possible" for A2Z Financial Services with the implementation of SOA using IBM Information Server, WebSphere Process Server, and Rational Application Developer. Without these concepts and technologies, A2Z Financial Services would most likely have implemented technologies of the day that did not easily lend themselves to the creation of reusable assets to be consumed by applications.

A2Z Financial Services' immediate requirement is to set up a self service Web site that provides functionality such as the ability to:

1. Open a brokerage or credit card account.

2. Place trades on the brokerage account.

3. Make payments on the credit card account.

4. Make changes to user profiles such as an address, telephone numbers, and e-mail addresses.

5. View the status of each account — balances, positions, and transactions.

Note: The CSR interface would also need to be modified to provide a consistent view of information as seen by the customer. This change might be transitioned in later, depending upon available personnel resources and other business priorities.

2.3 Environment configuration

The applications of our fictitious company, A2Z Financial Services, are implemented on Microsoft Windows 2003 Server and IBM AIX operating system platforms as shown in Figure 2-1 on page 33.

Given the functionality of IBM Information Server (as described in Chapter 1, "IBM Information Server architecture" on page 1) and WebSphere Process Server (as described in Appendix B, "WebSphere Integration Developer overview" on page 459), A2Z Financial Services chose the configuration shown in Figure 2-2 on page 37 as its solution to address its business requirements. An enterprise portal using WebSphere Portal Server enables authorized customers to access A2Z Financial Services' self service solution.

IBM Information Server was chosen for its ability to create SOA services of certain core functions implemented as DB2 stored procedures, DB2 federated queries, and DataStage and QualityStage jobs. These constitute existing functions in the "legacy" environment, as well as new functions that are reusable in the customer self service application and a revised CSR application.

Note: It is assumed that the existing "reusable" functions were modularly constructed as DB2 stored procedures that were accessed using SQL APIs. Potentially reusable SQL queries might or might not be implemented in DB2 stored procedures — if not, the queries are typically shared in a query tool or embedded in a single application that gets invoked from other applications.

If potentially and actually reusable functions are not available as DB2 stored procedures, federated queries, DataStage, or QualityStage jobs, consider rewriting them as such, in order for IBM Information Server to be able to convert them into SOA services.

WebSphere Process Server was chosen for its complementary functionality to IBM Information Server, as follows:

► Aggregate SOA services (both IBM Information Server are generated as well as otherwise) into a larger business process SOA service.

► Support is provided for additional binding over those supported by IBM Information Server such as Messaging Binding (MQ JMS Binding).

► Support is provided for both sync and async invocations of an SOA service (IBM Information Server only supports the sync invocation). The async invocation is particularly relevant for long running tasks.

► The security function allows only authorized applications to invoke a service using a particular interface. (However, we did not use this functionality.)

Important: Organizations need to ensure that services providing critical customer information be protected from unauthorized applications and users. Multiple levels of security are typically used involving authentication of the user, user authorization to access specific applications, and application authorization to access specific services. As indicated earlier, a white paper is currently being developed to provide you with guidelines on implementing authentication, access control, and encryption security within an IBM Information Server environment. A reference to this white paper will be provided here when it becomes publicly available.

Figure 2-2 on page 37 shows the configuration used in the A2Z Financial Services' self service application which includes the following features:

► A Microsoft Windows 2003 server (swiss.itsosj.sanjose.ibm.com — 9.43.86.72) provides A2Z Financial Services' enterprise portal through which authorized customers will access the self service solution.

► WebSphere Process Server (lead.itsosj.sanjose.ibm.com — 9.43.86.68) is installed on a separate Microsoft Windows 2003 server. WebSphere MQ is also installed on this server.

► A single Microsoft Windows 2003 server (radon.itsosj.sanjose.ibm.com — 9.43.86.70) is used for the IBM Information Server. This includes DataStage, QualityStage, and Federation Server.

► A single Microsoft Windows 2003 server (boron.itsosj.sanjose.ibm.com — 9.43.86.63) runs the brokerage application.

► A single IBM AIX 5.2 server (Jamaica.itsosj.sanjose.ibm.com — 9.43.86.55) runs the credit card, operational data store, and enterprise data warehouse applications.

► A single Microsoft Windows 2003 server (dyn-9-152-130-81.boeblingen.de.ibm.com — 9.152.130.81) runs the WebSphere Server Registry and Repository (WSRR).

> **Attention:** Our configuration in Figure 2-2 is meant to represent the eclectic mix of operating systems and platforms that are typical of large organizations, and how IBM Information Server integrates into such an environment. Therefore, you should not conclude that we are making recommendations about configuring your environment in this manner, or that it will deliver the scalability and performance requirements of your business solution.

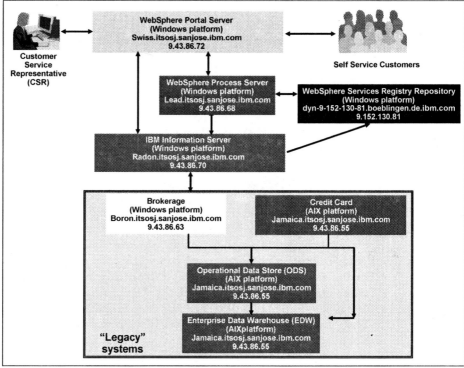

Figure 2-2   A2Z Financial Services' Internet era

2.4 Step-by-step approach

In this section, we document the step-by-step set up of A2Z Financial Services' self service environment.

At a macro level, the tasks that needed to be performed included:

► Creating information services over existing business functions such as opening brokerage or credit card account, placing trades on the brokerage account, and viewing the status of each customer account. The existing business functions may be implemented in "legacy" systems as database stored procedures, DataStage jobs, QualityStage job, and federated SQL queries. Such services execute on the IBM Information Server.

► Creating information services for new functions for the self service solution such as auditing all customer activity and validating addresses. The new business functions may be implemented as database stored procedures, DataStage jobs, QualityStage job, and federated SQL queries. Such services also execute on the IBM Information Server.

▶ Creating aggregation services using WID that included information services as well as other "legacy" services such as a stock quote service. Such services execute on a WebSphere Process Server and invoke information services on the IBM Information Server.

▶ Optionally registering information services into a WebSphere Service Registry and Repository (WSRR) — for organizations that already have an advanced SOA infrastructure with WSRR implemented. The WSRR server is typically isolated from the data and application servers.

▶ Developing the self service client applications that leverage the services (both information services as well as WID generated services) defined in the earlier steps from enterprise portal environments such as WebSphere Portal Server and Microsoft Internet Information Server.

Figure 2-3 lists the main steps involved in setting up the A2Z Financial Services' self service environment. In the first step, we prepare a federation database on the federation server component of IBM Information Server — to define SOA service wrappers around stored procedures and federated queries, the federation server component of IBM Information Server needs to be aware of these queries and stored procedures. This is followed by a second step where we identify and create the "core" information management processes that we are going to create an SOA service wrapper for using the WISD component of IBM Information Server. In the third step, we create IBM Information Server services for them. In the fourth step, we build aggregate SOA services (Service Component Architecture modules) that combine the IBM Information Server SOA services into a larger business process using WebSphere Integration Developer. Finally, in the fifth step, we develop applications to consume the SOA services we just created.

Each of these steps is described in detail in the following sections.

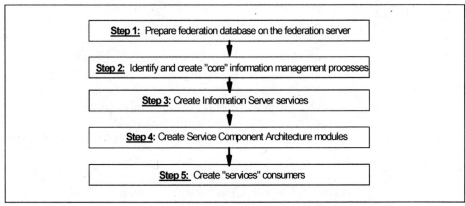

Figure 2-3   Step-by-step set up of A2Z Financial Services self service environment

2.5 Step 1: Prepare federation database on the federation server

To define SOA service wrappers around stored procedures and federated queries, the federation server component of IBM Information Server needs to be aware of these queries and stored procedures. You therefore need to prepare the federation server environment by creating a database with the appropriate options (FEDERATED YES in the database manager configuration) and defining the appropriate nicknames as follows:

1. Create a database such as FEDDB.

2. Ensure that the FEDERATED YES option in the database manager configuration file is enabled.

3. Create a DRDA® wrapper, since we need to access DB2 databases related to the Brokerage, Credit Card, operational data store and enterprise data warehouse applications. For other databases, appropriate wrappers such as NET8 (Oracle) and MSSQLODBC3 (Microsoft SQL Server) would need to be defined.

4. Define the server names corresponding to the location of the remote databases with the authentication details.

5. Define how user names provided at the federation should be mapped to usernames at the remote servers.

6. Create nicknames in the federation database (FEDDB) for the tables or views in the remote servers. These nicknames will be used in federated queries.

7. Define federated stored procedures in the federated database (FEDDB) corresponding to stored procedures[3] on the remote databases. These federated stored procedures are somewhat like nicknames, in that they can be invoked as if they were local to the federated database. The federation server component of IBM Information Server (radon.itsosj.sanjose.ibm.com) needs to be configured to access the brokerage and credit card stored procedures before the WebSphere Information Services Director (WISD) component of IBM Information Server can generate an SOA service wrapper for it.

Example 2-1, Example 2-2, and Example 2-3 show the commands used to prepare the federated database on the federation server.

---

[3] DB2 stored procedures support the brokerage and credit card applications running on the Microsoft Windows (boron.itsosj.sanjose.ibm.com) and IBM AIX (jamaica.itsosj.sanjose.ibm.com) platforms respectively.

We can now proceed to create the "core" information management services as described in "Step 2: Identify and create "core" information management processes" on page 44.

Example 2-1   Define the Brokerage and CreditCard servers

```
CREATE DATABASE FEDDB AUTOMATIC STORAGE YES  ON 'C:\' DBPATH ON 'C:\' USING CODESET
IBM-1252 TERRITORY US COLLATE USING SYSTEM PAGESIZE 4096;
CONNECT TO FEDDB;

UPDATE DBM CFG USING FEDERATED YES:

CREATE WRAPPER DRDA LIBRARY 'db2drda.dll';


CREATE SERVER ODS TYPE DB2/UDB VERSION '8.2' WRAPPER DRDA AUTHID "db2inst1" PASSWORD
"db2inst1" OPTIONS( ADD DBNAME 'ODS');

CREATE SERVER CCA TYPE DB2/UDB VERSION '8.2' WRAPPER DRDA AUTHID "db2inst1" PASSWORD
"db2inst1" OPTIONS( ADD DBNAME 'CCA');

CREATE SERVER EDW TYPE DB2/UDB VERSION '8.2' WRAPPER DRDA AUTHID "db2inst1" PASSWORD
"db2inst1" OPTIONS( ADD DBNAME 'EDW');

CREATE SERVER BROKRAGE TYPE DB2/UDB VERSION '9.1' WRAPPER DRDA AUTHID "db2admin"
PASSWORD "db2admin" OPTIONS( ADD DBNAME 'BROKRAGE');

CREATE USER MAPPING FOR DB2ADMIN SERVER ODS OPTIONS ( ADD REMOTE_AUTHID 'db2inst1',
ADD  REMOTE_PASSWORD 'db2inst1') ;
CREATE USER MAPPING FOR ADMINISTRATOR SERVER ODS OPTIONS ( ADD REMOTE_AUTHID
'db2inst1', ADD  REMOTE_PASSWORD 'db2inst1') ;
CREATE USER MAPPING FOR GUEST SERVER ODS OPTIONS ( ADD REMOTE_AUTHID 'db2inst1', ADD
REMOTE_PASSWORD 'db2inst1') ;
CREATE USER MAPPING FOR MKSSSHD SERVER ODS OPTIONS ( ADD REMOTE_AUTHID 'db2inst1',
ADD  REMOTE_PASSWORD 'db2inst1') ;
CREATE USER MAPPING FOR SUITEADMIN SERVER ODS OPTIONS ( ADD REMOTE_AUTHID 'db2inst1',
ADD  REMOTE_PASSWORD 'db2inst1') ;
CREATE USER MAPPING FOR SUITEUSER SERVER ODS OPTIONS ( ADD REMOTE_AUTHID 'db2inst1',
ADD  REMOTE_PASSWORD 'db2inst1') ;
CREATE USER MAPPING FOR SUPPORT_388945A0 SERVER ODS OPTIONS ( ADD REMOTE_AUTHID
'db2inst1', ADD  REMOTE_PASSWORD 'db2inst1') ;
CREATE USER MAPPING FOR TDSITSO SERVER ODS OPTIONS ( ADD REMOTE_AUTHID 'db2inst1',
ADD  REMOTE_PASSWORD 'db2inst1') ;
CREATE USER MAPPING FOR WASADMIN SERVER ODS OPTIONS ( ADD REMOTE_AUTHID 'db2inst1',
ADD  REMOTE_PASSWORD 'db2inst1') ;
```

```
CREATE USER MAPPING FOR XMETA SERVER ODS OPTIONS ( ADD REMOTE_AUTHID 'db2inst1', ADD
REMOTE_PASSWORD 'db2inst1') ;

CREATE USER MAPPING FOR ADMINISTRATOR SERVER CCA OPTIONS ( ADD REMOTE_AUTHID
'db2inst1', ADD  REMOTE_PASSWORD 'db2inst1') ;
CREATE USER MAPPING FOR DB2ADMIN SERVER CCA OPTIONS ( ADD REMOTE_AUTHID 'db2inst1',
ADD  REMOTE_PASSWORD 'db2inst1') ;
CREATE USER MAPPING FOR GUEST SERVER CCA OPTIONS ( ADD REMOTE_AUTHID 'db2inst1', ADD
REMOTE_PASSWORD 'db2inst1') ;
CREATE USER MAPPING FOR MKSSSHD SERVER CCA OPTIONS ( ADD REMOTE_AUTHID 'db2inst1',
ADD  REMOTE_PASSWORD 'db2inst1') ;
CREATE USER MAPPING FOR SUITEADMIN SERVER CCA OPTIONS ( ADD REMOTE_AUTHID 'db2inst1',
ADD  REMOTE_PASSWORD 'db2inst1') ;
CREATE USER MAPPING FOR SUITEUSER SERVER CCA OPTIONS ( ADD REMOTE_AUTHID 'db2inst1',
ADD  REMOTE_PASSWORD 'db2inst1') ;
CREATE USER MAPPING FOR SUPPORT_388945A0 SERVER CCA OPTIONS ( ADD REMOTE_AUTHID
'db2inst1', ADD  REMOTE_PASSWORD 'db2inst1') ;
CREATE USER MAPPING FOR TDSITSO SERVER CCA OPTIONS ( ADD REMOTE_AUTHID 'db2inst1',
ADD  REMOTE_PASSWORD 'db2inst1') ;
CREATE USER MAPPING FOR WASADMIN SERVER CCA OPTIONS ( ADD REMOTE_AUTHID 'db2inst1',
ADD  REMOTE_PASSWORD 'db2inst1') ;
CREATE USER MAPPING FOR XMETA SERVER CCA OPTIONS ( ADD REMOTE_AUTHID 'db2inst1', ADD
REMOTE_PASSWORD 'db2inst1') ;

CREATE USER MAPPING FOR ADMINISTRATOR SERVER EDW OPTIONS ( ADD REMOTE_AUTHID
'db2inst1', ADD  REMOTE_PASSWORD 'db2inst1') ;
CREATE USER MAPPING FOR DB2ADMIN SERVER EDW OPTIONS ( ADD REMOTE_AUTHID 'db2inst1',
ADD  REMOTE_PASSWORD 'db2inst1') ;
CREATE USER MAPPING FOR GUEST SERVER EDW OPTIONS ( ADD REMOTE_AUTHID 'db2inst1', ADD
REMOTE_PASSWORD 'db2inst1') ;
CREATE USER MAPPING FOR MKSSSHD SERVER EDW OPTIONS ( ADD REMOTE_AUTHID 'db2inst1',
ADD  REMOTE_PASSWORD 'db2inst1') ;
CREATE USER MAPPING FOR SUITEADMIN SERVER EDW OPTIONS ( ADD REMOTE_AUTHID 'db2inst1',
ADD  REMOTE_PASSWORD 'db2inst1') ;
CREATE USER MAPPING FOR SUITEUSER SERVER EDW OPTIONS ( ADD REMOTE_AUTHID 'db2inst1',
ADD  REMOTE_PASSWORD 'db2inst1') ;
CREATE USER MAPPING FOR SUPPORT_388945A0 SERVER EDW OPTIONS ( ADD REMOTE_AUTHID
'db2inst1', ADD  REMOTE_PASSWORD 'db2inst1') ;
CREATE USER MAPPING FOR TDSITSO SERVER EDW OPTIONS ( ADD REMOTE_AUTHID 'db2inst1',
ADD  REMOTE_PASSWORD 'db2inst1') ;
CREATE USER MAPPING FOR WASADMIN SERVER EDW OPTIONS ( ADD REMOTE_AUTHID 'db2inst1',
ADD  REMOTE_PASSWORD 'db2inst1') ;
CREATE USER MAPPING FOR XMETA SERVER EDW OPTIONS ( ADD REMOTE_AUTHID 'db2inst1', ADD
REMOTE_PASSWORD 'db2inst1') ;
```

```
CREATE USER MAPPING FOR ADMINISTRATOR SERVER BROKRAGE OPTIONS ( ADD REMOTE_AUTHID
'db2admin', ADD  REMOTE_PASSWORD 'db2admin') ;
CREATE USER MAPPING FOR DB2ADMIN SERVER BROKRAGE OPTIONS ( ADD REMOTE_AUTHID
'db2admin', ADD  REMOTE_PASSWORD 'db2admin') ;
CREATE USER MAPPING FOR GUEST SERVER BROKRAGE OPTIONS ( ADD REMOTE_AUTHID 'db2admin',
ADD  REMOTE_PASSWORD 'db2admin') ;
CREATE USER MAPPING FOR MKSSSHD SERVER BROKRAGE OPTIONS ( ADD REMOTE_AUTHID
'db2admin', ADD  REMOTE_PASSWORD 'db2admin') ;
CREATE USER MAPPING FOR SUITEADMIN SERVER BROKRAGE OPTIONS ( ADD REMOTE_AUTHID
'db2admin', ADD  REMOTE_PASSWORD 'db2admin') ;
CREATE USER MAPPING FOR SUITEUSER SERVER BROKRAGE OPTIONS ( ADD REMOTE_AUTHID
'db2admin', ADD  REMOTE_PASSWORD 'db2admin') ;
CREATE USER MAPPING FOR SUPPORT_388945A0 SERVER BROKRAGE OPTIONS ( ADD REMOTE_AUTHID
'db2admin', ADD  REMOTE_PASSWORD 'db2admin') ;
CREATE USER MAPPING FOR TDSITSO SERVER BROKRAGE OPTIONS ( ADD REMOTE_AUTHID
'db2admin', ADD  REMOTE_PASSWORD 'db2admin') ;
CREATE USER MAPPING FOR WASADMIN SERVER BROKRAGE OPTIONS ( ADD REMOTE_AUTHID
'db2admin', ADD  REMOTE_PASSWORD 'db2admin') ;
CREATE USER MAPPING FOR XMETA SERVER BROKRAGE OPTIONS ( ADD REMOTE_AUTHID 'db2admin',
ADD  REMOTE_PASSWORD 'db2admin') ;


CREATE NICKNAME EDW.CUSTXREF FOR EDW.EDW.CUSTXREF;
CREATE NICKNAME EDW.CUSTOMER FOR EDW.EDW.CUSTOMER;
CREATE NICKNAME EDW.ADDRESS FOR EDW.EDW.ADDRESS;
CREATE NICKNAME EDW.BROKERACCOUNT FOR EDW.EDW.BROKERACCOUNT;
CREATE NICKNAME EDW.BROKERORDERS FOR EDW.EDW.BROKERORDERS;
CREATE NICKNAME EDW.CARDDETAILS FOR EDW.EDW.CARDDETAILS;
CREATE NICKNAME EDW.CREDITDETAILS FOR EDW.EDW.CREDITDETAILS;
CREATE NICKNAME EDW.CARDTRANSACTIONS FOR EDW.EDW.CARDTRANSACTIONS;
CREATE NICKNAME EDW.CARDTRANSATIONS FOR EDW.EDW.CARDTRANSATIONS;
CREATE NICKNAME EDW.CARDPAYMENT FOR EDW.EDW.CARDPAYMENT;
CREATE NICKNAME EDW.BROKERPOSITIONS FOR EDW.EDW.BROKERPOSITIONS;

CREATE NICKNAME CCA.CUSTOMER FOR CCA.CCA.CUSTOMER;
CREATE NICKNAME CCA.CARDDETAILS FOR CCA.CCA.CARDDETAILS;
CREATE NICKNAME CCA.TRANSACTIONS FOR CCA.CCA.TRANSACTIONS;
CREATE NICKNAME CCA.PAYMENTS FOR CCA.CCA.PAYMENTS;

CREATE NICKNAME BROKERAGE.CUSTOMER FOR BROKRAGE.BROKERAGE.CUSTOMER;
CREATE NICKNAME BROKERAGE.ADDRESS FOR BROKRAGE.BROKERAGE.ADDRESS;
CREATE NICKNAME BROKERAGE.ACCOUNT FOR BROKRAGE.BROKERAGE.ACCOUNT;
CREATE NICKNAME BROKERAGE.ORDERS FOR BROKRAGE.BROKERAGE.ORDERS;
CREATE NICKNAME BROKERAGE.POSITIONS FOR BROKRAGE.BROKERAGE.POSITIONS;
```

```
CREATE NICKNAME ODS.CUSTOMER FOR ODS.ODS.CUSTOMER;
CREATE NICKNAME ODS.ADDRESS FOR ODS.ODS.ADDRESS;
CREATE NICKNAME ODS.BROKERACCOUNT FOR ODS.ODS.BROKERACCOUNT;
CREATE NICKNAME ODS.CUSTXREF FOR ODS.ODS.CUSTXREF;
CREATE NICKNAME ODS.BROKERORDERS FOR ODS.ODS.BROKERORDERS;
CREATE NICKNAME ODS.CARDDETAILS FOR ODS.ODS.CARDDETAILS;
CREATE NICKNAME ODS.CARDTRANSACTIONS FOR ODS.ODS.CARDTRANSACTIONS;
CREATE NICKNAME ODS.CARDPAYMENTS FOR ODS.ODS.CARDPAYMENTS;
CREATE NICKNAME ODS.BROKERPOSITIONS FOR ODS.ODS.BROKERPOSITIONS;

DISCONNECT FEDDB;
```

Example 2-2   Define the Brokerage federated stored procedures

```
CONNECT TO FEDDB USER xxxxx USING yyyy;

CREATE PROCEDURE DB2ADMIN.BROKERAGE.PLACETRADE SOURCE BROKERAGE.PLACETRADE FOR SERVER
BROKRAGE;

CREATE PROCEDURE DB2ADMIN.BROKERAGE.OPENBROKERAGEACCOUNT SOURCE
BROKERAGE.OPENBROKERAGEACCOUNT FOR SERVER BROKRAGE;

CREATE PROCEDURE DB2ADMIN.BROKERAGE.BRO_ADDADDRESS SOURCE BROKERAGE.BRO_ADDADDRESS
FOR SERVER BROKRAGE;

CREATE PROCEDURE DB2ADMIN.BROKERAGE.BRO_ADDCUSTOMER SOURCE BROKERAGE.BRO_ADDCUSTOMER
FOR SERVER BROKRAGE;

CREATE PROCEDURE DB2ADMIN.BROKERAGE.BRO_UPDATEACCOUNT SOURCE
BROKERAGE.BRO_UPDATEACCOUNT FOR SERVER BROKRAGE;

CREATE PROCEDURE DB2ADMIN.BROKERAGE.BRO_UPDATEADDRESS SOURCE
BROKERAGE.BRO_UPDATEADDRESS FOR SERVER BROKRAGE;

CREATE PROCEDURE DB2ADMIN.BROKERAGE.BRO_UPDATECUSTOMER SOURCE
BROKERAGE.BRO_UPDATECUSTOMER FOR SERVER BROKRAGE;

DISCONNECT FEDDB;
```

Example 2-3   Define the CreditCard federated stored procedures

```
CONNECT TO FEDDB USER xxxxx USING yyyy;

CREATE PROCEDURE DB2ADMIN.CCA_ADDCUSTOMER SOURCE CCA.CCA_ADDCUSTOMER FOR SERVER CCA;
```

```
CREATE PROCEDURE DB2ADMIN.CCA_ADDCARDDETAILS SOURCE CCA.CCA_ADDCARDDETAILS FOR SERVER
CCA;

DISCONNECT FEDDB;
```

2.6 Step 2: Identify and create "core" information management processes

After the federation database has been prepared on the federation server, you should create any DataStage jobs, QualityStage jobs, federated queries, and stored procedures that you would like IBM Information Server to create SOA services for.

In our A2Z Financial Services self service scenario, we had to create DataStage jobs, QualityStage jobs, federated queries, and stored procedures as described in the following sections.

2.6.1 Create DataStage and QualityStage jobs

> **Attention:** For both DataStage and QualityStage jobs that you want to enable as information services, you need to check the box Enabled for Information Services. Right-click the **StandardizeAddress** job, and select **Properties** as shown in Figure 2-4. Check the box, Allow Multiple Instance, which then allows you to check the box, **Enabled for Information Services**, as shown in Figure 2-5. Click **OK**.

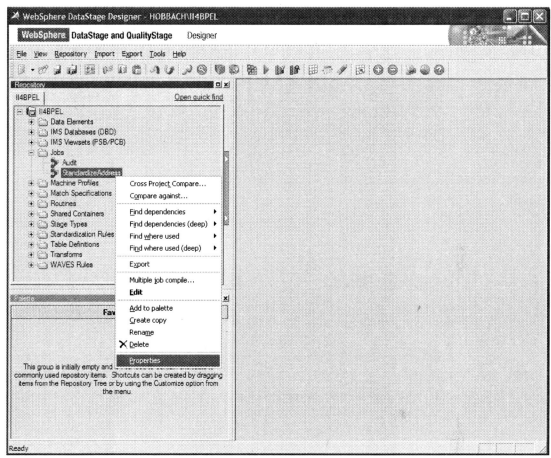

Figure 2-4   Enable DataStage/QualityStage jobs as an information service 1/2

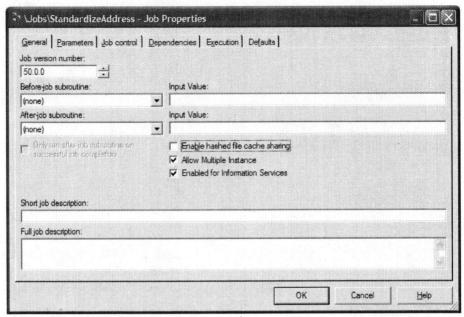

Figure 2-5   Enable DataStage/QualityStage jobs as an information service 2/2

To implement the self service functionality, we defined the need for two functions as follows:

► An audit trail function to record all actions taken by the customer. This function can be delivered using DataStage capabilities and exposed as an information service called AuditService. It is used by a number of self service business functions such as performing a trade and opening a brokerage account as described in "Step 5: Create "services" consumers" on page 307.

► Implement a new standardization function for addresses entered by the customer. This function can be delivered using QualityStage capabilities and exposed as an information service called StandardizeAddressService. It is used by a number of self service business functions such as opening a brokerage account and updating credit card customer information as described in "Step 5: Create "services" consumers" on page 307.

These are briefly described here.

Note: It is not our objective to explain the flows shown here. We assume that you are familiar with DataStage and QualityStage functionality and flows.

Audit DataStage job

Figure 2-6 on page 48 through Figure 2-17 on page 54 show the DataStage flow we designed for the audit trail function.

> **Note:** As mentioned earlier, the invocation of an IBM Information Server SOA service is synchronous, and requires a request/response model. If there is no response received by the invoker of the service, the requester will wait until a response is received from the service. To address this limitation, we needed to have the audit trail function send a response back to the invoker even though the normal semantics of an audit trail is to submit a request and not wait for the action to complete. This is implemented via the WISD_Output stage in Figure 2-6.

Figure 2-6 shows the overall flow of the function,

Figure 2-7 through Figure 2-9 on page 49 show the properties of the WISD_Input stage.

Figure 2-10 on page 50 through Figure 2-11 on page 51 show the properties of the Transformer stage.

Figure 2-12 on page 52 shows the properties of the WISD_Output stage.

In Figure 2-13 on page 52, we returned the application key (AppKey) as an output of the Audit trail job — we are not interested in the returned value, but must ensure that the WISD_Output stage job is not empty for the restriction described in "Client application access to services" on page 18.

Figure 2-14 on page 53 through Figure 2-17 on page 54 show the properties of the Audit_File stage.

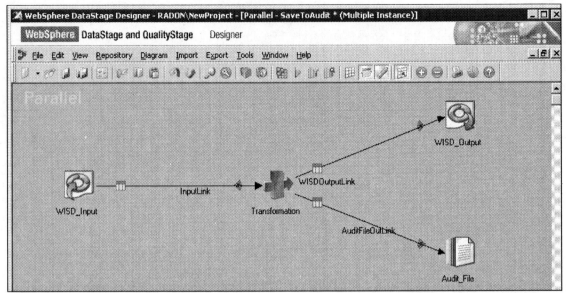

Figure 2-6   Audit trail DataStage flow 1/12

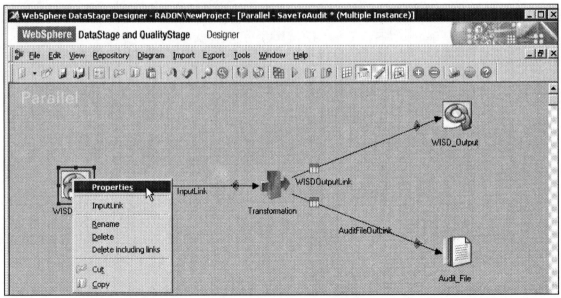

Figure 2-7   Audit trail DataStage flow 2/12

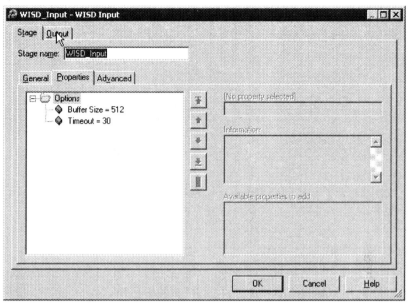

Figure 2-8   Audit trail DataStage flow 3/12

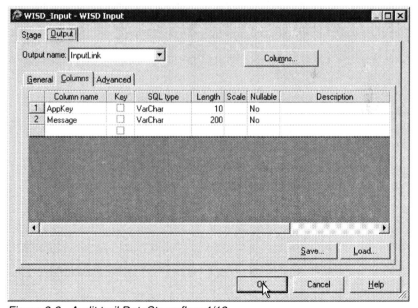

Figure 2-9   Audit trail DataStage flow 4/12

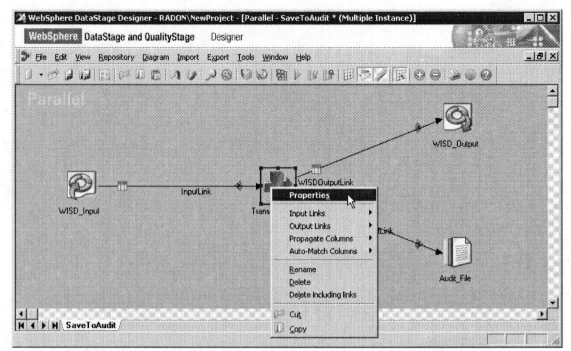

Figure 2-10   Audit trail DataStage flow 5/12

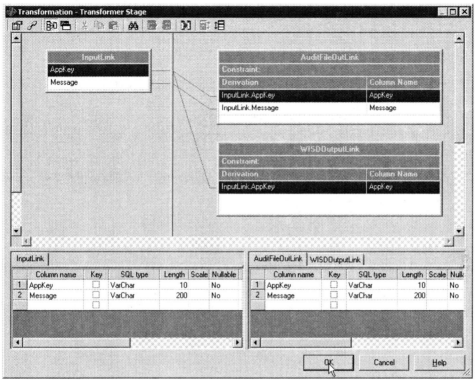

Figure 2-11   Audit trail DataStage flow 6/12

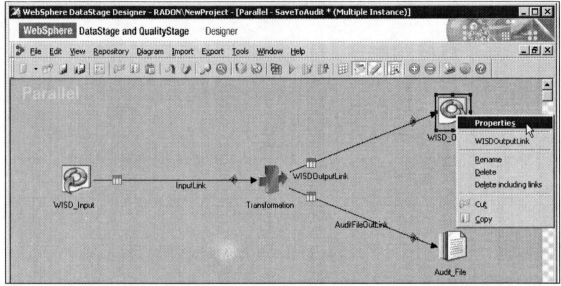

Figure 2-12   Audit trail DataStage flow 7/12

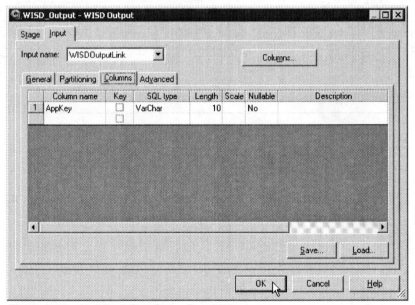

Figure 2-13   Audit trail DataStage flow 8/12

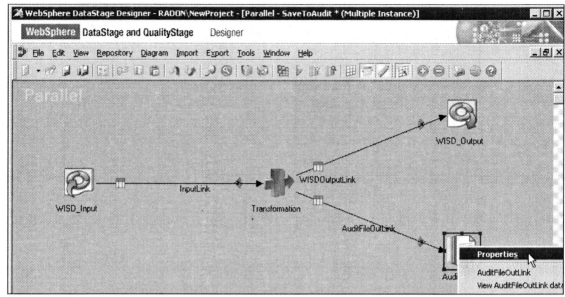

Figure 2-14   Audit trail DataStage flow 9/12

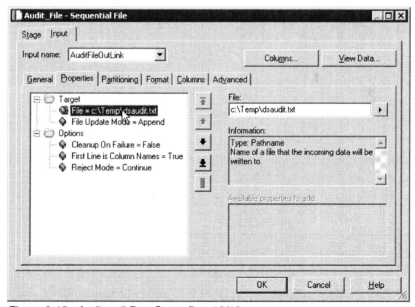

Figure 2-15   Audit trail DataStage flow 10/12

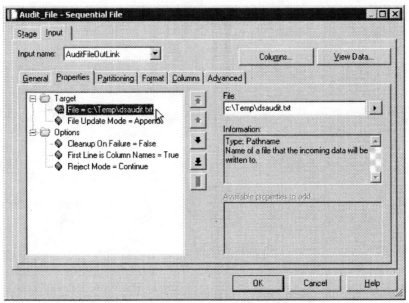

Figure 2-16   Audit trail DataStage flow 11/12

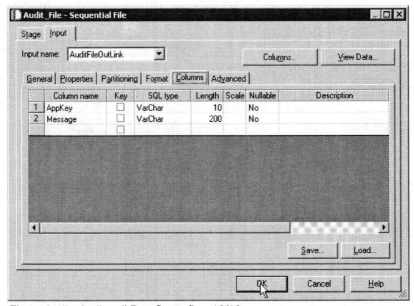

Figure 2-17   Audit trail DataStage flow 12/12

StandardizeAddress QualityStage job

Figure 2-18 on page 55 through Figure 2-26 on page 59 show the QualityStage job flow we designed for the standardize address function.

Figure 2-18 shows the overall flow of the function,

Figure 2-19 on page 56 through Figure 2-20 on page 56 show the properties of the InputAddress stage.

Figure 2-21 on page 57 through Figure 2-22 on page 57 show the properties of the StandardizeAddressFields stage.

Figure 2-23 on page 58 through Figure 2-24 on page 58 through show the properties of the PrepareForOutput stage.

Figure 2-25 on page 59 through Figure 2-26 on page 59 show the properties of the ReturnAddress stage.

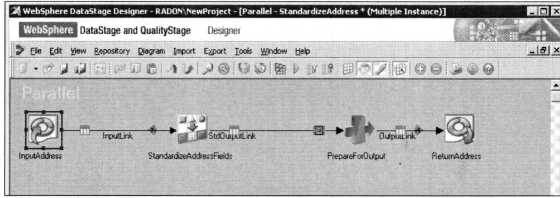

Figure 2-18 Standardize address QualityStage flow 1/9

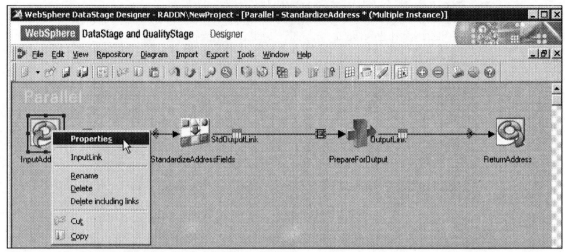

Figure 2-19   Standardize address QualityStage flow 2/9

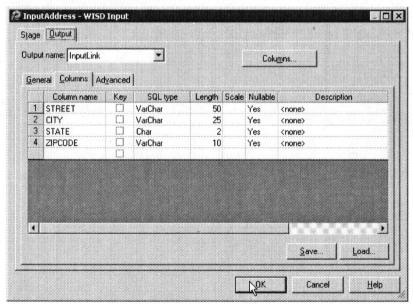

Figure 2-20   Standardize address QualityStage flow 3/9

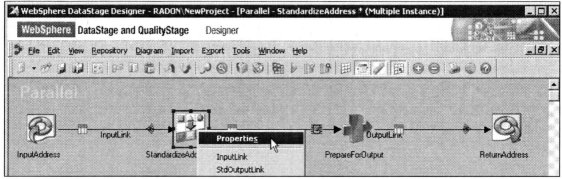

Figure 2-21   Standardize address QualityStage flow 4/9

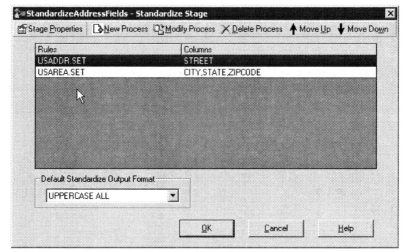

Figure 2-22   Standardize address QualityStage flow 5/9

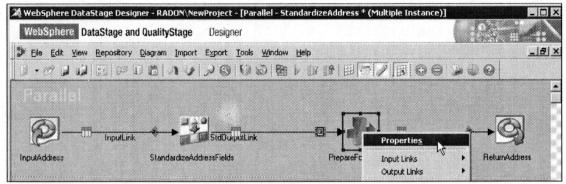

Figure 2-23 Standardize address QualityStage flow 6/9

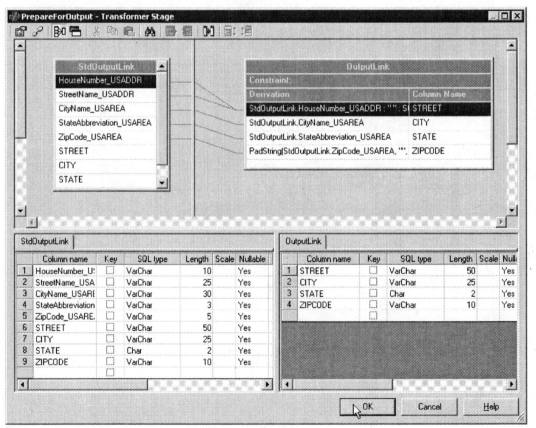

Figure 2-24 Standardize address QualityStage flow 7/9

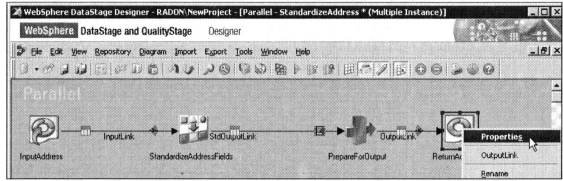

Figure 2-25   Standardize address QualityStage flow 8/9

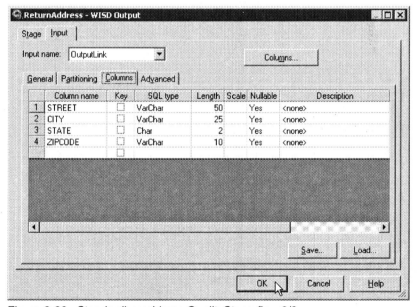

Figure 2-26   Standardize address QualityStage flow 9/9

2.6.2 Create federated queries

To implement the self service functionality, we defined the need for a number of federated queries as follows:

▶ A lookup of a customer ID on the Brokerage and CreditCard systems. The social security number of the customer is used as the self service customer's login id. Example 2-4 shows two queries that look up the actual customer ID in the Brokerage and CreditCard systems for a given social security number.

Example 2-4   Look up CUSTOMER ID on the Brokerage and CreditCard systems

```
-- lookupBrokerageCustomerID
SELECT A.CUSTID FROM BROKERAGE.CUSTOMER A WHERE A.SSNUMB = ?

-- lookupCreditCardCustomerID
SELECT A.CUSTID FROM CCA.CUSTOMER A WHERE A.SSNUMB = ?
```

► Two federated queries against the Brokerage system that list the positions held in an account and the cost basis of the positions. These are not shown here.

► Two federated queries against the CreditCard system that list the transactions associated with a particular account. One query (for platinum or high value customers) provides this information from the operational system, the operational data store and the enterprise data warehouse. The second query (for gold or medium value customers) only provides this information from the operational data store and the enterprise data warehouse. Example 2-5 shows the two queries.

We can now proceed to create the Information Server services as described in "Step 3: Create Information Server services" on page 62.

Example 2-5   CreditCard application queries

```
--Platinum Customers all 3 systems
WITH CUST AS (SELECT CUSTOMERID, CCCUSTID FROM ODS.CUSTXREF WHERE CCCUSTID = ?)

(SELECT A.AMOUNT,A.TRANDATE AS TRANDATE, 'ODS' AS SOURCE
FROM ODS.CARDTRANSACTIONS A, ODS.CARDDETAILS B, CUST
WHERE A.CARDDETAILSFK=B.CARDNUMBER AND B.CARDCUSTID=CUST.CCCUSTID)

UNION

(SELECT A.AMOUNT, A.TRANDATE AS TRANDATE, 'OPS' AS SOURCE
FROM CCA.TRANSACTIONS A, CCA.CARDDETAILS B,CUST
WHERE A.CARDDETAILSFK=B.CARDNUMBER AND B.CUSTOMERFK=CUST.CCCUSTID)

UNION

(SELECT A.AMOUNT, A.TRANDATE AS TRANDATE, 'EDW' AS SOURCE
FROM EDW.CARDTRANSACTIONS A, EDW.CARDDETAILS B, CUST
WHERE A.CARDDETAILSFK=B.CARDNUMBER AND B.CARDCUSTID=CUST.CCCUSTID)

--Gold Customers no operational systems
WITH CUST AS (SELECT CUSTOMERID, CCCUSTID FROM ODS.CUSTXREF WHERE CCCUSTID = ?)
```

```
(SELECT A.AMOUNT, A.TRANDATE AS TRANDATE, 'ODS' AS SOURCE
FROM ODS.CARDTRANSACTIONS A, ODS.CARDDETAILS B, CUST
WHERE A.CARDDETAILSFK=B.CARDNUMBER AND B.CARDCUSTID=CUST.CCCUSTID)

UNION

(SELECT A.AMOUNT, A.TRANDATE AS TRANDATE, 'EDW' AS SOURCE
FROM EDW.CARDTRANSACTIONS A, EDW.CARDDETAILS B, CUST
WHERE A.CARDDETAILSFK=B.CARDNUMBER AND B.CARDCUSTID=CUST.CCCUSTID)
```

2.6.3 Create stored procedures

An authorization service needed to be created for the self service solution to
validate a customer logging in with a social security number. We chose to write
an SQL stored procedure (shown in Example 2-6 on page 61) to perform this
function, and use IBM Information Server to generate an SOA service of it.

> **Attention:** In the real world, it is highly unlikely that you would implement an
> authorization service using a stored procedure. We did so for expedience.

Example 2-6   SQL stored procedure authorizeaction

```
CREATE PROCEDURE feddb.authorizeaction(IN p_ssnumb VARCHAR(13),
                                IN action VARCHAR(40),
                                OUT AUTHORIZED INTEGER)
LANGUAGE SQL
P1: BEGIN
   DECLARE CUSTID VARCHAR(20) DEFAULT '--';

   SET AUTHORIZED = 0;

   IF SUBSTR(ACTION, 1, 9) = 'Brokerage' THEN
       SELECT B.CUSTID INTO CUSTID FROM BROKERAGE.CUSTOMER AS B WHERE B.SSNUMB =
p_ssnumb;
       IF CUSTID<>'--' THEN
          SET AUTHORIZED = 1;
       END IF;
   END IF;

   IF ACTION = 'CreditCard' THEN
      SELECT C.CUSTID INTO CUSTID FROM CCA.CUSTOMER AS C WHERE C.SSNUMB = p_ssnumb;
      IF CUSTID<>'--' THEN
         SET AUTHORIZED = 1;
```

```
      END IF;
    END IF;

END P1@
```

2.7 Step 3: Create Information Server services

IBM Information Server enables you to create SOA service wrappers around stored procedures, federated queries, DataStage job, and QualityStage jobs with EJB and/or SOAP over HTTP bindings.

Our A2Z Financial Services' self service scenario had the following items around which SOA services had to be defined:

1. AuditService for the Audit DataStage job described in "Audit DataStage job" on page 47.

2. StandardizeAddressService for the StandardizeAddress QualityStage job described in "StandardizeAddress QualityStage job" on page 55.

3. CustomerIdLookupService for the lookupBrokerageCustomerID and lookupCreditCard CustomerID SQL queries described in "Create federated queries" on page 59.

4. AuthorizationService for the isAuthorizedFor stored procedure described in "Create stored procedures" on page 61.

5. CardMaintenanceService for the updateCardDetails and updateCustomer federated stored procedures for the CreditCard system.

6. CardStatusPlatinumService for the getTransactions platinum federated query for the CreditCard system.

7. CardStatusService for the getTransactions gold federated query for the CreditCard system.

8. AccountStatusPlatinumService for the getPositions platinum and the getBalances platinum federated queries for the Brokerage system.

9. AccountStatusService for the getPositions and the getBalances federated queries for the Brokerage system.

10. placeTradesService for the Trade federated stored procedure for the Brokerage system.

11. AccountMaintenanceService for the updateAccount, updateAddress, and the updateCustomer federated stored procedures for the Brokerage system.

12. NewCardService for the addNewCustomer and addCardDetails federated stored procedures for the CreditCard system.

13. NewAccountService for the addNewCustomer, addNewAccount, and addCustomerAddress federated stored procedures for the Brokerage system.

> **Attention:** In the following sections, we describe one example of the creation, deployment and testing of an SOA service generated from each source type such as stored procedure, federated query, and a DataStage job.

Figure 2-27 shows the main steps in creating an SOA service using IBM Information Server. These are described in more detail as follows:

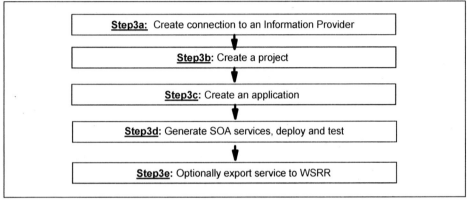

Figure 2-27 Steps in creating SOA services

> **Attention:** In all the following sections, to avoid overburdening you with excessive screen captures, we have *not* included all the panels that you would typically navigate through in order to perform the desired function. Instead we have focused on including select screen captures (and in some cases, just portions of them) that highlight the key items of interest, thereby skipping both initial screen captures, as well as some intervening ones, in the process.

2.7.1 Step 3a: Create connection to an Information Provider

You need to create a connection to an Information Provider before being able to generate an SOA service. There are two types of Information Providers — a "DataStage and QualityStage" type for DataStage and QualityStage jobs, and a "DB2 or Federation Server" type for stored procedures and federated queries.

Figure 2-28 through Figure 2-37 describe the creation and testing of a "DB2 or Federation Server" type of information provider:

1. Launch the IBM Information Server console by clicking **Start** → **Programs** → **IBM Information Server** → **IBM Information Server Console** and then provide login information as shown in Figure 2-28.

2. Click **Home**, expand **Configuration**, and click **Information Services Connections** as shown in Figure 2-29 on page 65.

3. Then click **New** under Tasks column in Figure 2-30 on page 66 to create a new Information Services connection.

4. Provide details of the Connection Name (we chose FEDDB since this connection will access the FEDDB database), Information Provider Type ("DB2 or Federation Server" from the drop-down list) as shown in Figure 2-31 on page 66.

5. Then provide details of the Agent Host (RADON from the drop-down list which is where IBM Information Server is installed), Database Host (RADON where the database is installed) and its Port (50000) as shown in Figure 2-32 on page 67.

6. Click **Add** to add databases to the list of databases. Provide database details (FEDDB) along with the User Name and Password to access it, and click **OK** as shown in Figure 2-33 on page 68.

> **Note:** JDBC Connection Properties such as isolation levels may be specified in Figure 2-33 on page 68 to override defaults used by IBM Information Server.

7. Highlight the FEDDB database in the Database box, and click **Test** to ensure that the database has been configured correctly as shown in Figure 2-34 on page 69 and Figure 2-35 on page 70. Click **OK** in Figure 2-35 on page 70.

8. After successful validation, click **Save & Enable** to complete the definition of the Information Provider as shown in Figure 2-36 on page 71 and Figure 2-37 on page 72.

> **Note:** While we chose to access only a single database (FEDDB) on the database server (RADON), you can in fact access all the databases on the database server. You have to add the databases of interest on the database server as was done with FEDDB as shown in Figure 2-31 on page 66 through Figure 2-33 on page 68.

We can now proceed to create a project as described in "Step 3b: Create a project" on page 72.

Note: The creation of a DataStage and QualityStage type of information provider is not shown here. It is somewhat similar to that of creating the "DB2 or Federation Server" type, with the following differences:

► It does not have the database configuration aspect.

► With DataStage & QualityStage, the connection should already be there, and it just needs to be enabled (which just consists of adding a user/password). You do not need to create a new "DataStage and QualityStage" connection.

Figure 2-28   Login to the IBM Information Server console

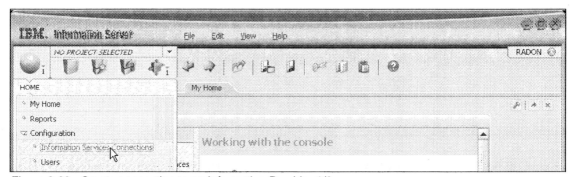

Figure 2-29   Create connection to an Information Provider 1/9

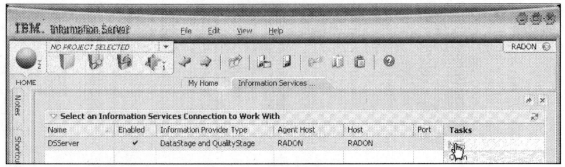

Figure 2-30   Create connection to an Information Provider 2/9

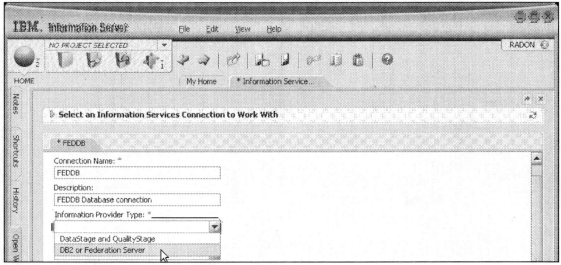

Figure 2-31   Create connection to an Information Provider 3/9

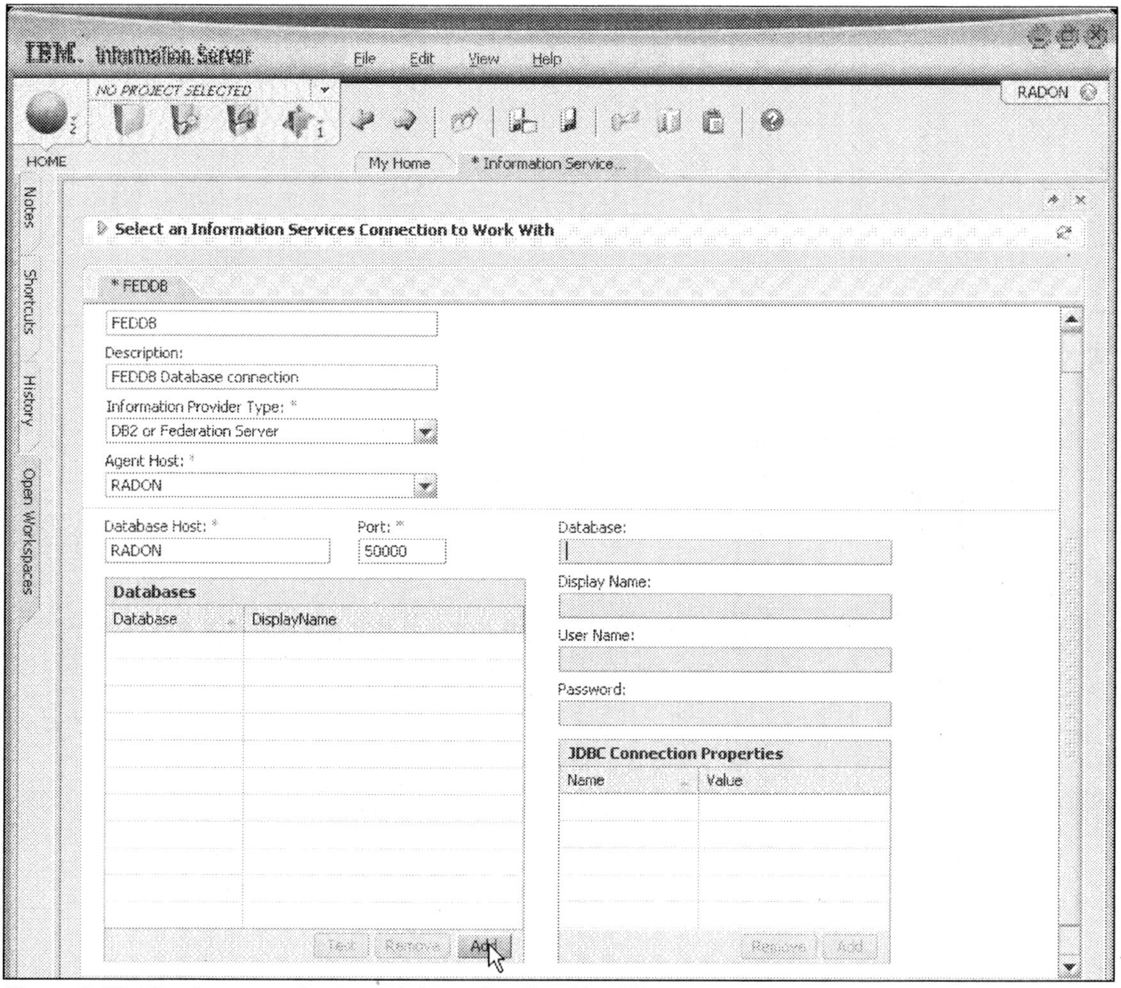

Figure 2-32   Create connection to an Information Provider 4/9

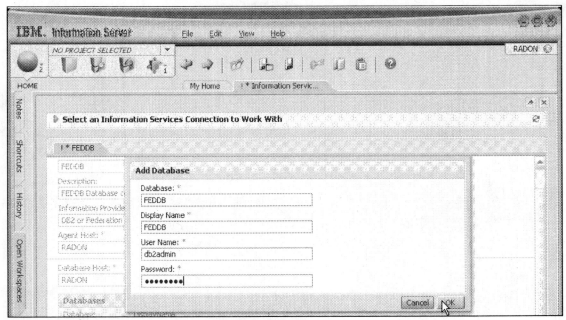

Figure 2-33   Create connection to an Information Provider 5/9

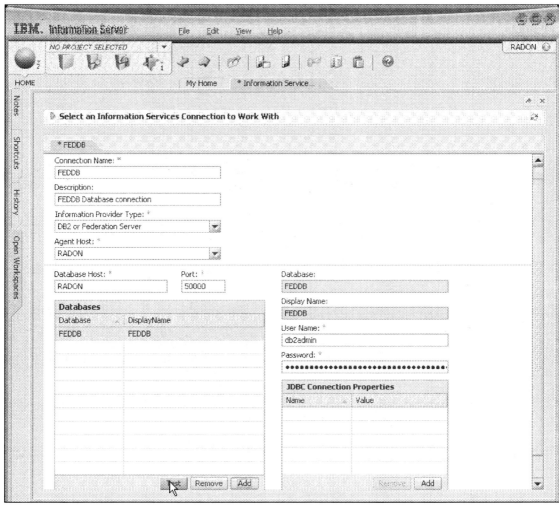

Figure 2-34   Create connection to an Information Provider 6/9

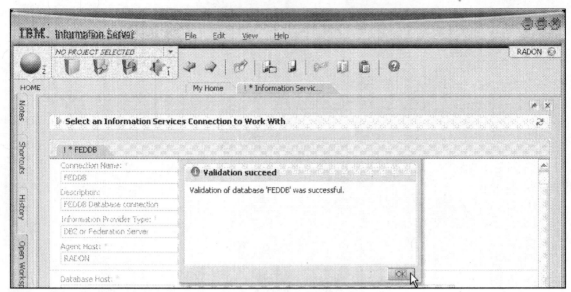

Figure 2-35   Create connection to an Information Provider 7/9

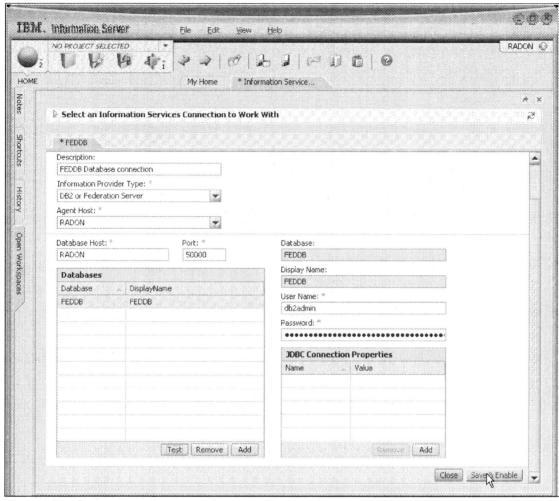

Figure 2-36   Create connection to an Information Provider 8/9

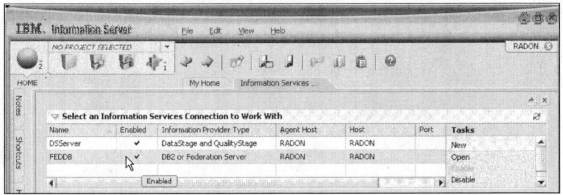

Figure 2-37   Create connection to an Information Provider 9/9

2.7.2 Step 3b: Create a project

To create an SOA service using IBM Information Server, you need to create a project and an application. While the application is a deployable unit[4], a project is a mechanism for grouping SOA services together in a logical unit. A project is a collaborative environment that you use to design applications, services, and operations. Proceed as follows:

1. After logging in to the IBM Information Server Console, click **New Project** as shown in Figure 2-38.

2. Provide the Name (A2ZProject) in Figure 2-39 on page 73 and click **OK**.

3. Provide a Description (A2Z Financial Services) and click **Save** to complete the definition of the project.

We can now proceed to create an application under this project as described in "Step 3c: Create an application" on page 75.

---

[4] An application becomes a ".ear" file that gets deployed on the WebSphere Application Server associated with IBM Information Server.

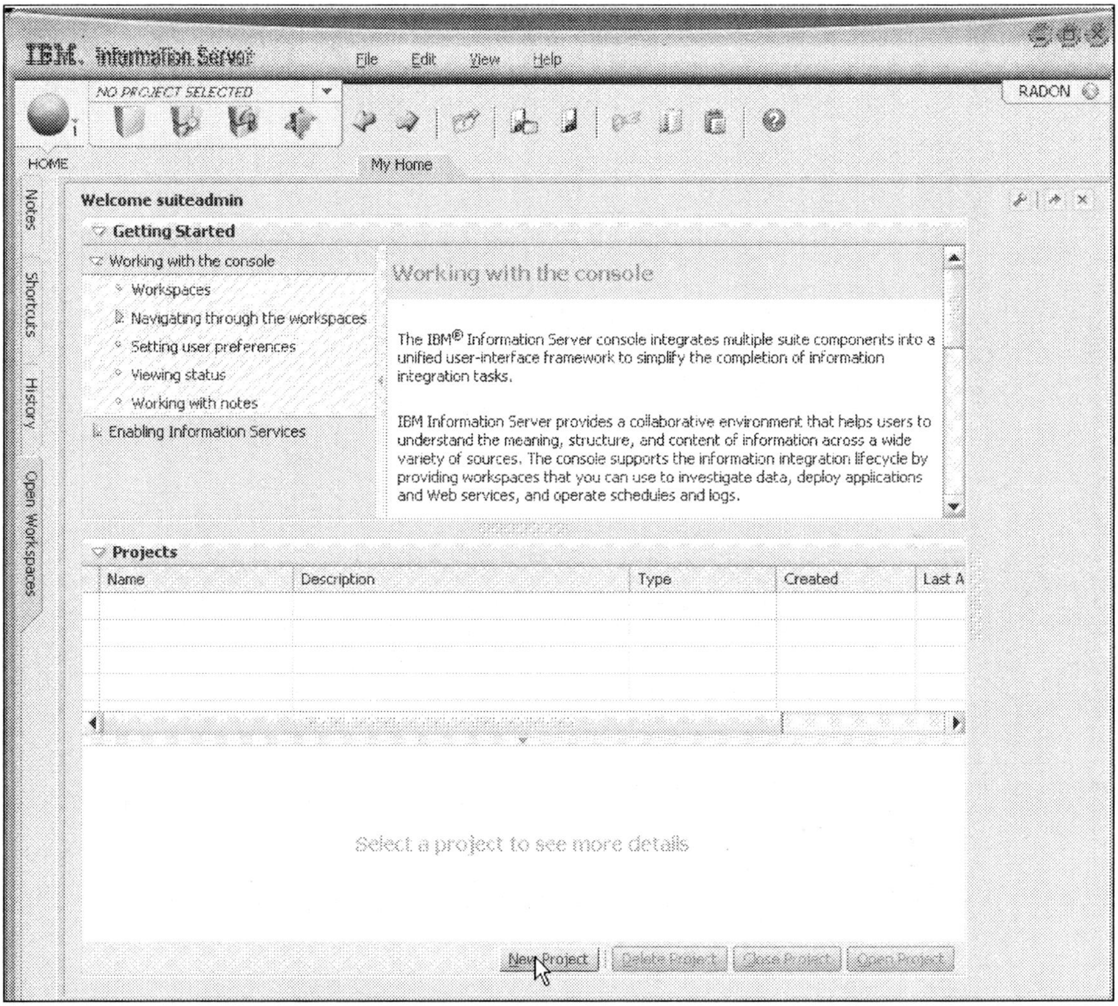

Figure 2-38   Create a new project 1/3

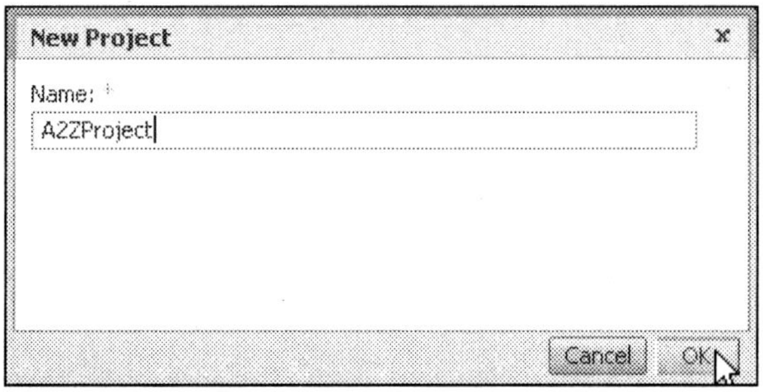

Figure 2-39   Create a new project 2/3

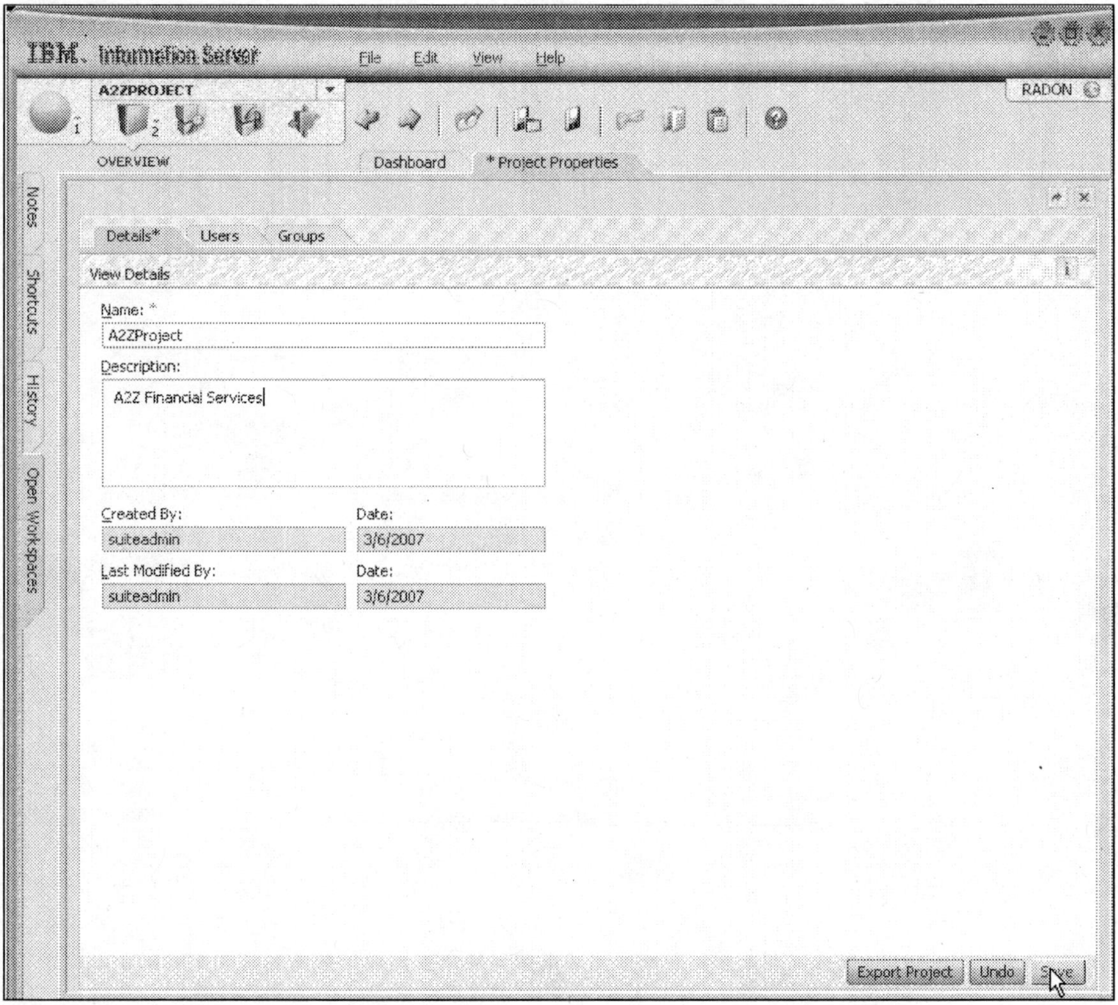

Figure 2-40 Create a new project 3/3

2.7.3 Step 3c: Create an application

To create an application, proceed as follows:

1. After saving the project definition, click **Information Services Application** under the Develop icon as shown in Figure 2-41.

2. Click **New** under the Tasks column to create a new Information Services Application to work with as shown in Figure 2-42 on page 76.

3. Provide details of the application such as Name (CommonServicesApp) and Description (Common services used by the brokerage and credit card applications) and click **Save Application** to complete the definition as shown in Figure 2-43 on page 77.

> **Note:** An application is a deployable unit, in that a ".ear" file is created for each application, and appears as an installed application when viewed from the WebSphere Application Server Administrative Console. We create three applications (BrokerageApp, CreditCardApp, and CommonServicesApp) in this project. After services have been defined in each of these applications, and deployed, these applications will appear in the WebSphere Application Server Administrative Console as shown in Figure 2-44 on page 78.

We can now proceed to generate the various SOA services, deploy and test them as described in "Step 3d: Generate SOA services, deploy, and test" on page 78.

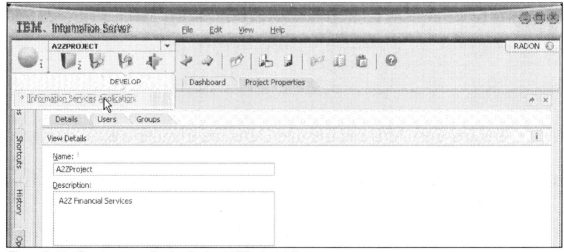

Figure 2-41   Create an application in the A2ZProject 1/3

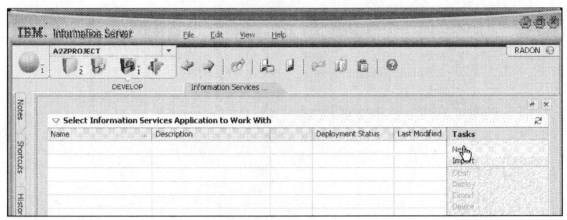

Figure 2-42   Create an application in the A2ZProject 2/3

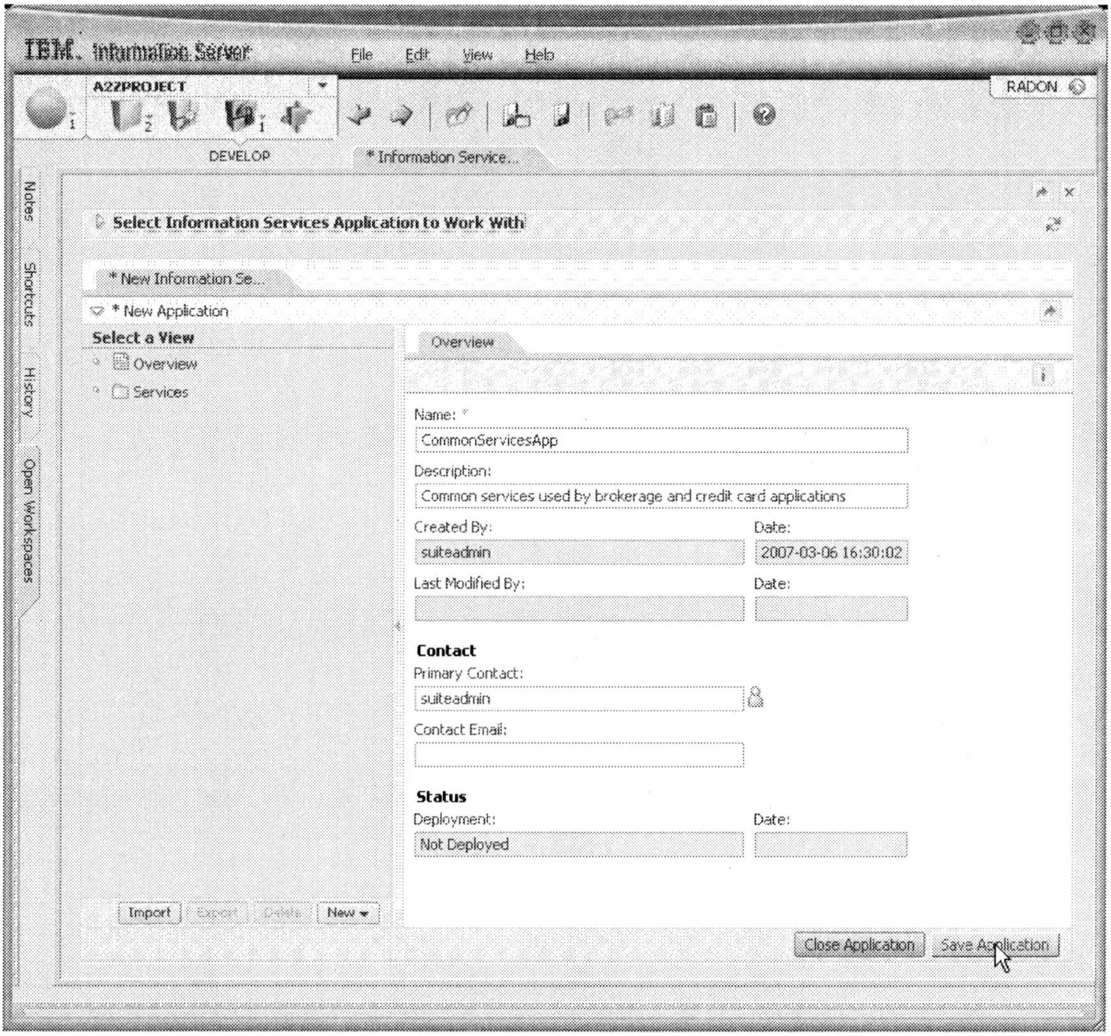

Figure 2-43 Create an application in the A2ZProject 3/3

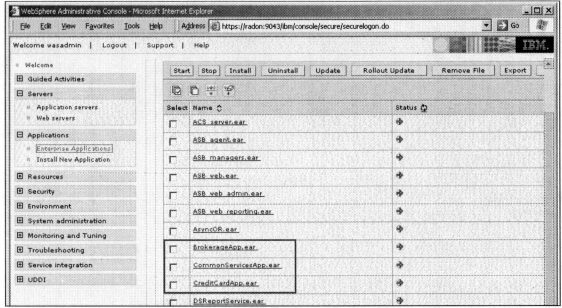

Figure 2-44   IBM Information Server deployed applications in WebSphere Application Server

2.7.4 Step 3d: Generate SOA services, deploy, and test

The A2Z Financial Services' self service application has 22 processes that require SOA services to be defined for them. As described earlier, they are a combination of DataStage, QualityStage, federated queries and stored procedures. In this section, we show the definition of services for each type of process, the deployment of one of these services, and a test that involves SOAP over HTTP and EJB bindings.

This section includes the following topics:

► Generate a stored procedure service
► Deploy the stored procedure service
► Test the stored procedure service (SOAP over HTTP binding)
► Test the stored procedure service (EJB binding)
► Generate a DataStage QualityStage service
► Generate a federated query service
► List of all deployed services

Generate a stored procedure service

Figure 2-45 on page 80 through Figure 2-57 on page 91 describe the steps involved in generating an SOA service of a stored procedure with SOAP over HTTP and EJB bindings:

1. After creating an application, expand Services and select **New Service** for the CommonServicesApp application as shown in Figure 2-45.

2. Provide details such as the Name (AuthorizationService) and Description (Authorization Service) and click **Save Application** as shown in Figure 2-46 on page 81.

3. Expand Operations, double-click **newOperation1** and then modify the Name field to isAuthorizedFor and Description field (Checks if user is authorized for an action) as shown in Figure 2-47 on page 82. Click **Select** to select an information provider.

4. Select **DB2 or Federation Server** as the Information Provider Type from the drop-down list (Figure 2-48 on page 82), and Stored Procedure from the Subtype drop-down list as shown in Figure 2-49 on page 83.

5. Select **FEDDB** in the Select a Database column, and highlight AUTHORIZEACTION in the "Select a Stored Procedure", and click **OK** as shown in Figure 2-50 on page 84.

6. The output of the isAuthorizedFor operation is shown in Figure 2-51 on page 85.

7. Click **Save Application** to save the changes as shown in Figure 2-52 on page 86.

8. Next specify the bindings for the service. Double-click **Bindings** for the AuthorizationService in Figure 2-53 on page 87.

9. Click **Attach Bindings** and select **SOAP over HTTP** and **EJB** as shown in Figure 2-54 on page 88 and Figure 2-55 on page 89.

10. Click **Save Application** to save these changes as shown in Figure 2-56 on page 90, and click **Yes** on the prompt to confirm the unsaved changes before releasing the edit lock as shown in Figure 2-57 on page 91.

> **Note:** Multiple bindings can be defined depending upon the environments (J2EE and/or .NET) in which client applications consuming these services operate. We chose both bindings to demonstrate this capability.

We can now proceed to deploy the generated SOA service as described in "Deploy the stored procedure service" on page 91.

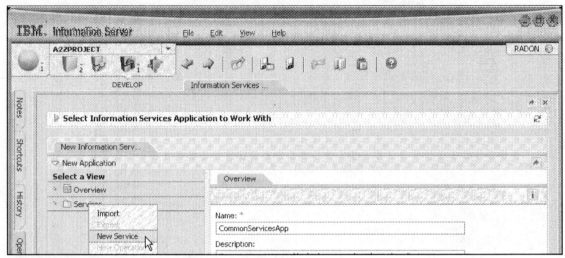

Figure 2-45   Generate a stored procedure service 1/13

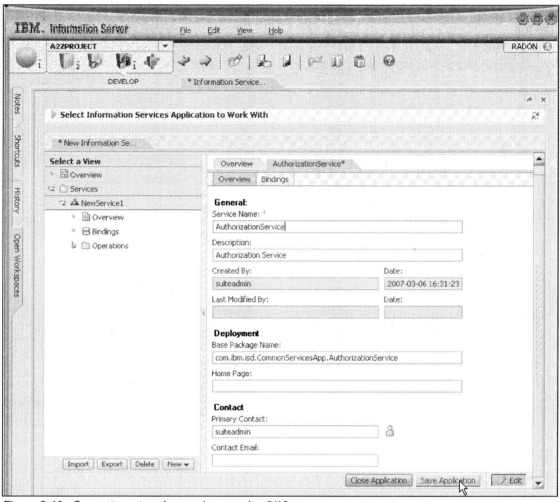

Figure 2-46   Generate a stored procedure service 2/13

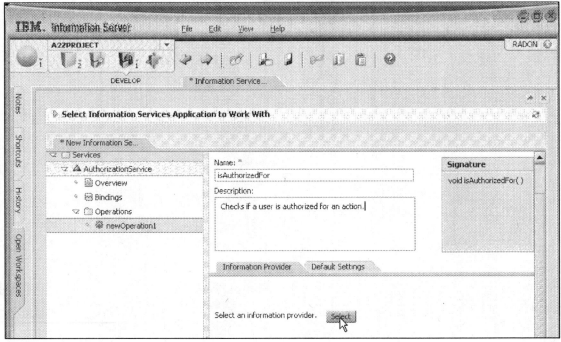

Figure 2-47   Generate a stored procedure service 3/13

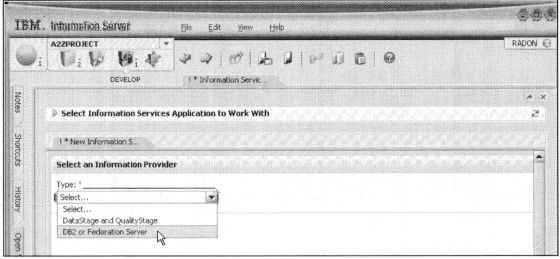

Figure 2-48   Generate a stored procedure service 4/13

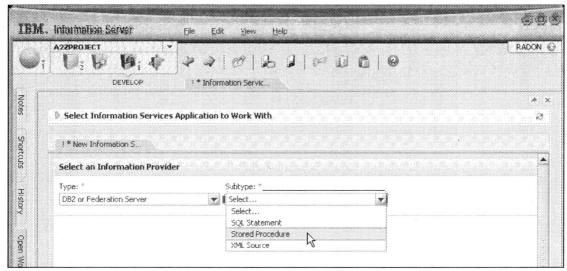

Figure 2-49   Generate a stored procedure service 5/13

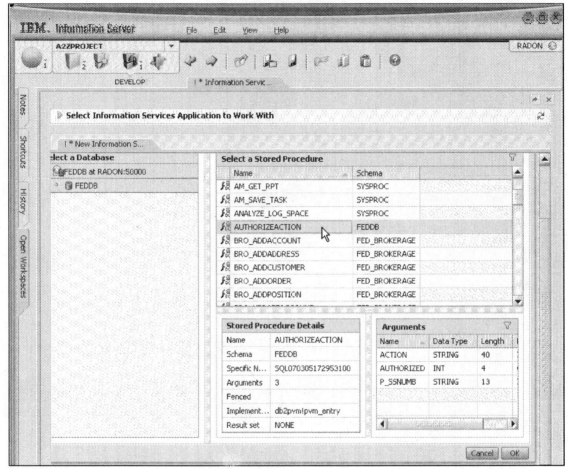

Figure 2-50   Generate a stored procedure service 6/13

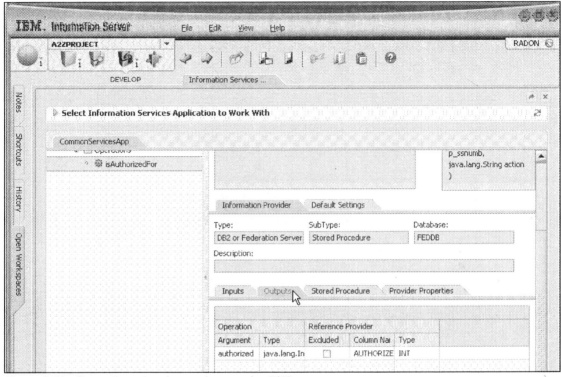

Figure 2-51   Generate a stored procedure service 7/13

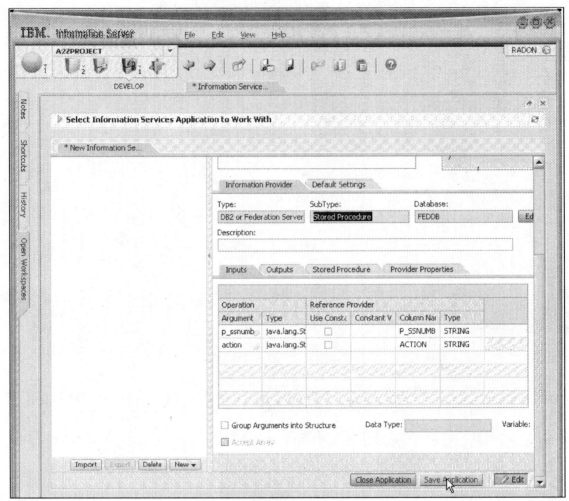

Figure 2-52   Generate a stored procedure service 8/13

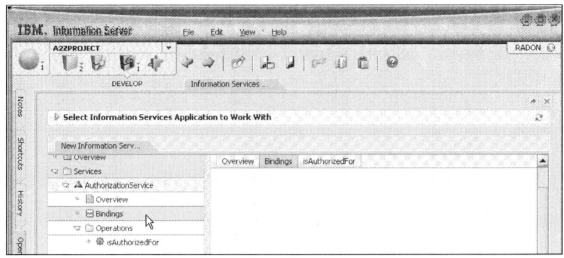

Figure 2-53   Generate a stored procedure service 9/13

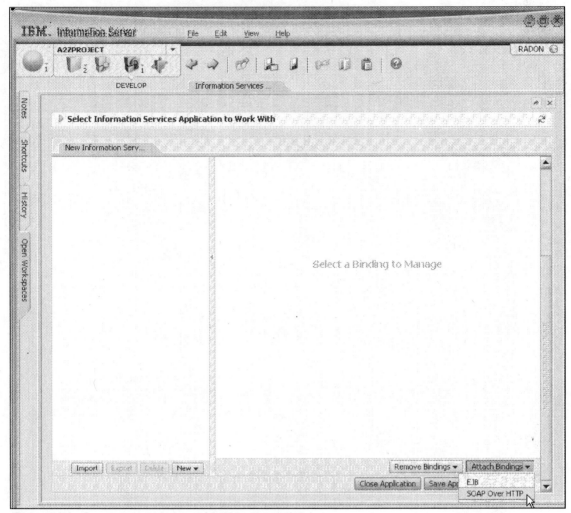

Figure 2-54   Generate a stored procedure service 10/13

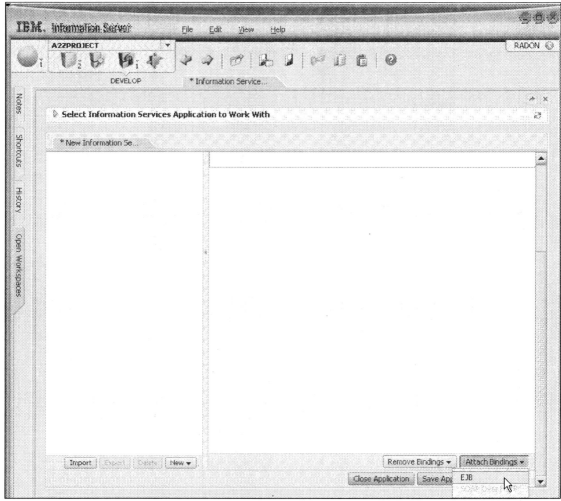

Figure 2-55   Generate a stored procedure service 11/13

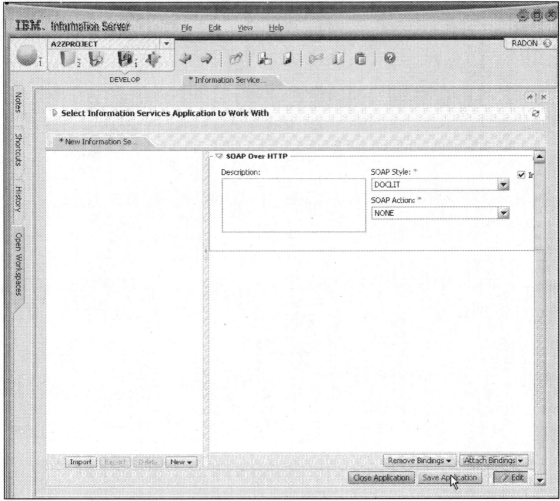

Figure 2-56   Generate a stored procedure service 12/13

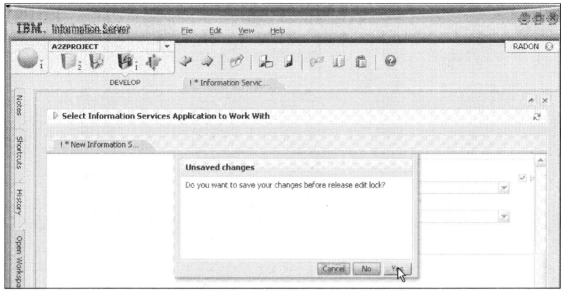

Figure 2-57   Generate a stored procedure service 13/13

Deploy the stored procedure service

To deploy the stored procedure service, proceed as follows:

1. To deploy the saved CommonServicesApp, switch to edit by clicking **Edit** in Figure 2-58.

2. Then select and right-click **CommonServicesApp**, and select **Deploy** as shown in Figure 2-59 on page 93. Confirm the services, bindings and operations to include in this deployment by checking the appropriate boxes. We chose not to exclude any bindings or operations.

3. Click **Deploy** as shown in Figure 2-60 on page 94.

4. When deployment is completed, the status of the CommonServicesApp has a Deployment Status of Deployed as shown in Figure 2-61 on page 95.

We can now proceed to test the SOAP over HTTP binding of this deployed service as described in "Test the stored procedure service (SOAP binding)" on page 95.

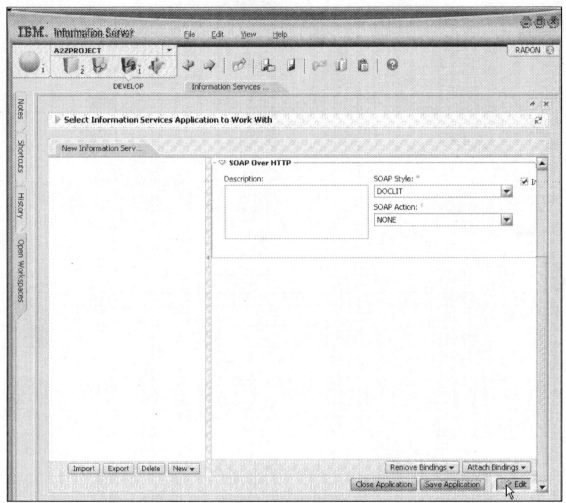

Figure 2-58   Deploy the stored procedure 1/4

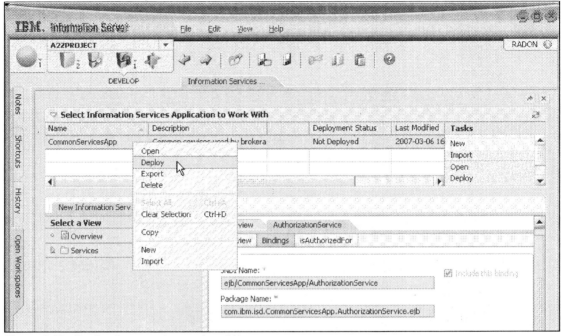

Figure 2-59   Deploy the stored procedure 2/4

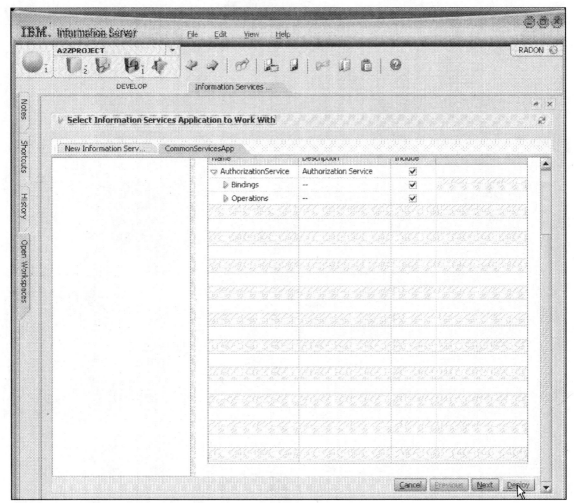

Figure 2-60   Deploy the stored procedure 3/4

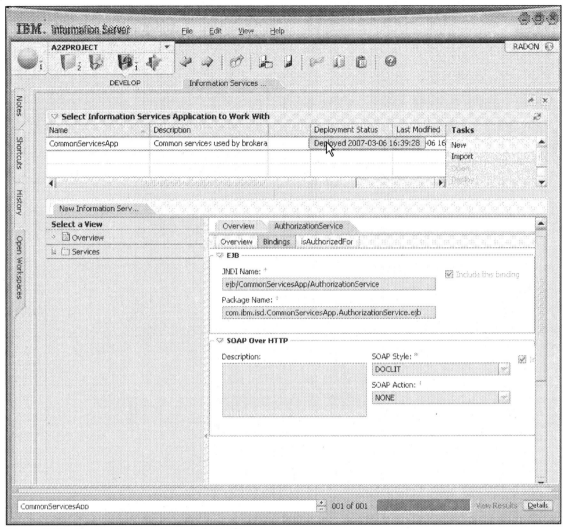

Figure 2-61   Deploy the stored procedure 4/4

Test the stored procedure service (SOAP binding)

The AuthorizationService was deployed with both SOAP over HTTP and EJB bindings. In this step, we test the deployed stored procedure service using SOAP over HTTP bindings. Figure 2-62 on page 97 through Figure 2-74 on page 106 show the process for testing the deployed service using SOAP over HTTP.

To test the service, we need to identify the location of the WSDL describing the deployed service as shown in Figure 2-62 through Figure 2-67 on page 100. The Rational Application Developer (RAD) tool is then used to test this service as shown in Figure 2-68 on page 102 through Figure 2-74 on page 106.

Figure 2-62 through Figure 2-67 on page 100 show the steps to find the WSDL:

1. Use the Web console interface to login to the IBM Information Server by typing the `http://radon:9080/` URL as shown in Figure 2-62. Provide the User Name and Password, and click **Enter**.

2. Select the Information Services Catalog tab in the IBM Information Server Welcome page as shown in Figure 2-63 on page 98.

3. Click **Manage Deployed Services** in Figure 2-64 on page 98 to view all the deployed services as shown in Figure 2-65 on page 99. Check AuthorizationService in the Name column and click **Open.**

4. Select Bindings in the Select a View column, and click **Open WSDL Document** in Figure 2-66 on page 99 to view the contents of the AuthorizationService WSDL document (Figure 2-67 on page 100).

5. The highlighted URL in the Address bar is the location of the AuthorizationService WSDL document to be used in testing the stored procedure service using SOAP over HTTP binding. Example 2-7 on page 101 shows the contents of the AuthorizationService WSDL document.

Figure 2-68 on page 102 through Figure 2-74 on page 106 describe the steps for testing the AuthorizationService stored procedure service using RAD:

1. After launching RAD, the Web Services Explorer is only available if the Web Services Developer is enabled — this can be done by selecting Preferences from the Window menu bar as shown in Figure 2-68 on page 102, checking the Web Services Developer (locked) box under Capabilities and clicking **OK** as shown in Figure 2-69 on page 103.

2. Click **Launch the Web Services Explorer** from the Run menu bar as shown in Figure 2-70 on page 103.

3. Click the appropriate icon to get the WSDL Main button, highlight it and type[5] in the location of the AuthorizationService WSDL file identified in Figure 2-67 on page 100:

   `(http://radon:9080/wisd/CommonServicesApp/AuthorizationService/wsdl/`
   `AuthorizationService.wsdl)`

4. Click **Go** as shown in Figure 2-71 on page 104.

---

[5] Or copy and paste the URL from the browser used to navigate to the WSDL location

5. Expand AuthorizationService in the Navigator pane in Figure 2-72 on page 104, highlight the AuthorizationServiceSOAPSoapBinding and then click **isAuthorizedFor** operation.

6. Provide a string argument for the ssnumb field (611-320-3978) and a string argument for the action field (Brokerage_OpenAccount) in Figure 2-73 on page 105 and click **Go**.

7. Figure 2-74 on page 106 shows the Status of this request as being successful with "isAuthorizedForReturn (int) 0".

> **Note:** While we used the RAD tool to test this service, you may use any of the numerous freeware and commercially available tools available to test a SOAP over HTTP service.

We can now proceed to test the stored procedure service using the generated EJB binding as described in "Test the stored procedure service (EJB binding)" on page 106.

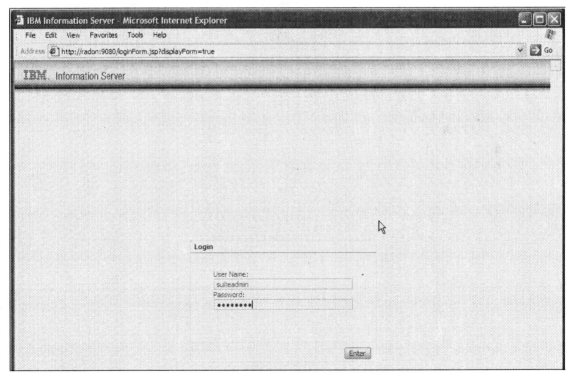

Figure 2-62   Determine location of the AuthorizationService stored procedure service WSDL 1/6

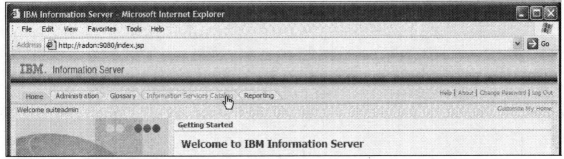

Figure 2-63   Determine location of the AuthorizationService stored procedure service WSDL 2/6

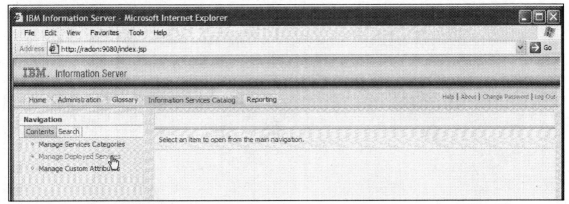

Figure 2-64   Determine location of the AuthorizationService stored procedure service WSDL 3/6

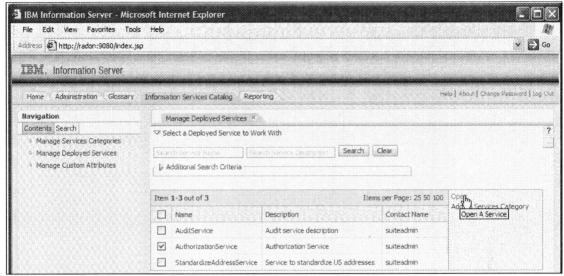

Figure 2-65   Determine location of the AuthorizationService stored procedure service WSDL 4/6

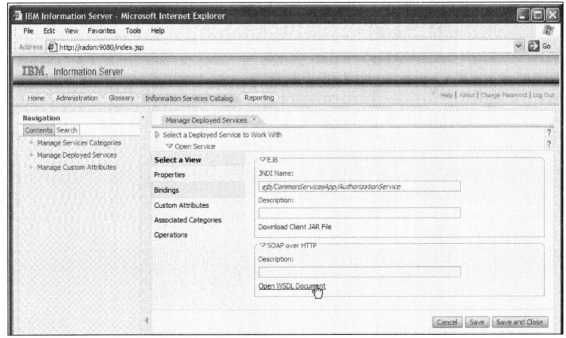

Figure 2-66   Determine location of the AuthorizationService stored procedure service WSDL 5/6

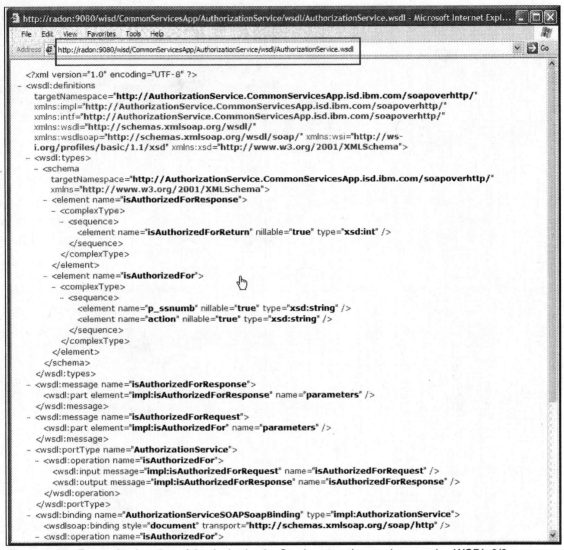

Figure 2-67   Determine location of the AuthorizationService stored procedure service WSDL 6/6

Example 2-7 AuthorizationService WSDL document

```
<?xml version="1.0" encoding="UTF-8" ?>
- <wsdl:definitions
targetNamespace="http://AuthorizationService.CommonServicesApp.isd.ibm.com/soapoverht
tp/"
xmlns:impl="http://AuthorizationService.CommonServicesApp.isd.ibm.com/soapoverhttp/"
xmlns:intf="http://AuthorizationService.CommonServicesApp.isd.ibm.com/soapoverhttp/"
xmlns:wsdl="http://schemas.xmlsoap.org/wsdl/"
xmlns:wsdlsoap="http://schemas.xmlsoap.org/wsdl/soap/"
xmlns:wsi="http://ws-i.org/profiles/basic/1.1/xsd"
xmlns:xsd="http://www.w3.org/2001/XMLSchema">
- <wsdl:types>
- <schema
targetNamespace="http://AuthorizationService.CommonServicesApp.isd.ibm.com/soapoverht
tp/" xmlns="http://www.w3.org/2001/XMLSchema">
- <element name="isAuthorizedForResponse">
- <complexType>
- <sequence>
  <element name="isAuthorizedForReturn" nillable="true" type="xsd:int" />
  </sequence>
  </complexType>
  </element>
- <element name="isAuthorizedFor">
- <complexType>
- <sequence>
  <element name="p_ssnumb" nillable="true" type="xsd:string" />
  <element name="action" nillable="true" type="xsd:string" />
  </sequence>
  </complexType>
  </element>
  </schema>
  </wsdl:types>
- <wsdl:message name="isAuthorizedForResponse">
  <wsdl:part element="impl:isAuthorizedForResponse" name="parameters" />
  </wsdl:message>
- <wsdl:message name="isAuthorizedForRequest">
  <wsdl:part element="impl:isAuthorizedFor" name="parameters" />
  </wsdl:message>
- <wsdl:portType name="AuthorizationService">
- <wsdl:operation name="isAuthorizedFor">
  <wsdl:input message="impl:isAuthorizedForRequest" name="isAuthorizedForRequest" />
  <wsdl:output message="impl:isAuthorizedForResponse" name="isAuthorizedForResponse"
/>
  </wsdl:operation>
```

```
    </wsdl:portType>
-   <wsdl:binding name="AuthorizationServiceSOAPSoapBinding"
    type="impl:AuthorizationService">
      <wsdlsoap:binding style="document" transport="http://schemas.xmlsoap.org/soap/http"
    />
-     <wsdl:operation name="isAuthorizedFor">
        <wsdlsoap:operation soapAction="" />
-       <wsdl:input name="isAuthorizedForRequest">
          <wsdlsoap:body use="literal" />
        </wsdl:input>
-       <wsdl:output name="isAuthorizedForResponse">
          <wsdlsoap:body use="literal" />
        </wsdl:output>
      </wsdl:operation>
    </wsdl:binding>
-   <wsdl:service name="AuthorizationService">
-     <wsdl:port binding="impl:AuthorizationServiceSOAPSoapBinding"
    name="AuthorizationServiceSOAP">
        <wsdlsoap:address
    location="http://radon:9080/wisd/CommonServicesApp/AuthorizationService" />
      </wsdl:port>
    </wsdl:service>
    </wsdl:definitions>
```

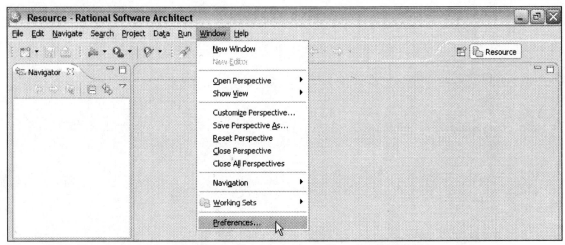

Figure 2-68   Test AuthorizationService stored procedure service using RAD 1/7

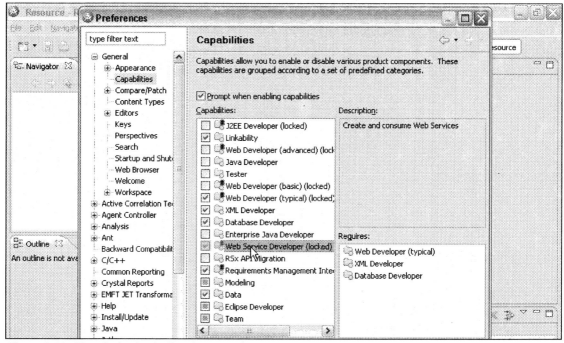

Figure 2-69   Test AuthorizationService stored procedure service using RAD 2/7

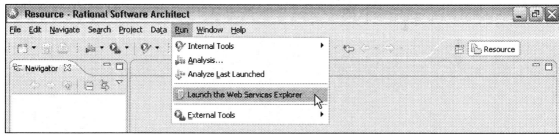

Figure 2-70   Test AuthorizationService stored procedure service using RAD 3/7

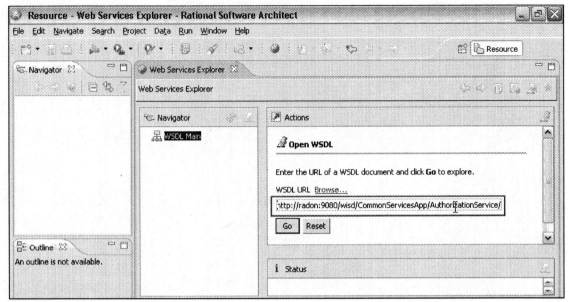

Figure 2-71   Test AuthorizationService stored procedure service using RAD 4/7

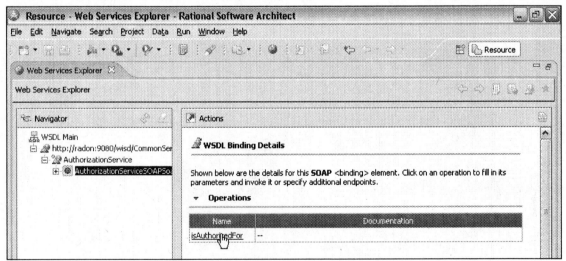

Figure 2-72   Test AuthorizationService stored procedure service using RAD 5/7

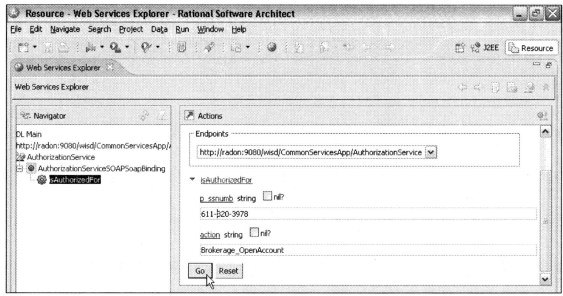

Figure 2-73   Test AuthorizationService stored procedure service using RAD 6/7

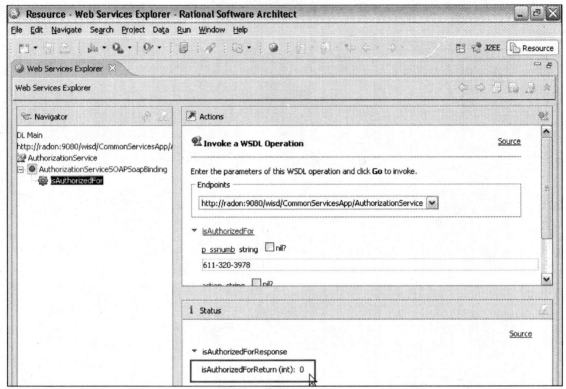

Figure 2-74   Test AuthorizationService stored procedure service using RAD 7/7

Test the stored procedure service (EJB binding)

When a service is created with an EJB binding, you can download a Client JAR file that can be imported into your EJB client to access the service. This is similar to the WSDL document for a service generated with SOAP over HTTP bindings, but unlike the case of SOAP over HTTP binding, you need to create a test EJB client that uses the downloaded client JAR file to test access to the SOA service.

Here again, we first show how to download the Client JAR file from IBM Information Server, and then use RAD tool to create a test EJB client to access the service using the Client JAR file.

Figure 2-75 on page 108 through Figure 2-77 on page 109 describe the steps to download the EJB Client JAR file for a given service.

After logging in to the Information Server Web Console, you navigate to the Information Services Catalog tab, check the service AuthorizationService, and click **Open** as shown in Figure 2-62 on page 97 through Figure 2-65 on page 99.

Then proceed as follows:

1. Expand the Bindings and EJB button as shown in Figure 2-75 on page 108, and note the JNDI Name (ejb/CommonServicesApp/AuthorizationService). Click **Download Client JAR file.**

2. At the prompt shown in Figure 2-76 on page 109, save the Client JAR file (default name CommonServicesApp_client.jar in this case) to an appropriate directory (C:\temp\clientjar in this case) as shown in Figure 2-77 on page 109.

Figure 2-78 on page 110 through Figure 2-99 on page 125 describe the steps using the RAD tool to develop a Java EJB client that imports the IBM Information Server generated Client JAR file, and performs a test of the AuthorizationService using EJB bindings.

> **Note:** It is not our objective to teach you RAD tool usage, and therefore the steps are described cursorily. For information on RAD., refer to the Web site `http://www.ibm.com/software/awdtools/developer/application/`

Proceed as follows:

1. After launching RAD, from the Java perspective (highlighted), right-click in the left pane, and select **New** and **Project** as shown in Figure 2-78 on page 110.

2. Create a new Java project named EJBClientTest as shown in Figure 2-79 on page 110 and Figure 2-81 on page 112.

3. The server runtime (which includes all required J2EE classes such as InitialContext) must be added to the classpath as shown in Figure 2-82 on page 113 through Figure 2-86 on page 116.

4. Next, import the CommonServicesApp_client.jar file generated (Figure 2-87 on page 116 through Figure 2-89 on page 118) and add it to the Java Build Path as shown in Figure 2-90 on page 119 through Figure 2-93 on page 121.

5. Then create a new Java Class named test as shown in Figure 2-94 on page 121 through Figure 2-95 on page 122.

6. The Test.java source shown in Figure 2-96 on page 123 is coded to reference the proper INITIAL_CONTEXT_FACTORY (com.ibm.websphere.naming.WsnInitialContextFactory) and PROVIDER_URL (iiop://radon:2809). The isAuthorizedFor method is invoked with social security number 611-32-3978 followed by a message "***Authorization test result:" with the result of the invocation.

Note: The following two import statements are derived from the IBM Information Server generated CommonServicesApp_client.jar file:

► com.ibm.isd.CommonServicesApp.AuthorizationService. AuthorizationService

► com.ibm.isd.CommonServicesApp.AuthorizationService.server. AuthorizationServiceHome

The JNDI Name is obtained from Figure 2-75 on page 108, and the EJB Home and Interface classes from the CommonServicesApp_client.jar file contents shown in Figure 2-97 on page 124.

7. This Test.java is then executed as a Java Application and its results viewed as shown in Figure 2-98 on page 125 and Figure 2-99 on page 125.

We can now proceed to generate a DataStage service as described in "Generate a DataStage QualityStage service" on page 126.

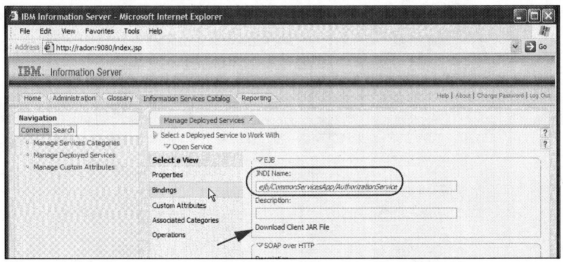

Figure 2-75   Download AuthorizationService stored procedure service Client JAR file 1/3

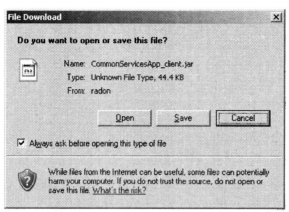

Figure 2-76   Download AuthorizationService stored procedure service Client JAR file 2/3

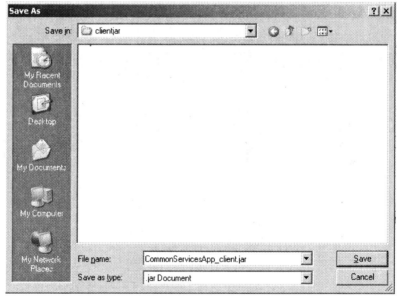

Figure 2-77   Download AuthorizationService stored procedure service Client JAR file 3/3

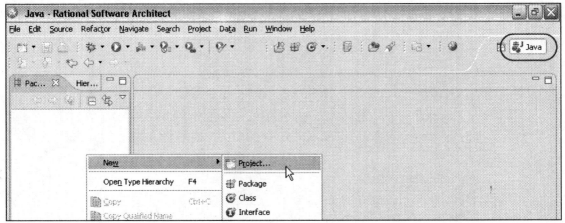

Figure 2-78   Test AuthorizationService EJB binding using RAD 1/22

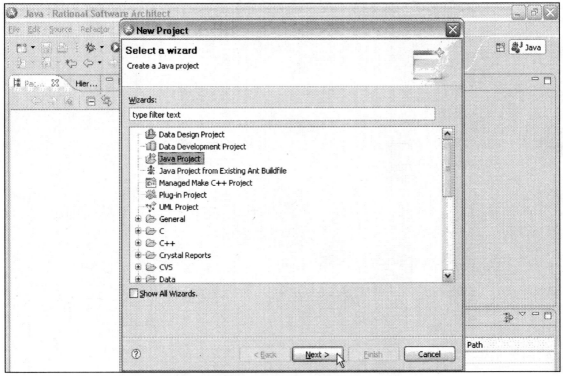

Figure 2-79   Test AuthorizationService EJB binding using RAD 2/22

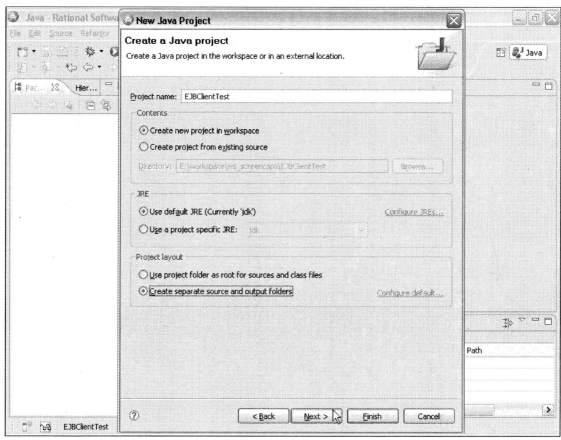

Figure 2-80   Test AuthorizationService EJB binding using RAD 3/22

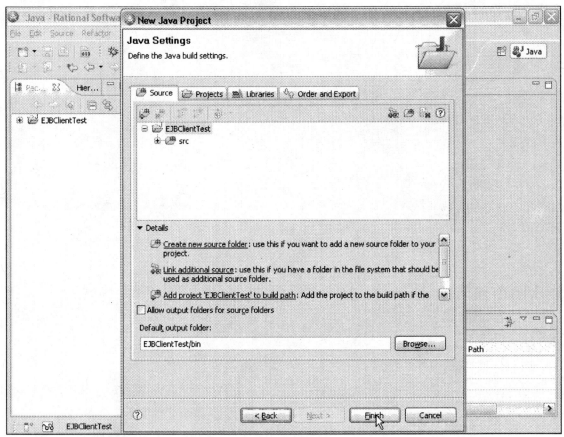

Figure 2-81   Test AuthorizationService EJB binding using RAD 4/22

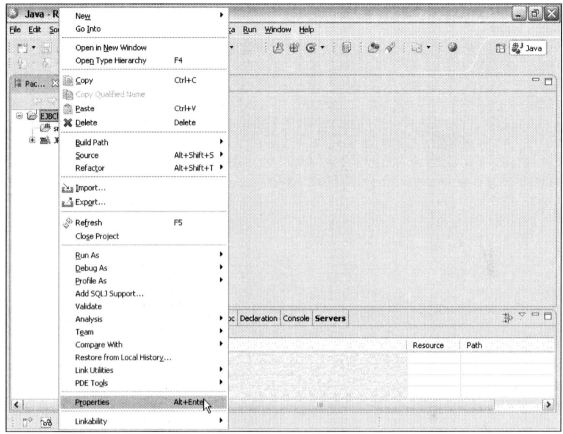

Figure 2-82   Test AuthorizationService EJB binding using RAD 5/22

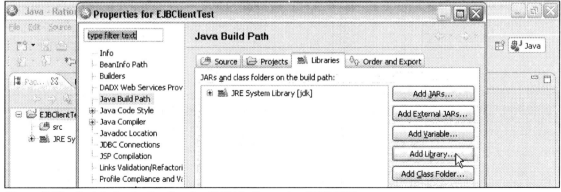

Figure 2-83   Test AuthorizationService EJB binding using RAD 6/22

Chapter 2. Financial services business scenario   **113**

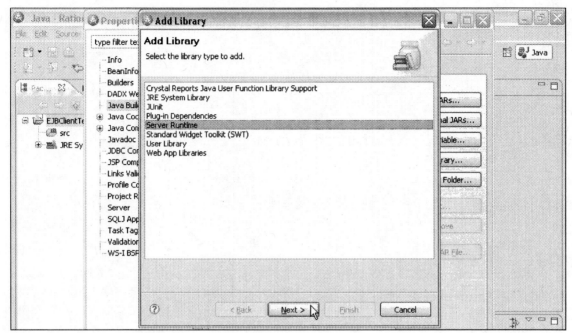

Figure 2-84   Test AuthorizationService EJB binding using RAD 7/22

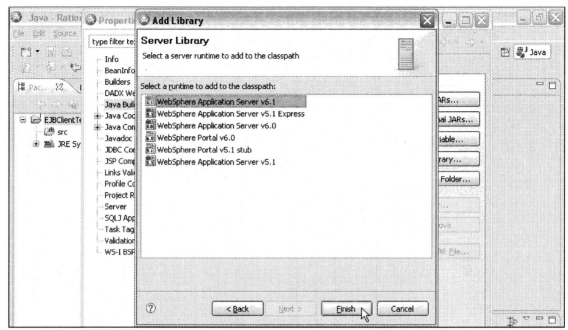

Figure 2-85   Test AuthorizationService EJB binding using RAD 8/22

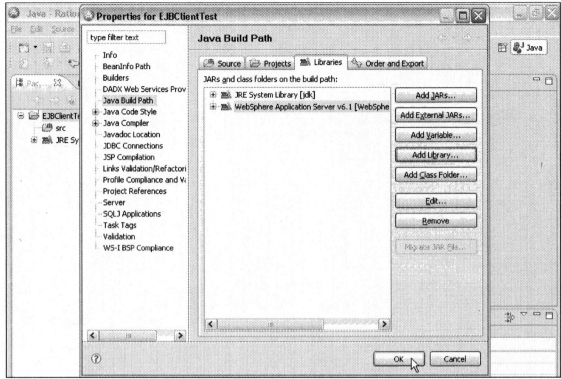

Figure 2-86   Test AuthorizationService EJB binding using RAD 9/22

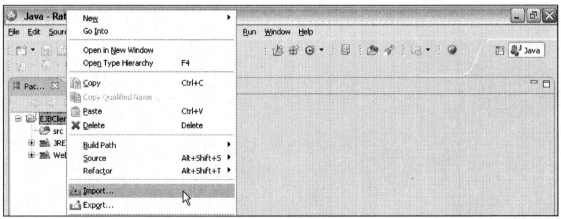

Figure 2-87   Test AuthorizationService EJB binding using RAD 10/22

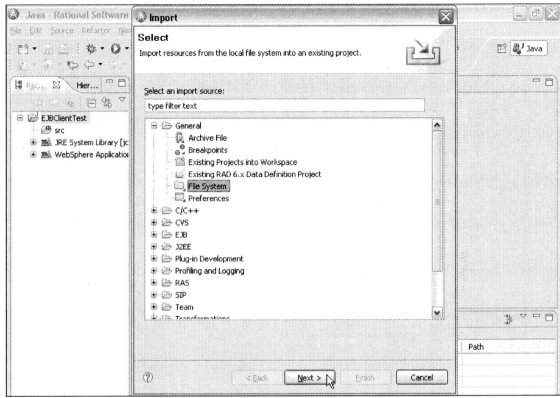

Figure 2-88   Test AuthorizationService EJB binding using RAD 11/22

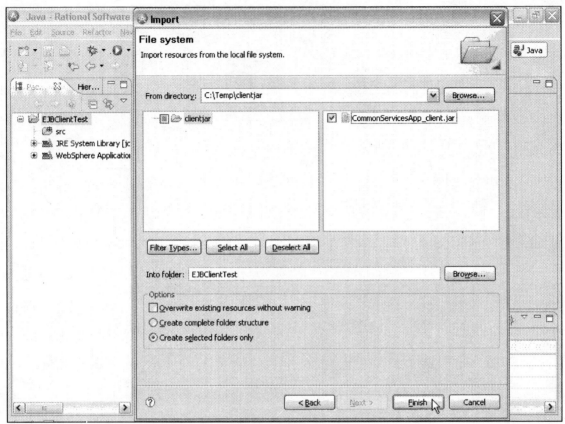

Figure 2-89   Test AuthorizationService EJB binding using RAD 12/22

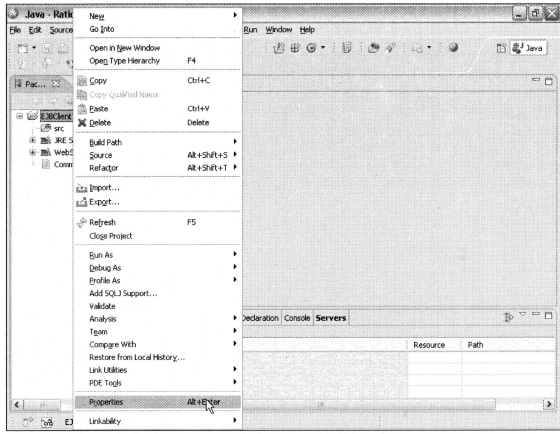

Figure 2-90   Test AuthorizationService EJB binding using RAD 13/22

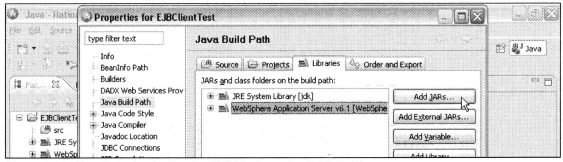

Figure 2-91   Test AuthorizationService EJB binding using RAD 14/22

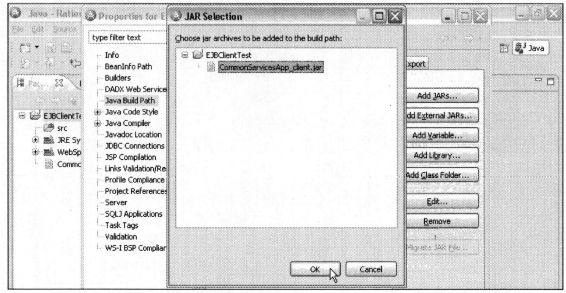

Figure 2-92   Test AuthorizationService EJB binding using RAD 15/22

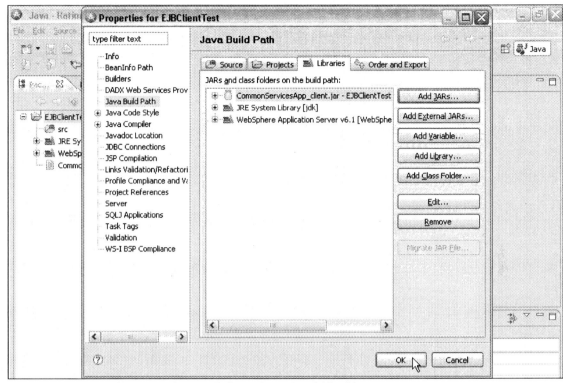

Figure 2-93   Test AuthorizationService EJB binding using RAD 16/22

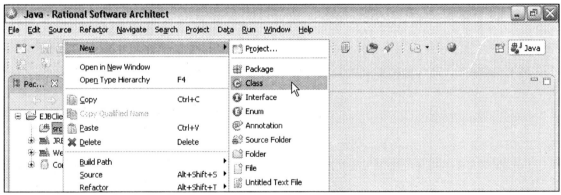

Figure 2-94   Test AuthorizationService EJB binding using RAD 17/22

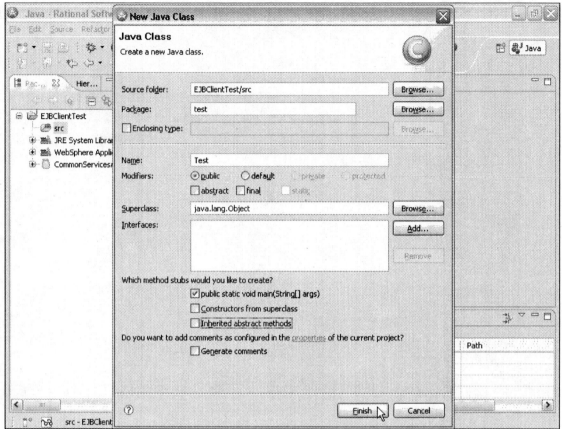

Figure 2-95   Test AuthorizationService EJB binding using RAD 18/22

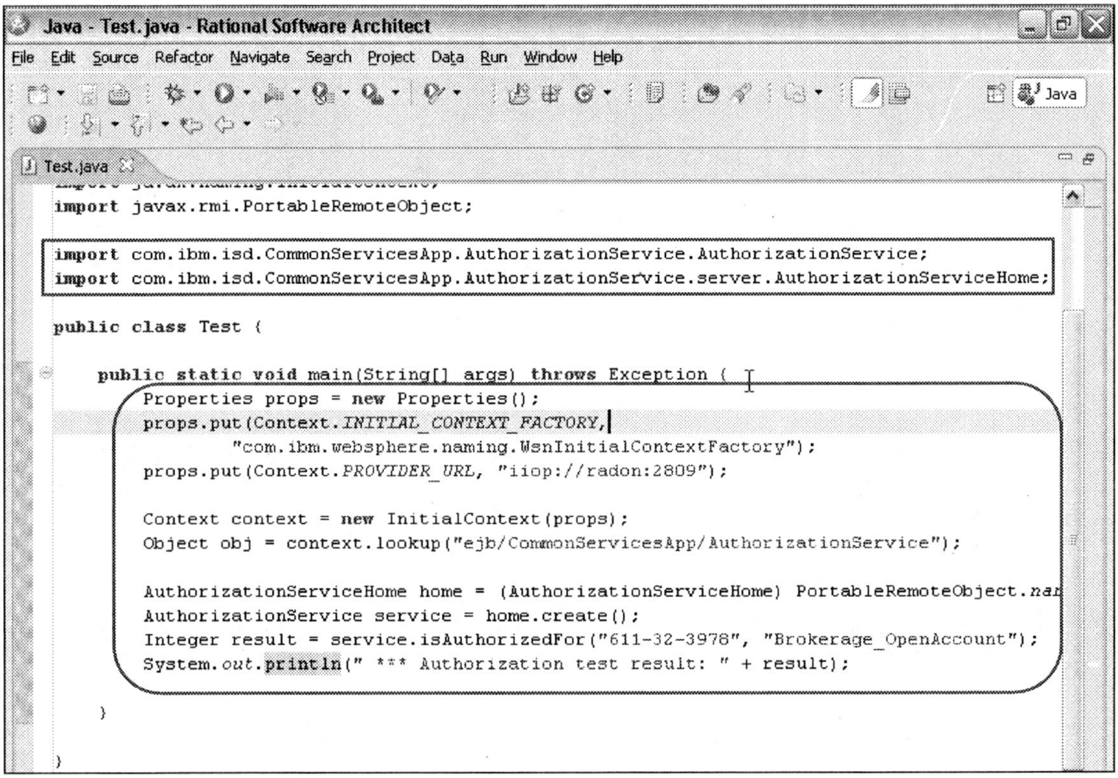
Java - Test.java - Rational Software Architect
File Edit Source Refactor Navigate Search Project Data Run Window Help
Java
Test.java
import javax.rmi.PortableRemoteObject;
import com.ibm.isd.CommonServicesApp.AuthorizationService.AuthorizationService;
import com.ibm.isd.CommonServicesApp.AuthorizationService.server.AuthorizationServiceHome;
public class Test {
public static void main(String[] args) throws Exception {
Properties props = new Properties();
props.put(Context.INITIAL_CONTEXT_FACTORY,
"com.ibm.websphere.naming.WsnInitialContextFactory");
props.put(Context.PROVIDER_URL, "iiop://radon:2809");
Context context = new InitialContext(props);
Object obj = context.lookup("ejb/CommonServicesApp/AuthorizationService");
AuthorizationServiceHome home = (AuthorizationServiceHome) PortableRemoteObject.nar
AuthorizationService service = home.create();
Integer result = service.isAuthorizedFor("611-32-3978", "Brokerage_OpenAccount");
System.out.println(" *** Authorization test result: " + result);
}
}

Figure 2-96 Test AuthorizationService EJB binding using RAD 19/22

Figure 2-97   Test AuthorizationService EJB binding using RAD 20/22

Name	Modified	Size	Ratio	Packed	Path
Manifest.mf	3/6/2007 7:17 PM	94	14%	81	meta-inf\
AuditService.class	3/6/2007 7:17 PM	259	30%	182	com\ibm\isd\CommonServices.
AuditServiceHome.class	3/6/2007 7:17 PM	366	40%	221	com\ibm\isd\CommonServices.
AuditServiceRemote.class	3/6/2007 7:17 PM	257	38%	159	com\ibm\isd\CommonServices.
_AuditServiceHome_Stub.class	3/6/2007 7:17 PM	7,796	61%	3,029	com\ibm\isd\CommonServices.
_AuditServiceRemote_Stub.class	3/6/2007 7:17 PM	8,095	57%	3,506	com\ibm\isd\CommonServices.
_AuditService_Stub.class	3/6/2007 7:17 PM	3,827	56%	1,672	com\ibm\isd\CommonServices.
AuthorizationService.class	3/6/2007 7:17 PM	311	36%	199	com\ibm\isd\CommonServices.
AuthorizationServiceHome.class	3/6/2007 7:17 PM	406	45%	225	com\ibm\isd\CommonServices.
AuthorizationServiceRemote.class	3/6/2007 7:17 PM	297	44%	167	com\ibm\isd\CommonServices.
_AuthorizationServiceHome_Stub.class	3/6/2007 7:17 PM	7,980	62%	3,035	com\ibm\isd\CommonServices.
_AuthorizationServiceRemote_Stub.class	3/6/2007 7:17 PM	8,440	57%	3,621	com\ibm\isd\CommonServices.
_AuthorizationService_Stub.class	3/6/2007 7:17 PM	4,216	57%	1,799	com\ibm\isd\CommonServices.
CustomerIDLookupService.class	3/6/2007 7:17 PM	358	39%	220	com\ibm\isd\CommonServices.
CustomerIDLookupServiceHome.class	3/6/2007 7:17 PM	421	45%	231	com\ibm\isd\CommonServices.
CustomerIDLookupServiceRemote.class	3/6/2007 7:17 PM	312	45%	171	com\ibm\isd\CommonServices.
_CustomerIDLookupServiceHome_Stub.class	3/6/2007 7:17 PM	8,049	62%	3,046	com\ibm\isd\CommonServices.
_CustomerIDLookupServiceRemote_Stub.class	3/6/2007 7:17 PM	8,897	59%	3,624	com\ibm\isd\CommonServices.
_CustomerIDLookupService_Stub.class	3/6/2007 7:17 PM	4,652	61%	1,836	com\ibm\isd\CommonServices.
StandardizeAddressServiceHome.class	3/6/2007 7:17 PM	431	46%	233	com\ibm\isd\CommonServices.
StandardizeAddressServiceRemote.class	3/6/2007 7:17 PM	322	47%	171	com\ibm\isd\CommonServices.
_StandardizeAddressServiceHome_Stub.class	3/6/2007 7:17 PM	8,095	62%	3,050	com\ibm\isd\CommonServices.
_StandardizeAddressServiceRemote_Stub.class	3/6/2007 7:17 PM	8,964	59%	3,688	com\ibm\isd\CommonServices.
StandardizeAddressService.class	3/6/2007 7:17 PM	423	51%	207	com\ibm\isd\CommonServices.
StandardizedAddress.class	3/6/2007 7:17 PM	1,240	59%	503	com\ibm\isd\CommonServices.
_StandardizeAddressService_Stub.class	3/6/2007 7:17 PM	4,720	61%	1,818	com\ibm\isd\CommonServices.

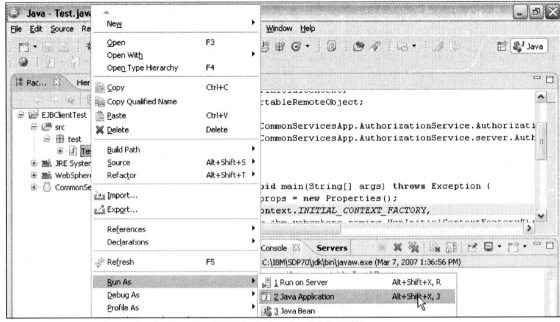

Figure 2-98   Test AuthorizationService EJB binding using RAD 21/22

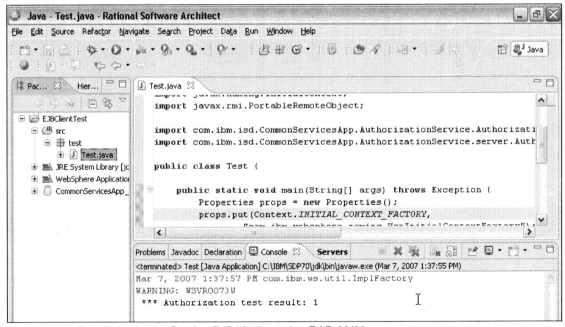

Figure 2-99   Test AuthorizationService EJB binding using RAD 22/22

Generate a DataStage QualityStage service

Figure 2-100 through Figure 2-103 on page 129 describe some of the steps involved in generating an SOA service of a DataStage QualityStage job.

> **Note:** Since the naming of the service, association of bindings, deployment, and testing are identical to those described in "Generate a stored procedure service" on page 79, we have excluded those screen captures here.

Proceed as follows:

1. After naming the StandardizeAddress, expand Operations for this service, modify the Name (standardizeAddress), Description (Standardize Address) and click **Select** to Select an information provider as shown in Figure 2-100.

2. Select **DataStage and QualityStage** for the Type field from the drop-down list in Figure 2-101 on page 127.

3. From the CommonServiceApp application tab, select DataStage job **StandardizeAddress**, Host (RADON) and Port (31538) and click **OK** as shown in Figure 2-102 on page 128.

4. Modify the Data Type field for the Outputs of this job as StandardizedAddress in Figure 2-103 on page 129 — this is the name of the complex data type for the group of arguments (see checked box), and we chose to give it a name of our choice.

5. Click **Save Application** to complete this portion of the definition of the service. As mentioned earlier, the association of bindings, deployment and test of the service is not repeated here again.

We can now proceed to deploy the generate a federated query SOA service as described in "Generate a federated query service" on page 129.

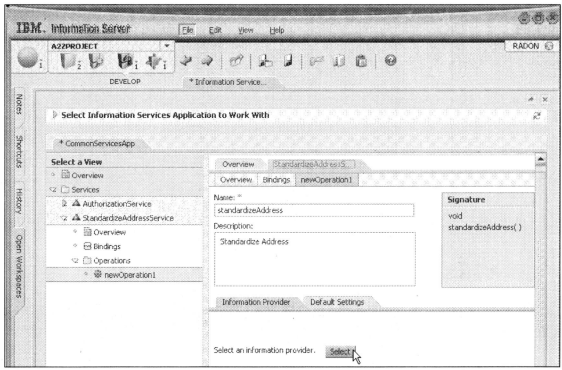

Figure 2-100   Generate a DataStage QualityStage service 1/4

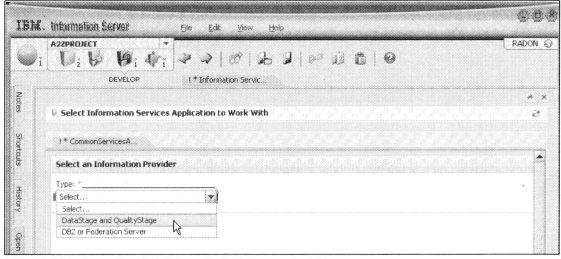

Figure 2-101   Generate a DataStage QualityStage service 2/4

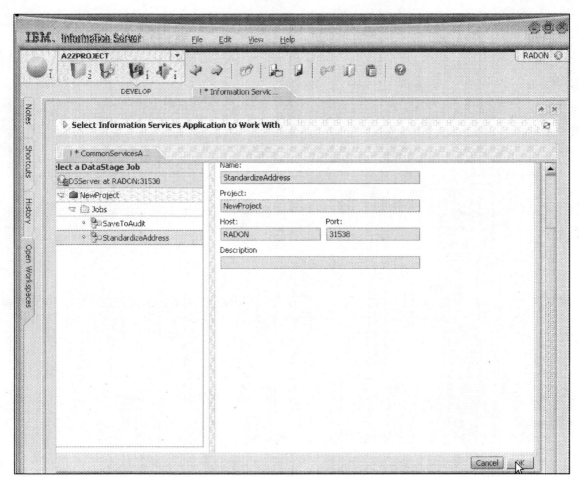

Figure 2-102   Generate a DataStage QualityStage service 3/4

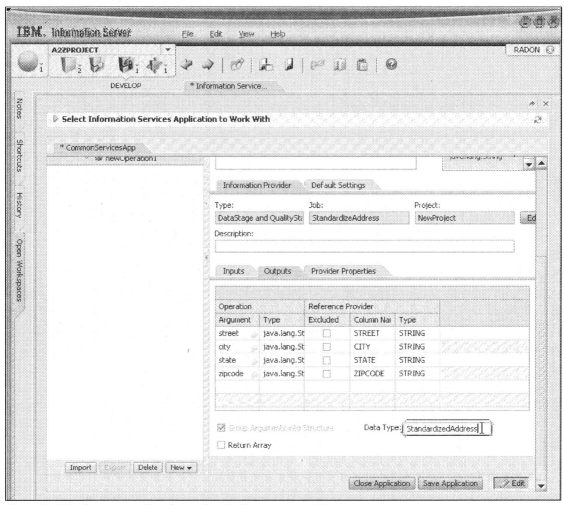

Figure 2-103   Generate a DataStage QualityStage service 4/4

Generate a federated query service

Figure 2-104 through Figure 2-109 on page 136 describe some of the steps involved in generating an SOA service of a federated query.

Note: Since the naming of the service, association of bindings, deployment, and testing are identical to those described in "Generate a stored procedure service" on page 79, we have excluded those screen captures here.

Proceed as follows:

1. After naming the CardStatusPlatinumService, from the New Information Services Application tab, expand Operations for this service, modify the Name (getTransactions), Description (Retrieves the transactions for the Platinum customers) and click **Select** to Select an information provider as shown in Figure 2-104.

2. Select **DB2 or Federation Server** for the Type field from the drop-down list, **SQL Statement** from the Subtype field drop-down list, **Create SQL Statement** from the Action field drop-down list, and **Select** from the SQL Type drop-down list as shown in Figure 2-105 on page 132.

> **Note:** Instead of choosing the Create SQL Statement from the drop-down list, we could have chosen the Browse Databases option to build the SQL statement using the GUI. For convenience, we chose to type in the SQL statement ourselves.

3. Select **FEDDB** from the Select a Database column, and key in the SQL statement for which the SOA service is to be built as shown in Figure 2-106 on page 133 and Figure 2-107 on page 134.

4. Click **OK** in Figure 2-107 on page 134. Under the Inputs tab, modify the Argument column value to customerId (from the default arg1) as shown in Figure 2-108 on page 135.

5. Under the Outputs tab, modify the Data Type field for the Outputs of this job as CardStatusPlatinumServiceOut in Figure 2-109 on page 136 — this is the name of the complex data type for the group of arguments (see checked box) and Return Array (see checked box), and we chose to give it a name of our choice.

6. Click **Save Application** to complete this portion of the definition of the service. As mentioned earlier, the association of bindings, deployment, and test of the service is not repeated here again.

We can now proceed to list all the deployed services for the A2Z Financial Services organization as described in "List all deployed services" on page 136.

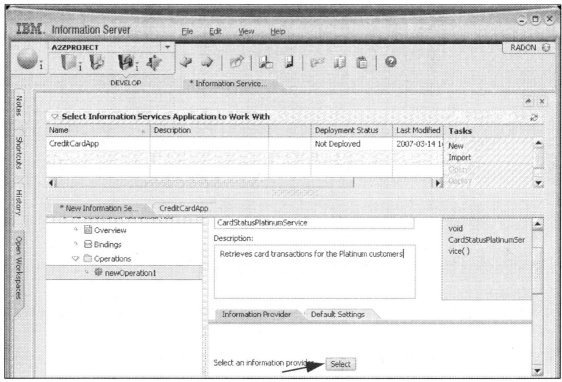

Figure 2-104   Generate a federated query service 1/6

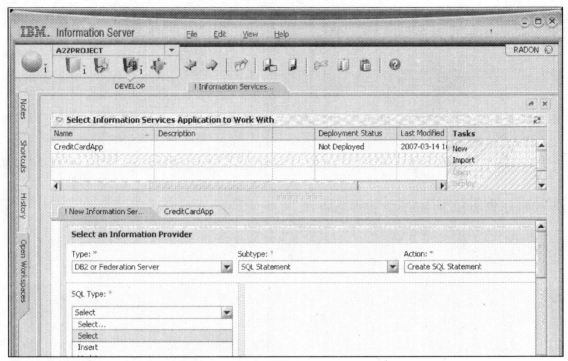

Figure 2-105   Generate a federated query service 2/6

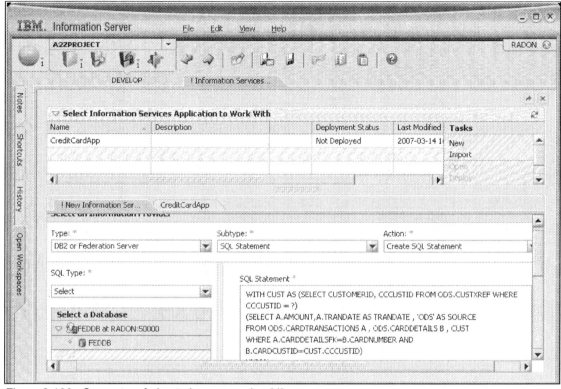

Figure 2-106   Generate a federated query service 3/6

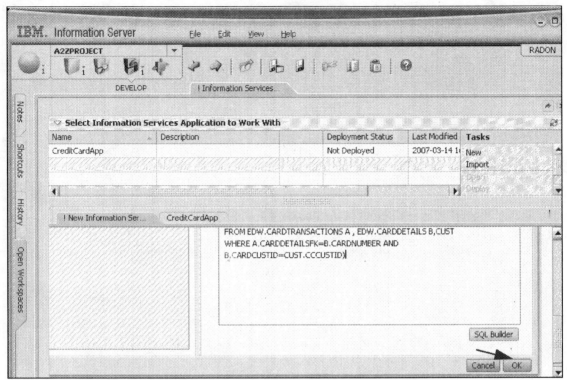

Figure 2-107   Generate a federated query service 4/6

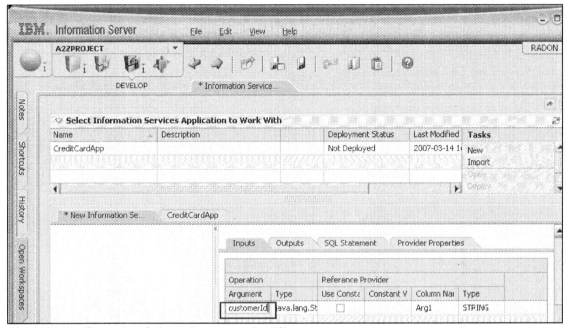

Figure 2-108   Generate a federated query service 5/6

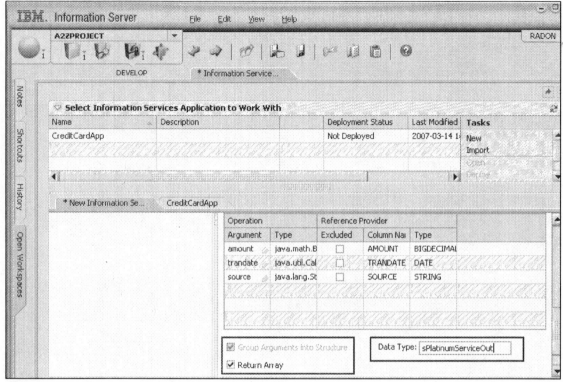

Figure 2-109   Generate a federated query service 6/6

List all deployed services

As described earlier, 13 services were generated for the 22 functions suitable for the A2Z Financial Services company. We generated and deployed all 13 services (with SOAP over HTTP and EJB bindings) as shown in Figure 2-110 and Figure 2-111 on page 138.

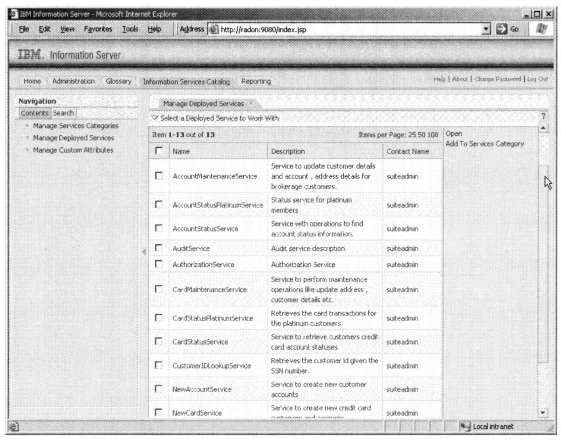

Figure 2-110   A2Z Financial Services IBM Information Server services 1/2

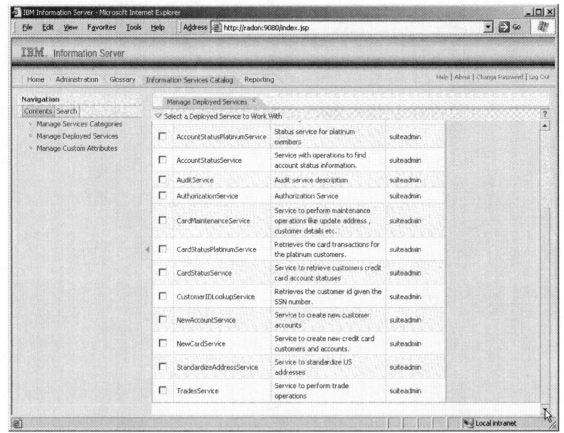

Figure 2-111   A2Z Financial Services IBM Information Server services 2/2

2.7.5 Step 3e: Optionally export service to WSRR

This is an optional step that you should perform if you want to export the IBM Information Server generated services to a WebSphere Service Registry and Repository (WSRR).

> **Note:** In a future release, an option will be provided to automatically publish an IBM Information Server service to a WSRR.

In the following panels, we describe the steps involved in exporting the AccountStatusPlatinumService to a WSRR.

Figure 2-112 on page 139 through Figure 2-115 on page 141 show the save of the AccountStatusPlatinumService.wsdl file to a file system directory from the IBM Information Server Web Console interface.

Figure 2-116 on page 141 through Figure 2-122 on page 146 show a successful login to WSRR's secure server (9.152.130.81), the import of the WSDL file to the WSRR, and a query showing successful registration of two IBM Information Server services in the WSRR.

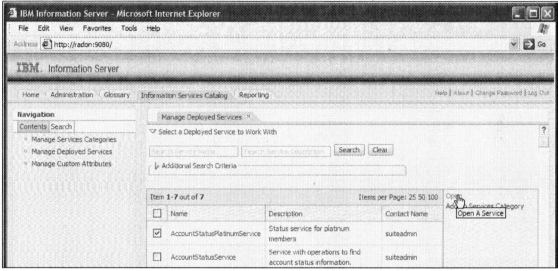

Figure 2-112   Export the AccountStatusPlatinumService to a WSRR 1/11

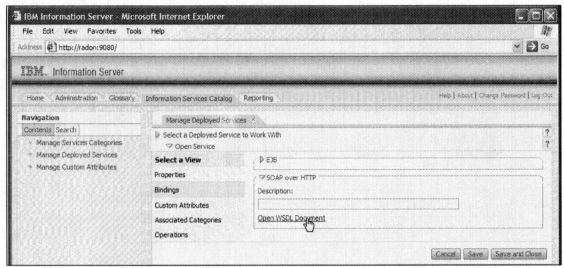

Figure 2-113   Export the AccountStatusPlatinumService to a WSRR 2/11

Figure 2-114   Export the AccountStatusPlatinumService to a WSRR 3/11

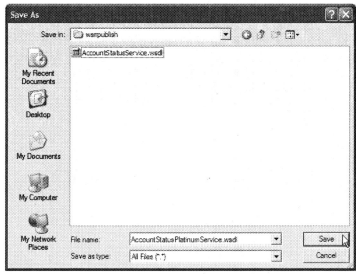

Figure 2-115   Export the AccountStatusPlatinumService to a WSRR 4/11

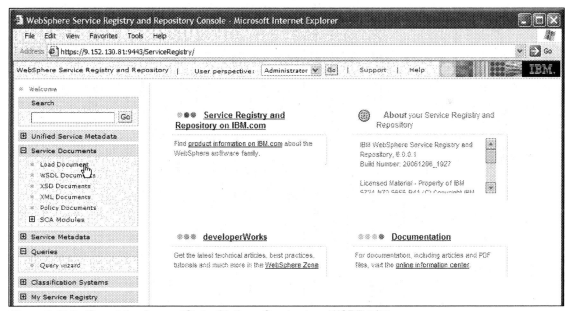

Figure 2-116   Export the AccountStatusPlatinumService to a WSRR 5/11

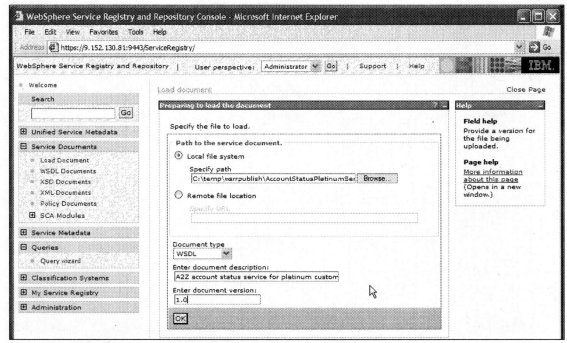

Figure 2-117   Export the AccountStatusPlatinumService to a WSRR 6/11

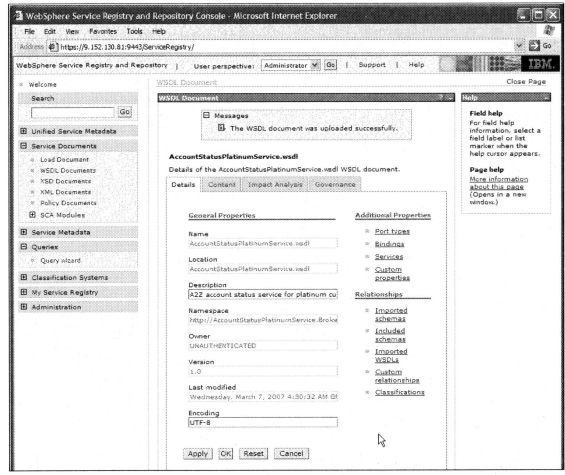

Figure 2-118   Export the AccountStatusPlatinumService to a WSRR 7/11

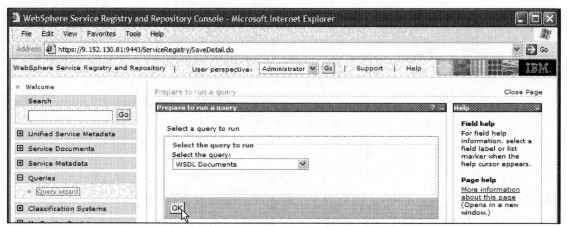

Figure 2-119   Export the AccountStatusPlatinumService to a WSRR 8/11

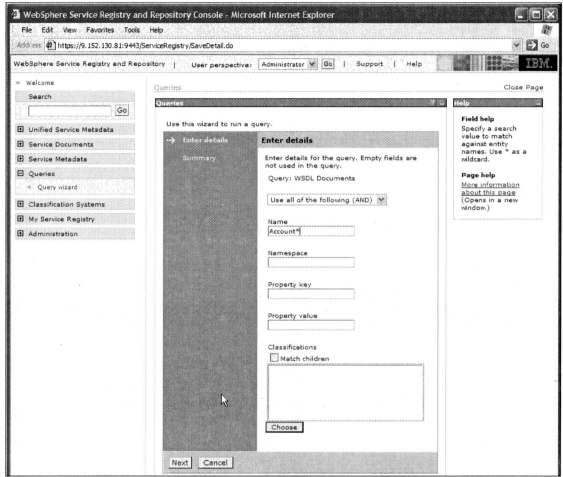

Figure 2-120   Export the AccountStatusPlatinumService to a WSRR 9/11

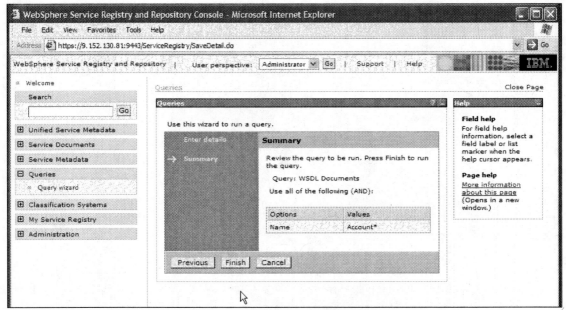

Figure 2-121   Export the AccountStatusPlatinumService to a WSRR 10/11

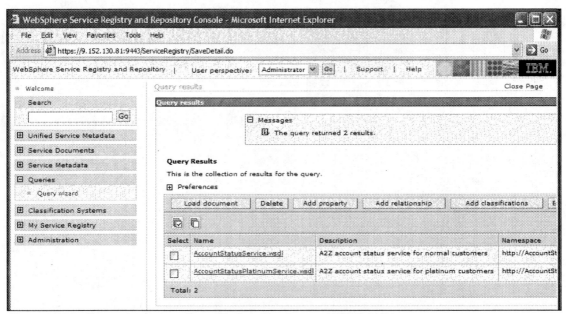

Figure 2-122   Export the AccountStatusPlatinumService to a WSRR 11/11

2.8 Step 4: Create Service Component Architecture modules

As mentioned earlier, we included WebSphere Process Server in the A2Z Financial Services' self service solution for its complementary functionality to IBM Information Server. In particular, its support for aggregating SOA services (both IBM Information Server generated as well as otherwise) into a larger business process SOA service, support for both sync and async invocations of an SOA service. The service aggregation feature simplifies application development, while the other features support a more diverse infrastructure.

WebSphere Integration Developer (WID) is the tooling for developing Service Component Architecture (SCA) modules which are the deployable units in WebSphere Process Server. An enterprise archive (.ear) file is generated from a module, which is then deployed on WebSphere Application Server (WAS) and appears as an application in the WAS Administrative Console.

As described in Appendix B, "WebSphere Integration Developer overview" on page 459, the SCA module assembly contains a diagram of the integrated business application consisting of components and wires that connect them. Services become components that can be dropped into an assembly diagram that forms a module. Services may be implemented using a variety of programming paradigms such as process-flow style business process execution language (BPEL) processes, state machine-style event management, and declarative business rules style.

> **Note:** We installed the Interim Fix 003 without which the modules could not be built, and the optional feature IBM Information Server Plug-In for WID that contains the IBM Information Server activity for BPEL processes and the Enterprise Service Discovery Wizard extension for IBM Information Server. These packages can be downloaded from
> `http://www-306.ibm.com/software/integration/wid/support/`

In our A2Z Financial Services' self service solution, we chose to use the BPEL style implementation in the following SCA modules that are created and deployed on the WebSphere Process Server (lead.itsosj.sanjose.ibm.com):

► **A2ZSCA_Brokerage:**

This module includes multiple business processes that are exposed as an SOA service using different bindings, as follows:

a. PlaceTradeProcess is a business process that places a trade in the Brokerage system. The PlaceTradeProcess is exposed as a service using SOAP over HTTP binding, and invokes the following Information Server services:

   i. AuthorizationService

   ii. TradesService

   iii. AuditService

> **Note:** Even though the PlaceTradeProcess is exposed using SOAP over HTTP binding, the Information Server services it consumes may be accessed using a combination of EJB binding and SOAP over HTTP binding.

b. OpenAccountProcess is a business process that opens an account in the Brokerage system. The OpenAccountProcess is exposed as a service using JMS binding, and invokes the following Information Server services:

   i. AuthorizationService

   ii. StandardizeAddressService

   iii. NewAccountService

   iv. AuditService

c. GetBalancesProcess is a business process that gets the balances in the Brokerage system. The GetBalancesProcess is exposed as a service using SCA binding, and invokes the following Information Server services:

   i. AuthorizationService

   ii. AccountStatusService

   iii. AuditService

d. GetPositionsProcess is a business process that gets the positions in the Brokerage system. The GetPositionsProcess is exposed as a service using SOAP over HTTP binding, and invokes the following Information Server services:

   i. AuthorizationService

   ii. AccountStatusPlatinumService and AccountStatusService

   iii. LegacyStockQuoteService[6]

---

[6] This is not an IBM Information Server service. GetPositionsProcess consumes this service using SOAP over HTTP binding.

▶ **A2ZSCA_CreditCard:**

– This module includes multiple business processes that are exposed as an SOA service using different bindings such as NewCardService, CardStatusPlatinumService, CardStatusService, and CardMaintenanceService.

– The creation of this module is not shown here, but the CardStatusPlatinumService and CardStatusService are imported by the A2ZSCAccountStatusMediation module.

▶ **A2ZSCA_AccountStatusMediation**

– This module also invokes a number of services linked together using a number of artifacts. The objective with this module was to showcase the capabilities of a mediation flow which responds to a service request (GetAccountStatus) and routes it to another service (gold or platinum service depending upon the customer's status) that is designed to handle it. Mediation modules and mediation flows are used in the WebSphere Enterprise Bus.

– This module is exposed as a single interface service using SCA binding, and invokes the following Information Server services:

   i. AuthorizationService

   ii. AccountStatusPlatinumService and AccountStatusService

   iii. CardStatusPlatinumService and CardStatusService

   iv. CustomerIdLookupService

> **Note:** We chose to only define representative SCA modules to showcase async capabilities and various bindings support such as JMS, SCA, and SOAP over HTTP.

Figure 2-123 on page 150 shows these modules as deployed applications in the WAS Administrative Console.

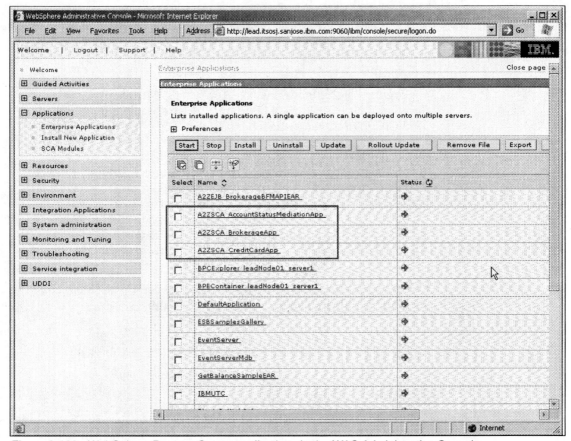

Figure 2-123   WebSphere Process Server applications in the WAS Administrative Console

In the following sections, we describe the following topics:

► A2ZSCA_Brokerage module creation

► A2ZSCA_AccountStatusMediation module creation

► Testing the business processes

> **Attention:** Our intention is to expose the capabilities of WebSphere
> Integration Developer to you as an Information Management specialist, but not
> provide the kind of detailed information that could be considered a tutorial. You
> should refer to the numerous sources of WebSphere Integration Developer
> documentation for a comprehensive understanding of its functionality and
> guidelines of usage.

2.8.1 A2ZSCA_Brokerage module creation

Figure 2-124 shows the typical steps involved in creating a business integration (SCA) module, and deploying and testing an exposed interface. Each of these steps is covered briefly as described in the following sections.

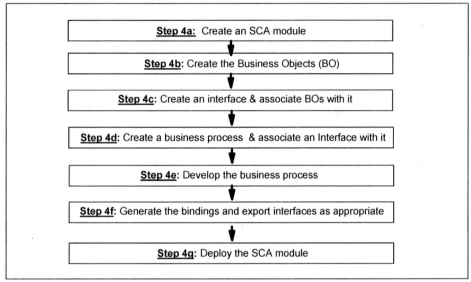

Figure 2-124   Typical steps in creating an SCA module and associated objects

Step 4a: Create an SCA module

To create an SCA module, proceed as follows:

1. Launch WebSphere Integration Developer by selecting **Start** → **Programs** → **IBM WebSphere** → **Integration DeveloperV6.0.2** → **WebSphere Integration Developer V6.0.2.**

2. Switch to the Business Integration perspective, right-click in the left pane and select **New** and **Module** as shown in Figure 2-125.

3. Then provide the Module name (A2ZSCA_Brokerage) and click **Finish** to complete the definition of the module.

We can now proceed to create the business objects as described in "Step 4b: Create the Business Objects (BO)" on page 152.

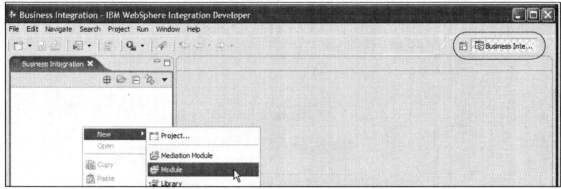

Figure 2-125   Create an SCA module 1/2

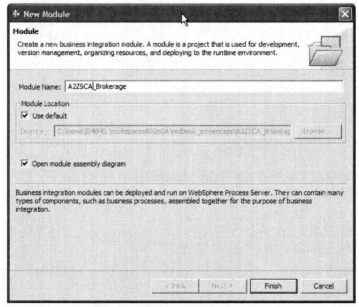

Figure 2-126   Create an SCA module 2/2

Step 4b: Create the Business Objects (BO)

A Business Object provides a universal data description. They are used for data
going in and out of services, and are based on the Service Data Objects (SDO)
standard. In this step, we define two BOs called PlaceTradeInput and
PlaceTradeOutput with appropriate attributes as shown in Figure 2-127 through
Figure 2-133 on page 157.

Proceed as follows:

1. Right-click **Data Types**, and select **New and Business Object** as shown in Figure 2-127.

2. Provide the Name (PlaceTradeInput) and click **Finish** as shown in Figure 2-128 on page 154.

3. Select the **PlaceTradeInput** tab, and click the icon corresponding to Add an attribute to a business object to get a default name of attribute1 with a string attribute.

4. Select the **Properties** tab in the lower right hand pane to view greater details of this attribute.

5. Modify the Name to ssnumb as shown in Figure 2-129 on page 154 and Figure 2-130 on page 155.

6. Repeat the click icon process to add the remaining attributes as shown in Figure 2-131 on page 156.

7. Add another BO named PlaceTradeOutput with its attributes as shown in Figure 2-132 on page 156 and Figure 2-133 on page 157.

We can now proceed to create an interface as described in "Step 4c: Create an interface and associate BOs with it" on page 157.

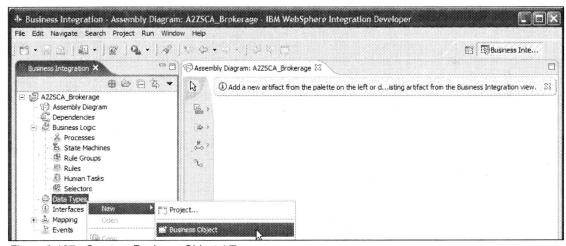

Figure 2-127   Create a Business Object 1/7

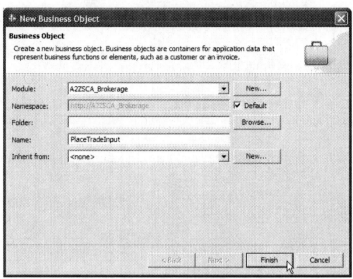

Figure 2-128   Create a Business Object 2/7

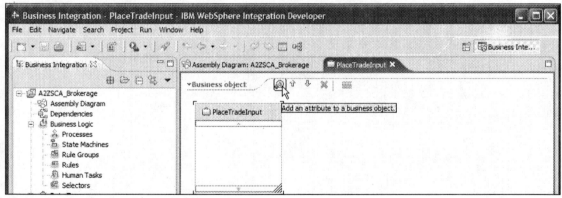

Figure 2-129   Create a Business Object 3/7

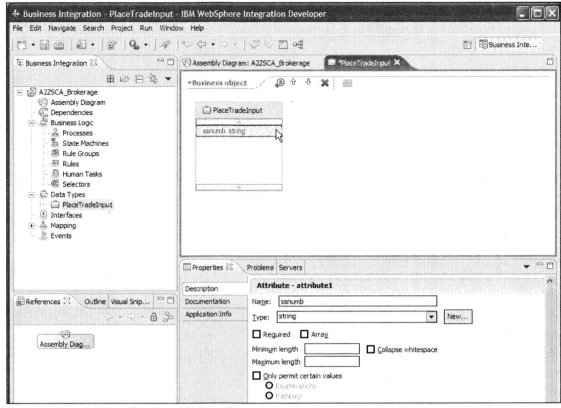

Figure 2-130   Create a Business Object 4/7

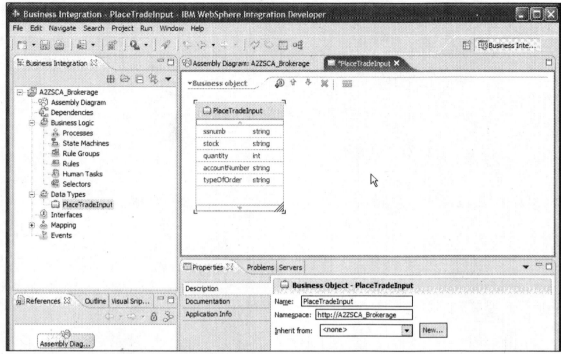

Figure 2-131   Create a Business Object 5/7

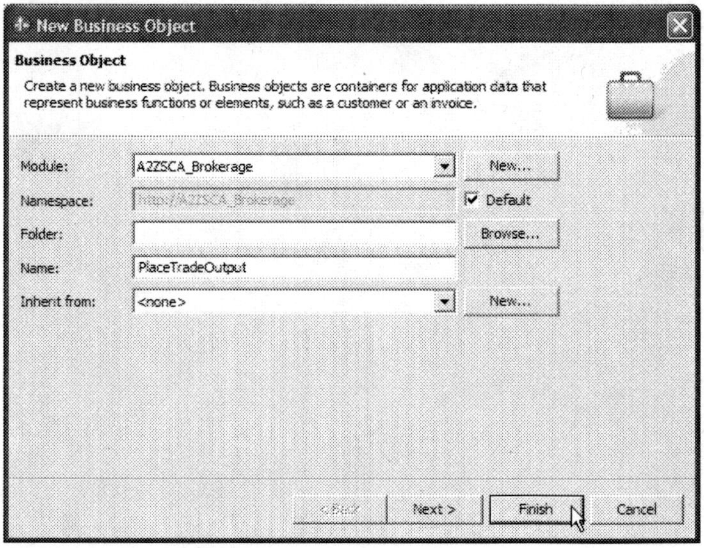

Figure 2-132   Create a Business Object 6/7

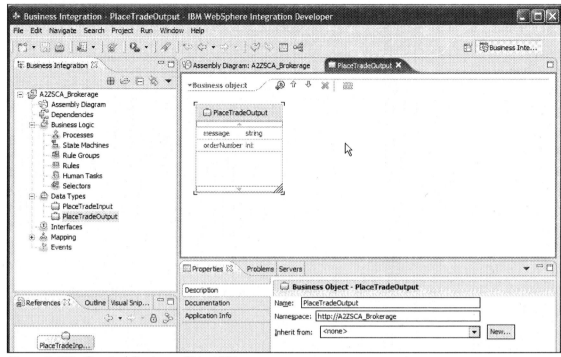

Figure 2-133   Create a Business Object 7/7

Step 4c: Create an interface and associate BOs with it

The interface defines the operations that can be called and the data that can be passed, such as input arguments, returned values, and exceptions. Interfaces can be of two types — a WSDL Port Type or a Java-type.

> **Note:** An SCA component can have multiple interfaces, but they must all be of the same type. You can also apply a role-based permission qualifier to an interface so that only authorized applications can invoke the service with that interface. If operations associated with an interface require different levels of permission, you must define separate interfaces to control their access. We did not implement any role-based permissions.

The data that can be passed can be entered individually or associated with a Business Object, which is what we chose to do. Figure 2-134 on page 158 through Figure 2-138 on page 160 show the creation of an interface called TradesInterface, an operation called placeTrade, and the association of the PlaceTradeInput and PlaceTradeOutput BOs with the interface.

Proceed as follows:

1. Right-click **Interfaces** and select **New** and **Interface** as shown in Figure 2-134 on page 158.

2. Provide a Name (TradesInterface) and click **Finish** as shown in Figure 2-135 on page 159.

3. Click the icon to Add Request Response Operation as shown in Figure 2-136 on page 159.

4. Modify the default operation1 to placeTrade, and select and click **string** under the Type column in the Input(s) column to view the list of available data types as shown in Figure 2-137 on page 160.

5. Select **PlaceTradeInput**. Then select **PlaceTradeOutput** for the data type for Output(s) as shown in Figure 2-138 on page 160.

We can now proceed to create a Business Process as described in "Step 4d: Create a business process and associate an Interface with it" on page 160.

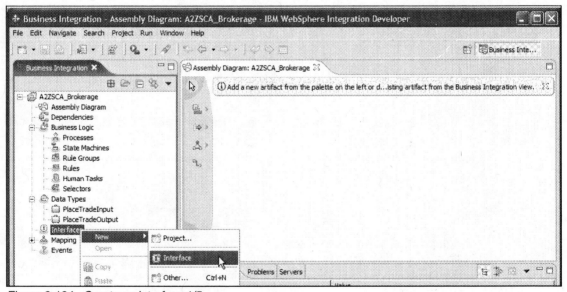

Figure 2-134   Create an interface 1/5

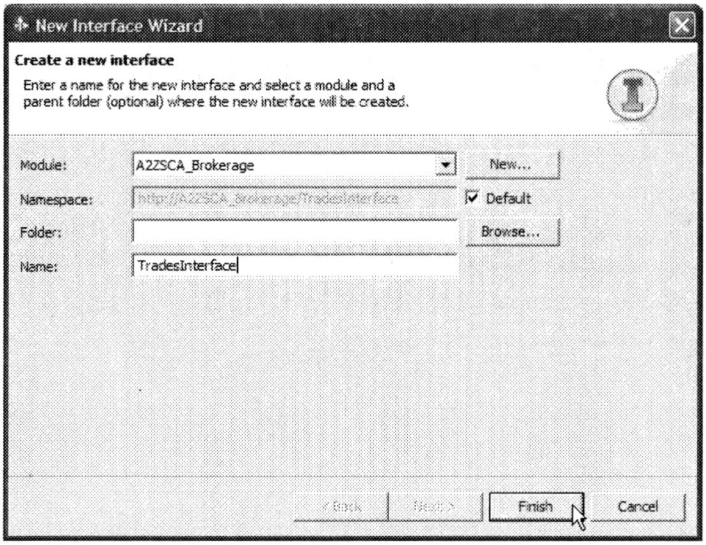

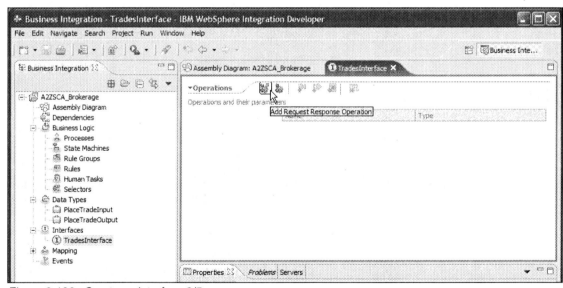

Figure 2-135   Create an interface 2/5

Figure 2-136   Create an interface 3/5

Figure 2-137   Create an interface 4/5

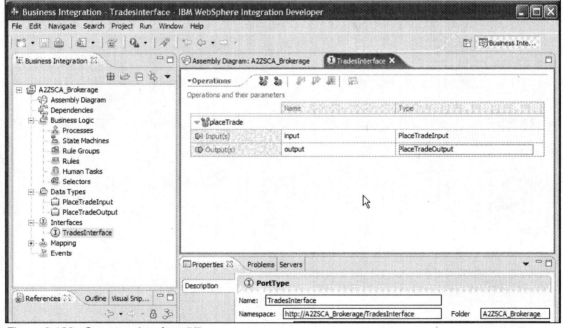

Figure 2-138   Create an interface 5/5

Step 4d: Create a business process and associate an Interface with it

A business process provides the primary means for coordinating enterprise services and describing your business logic. It consists of a series of activities or steps that are executed in a specific order, sequentially or in parallel. The business process editor is a visual construction tool that allows you to quickly author a business process based on the BPEL standard. A business process itself is a service. You can use it to coordinate reusable subprocesses or other services which may have any other implementation type.

In this section, we create a business process called PlaceTradeProcess and associate the TradesInterface with it as shown in Figure 2-139 on page 161 through Figure 2-144 on page 164:

1. Right-click **Processes** and select **New and Business Process** as shown in Figure 2-139 on page 161.

2. Provide the Name (PlaceTradeProcess) and click **Next** as shown in Figure 2-140 on page 162.

3. Then the TradesInterface is located and associated with the PlaceTradeProcess as shown in Figure 2-141 on page 162 through Figure 2-144 on page 164.

4. Click **Finish** in Figure 2-143 on page 164.

5. The new process appears in the left pane as shown in Figure 2-144 on page 164.

We can now proceed to develop the PlaceTradeProcess as described in "Step 4e: Develop the business process" on page 165.

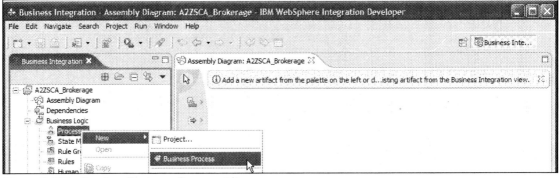

Figure 2-139   Create a Business Process 1/6

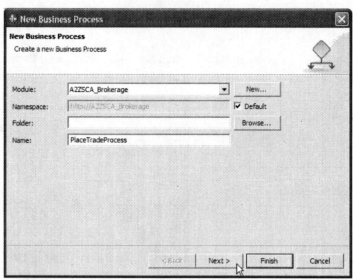

Figure 2-140   Create a Business Process 2/6

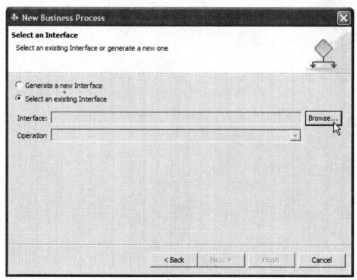

Figure 2-141   Create a Business Process 3/6

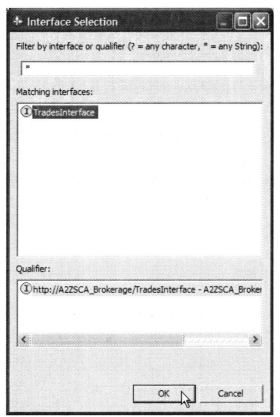

Figure 2-142   Create a Business Process 4/6

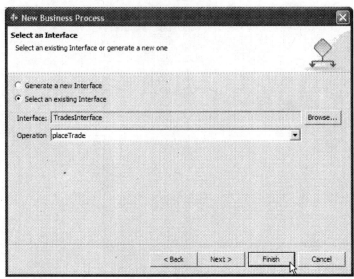

Figure 2-143   Create a Business Process 5/6

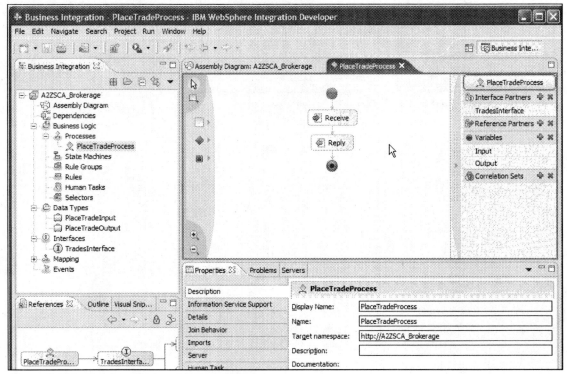

Figure 2-144   Create a Business Process 6/6

Step 4e: Develop the business process

In this step, we develop the implementation of the PlaceTradeProcess using the business process editor.

The PlaceTradeProcess accepts as input the social security number, account number, stock symbol, quantity, and order type as defined by the PlaceTradeInput business object, and a message and order number as output as defined by the PlaceTradeOutput business object. The PlaceTradeProcess performs the following functions:

1. It accepts input for placing an order, and invokes the AuthorizationService of IBM Information Server to determine whether the customer is authorized to perform the trade.

2. If authorized, it invokes the TradesService of IBM Information Server to perform the trade.

3. It then invokes the AuditService of IBM Information Server to log the action taken.

4. It finally returns a message back with a message and order number.

> **Note:** As described in Appendix B, "WebSphere Integration Developer overview" on page 459, WID provides powerful capabilities for developing the application using visual tools. It is *not* our intention to go through every step of developing the business logic. But we intend to focus on those aspects of developing the business logic related to IBM Information Server. But the code we developed is available for download from the IBM Redbooks Web site URL, `ftp://www.redbooks.ibm.com/redbooks/SG247402/`

In the following panels, we show WID being used to:

▶ Invoke an operation of the AuthorizationService IBM Information Server as shown in Figure 2-145 on page 166 through Figure 2-160 on page 178:

a. Click the Information Service icon as shown in Figure 2-145 on page 166 and drop it into the Assembly Diagram as shown in Figure 2-146 on page 167.

b. Then click **Browse** to provide details of the Information Server connection to the IBM Information Server on RADON.itsosj.sanjose.ibm.com as shown in Figure 2-147 on page 168. Click **Next**.

c. Select the isAuthorizedFor operation of the AuthorizationService, and click **Details** in Figure 2-148 on page 168 to view further details of the AuthorizationService as shown in Figure 2-149 on page 169 through Figure 2-152 on page 171.

d. Click **Finish** in Figure 2-152 on page 171.

e. Then specify the input and output variables for this operation as shown in Figure 2-153 on page 172 through Figure 2-160 on page 178 to complete the invocation of the isAuthorizedFor operation of the AuthorizationService in the business process.

► Invoke an operation of the placeTradesService IBM Information Server as shown in Figure 2-161 on page 179 through Figure 2-164 on page 182.

► Invoke an operation of the AuditService IBM Information Server as shown in Figure 2-165 on page 183 through Figure 2-168 on page 185.

Figure 2-169 on page 186 shows the final Assembly Diagram of business logic implementation of the PlaceTradeProcess.

> **Note:** A number of other business processes were also defined in the A2ZSCA_Brokerage module such as the OpenAccountProcess, the GetPositionsProcess, and the GetBalancesProcess. The GetPositionsProcess includes the LegacyStockQuoteService which is a non IBM Information Server that is imported from a WSDL as a Web Services binding as shown in Figure 2-170 on page 187 through Figure 2-176 on page 190.

We can now proceed to generate the bindings for the appropriate business processes as described in "Step 4f: Generate the bindings and export interfaces as appropriate" on page 190.

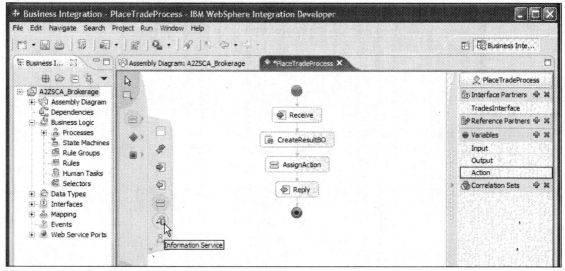

Figure 2-145   Developing the business process 1/32

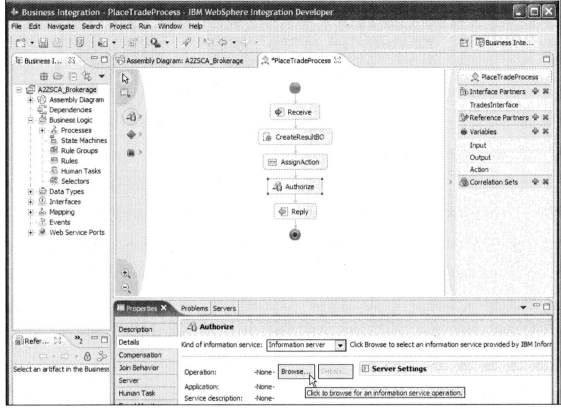

Figure 2-146   Develop the business process 2/32

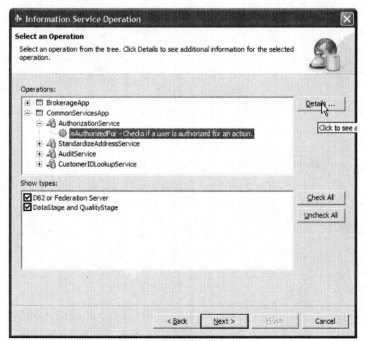

Figure 2-147   Develop the business process 3/32

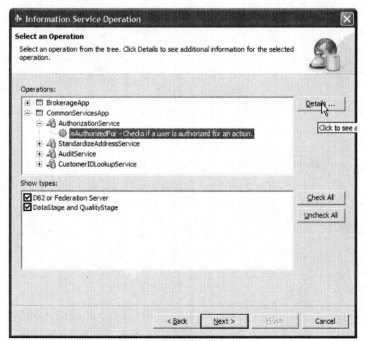

Figure 2-148   Develop the business process 4/32

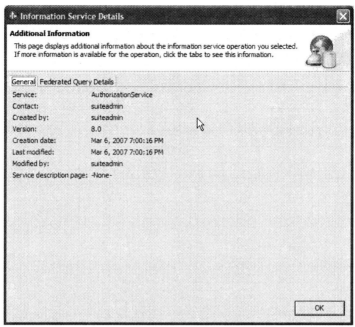

Figure 2-149   Develop the business process 5/32

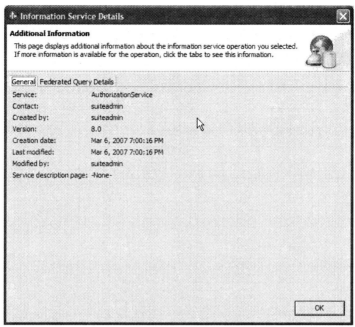

Figure 2-150   Develop the business process 6/32

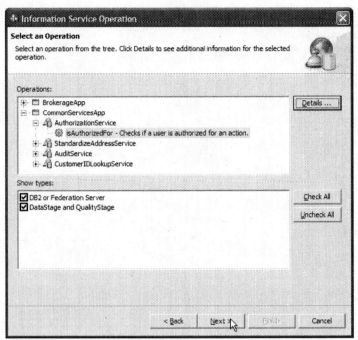

Figure 2-151   Develop the business process 7/32

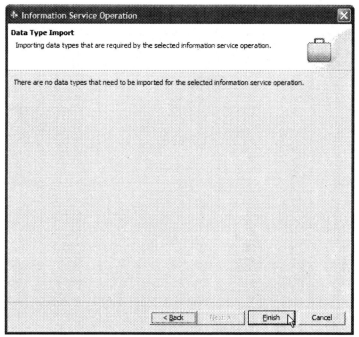

Figure 2-152   Develop the business process 8/32

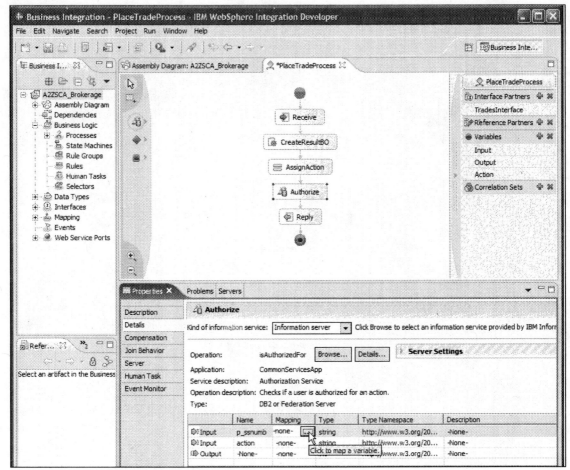

Figure 2-153   Develop the business process 9/32

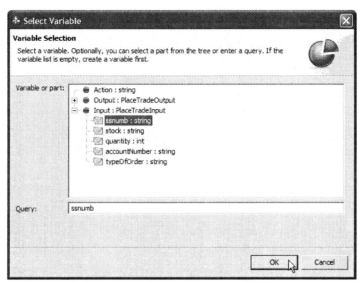

Figure 2-154   Develop the business process 10/32

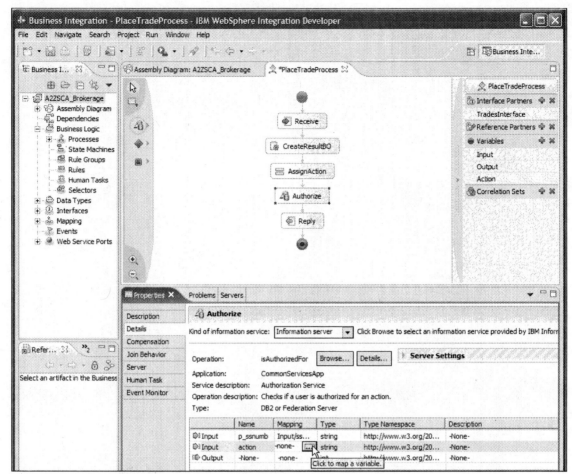

Figure 2-155   Develop the business process 11/32

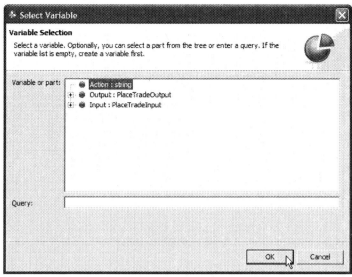

Figure 2-156   Develop the business process 12/32

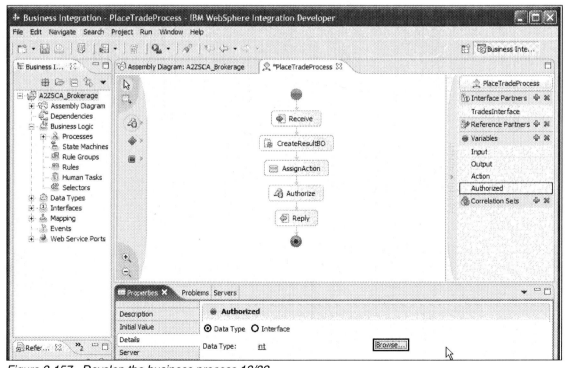

Figure 2-157   Develop the business process 13/32

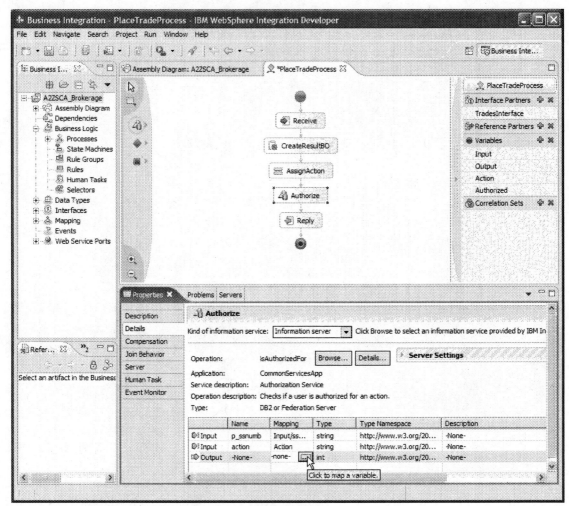

Figure 2-158   Develop the business process 14/32

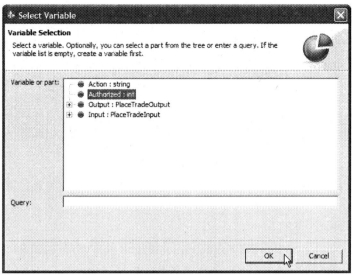

Figure 2-159   Develop the business process 15/32

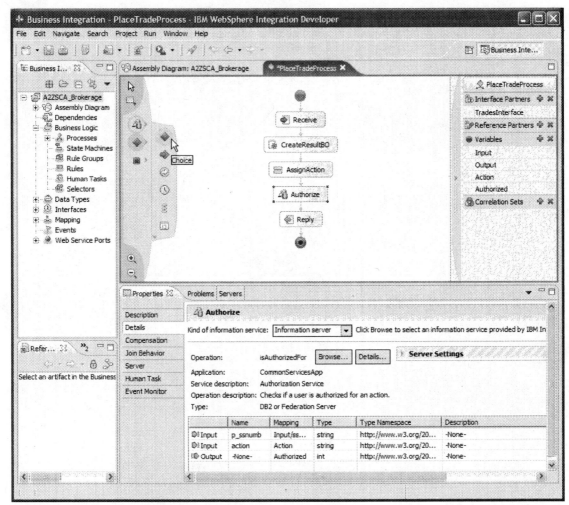

Figure 2-160   Develop the business process 16/32

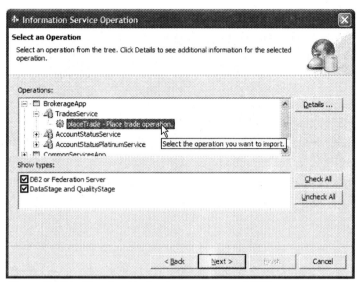

Figure 2-161   Develop the business process 17/32

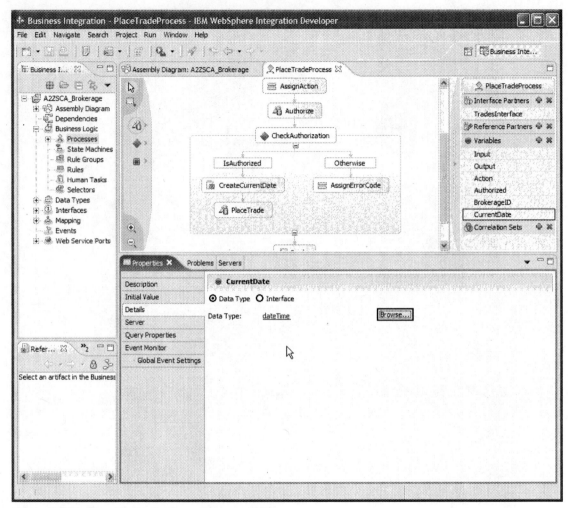

Figure 2-162   Develop the business process 18/32

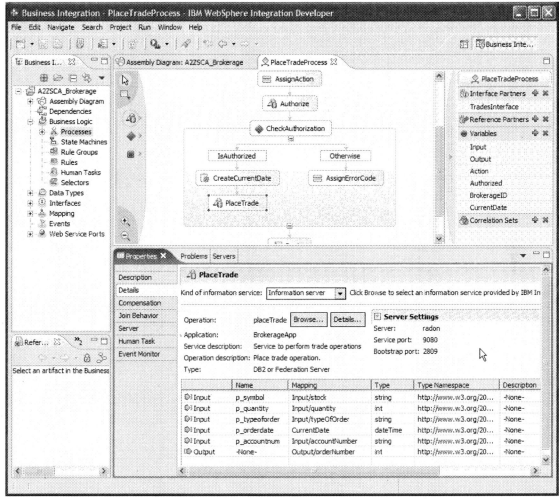

Figure 2-163   Develop the business process 19/32

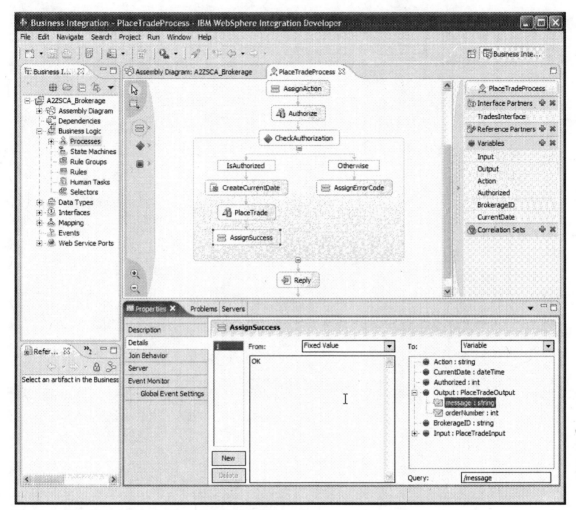

Figure 2-164   Develop the business process 20/32

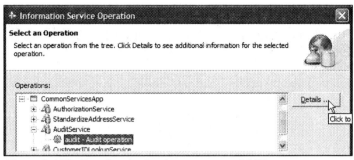

Figure 2-165   Develop the business process 21/32

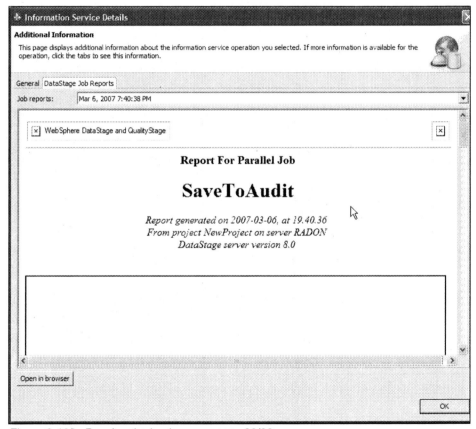

Figure 2-166   Develop the business process 22/32

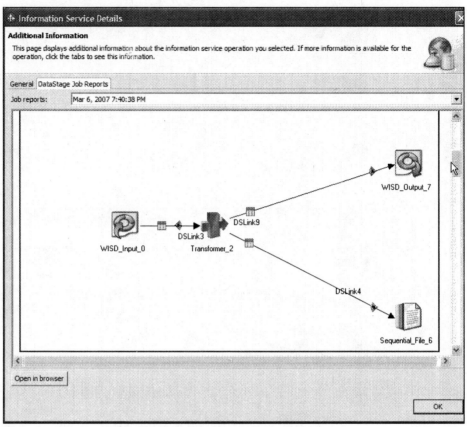

Figure 2-167   Develop the business process 23/32

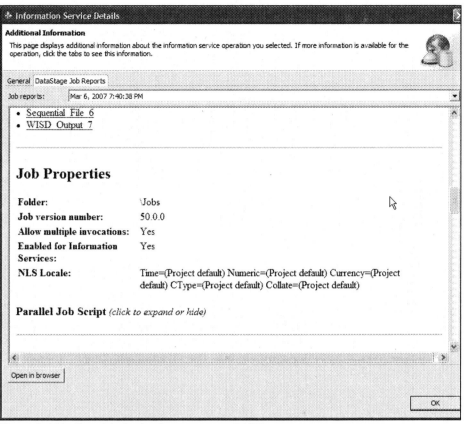

Figure 2-168   Develop the business process 24/32

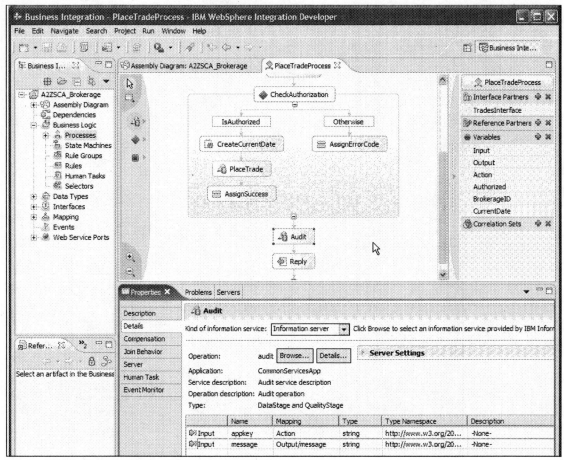

Figure 2-169   Develop the business process 25/32

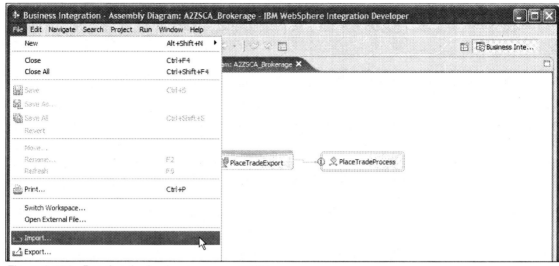

Figure 2-170   Develop the business process 26/32

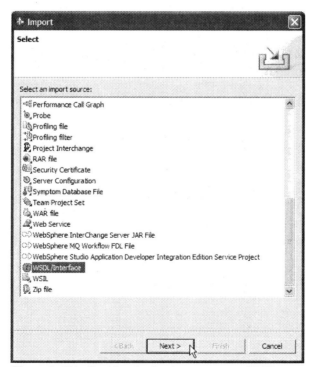

Figure 2-171   Develop the business process 27/32

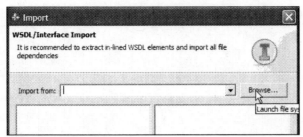

Figure 2-172   Develop the business process 28/32

Figure 2-173   Develop the business process 29/32

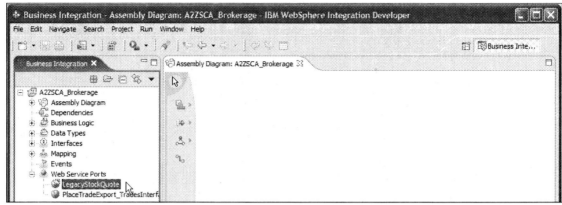

Figure 2-174   Develop the business process 30/32

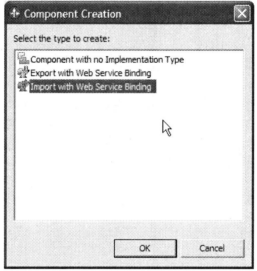

Figure 2-175   Develop the business process 31/32

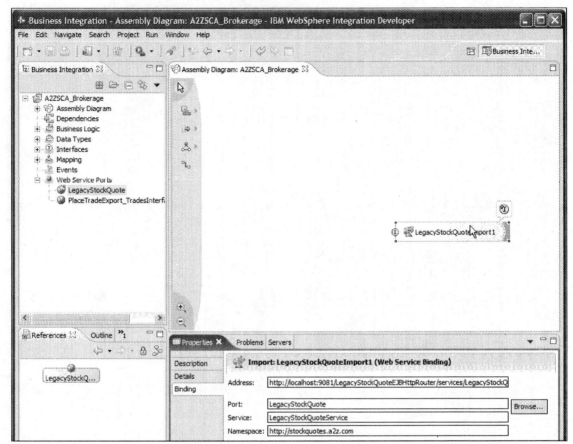

Figure 2-176   Develop the business process 32/32

Step 4f: Generate the bindings and export interfaces as appropriate

In this step, we generate bindings for the different business processes that will be invoked by client applications or components in other SCA modules.

> **Note:** WID supports Messaging Binding (JMS), Web Services Binding (SOAP over HTTP and SOAP over JMS), and SCA binding. It does *not* support EJB binding for exports.

As indicated in "Step 4e: Develop the business process" on page 165, the bindings for the PlaceTradeProcess, GetBalancesProcess, and the OpenAccountProcess processes are demonstrated here as follows:

▶ The PlaceTradeProcess created needs to become available as an external service with SOAP over HTTP binding, and therefore needs to be exported as described in Figure 2-177 on page 193 through Figure 2-187 on page 199:

   a. Open the Assembly Editor by double-clicking Assembly Diagram under the A2ZSCA_Brokerage module.

   b. Drag and drop the PlaceTradeProcess on the Assembly Diagram as shown in Figure 2-177 on page 193.

   c. Select the Export icon and click in the Assembly Diagram as shown in Figure 2-178 on page 193 and Figure 2-179 on page 194.

   d. Modify the default name of Export1 to PlaceTradeExport and connect it to the PlaceTradeProcess using Add Wire as shown in Figure 2-180 on page 194.

   e. Click **OK** on the prompt in Figure 2-181 on page 195 to establish the connection to the PlaceTradeProcess as shown in Figure 2-182 on page 195.

   f. Right-click **PlaceTradeExportHttpPort**, and select **Generate Binding** and **Web Service Binding** in Figure 2-183 on page 196.

   g. Then select **soap/http** and click **OK** as shown in Figure 2-184 on page 196.

   h. Right-click **PlaceTradeExport_TradesInterfaceHttp_service** under Web Server Ports, select **Export** as shown in Figure 2-185 on page 197, and click **Next** in Figure 2-186 on page 198 after selecting the WSDL/Interface.

   i. Check the box Merge dependent resources into the parent WSDL file and specify the To directory (C:\temp\exportwsdl), and click **Finish** as shown in Figure 2-187 on page 199.

▶ The GetBalancesProcess business process is consumed by the mediation flow component of the A2ZSCA_AccountStatus Mediation module (described in "A2ZSCA_AccountStatusMediation module creation" on page 226) using SCA binding:

   a. Select the Export icon and click in the Assembly Diagram. Modify the default name of Export1 to GetBalancesExport and connect it to the GetBalancesProcess using Add Wire as shown in Figure 2-188 on page 200.

   b. Click **OK** on the prompt in Figure 2-189 on page 200 to establish the connection to the GetBalancesProcess as shown in Figure 2-190 on page 201.

   c. Right-click **GetBalancesExport**, select **Generate Binding** and **SCA Binding** in Figure 2-190 on page 201 to complete the process of associating an SCA binding as shown in Figure 2-191 on page 201.

- The OpenAccountProcess business process is consumed by a client application in async mode since a client request to open an account may involve a long delay before a positive or negative response can be returned to the requester. Async mode processing is supported using JMS binding:

  a. Select the Export icon, click in the Assembly Diagram and modify the default name of Export1 to OpenAccountJMS as shown in Figure 2-192 on page 202 and Figure 2-193 on page 202.

  b. Connect OpenAccountJMS to the OpenAccountProcess using Add Wire as shown in Figure 2-194 on page 203 to establish the connection to the OpenAccountProcess.

  c. Right-click **OpenAccountJMS**, select **Generate Binding**, **Message Binding** and **MQ JMS Binding** as shown in Figure 2-195 on page 203:

  d. This selection requires certain configuration properties to be provided to deploy and execute the WebSphere MQ JMS Export service, such as the JNDI name for the connection factory (jms/MQCFLead), JNDI name for receive destination (jms/Q1lead), JNDI name for send destination (jms/Q2lead), and Receive destination listener port name (OpenAccountMQJMSListener) as shown in Figure 2-196 on page 204.

  e. These properties correspond to the underlying WebSphere MQ resources on the WebSphere MQ Server installed on lead.itsosj.sanjose.ibm.com that will be used as the messaging provider.

  f. Click **OK** in Figure 2-196 on page 204 to complete the configuration as shown in Figure 2-197 on page 205.

We can now proceed to deploy the A2ZSCA_Brokerage module on the WebSphere Process Server's WebSphere Application Server as described in "Step 4g: Deploy the SCA module" on page 205.

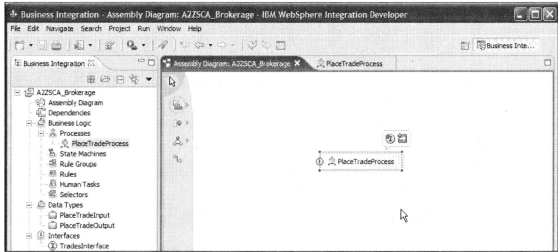

Figure 2-177   Export the service with SOAP over HTTP binding 1/11

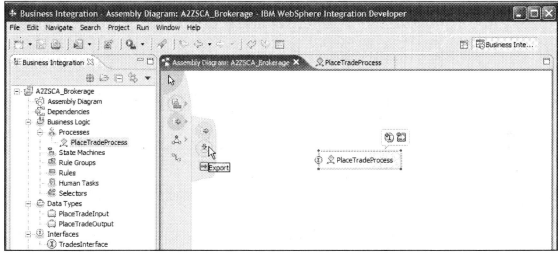

Figure 2-178   Export the service with SOAP over HTTP binding 2/11

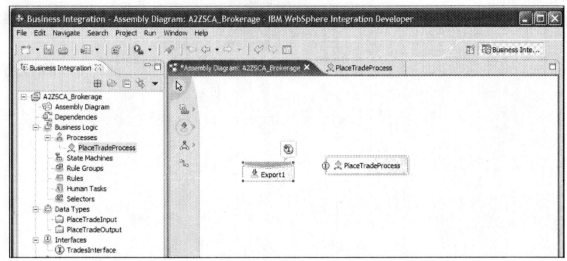

Figure 2-179   Export the service with SOAP over HTTP binding 3/11

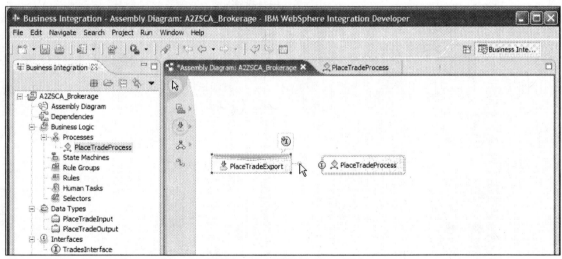

Figure 2-180   Export the service with SOAP over HTTP binding 4/11

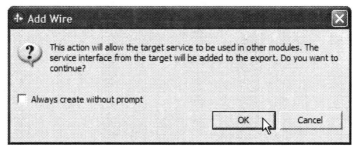

Figure 2-181 Export the service with SOAP over HTTP binding 5/11

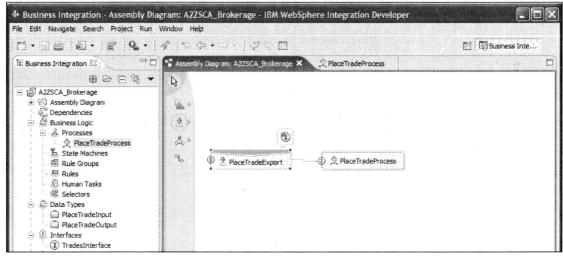

Figure 2-182 Export the service with SOAP over HTTP binding 6/11

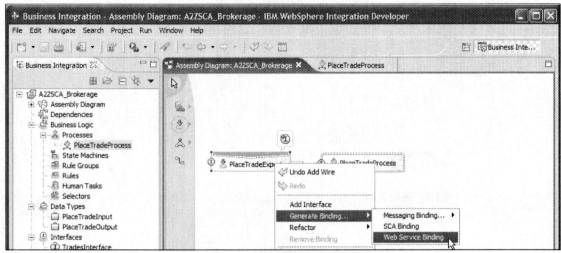

Figure 2-183   Export the service with SOAP over HTTP binding 7/11

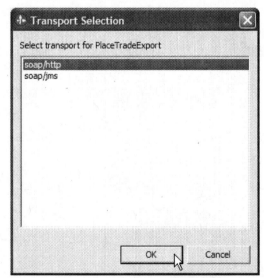

Figure 2-184   Export the service with SOAP over HTTP binding 8/11

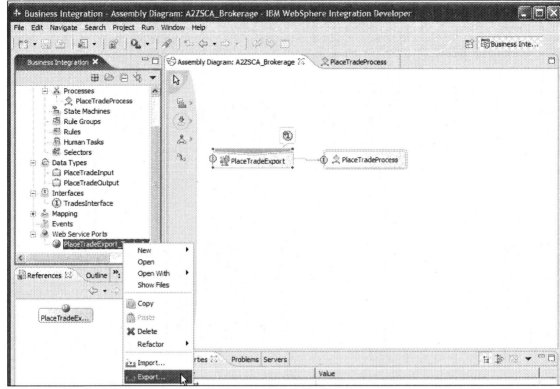

Figure 2-185   Export the service with SOAP over HTTP binding 9/11

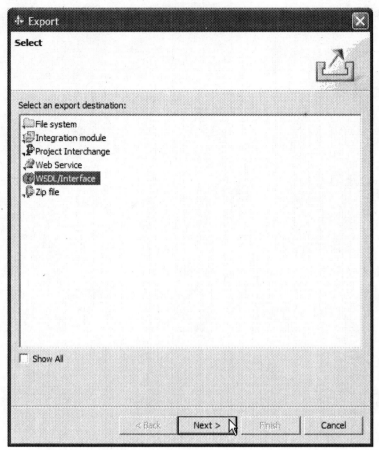

Figure 2-186   Export the service with SOAP over HTTP binding 10/11

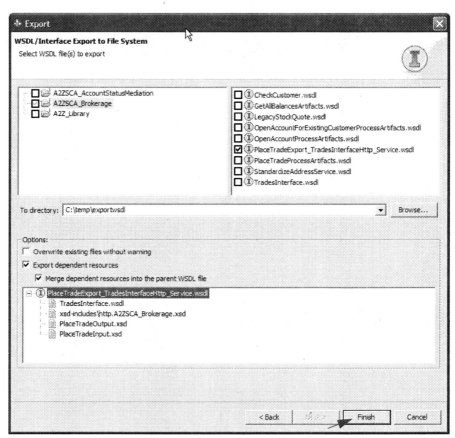

Figure 2-187   Export the service with SOAP over HTTP binding 11/11

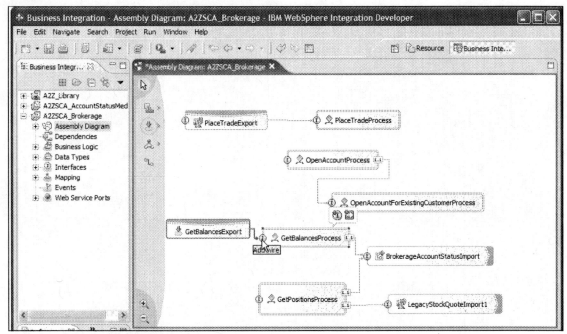

Figure 2-188   Generate SCA binding 1/4

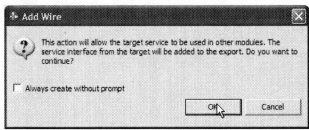

Figure 2-189   Generate SCA binding 2/4

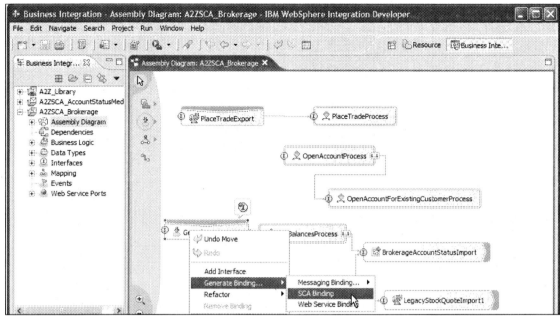

Figure 2-190   Generate SCA binding 3/4

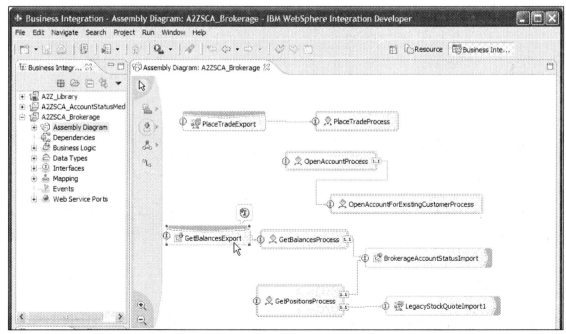

Figure 2-191   Generate SCA binding 4/4

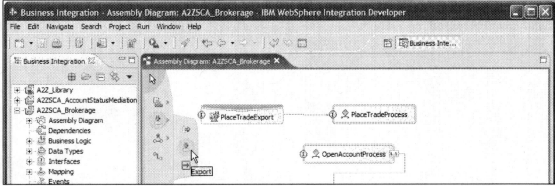

Figure 2-192   Generate the JMS binding 1/6

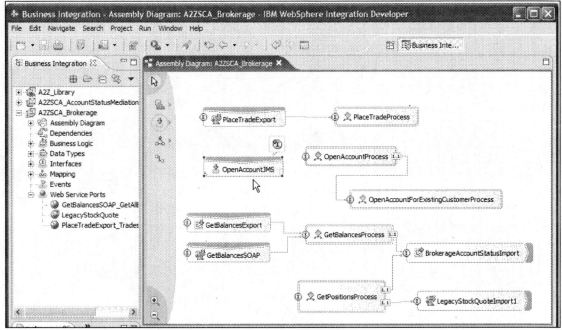

Figure 2-193   Generate the JMS binding 2/6

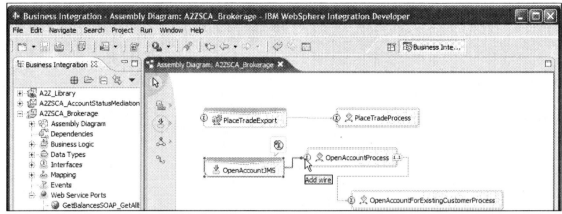

Figure 2-194   Generate the JMS binding 3/6

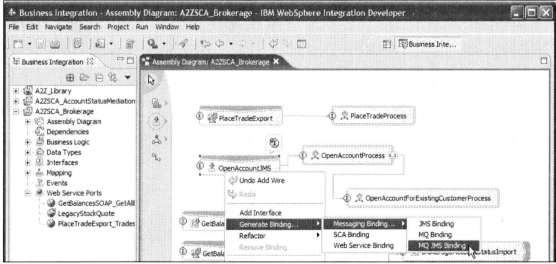

Figure 2-195   Generate the JMS binding 4/6

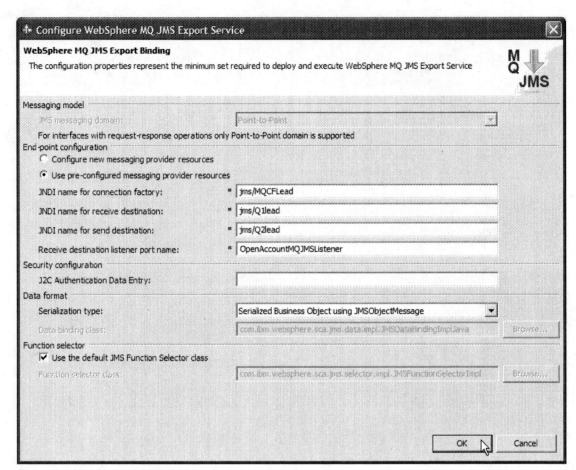

Figure 2-196   Generate the JMS binding 5/6

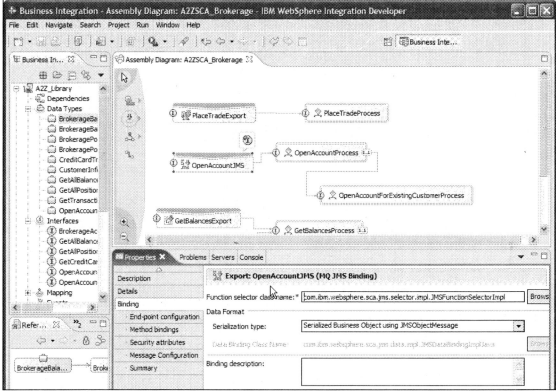

Figure 2-197   Generate the JMS binding 6/6

Step 4g: Deploy the SCA module

The SCA module is the deployable unit in WebSphere Process Server.
Figure 2-198 on page 207 through Figure 2-217 on page 225 describe all the
steps in deploying the A2ZSCA_Brokerage module on the WebSphere Process
Server WAS and starting the WAS application.

The steps involved are as follows:

1. Write "binding" code (A2ZOpenAccountDataBinding class), which converts a
   JMS message supplied by the client application to a Business Object to be
   passed to the component associated with the JMS Export.

2. After this component has finished processing, the binding code converts the
   output Business Object of the component to a JMS message. The client
   application must put a message in the format required by the input data
   binding class. Correspondingly, the client application must read the message
   in the format written by the output data binding class.

3. Configure JMS properties to associate the JMS binding input and output data binding format properties of the OpenAccountJMS export to the A2ZOpenAccountDataBinding class created in the previous step. This defines how the message put into the request queue by a client application is passed to the business process, and how the output parameters from the client application is written to the message queue, and the outgoing Business Object of the business process is written to the response message queue.

> **Note:** Therefore, the code in the A2ZOpenAccountDataBinding.read() method is the counterpart of the testWrite() method of the test client on page 251. Similarly, the readOpenAccount() method of the test client "matches" the method A2ZOpenAccountDataBinding.write().

4. Deploy the module by creating an Enterprise archive (.ear) file for the A2ZSCA_Brokerage module, installing it on the WAS, followed by starting the deployed application.

Write "binding" code

To write this code, proceed as follows:

1. Right-click **A2ZSCA_Brokerage** in WID, and select **New** and **Other** as shown in Figure 2-198 on page 207.
2. Select **Class** under Java and click **Next** as shown in Figure 2-199 on page 208.
3. Provide the name of the Package (a2z),the name of the Java class (A2ZOpenAccountDataBinding), and click **Finish** as shown in Figure 2-200 on page 209.

Example 2-8 on page 209 shows the A2ZOpenAccountDataBinding "binding" code we developed:

► The "read (Message jmsMessage)" class builds a business object from the client's MapMessage
► The "write (Message jmsMessage)" class reads the attributes of the output business object and puts it in a result MapMessage

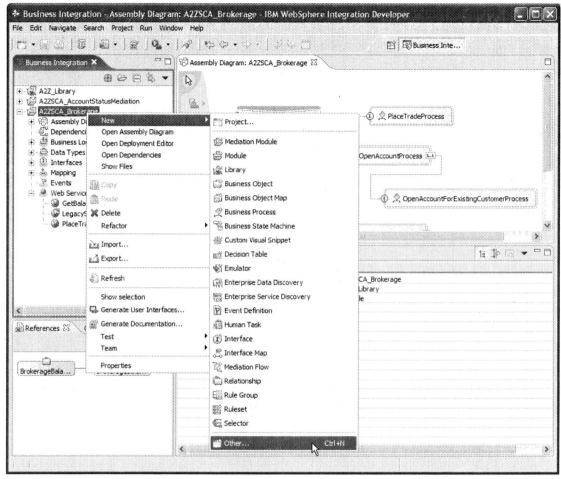

Figure 2-198   Write "binding" code 1/3

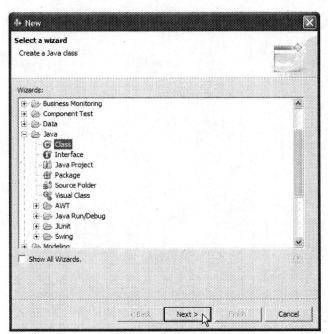

Figure 2-199   Write "binding" code 2/3

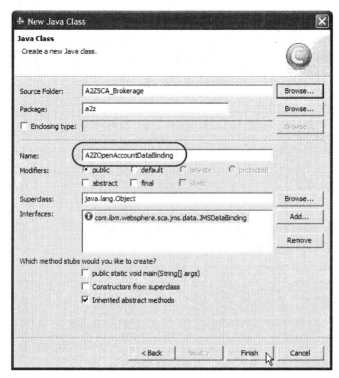

Figure 2-200   Write "binding" code 3/3

Example 2-8   A2ZOpenAccountDataBinding.java

```
/*
 * Created on Mar 8, 2007
 *
 */
package a2z;

import java.util.Date;

import javax.jms.JMSException;
import javax.jms.MapMessage;
import javax.jms.Message;

import com.ibm.websphere.sca.jms.data.JMSDataBinding;
import com.ibm.websphere.sca.sdo.DataFactory;

import commonj.connector.runtime.DataBindingException;
import commonj.sdo.DataObject;

/**
 * @author a2z
 *
```

```java
*/
public class A2ZOpenAccountDataBinding implements JMSDataBinding {

    private DataObject sdo = null;

    private boolean businessException = false;

    /* (non-Javadoc)
     * @see com.ibm.websphere.sca.jms.data.JMSDataBinding#getMessageType()
     */
    public int getMessageType() {
        return JMSDataBinding.MAP_MESSAGE;
    }

    /* (non-Javadoc)
     * @see com.ibm.websphere.sca.jms.data.JMSDataBinding#read(javax.jms.Message)
     */
    public void read(Message jmsMessage) throws JMSException {
        if (jmsMessage.propertyExists("IsBusinessException")) {
            businessException = jmsMessage.getBooleanProperty("IsBusinessException");
            // TODO Load fault data from message , set in jmsData and return
            return;
        }
        MapMessage mapMessage = (MapMessage) jmsMessage;

        // construct the operation BO
        sdo = DataFactory.INSTANCE.create("http://A2Z_Library/OpenAccount", "openAccount");
        sdo.setString("accountType", mapMessage.getString("accountType"));

        // construct the CustomerInfo BO from from the client's MapMessage
        DataObject customerInfo = sdo.createDataObject("customerInfo");
        customerInfo.setString("name",      mapMessage.getString("name"));
        customerInfo.setString("ssnumb",    mapMessage.getString("ssnumb"));
        // MapMessage does not support date, use java.util.Date.getTime() instead
        customerInfo.setDate("dob",         new Date(mapMessage.getLong("dob")) );
        customerInfo.setString("telephone", mapMessage.getString("telephone"));
        customerInfo.setString("street",    mapMessage.getString("street"));
        customerInfo.setString("city",      mapMessage.getString("city"));
        customerInfo.setString("state",     mapMessage.getString("state"));
        customerInfo.setString("zipcode",   mapMessage.getString("zipcode"));

    }


    /* (non-Javadoc)
     * @see com.ibm.websphere.sca.jms.data.JMSDataBinding#write(javax.jms.Message)
     */
    public void write(Message jmsMessage) throws JMSException {
        // read attributes of output BO and put it into result MapMessage
        MapMessage mapMessage = (MapMessage) jmsMessage;
        mapMessage.setString("message",         sdo.getString("message") );
        mapMessage.setString("newCustomerID",   sdo.getString("newCustomerID") );
        mapMessage.setString("newAccountNumber", sdo.getString("newAccountNumber") );
    }
```

```
/* (non-Javadoc)
 * @see com.ibm.websphere.sca.jms.data.JMSDataBinding#isBusinessException()
 */
public boolean isBusinessException() {
    return businessException;
}

/* (non-Javadoc)
 * @see com.ibm.websphere.sca.jms.data.JMSDataBinding#setBusinessException(boolean)
 */
public void setBusinessException(boolean b) {
    businessException = b;
}

/* (non-Javadoc)
 * @see commonj.connector.runtime.DataBinding#getDataObject()
 */
public DataObject getDataObject() throws DataBindingException {
    return sdo;
}

/* (non-Javadoc)
 * @see commonj.connector.runtime.DataBinding#setDataObject(commonj.sdo.DataObject)
 */
public void setDataObject(DataObject anSDO) throws DataBindingException {
    sdo = anSDO;
}

}
```

Configure JMS binding properties

The JMS binding input and output data binding format properties of the OpenAccountJMS export must be configured to specify the A2ZOpenAccountDataBinding class created earlier as shown in Figure 2-201 on page 212 through Figure 2-203 on page 214.

Proceed as follows:

1. Select **OpenAccountJMS export** in the Assembly Diagram, select the **Properties** tab, **Method** bindings, **OpenAccount**, and click **Show Advanced** as shown in Figure 2-201 on page 212.

2. Choose **User Supplied from the Serialization type** drop-down list (in the Input data binding format and Output data binding format), Input data binding class name (a2z.A2ZOpenAccountDataBinding), Output data binding class name (a2z.A2ZOpenAccountDataBinding) as shown in Figure 2-202 on page 213.

3. Select **Message Configuration** under Binding under Properties tab, and select Request Correlation ID to Correlation ID from the Response correlation scheme drop-down list as shown in Figure 2-279 on page 280.

4. This option allows you to specify how the response messages are related to the input. In our example, the Correlation ID is SSNumb as shown in the client application MQTest.java in Example 2-9 on page 276.

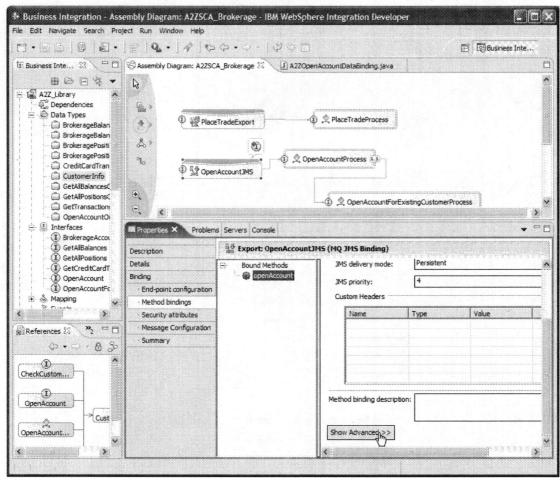

Figure 2-201   Configure JMS binding properties 1/3

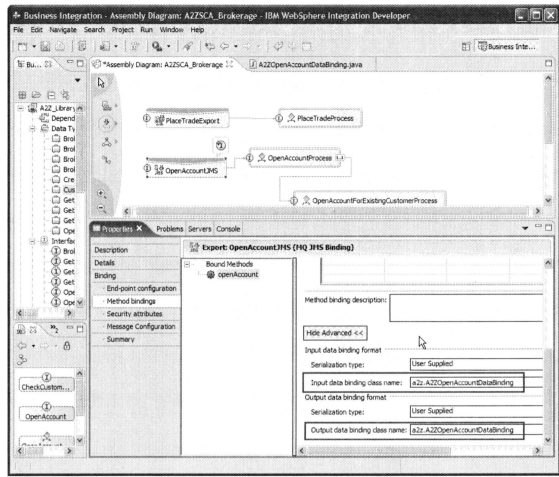

Figure 2-202   Configure JMS binding properties 2/3

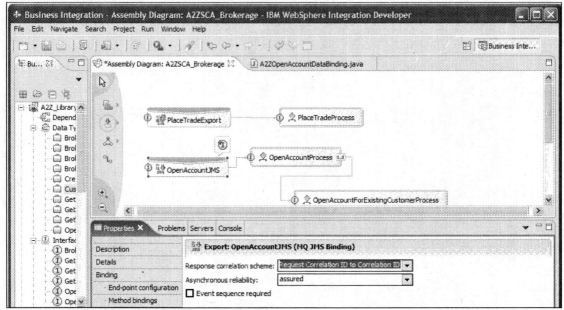

Figure 2-203   Configure JMS binding properties 3/3

Deploy

Proceed as follows:

1. From the File menu of WID, select **Export** as shown in Figure 2-204 on page 215.

2. Select the EAR file as the destination of the enterprise application project and click **Next** as shown in Figure 2-205 on page 216.

3. Specify the EAR project (A2ZSCA_BrokerageApp) and Destination (c:\Temp\A2ZSCA_BrokerageApp.ear) details for the export, and click **Finish** as shown in Figure 2-206 on page 217.

4. Next, login to the WebSphere Process Server WAS Administrative Console on lead.itsosj.sanjose.ibm.com as shown in Figure 2-207 on page 217.

5. Click **Install New Application**, specify the path on the Local file system (c:\temp\A2ZSCA_BrokerageApp.ear) as the location of the ".ear" file to be deployed, and click **Next** as shown in Figure 2-208 on page 218.

6. Choose the defaults for bindings and mappings and click **Next** in Figure 2-209 on page 219.

7. Click **Step 10** in Figure 2-210 on page 220 to proceed to the summary step, and click **Finish** in Figure 2-211 on page 221.

8. The next two screen captures, Figure 2-212 on page 222 and Figure 2-213 on page 223, show the successful progress of the installation.

9. Click **Save to Master Configuration** in Figure 2-213 on page 223, and **Save** again in Figure 2-214 on page 224 to complete the installation of this application.

Figure 2-215 on page 224 through Figure 2-217 on page 225 show the activation of the deployed A2ZXSCA_BrokerageApp application.

Proceed as follows:

1. Select **Enterprise Applications** in the WAS Administrative Console as shown in Figure 2-215 on page 224 to view all the installed applications.

2. Check the A2ZSCA_BrokerageApp application and click **Start** in Figure 2-216 on page 225 to activate the application.

3. The Status icon in Figure 2-217 on page 225 shows successful activation.

We can now proceed to test the processes created using WID as described in "Test the processes" on page 268.

Figure 2-204   Deploy the A2ZSCA_Brokerage module 1/14

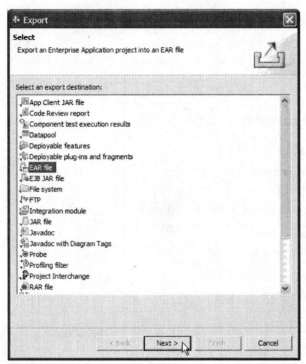

Figure 2-205   Deploy the A2ZSCA_Brokerage module 2/14

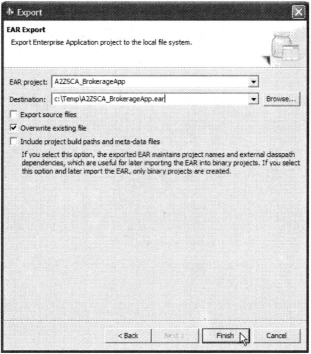

Figure 2-206   Deploy the A2ZSCA_Brokerage module 3/14

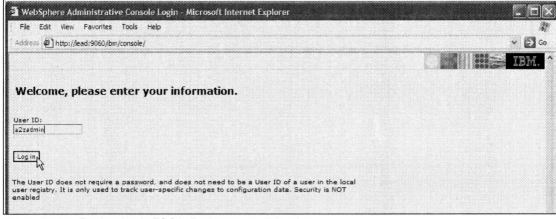

Figure 2-207   Deploy the A2ZSCA_Brokerage module 4/14

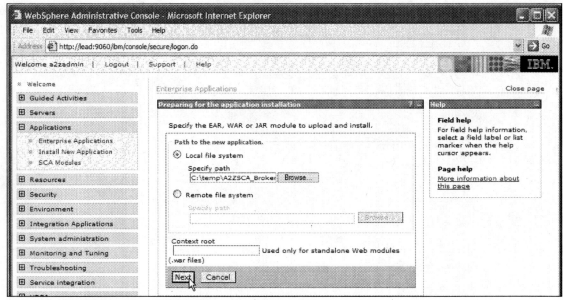

Figure 2-208   Deploy the A2ZSCA_Brokerage module 5/14

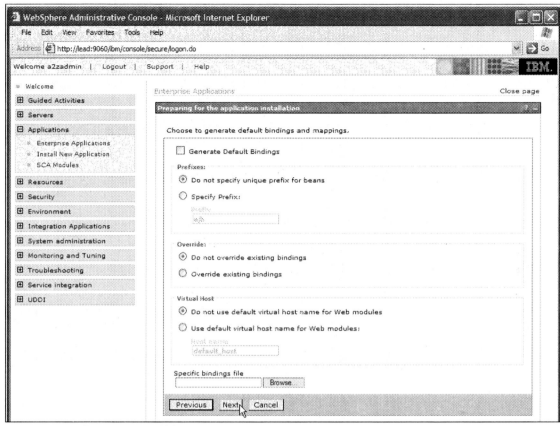

Figure 2-209   Deploy the A2ZSCA_Brokerage module 6/14

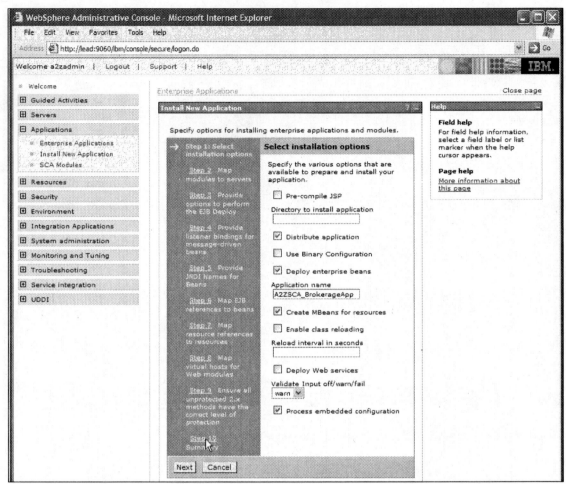

Figure 2-210   Deploy the A2ZSCA_Brokerage module 7/14

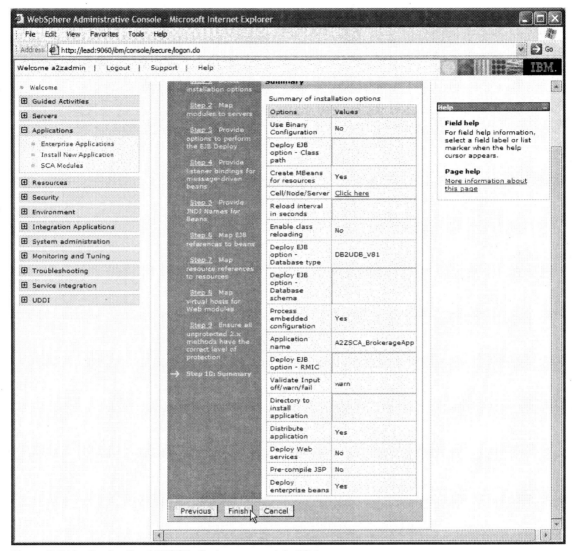

Figure 2-211   Deploy the A2ZSCA_Brokerage module 8/14

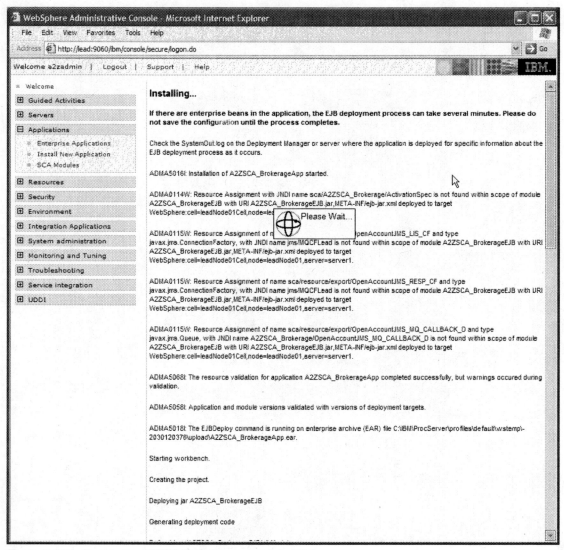

Figure 2-212   Deploy the A2ZSCA_Brokerage module 9/14

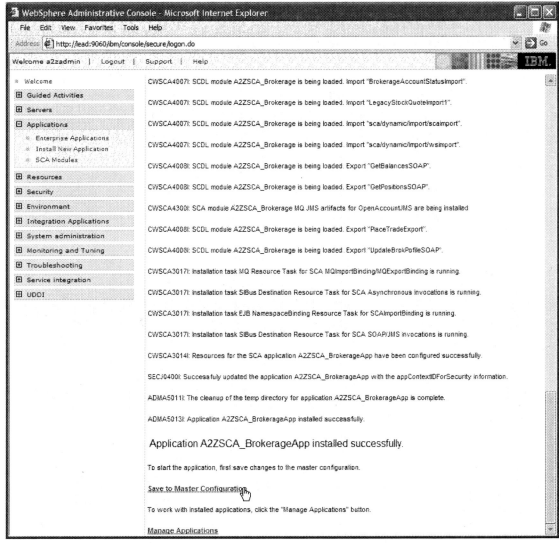

Figure 2-213   Deploy the A2ZSCA_Brokerage module 10/14

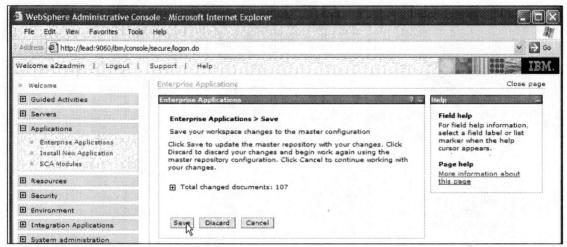

Figure 2-214   Deploy the A2ZSCA_Brokerage module 11/14

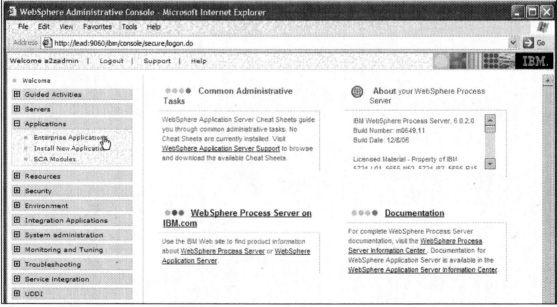

Figure 2-215   Deploy the A2ZSCA_Brokerage module 12/14

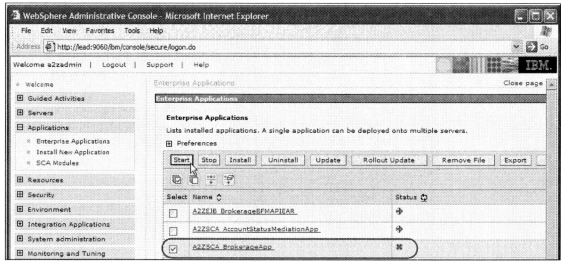

Figure 2-216 Deploy the A2ZSCA_Brokerage module 13/14

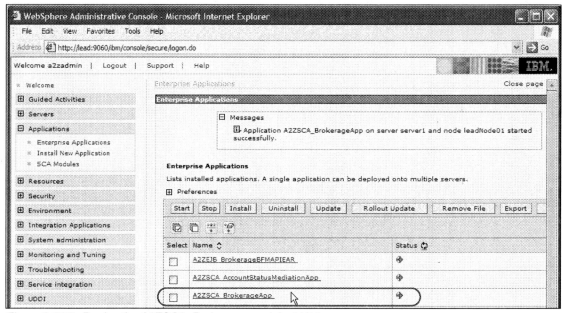

Figure 2-217 Deploy the A2ZSCA_Brokerage module 14/14

2.8.2 A2ZSCA_AccountStatusMediation module creation

As described earlier, the objective of this module was to showcase the capabilities of a mediation flow, which responds to a service request and routes it to another service that is designed to handle it. It also consumes (using SCA binding) the GetBalancesProcess service imported from the A2ZSCA_Brokerage module using SCA binding. The A2ZSCA_AccountStatusMediation module also imports with SOAP over HTTP bindings certain IBM Information Server services such as AccountStatusService and AccountStatusPlatinumService registered in the WSRR, and CardStatusService and CardStatusPlatinumService registered only in IBM Information Server.

> **Note:** A2ZSCA_AccountStatusMediation is a mediation module and its creation differs from that of a module containing processes. You need to select Mediation Module in Figure 2-125 on page 152 to create such a module.

In this step, we describe the import of some services from the WSRR, import of some services from IBM Information Server, and the creation of the mediation module.

▶ **Import some services from WSRR:**

Figure 2-218 on page 227 through Figure 2-232 on page 235 describe the steps in importing services from the WSRR which is located in the server at IP address 9.152.130.81.

We first have to define a connection (named A2ZRepository which is referred to in the import) to a WSRR in WID as shown in Figure 2-218 on page 227 through Figure 2-221 on page 229.

Proceed as follows:

a. From the Window menu in WID, select **Preferences** as shown in Figure 2-218 on page 227.

b. Add to the list of WSRRs by clicking **Add** in Figure 2-219 on page 228. Provide details such as Name (A2ZRepository), Host address (http://9.152.130.81:9080/WSRRCoreSDO/services/WSRRCoreSDOPort) and Description (Repository for A2Z services) of the WSRR where IBM Information Server generated services were exported to in "Step 3e: Optionally export service to WSRR" on page 138.

c. Click **Test Connection** and wait for the message, Test successful, as shown in Figure 2-220 on page 228, and click **OK**.

d. Figure 2-221 on page 229 shows the successful addition this repository to the list of WSRR servers.

e. After the successful test of the connection, right-click **Assembly Diagram** under A2ZSCA_AccountStatusMediation, and select **New** and **Enterprise Service Discovery** as shown in Figure 2-222 on page 229.

f. Select IBM WebSphere Service Registry and Repository as the resource adapter to use to discover a service and click **Next** in Figure 2-223 on page 230.

g. Select A2ZRepository from the Repository drop-down list and click **Next** in Figure 2-224 on page 231 to find and discover enterprise services.

h. Click **Edit Query** in Figure 2-225 on page 231 to specify query filter properties such as File type (Web services (WSDL)) in Figure 2-226 on page 232 and click **OK**.

i. Click **Execute Query** in Figure 2-227 on page 232 to view the results in Figure 2-228 on page 233.

j. Expand AccountStatusService.wsdl and click **Add to import list** as shown in Figure 2-228 on page 233 to import it into WID.

k. Click **OK** in Figure 2-229 on page 233 to confirm the import. Next, import the AccountStatusPlatinumService.wsdl service (not shown here) as well.

l. Click **Next** in Figure 2-230 on page 234 after both objects AccountStatusService and AccountStatusPlatinumService are selected for import.

m. Specify the Module (A2ZSCA_AccountStatusMediation) for the artifacts that will be generated in Figure 2-231 on page 235 and click **Finish**. This creates Web service ports for the two objects.

n. They then have to be imported into the A2ZSCA_AccountStatusMediation module's Assembly Diagram (Figure 2-232 on page 235) with Web Services bindings using drag and drop as shown in Figure 2-174 on page 189 through Figure 2-176 on page 190.

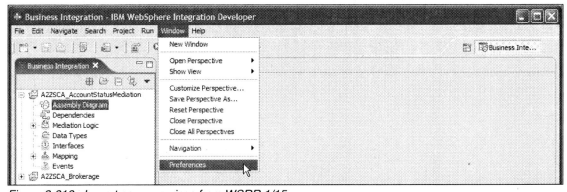

Figure 2-218   Import some services from WSRR 1/15

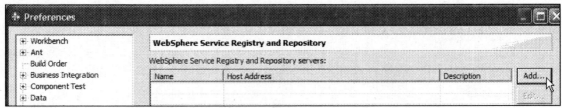

Figure 2-219   Import some services from WSRR 2/15

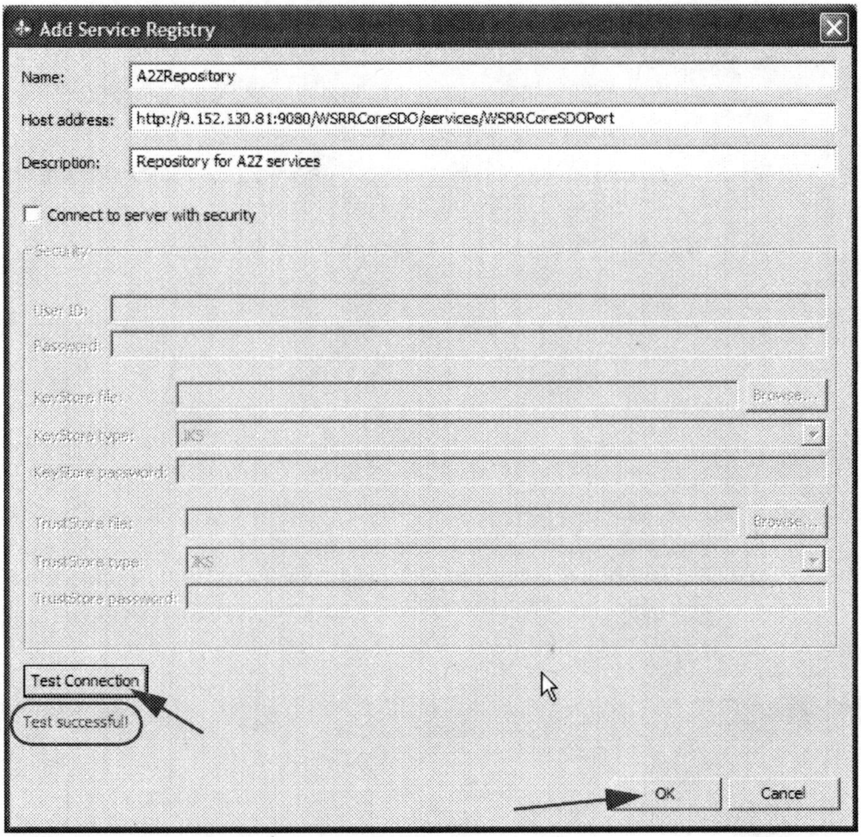

Add Service Registry

Name: A2ZRepository

Host address: http://9.152.130.81:9080/WSRRCoreSDO/services/WSRRCoreSDOPort

Description: Repository for A2Z services

☐ Connect to server with security

Security

User ID:

Password:

KeyStore file: Browse...

KeyStore type: JKS

KeyStore password:

TrustStore file: Browse...

TrustStore type: JKS

TrustStore password:

[Test Connection]

Test successful!

[OK]   [Cancel]

Figure 2-220   Import some services from WSRR 3/15

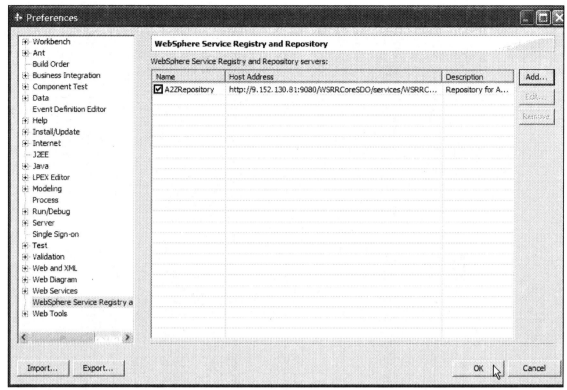

Figure 2-221   Import some services from WSRR 4/15

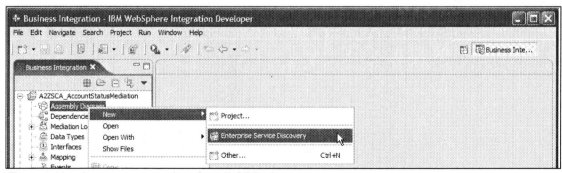

Figure 2-222   Import some services from WSRR 5/15

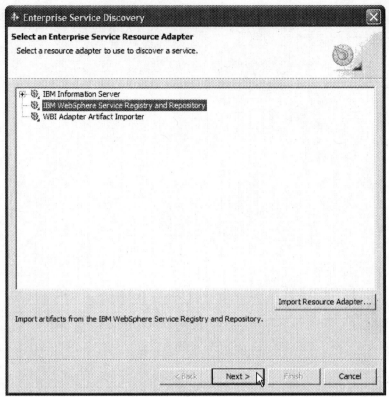

Figure 2-223   Import some services from WSRR 6/15

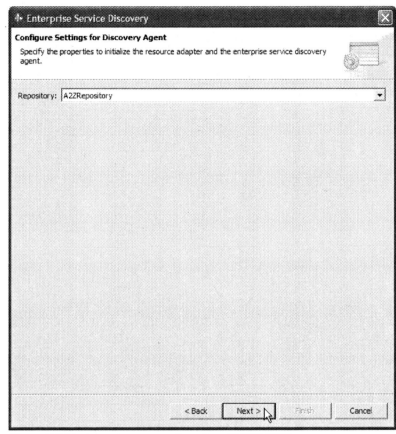

Figure 2-224   Import some services from WSRR 7/15

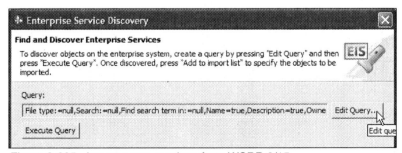

Figure 2-225   Import some services from WSRR 8/15

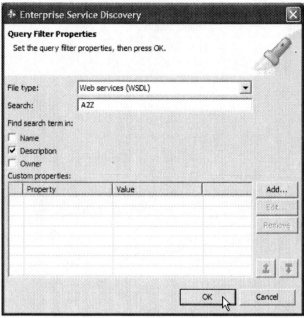

Figure 2-226   Import some services from WSRR 9/15

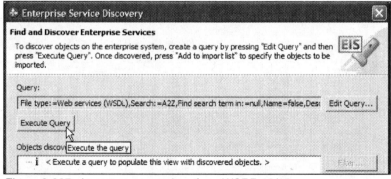

Figure 2-227   Import some services from WSRR 10/15

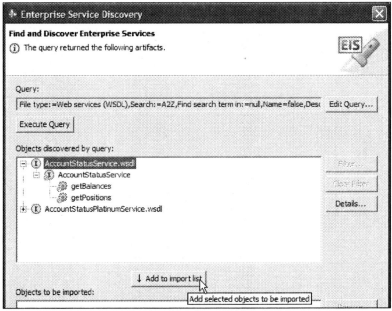

Figure 2-228   Import some services from WSRR 11/15

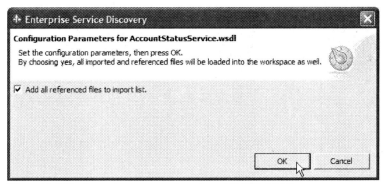

Figure 2-229   Import some services from WSRR 12/15

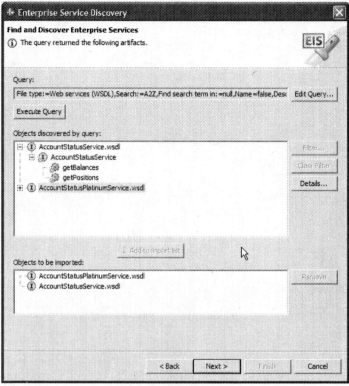

Figure 2-230   Import some services from WSRR 13/15

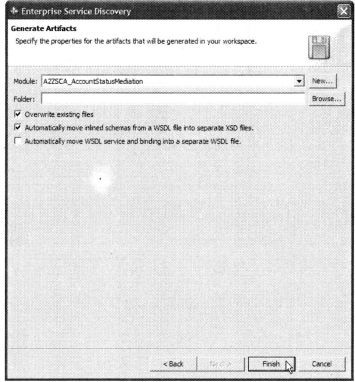

Figure 2-231   Import some services from WSRR 14/15

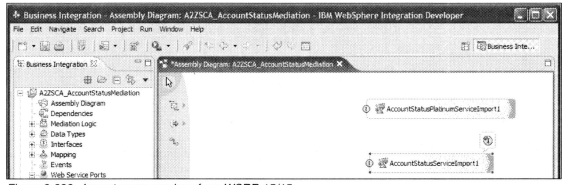

Figure 2-232   Import some services from WSRR 15/15

► **Import some services from IBM Information Server:**

Figure 2-233 on page 237 through Figure 2-245 on page 245 describe the steps in importing services from the IBM Information Server which is located in the server radon.itsosj.sanjose.ibm.com at IP address 9.43.86.70.

Proceed as follows:

a. Right-click **Assembly Diagram** under A2ZSCA_AccountStatusMediation, and select **New** and **Enterprise Service Discovery** as shown in Figure 2-233 on page 237.

b. Select IBM Information Server as the resource adapter to use to discover a service and click **Next** in Figure 2-234 on page 237.

c. Specify the properties for the discovery agent such as Host name (radon), User (suiteadmin), Password, HTTP port (9080) and Bootstrap port (2809) and click **Next** as shown in Figure 2-235 on page 238.

d. Click **Edit Query** in Figure 2-236 on page 239 to specify query filter properties such as Applications (CommonServicesApp and CreditCardApp) in Figure 2-237 on page 239 and click **OK**.

e. Click **Execute Query** in Figure 2-238 on page 240 to view the results in Figure 2-239 on page 240.

f. Select CardStatusPlatinumService and click **Details** to view more information of this service as shown in Figure 2-240 on page 241. Click **OK** to browse and select services in IBM Information Server.

g. Select CardStatusPlatinumService in Figure 2-241 on page 241 and click **Add to import list** to import it into WID. Import the CardStatusService service as well, as shown in Figure 2-242 on page 242.

h. Click **Next** as shown in Figure 2-243 on page 243. after both objects CardStatusService and CardStatusPlatinumService are selected for import.

i. Specify the Module (A2ZSCA_AccountStatusMediation) for the artifacts that will be generated in Figure 2-244 on page 244 and click **Finish**.

j. Figure 2-245 on page 245 shows the two objects imported into the A2ZSCA_AccountStatusMediation module's Assembly Diagram with Web Services bindings.

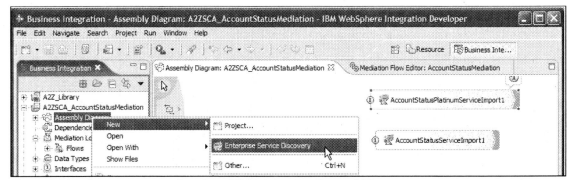

Figure 2-233 Import some services from IBM Information Server 1/13

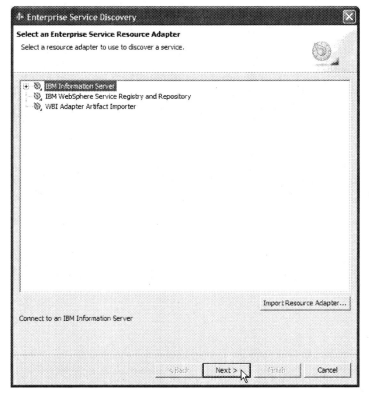

Figure 2-234 Import some services from IBM Information Server 2/13

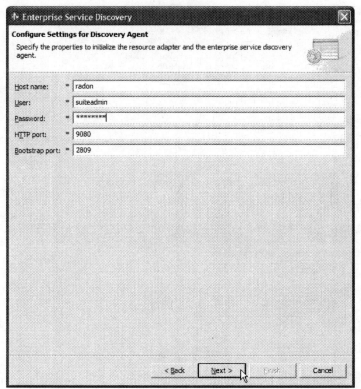

Figure 2-235 Import some services from IBM Information Server 3/13

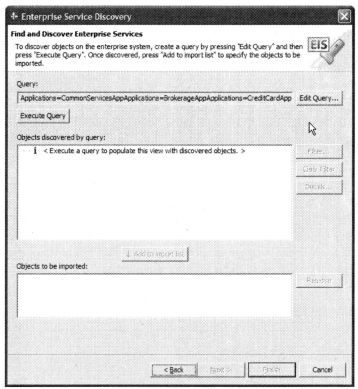

Figure 2-236   Import some services from IBM Information Server 4/13

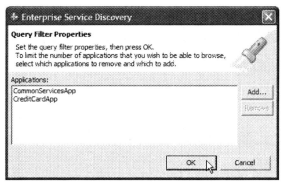

Figure 2-237   Import some services from IBM Information Server 5/13

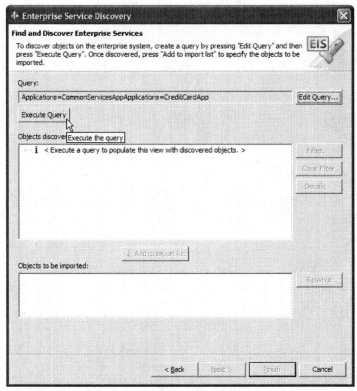

Figure 2-238   Import some services from IBM Information Server 6/13

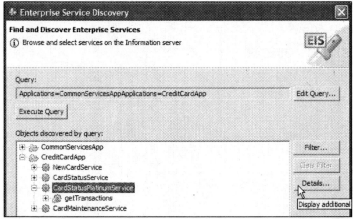

Figure 2-239   Import some services from IBM Information Server 7/13

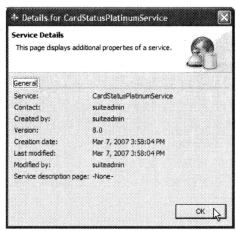

Figure 2-240   Import some services from IBM Information Server 8/13

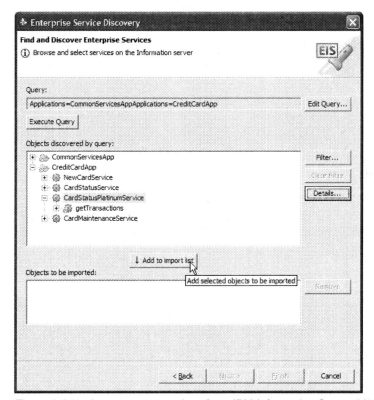

Figure 2-241   Import some services from IBM Information Server 9/13

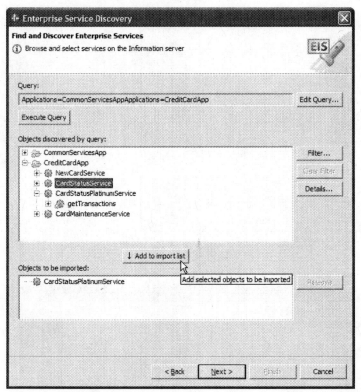

Figure 2-242 Import some services from IBM Information Server 10/13

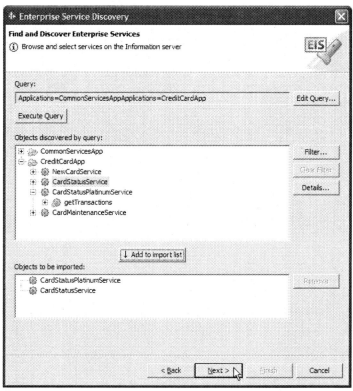

Figure 2-243   Import some services from IBM Information Server 11/13

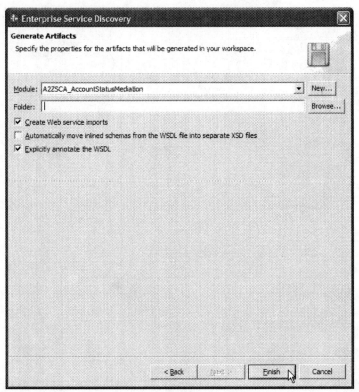

Figure 2-244   Import some services from IBM Information Server 12/13

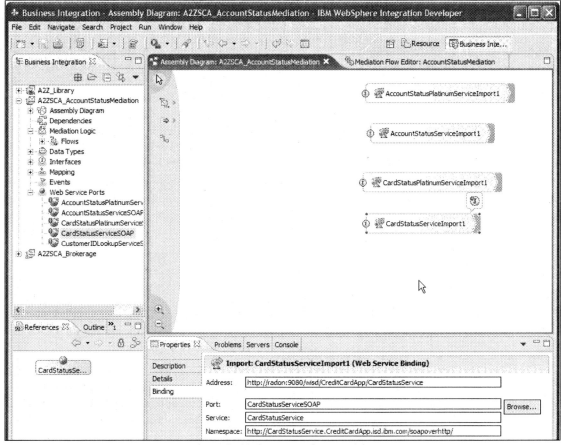

Figure 2-245 Import some services from IBM Information Server 13/13

▶ **Creation of the mediation flow:**

In this section, we provide a high level overview of the implementation of a mediation flow as shown in Figure 2-246 on page 247 through Figure 2-270 on page 267. Depending upon the customer's profile, the customer will be provided up to the second status of their accounts (for Platinum customers) or a slightly delayed status (for non-platinum customers). The customer's positions in the Brokerage system, and card transactions in the CreditCard system are shown as results of a request for account status. The AccountStatusMediation mediation flow is exposed with an SCA binding. A service CustomerIdLookupService is also used in this module — this service accepts as input the customer's social security number and returns the corresponding customer ids in the Brokerage and CreditCard systems.

Figure 2-246 on page 247 through Figure 2-250 on page 251 describe the creation of a Java service type called IsPlatinum which determines whether a customer is Platinum or not, and calls the CustomerIdLookupService to determine the respective customer ids for a given social security number.

Click the Java icon (Figure 2-246 on page 247) and drop it in the Assembly Diagram and modify the default name to IsPlatinum as shown in Figure 2-247 on page 248. Connect IsPlatinum to CustomerIdLookupServiceImport using Add Wire as shown. Choose the GetCustomerStatus interface for IsPlatinum from a filter of "get" as shown in Figure 2-248 on page 249. Click **OK**. Right-click **IsPlatinum** and select **Generate Implementation** in Figure 2-249 on page 250 to code the requirements of this service.

Figure 2-250 on page 251 shows the highlighted Java code which invokes the CustomerIdLookupService and extracts the customer ids from the Brokerage and CreditCard systems. It then determines whether the customer is Platinum or not. The result is a complex data type called DataObject.

Figure 2-251 on page 252 through Figure 2-255 on page 255 show the creation of a mediation flow component that is wired to AccountStatusPlatinumServiceImport1, AccountStatusServiceImport1, CardStatusPlatinumServiceImport1, CardStatusServiceImport1, and IsPlatinum components. This also shows the BrokerageAccountStatus interface for the IsPlatinum wire. Figure 2-255 on page 255 shows all the connections from the AccountStatusMediation component.

Figure 2-256 on page 255 and Figure 2-257 on page 256 show the assignment of the BrokerageAccountStatus and GetCreditCardTransactions interfaces to the AccountStatusMediation component. Right-click **AccountStatusMediation** and select **Generate Implementation** in Figure 2-256 on page 255, and check the boxes of both BrokerageAccountStatus and GetCreditCardTransactions in Figure 2-257 on page 256. Click **OK**.

Figure 2-258 on page 256 through Figure 2-260 on page 258 show the AccountStatusMediationExport of the AccountStatusMediation component with SCA binding.

Figure 2-261 on page 258 through Figure 2-270 on page 267 show the implementation of the AccountStatusMediation component. For each of the interfaces (BrokerageAccountStatus and GetCreditCardTransactions), logic is built using the visual tools to invoke the IsPlatinum service and route the service request to the Platinum or non-platinum service depending upon the Platinum status of a customer as established by the IsPlatinum service.

Figure 2-262 on page 259 through Figure 2-267 on page 264 show the logic implementation of the getAllBalances (Figure 2-262 on page 259 through Figure 2-264 on page 261) and getAllPositions (Figure 2-265 on page 262 through Figure 2-267 on page 264) operations of the BrokerageAccountStatus interface,

Likewise, Figure 2-268 on page 265 through Figure 2-270 on page 267 show the logic implementation of the getCreditCardTransaction operation of the GetCreditCardTransactions interface.

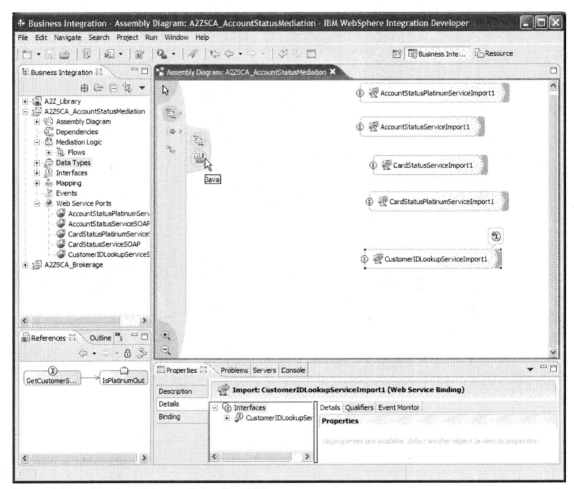

Figure 2-246   Creation of the mediation flow 1/25

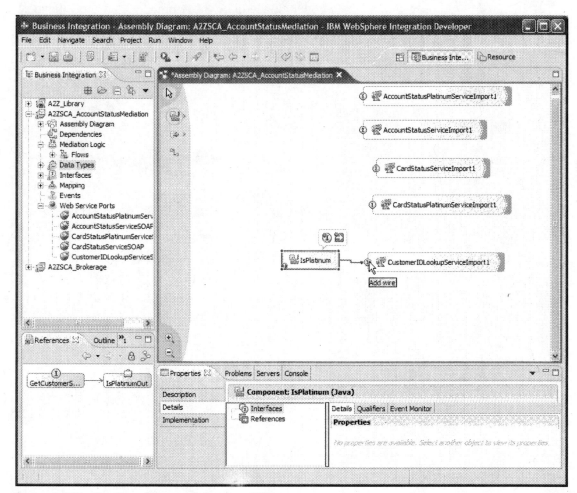

Figure 2-247   Creation of the mediation flow 2/25

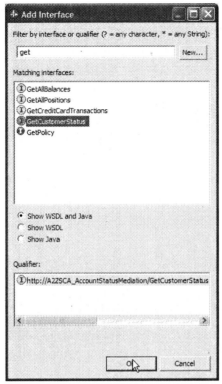

Figure 2-248   Creation of the mediation flow 3/25

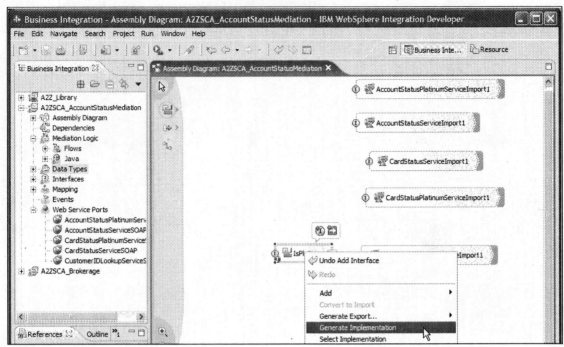

Figure 2-249   Creation of the mediation flow 4/25

File Edit Source Refactor Navigate Search Project Run Window Help

Assembly Diagram: A2ZSCA_AccountStatusMediation   IsPlatinumImpl.java ✕

```
    }

    /**
     * Method generated to support implementation of operation "IsPlatinum" defined for WSDL port type
     * named "interface.GetCustomerStatus".
     *
     * The presence of commonj.sdo.DataObject as the return type and/or as a parameter
     * type conveys that its a complex type. Please refer to the WSDL Definition for more information
     * on the type of input, output and fault(s).
     */
    public DataObject IsPlatinum(String ssnumb) {
        // get customer id looookup service reference
        CustomerIDLookupService lookupService = locateService_CustomerIDLookupServicePartner();
        // get the brokerage customer ID
        String brokerageID = lookupService.lookupBrokerageCustomerID(ssnumb);
        // get the credit card customer ID
        String creditCardID = lookupService.lookupCreditCardCustomerID(ssnumb);
        // a user is platinum if she has a brokerage account and a credit card account
        boolean isPlatinum = (brokerageID != null && creditCardID != null);

        // create result object
        DataObject result = DataFactory.INSTANCE.create("http://A2ZSCA_AccountStatusMediation",
                                                        "IsPlatinumOut");
        result.setBoolean("isPlatinum", isPlatinum);
        result.setString("brokerageID", brokerageID);
        result.setString("creditCardID", creditCardID);
        return result;
    }
```

Figure 2-250   Creation of the mediation flow 5/25

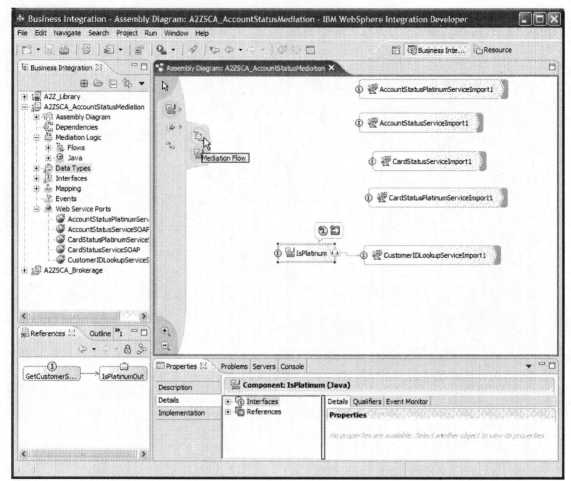

Figure 2-251   Creation of the mediation flow 6/25

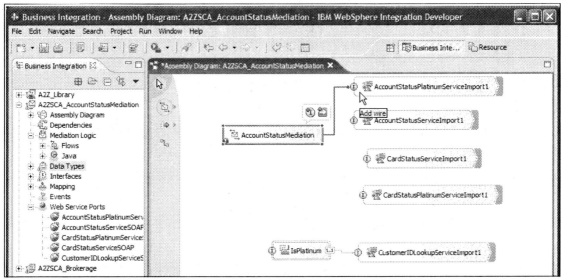

Figure 2-252   Creation of the mediation flow 7/25

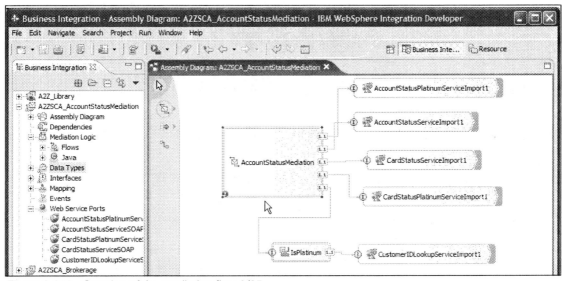

Figure 2-253   Creation of the mediation flow 8/25

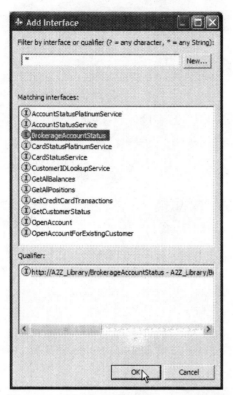

Figure 2-254   Creation of the mediation flow 9/25

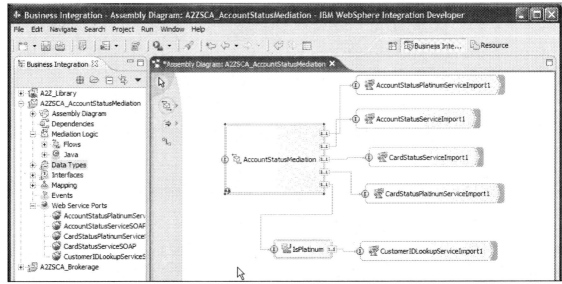

Figure 2-255 Creation of the mediation flow 10/25

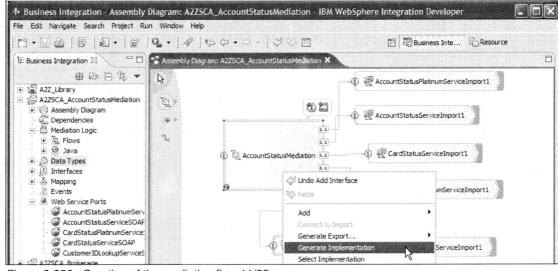

Figure 2-256 Creation of the mediation flow 11/25

Figure 2-257   Creation of the mediation flow 12/25

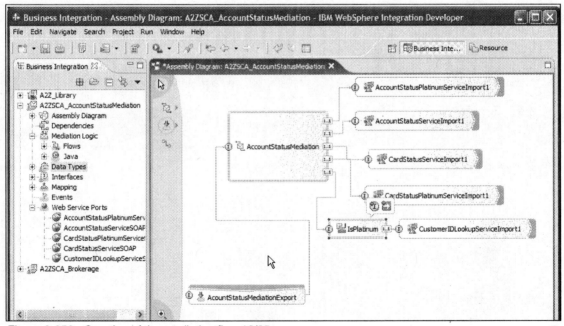

Figure 2-258   Creation of the mediation flow 13/25

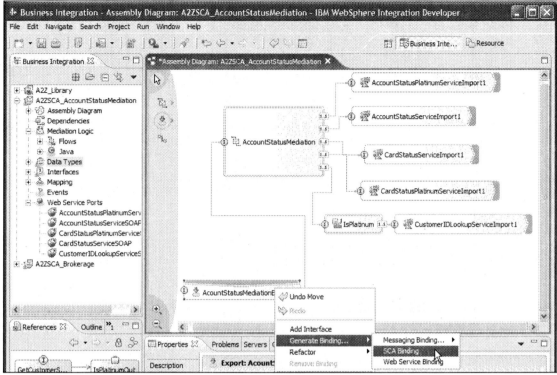

Figure 2-259   Creation of the mediation flow 14/25

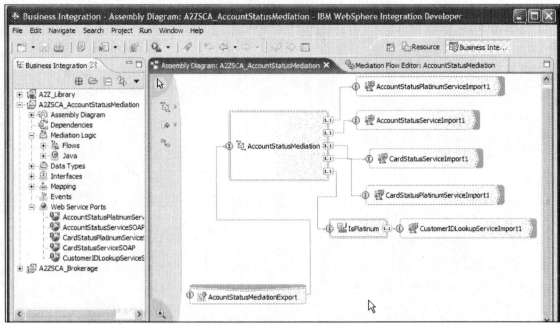

Figure 2-260   Creation of the mediation flow 15/25

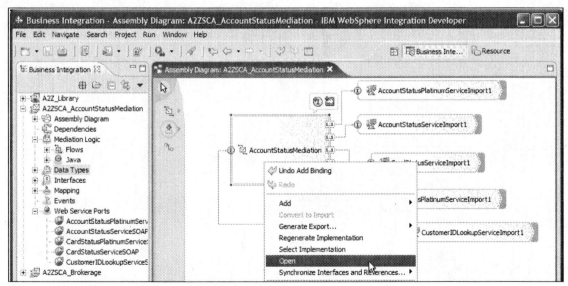

Figure 2-261   Creation of the mediation flow 16/25

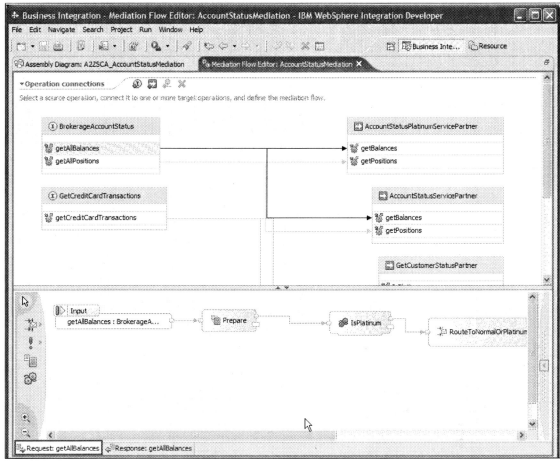

Figure 2-262   Creation of the mediation flow 17/25

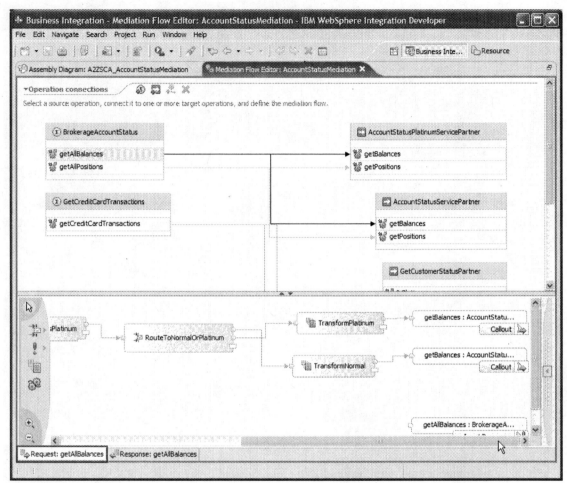

Figure 2-263   Creation of the mediation flow 18/25

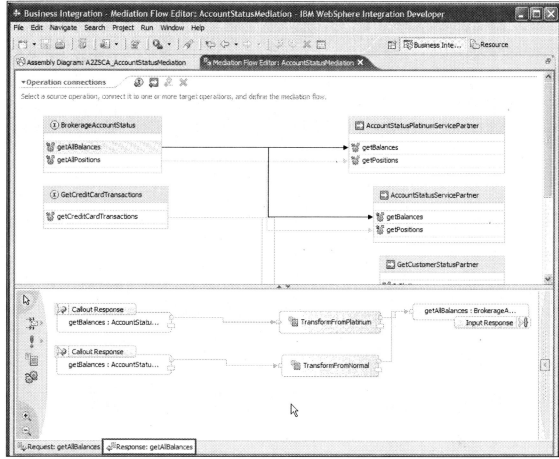

Figure 2-264   Creation of the mediation flow 19/25

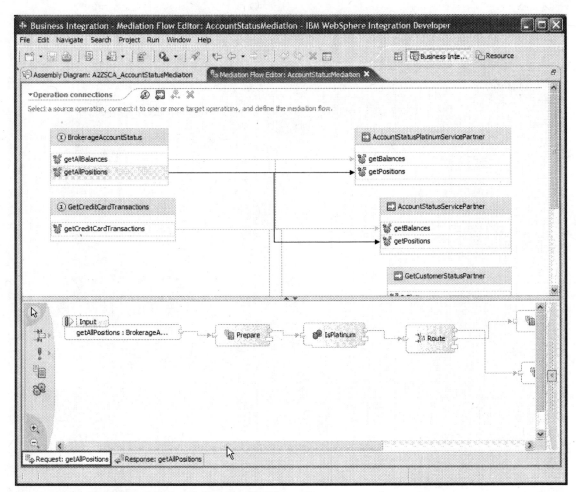

Figure 2-265   Creation of the mediation flow 20/25

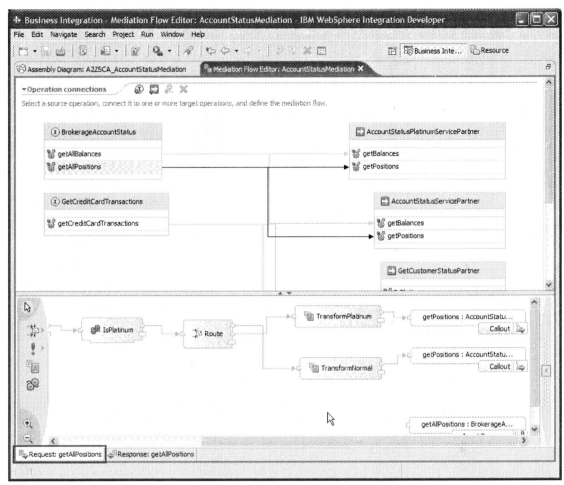

Figure 2-266   Creation of the mediation flow 21/25

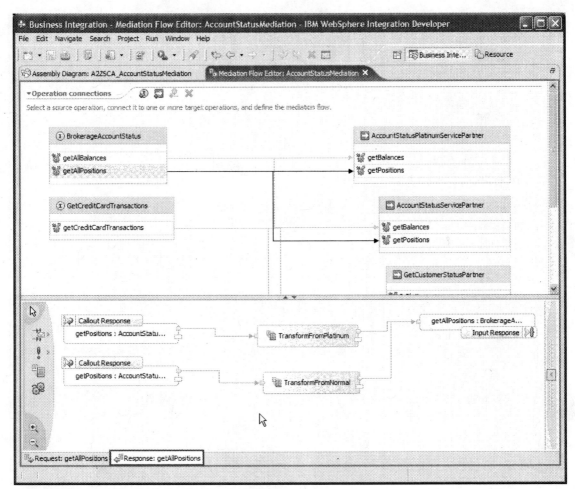

Figure 2-267   Creation of the mediation flow 22/25

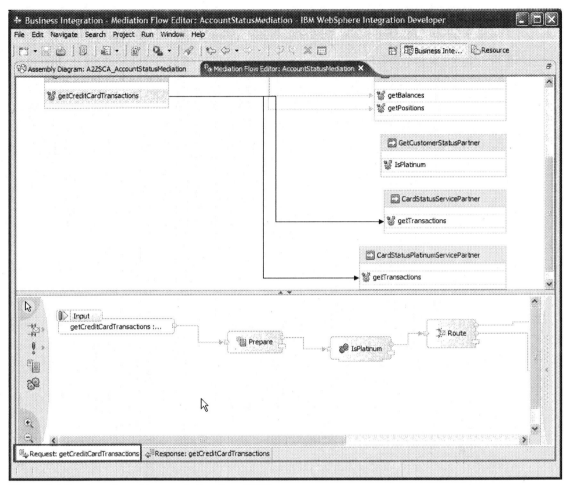

Figure 2-268   Creation of the mediation flow 23/25

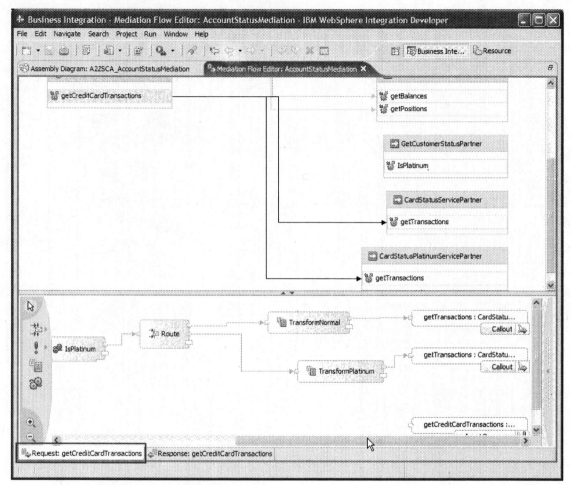

Figure 2-269   Creation of the mediation flow 24/25

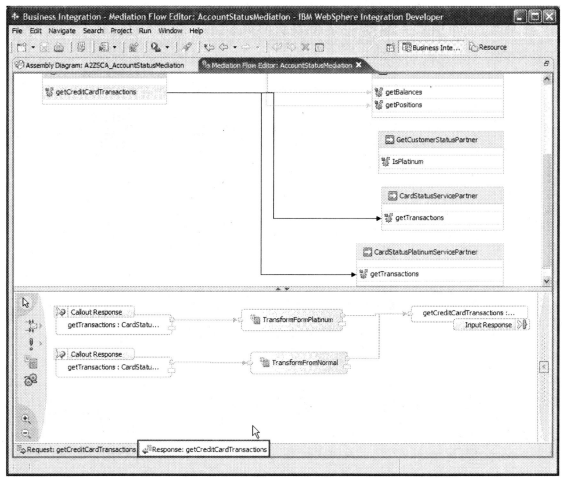

Figure 2-270   Creation of the mediation flow 25/25

2.8.3 Test the processes

In this step, we show how to test the SOAP over HTTP binding, SCA binding, and JMS binding of a component before making it available for consumption by client applications. Each of these test procedures is described here.

Test SOAP over HTTP binding process

WebSphere Integration Developer is built on Rational Application Developer, and therefore the same procedure described in "Test the stored procedure service (SOAP binding)" on page 95 to test processes with SOAP over HTTP binding can be applied here as well. After obtaining the location of the WSDL, you can follow the same steps as described in Figure 2-68 on page 102 through Figure 2-74 on page 106.

Test SCA binding process

In this step, we describe the steps involved in using WebSphere Integration Developer to test a component that has an SCA binding as shown in Figure 2-271 on page 269 through Figure 2-278 on page 275.

> **Note:** This procedure can be used to test processes that have other than SCA binding. The Business Process Choreographer (BPC) only requires that SCA components for the business processes be created.

Proceed as follows:

1. Select the Servers tab in WID as shown in Figure 2-271 on page 269.

2. If WebSphere Process Server v6.0 is stopped. start it by right-clicking the WebSphere Process Server v6.0, and clicking **Start** as shown in Figure 2-272 on page 270.

3. Right-click **WebSphere Process Server v6.0** and select **Add and Remove Projects** in Figure 2-273 on page 271 to configure it with desired modules.

4. Select A2ZSCA_Brokerage and click **Finish** to do so as shown in Figure 2-274 on page 272. This causes the A2ZSCA_Brokerage module to be deployed.

5. Next, right-click **WebSphere Process Server v6.0** and select **Launch** and **Business Process Choreographer Explorer** in Figure 2-275 on page 273.

6. Check PlaceTradeProcess in My Process Templates, and click **Start Instance** in Figure 2-276 on page 274.

7. Provide input details for the PlaceTradeProcess such as ssnumb (611-32-3978), stock (IBM), quantity (10), accountNumber (BA00010), and typeofOrder (B) and click **Submit** as shown in Figure 2-277 on page 274.

8. The results of this request are shown in Figure 2-278 on page 275, indicating successful execution.

> **Note:** There are other ways of testing the process that are not documented here.

We can now proceed to test the JMS bindings of a process as described in "Test JMS binding" on page 275.

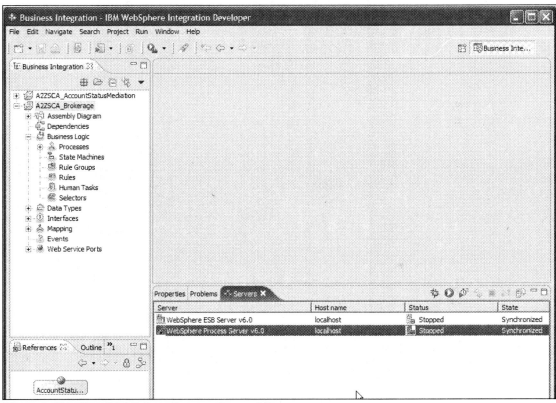

Figure 2-271   Start WebSphere Process Server 1/2

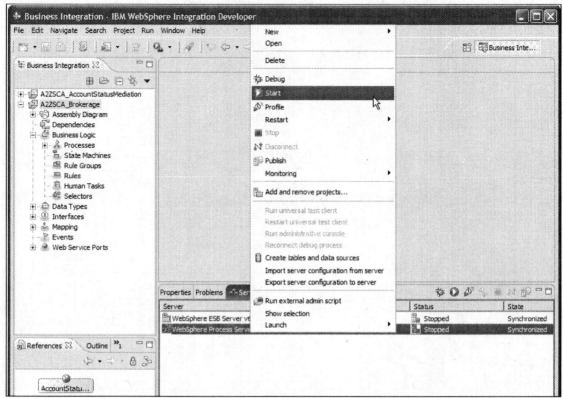

Figure 2-272   Start WebSphere Process Server 2/2

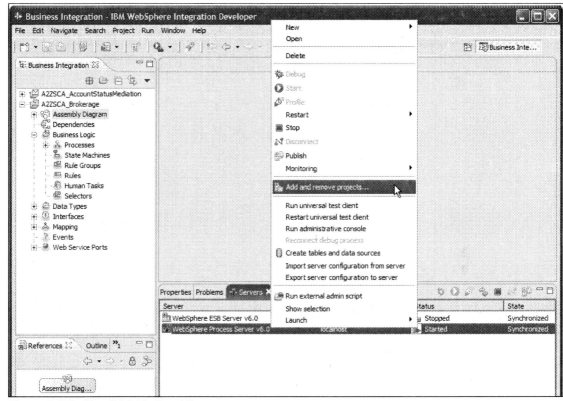

Figure 2-273   Test SCA binding 1/6

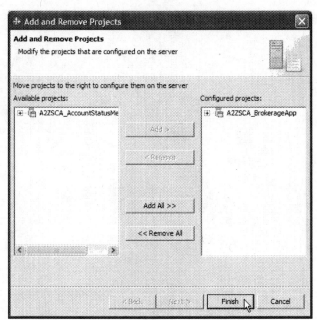

Figure 2-274   Test SCA binding 2/6

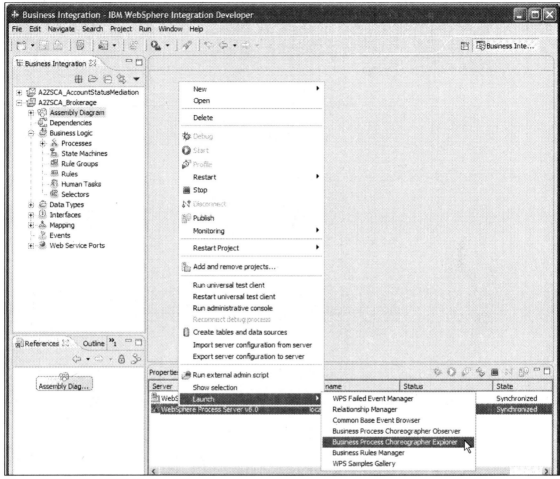

Figure 2-275   Test SCA binding 3/6

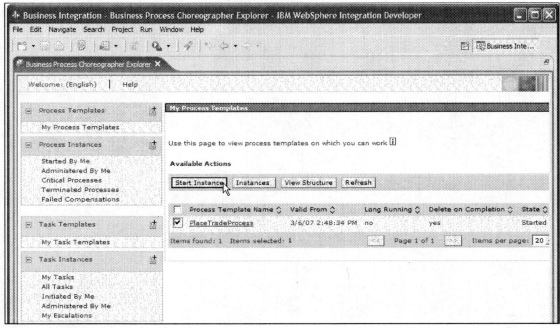

Figure 2-276   Test SCA binding 4/6

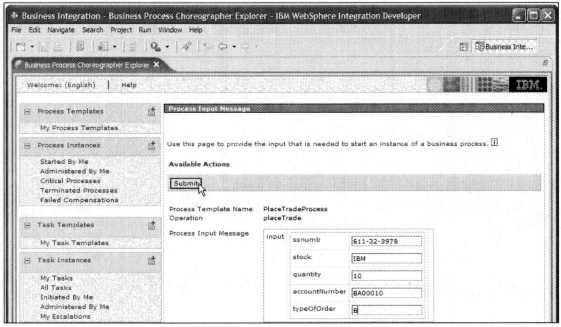

Figure 2-277   Test SCA binding 5/6

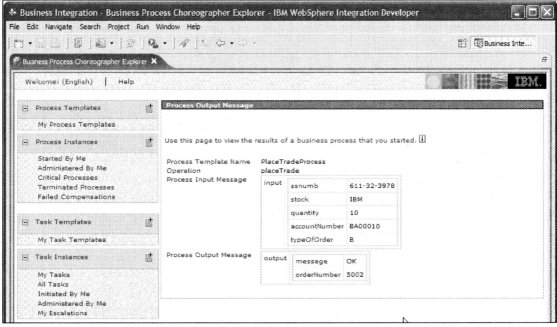

Figure 2-278   Test SCA binding 6/6

Test JMS binding

Testing a WID generated service with JMS bindings requires user-written code.

After the A2ZSCA_Brokerage module is deployed as described in "Step 4g: Deploy the SCA module" on page 205, we need to develop a client application to access the deployed service. Example 2-9 on page 276 shows the client code we developed to invoke the OpenAccountJMS service with JMS binding. It includes the following coding:

► Context for looking up JMS connection factory and queue — INITIAL_CONTEXT_FACTORY (com.ibm.websphere.naming.WsnInitialContextFactory) and PROVIDER_URL (iiop://lead:2809)

► writeOpenAccount (Map m) looks up the JNDI name (jms/MQCFLead) connection factory, and the specific queue (jms/Q1lead) to which it sends a message with the open account information from the Map m.

> **Note:** As mentioned earlier, it sets the JMSCorrelationID to the social security number field ssnumb.

► readOpenAccount () looks up the JNDI name (jms/MQCFLead) connection factory, and the specific queue (jms/Q2lead). It listens on this queue, and reads a message and writes its contents to a HashMap and also prints it contents.

The MQTest.java code writes a JMS message to open an account for "John Doe" with social security number of "111-11-1111" and other details which are hard coded in the program since this is just test code. It then waits on a response and prints the received message.

Figure 2-279 on page 280 through Figure 2-284 on page 285 describe the test using the RAD tool. Select MQTest.java in the a2z package, and then from the Run menu, select **Run As** and **Java Application** as shown in Figure 2-279 on page 280. The results of this execution are shown in Figure 2-280 on page 281, which prints the message written to the message queue and puts up the prompt "Press key to continue".

There is a human task interaction (RunCheck) in the OpenAccountProcess which approves or disapproves the request as shown in Figure 2-281 on page 282. The RunCheck task creates a task in the Human Task Manager component of WebSphere Process Server. For testing purposes, you cam use BPC Explorer to view all current tasks, claim a task, and complete it as shown in Figure 2-283 on page 284.

Figure 2-282 on page 283 through Figure 2-284 on page 285 show the use of Business Process Choreographer Explorer to put a message false (indicating a disapproval by a human of this open account request) in the canCreateAccount field as shown in Figure 2-284 on page 285. This puts a message in the JMS message queue. The user then presses a key to continue, which causes MQTest to consume this message and put out a message saying that an account cannot be created as shown in Figure 2-284 on page 285. This concludes a successful test of the WID generated service with JMS binding.

Example 2-9   MQTest.java

```
package a2z;

import java.util.Date;
import java.util.HashMap;
import java.util.Iterator;
import java.util.Map;
import java.util.Properties;

import javax.jms.MapMessage;
import javax.jms.Message;
import javax.jms.Queue;
import javax.jms.QueueConnection;
import javax.jms.QueueConnectionFactory;
```

```java
import javax.jms.QueueReceiver;
import javax.jms.QueueSender;
import javax.jms.QueueSession;
import javax.jms.Session;
import javax.naming.Context;
import javax.naming.InitialContext;

public class MQTest {

    /**
     * get a Context object for looking up JMS connection factories
     * and queue
     */
    static Context getContext() throws Exception {
        // create context for remote server where the JMS Queues are defined
        Properties props = new Properties();
        props.put(Context.INITIAL_CONTEXT_FACTORY,
                "com.ibm.websphere.naming.WsnInitialContextFactory");
        props.put(Context.PROVIDER_URL, "iiop://lead:2809");
        Context context = new InitialContext(props);
        return context;
    }

    /**
     * write the key-value pairs of the input as a
     * JMS MapMessage
     */
    public void writeOpenAccount(Map m) throws Exception {
        // lookup Queue
        Context ctx = getContext();
        Object o = ctx.lookup("jms/MQCFLead");
        QueueConnectionFactory queueConnectionFactory = (QueueConnectionFactory) o;
        o = ctx.lookup("jms/Q1lead");
        Queue queue = (Queue) o;
        // use standard JMS API to create message
        QueueConnection queueConnection = queueConnectionFactory.createQueueConnection();
        QueueSession session = queueConnection.createQueueSession(false,
                Session.AUTO_ACKNOWLEDGE);
        QueueSender sender = session.createSender(queue);
        MapMessage message = session.createMapMessage();
        // use SSNumber as correlation ID
        message.setJMSCorrelationID((String) m.get("ssnumb"));
        // the "TargetFunctionName" property is used by the MQ JMS binding
        //    use the name as indicated in the "native method" field
        //    of the "Method binding" tab
        message.setStringProperty("TargetFunctionName", "openAccount");

        // prepare MapMessage
        Iterator it = m.entrySet().iterator();
        while (it.hasNext()) {
            Map.Entry entry = (Map.Entry) it.next();
            Object value = entry.getValue();
            message.setObject((String) entry.getKey(), value);
        }
```

```
        System.out.println("Write message: " + message);
        sender.send(message);
        queueConnection.close();
    }


    /**
     * blocking read from the result queue
     */
    public Map readOpenAccount() throws Exception {
        Map result = null;
        Context ctx = getContext();
        // lookup Queue
        Object o = ctx.lookup("jms/MQCFLead");
        QueueConnectionFactory queueConnectionFactory = (QueueConnectionFactory) o;
        o = ctx.lookup("jms/Q2lead");
        Queue outQ = (Queue) o;
        QueueConnection outQConnection = queueConnectionFactory.createQueueConnection();
        outQConnection.start();

        // listen on queue
        QueueSession outSession = outQConnection.createQueueSession(false,
                Session.AUTO_ACKNOWLEDGE);
        QueueReceiver receiver = outSession.createReceiver(outQ);
        Message receivedMessage = receiver.receive();
        System.out.println("Received message: " + receivedMessage);

        // create output
        System.out.println("Message was delivered for SSnumber: "
                        + receivedMessage.getJMSCorrelationID());
        if (receivedMessage instanceof MapMessage) {
            MapMessage mm = (MapMessage) receivedMessage;
            result = new HashMap();
            result.put("message", mm.getString("message"));
            result.put("newCustomerID", mm.getString("newCustomerID"));
            result.put("newAccountNumber", mm.getString("newAccountNumber"));
        }
        outQConnection.close();
        return result;
    }

    public void testWrite() throws Exception {
        // prepare example open account request
        Map m = new HashMap();
        m.put("name", "John Doe");
        m.put("ssnumb", "111-11-1111");
        m.put("dob", new Long(new Date().getTime()));
        m.put("telephone", "4711");
        m.put("street", "555 Bailey Avenue");
        m.put("city", "San Jose");
        m.put("state", "CA");
        m.put("zipcode", "95119");
        m.put("accountType", "A");
        System.out.println("Input: " + m);
        writeOpenAccount(m);
```

```
    }

    public void testRead() throws Exception {
        Map m = readOpenAccount();
        System.out.println("result: " + m);
    }

    public static void main(String[] args) {
        try {
            MQTest newAccount = new MQTest();
            newAccount.testWrite();
            System.out.println("Press key to continue...");
            System.in.read();
            System.out.println("done");
            newAccount.testRead();
        } catch (Exception e) {
            e.printStackTrace();
        }
    }

}
```

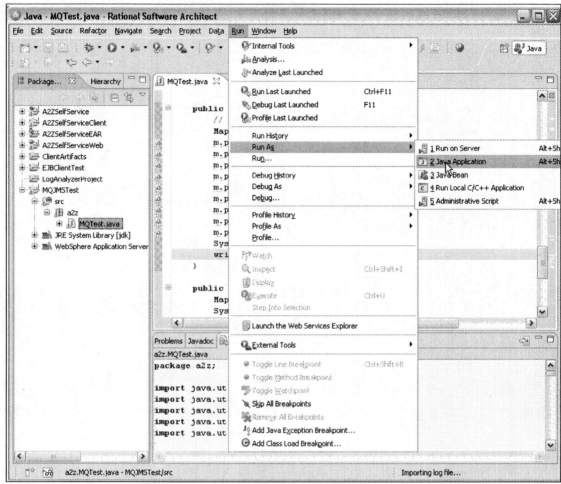

Figure 2-279   Test MQTest.java client code 1/6

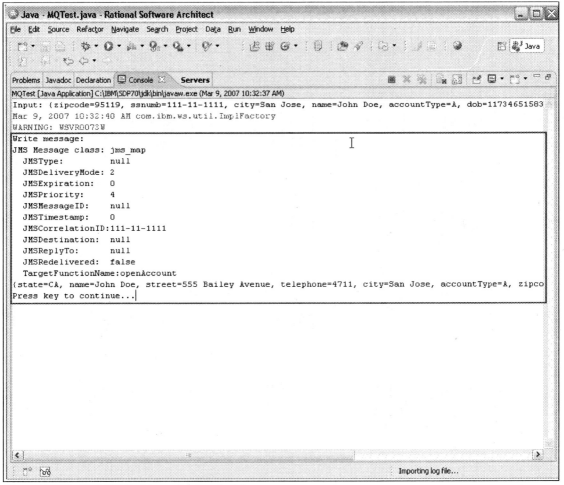

Figure 2-280   Test MQTest.java client code 2/6

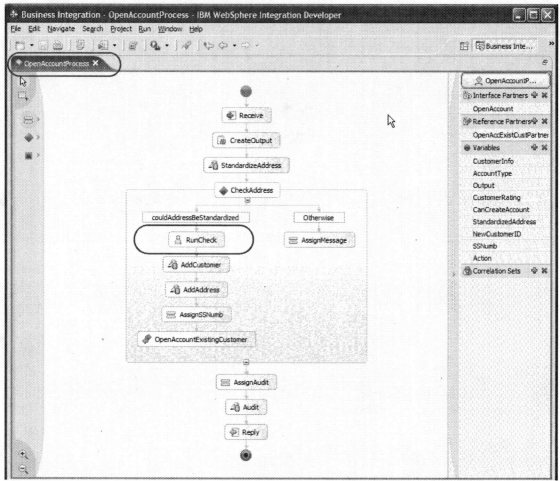

Figure 2-281   Test MQTest.java client code 3/6

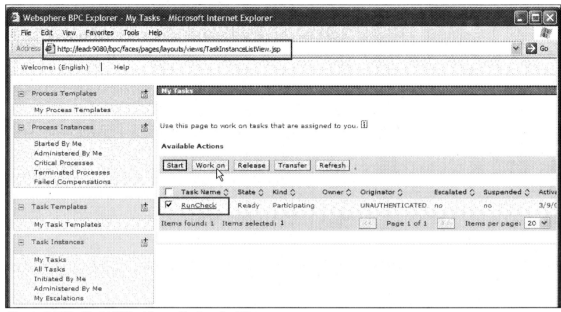

Figure 2-282   Test MQTest.java client code 4/6

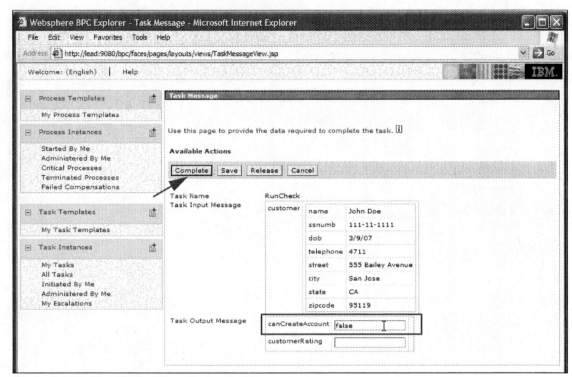

Figure 2-283   Test MQTest.java client code 5/6

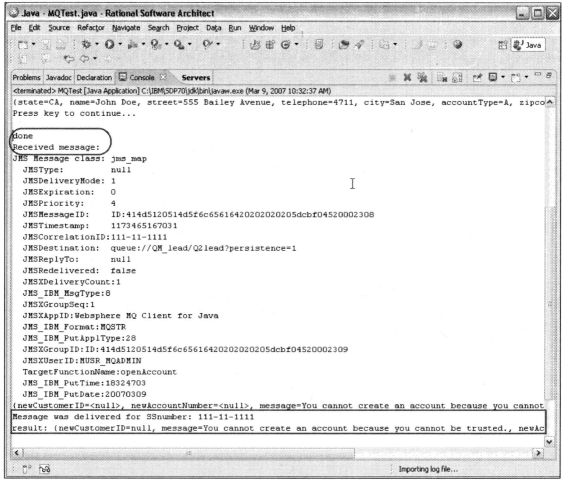

```
Java - MQTest.java - Rational Software Architect
File  Edit  Source  Refactor  Navigate  Search  Project  Data  Run  Window  Help

Problems  Javadoc  Declaration  Console  Servers
<terminated> MQTest [Java Application] C:\IBM\SDP70\jdk\bin\javaw.exe (Mar 9, 2007 10:32:37 AM)
(state=CA, name=John Doe, street=555 Bailey Avenue, telephone=4711, city=San Jose, accountType=A, zipco
Press key to continue...

done
Received message:
JMS Message class: jms_map
   JMSType:        null
   JMSDeliveryMode: 1
   JMSExpiration:  0
   JMSPriority:    4
   JMSMessageID:   ID:414d5120514d5f6c65616420202020205dcbf04520002308
   JMSTimestamp:   1173465167031
   JMSCorrelationID:111-11-1111
   JMSDestination: queue://QM_lead/Q2lead?persistence=1
   JMSReplyTo:     null
   JMSRedelivered: false
   JMSXDeliveryCount:1
   JMS_IBM_MsgType:8
   JMSXGroupSeq:1
   JMSXAppID:Websphere MQ Client for Java
   JMS_IBM_Format:MQSTR
   JMS_IBM_PutApplType:28
   JMSXGroupID:ID:414d5120514d5f6c65616420202020205dcbf04520002309
   JMSXUserID:MUSR_MQADMIN
   TargetFunctionName:openAccount
   JMS_IBM_PutTime:18324703
   JMS_IBM_PutDate:20070309
(newCustomerID=<null>, newAccountNumber=<null>, message=You cannot create an account because you cannot
Message was delivered for SSnumber: 111-11-1111
result: (newCustomerID=null, message=You cannot create an account because you cannot be trusted., newAc

                                                              Importing log file...
```

Figure 2-284   Test MQTest.java client code 6/6

Test EJB using WID

We mentioned earlier that you cannot generate (export) EJB binding for a
component using WID. However, it is possible to use the universal test client of
WID to test an EJB, which is what is described here.

These are the main steps involved:

1. Create a standalone reference
2. Develop a facade session bean to access the standalone reference
3. Associate the EJB project with the WID module
4. Invoke the universal test client

Create a standalone reference

A stand-alone reference is what is referenced by the facade session bean, and its creation is shown in Figure 2-285 on page 286 through Figure 2-290 on page 288.

Proceed as follows:

1. Click the Stand-alone References icon in WID as shown in Figure 2-285 on page 286.

2. Drag and drop it into the Assembly Diagram, and connect it to the PlaceTradeProcess using Add Wire as shown in Figure 2-286 on page 287.

3. Click **OK** on the prompts in Figure 2-287 on page 287 and Figure 2-288 on page 287.

4. Click **No** in Figure 2-289 on page 287 to stay with the WSDL interface.

5. This completes the generation of the standalone reference to the PlaceTradeProcess as shown in Figure 2-290 on page 288.

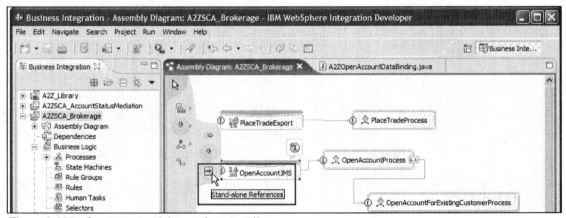

Figure 2-285   Create a standalone reference 1/6

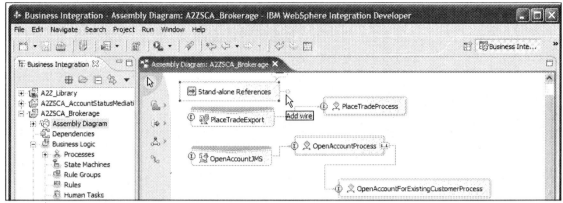

Figure 2-286 Create a standalone reference 2/6

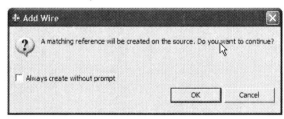

Figure 2-287 Create a standalone reference 3/6

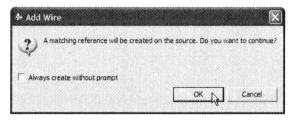

Figure 2-288 Create a standalone reference 4/6

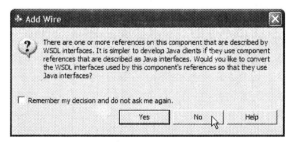

Figure 2-289 Create a standalone reference 5/6

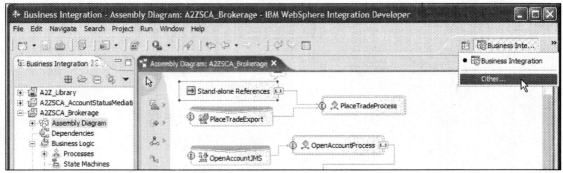

Figure 2-290   Create a standalone reference 6/6

Develop a facade session bean to access the standalone reference

Figure 2-291 on page 289 through Figure 2-301 on page 295 show the creation of an EJB project A2ZEJB_BrokerageSCAAPI and the facade session bean BrokerageFacadeBean that invokes the PlaceTradeProcess:

1. The facade session bean uses a standalone reference to access the relevant component.

2. Switch to the J2EE perspective in WID as shown in Figure 2-290 on page 288 and Figure 2-291 on page 289.

Figure 2-292 on page 289 through Figure 2-293 on page 290 show the creation of an EJB project:

1. Right-click **EJB Projects** and select **New** and **EJB Project** as shown in Figure 2-292 on page 289.

2. Provide details such as Name (A2ZEJB_BrokerageSCAAPI) and click **Finish**.

Figure 2-294 on page 290 through Figure 2-301 on page 295 show the creation of the facade session bean BrokerageFacadeBean. Expand to view the newly created EJB project A2ZEJB_BrokerageSCAAPI in the navigation pane:

1. Right-click **Session Bean** and select **New** as shown in Figure 2-294 on page 290.

2. Provide the session bean details such as Bean name (BrokerageFacade) and click **Next** in Figure 2-295 on page 291.

3. Check the Remote client view box, and provide details of the Remote home interface (a2z.BrokerageFacadeHome) and Remote interface (a2z.BrokerageFacade) and click Next in Figure 2-296 on page 292.

4. Click **Next** in Figure 2-297 on page 293, and **Finish** in Figure 2-298 on page 294 to create the session bean.

Figure 2-299 on page 294 through Figure 2-301 on page 295 show the development of the code for the session bean. The entire code of the BrokerageFacadeBean using the SCA API to access the standalone reference that accesses PlaceTradeProcess is shown in Example 2-10 on page 296.

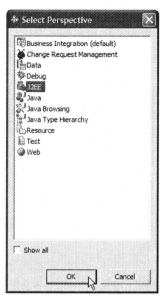

Figure 2-291   Create a facade session bean in A2ZEJB_BrokerageSCAAPI project 1/11

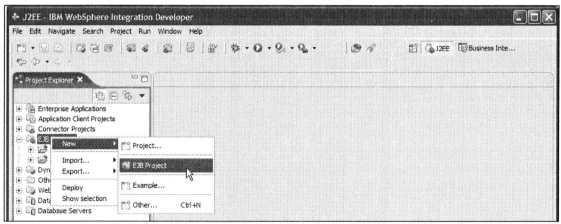

Figure 2-292   Create a facade session bean in A2ZEJB_BrokerageSCAAPI project 2/11

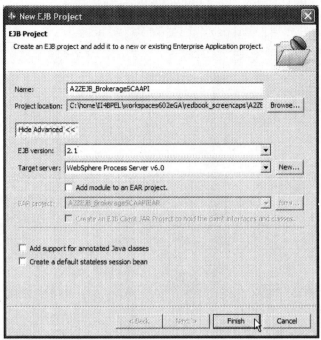

Figure 2-293   Create a facade session bean in A2ZEJB_BrokerageSCAAPI project 3/11

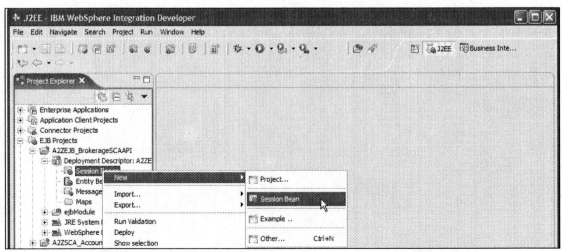

Figure 2-294   Create a facade session bean in A2ZEJB_BrokerageSCAAPI project 4/11

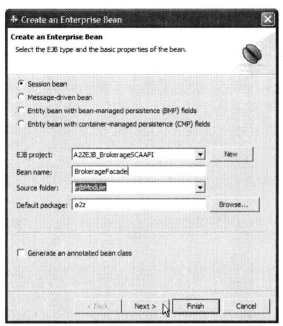

Figure 2-295   Create a facade session bean in A2ZEJB_BrokerageSCAAPI project 5/11

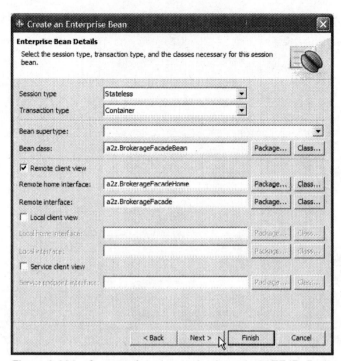

Figure 2-296   Create a facade session bean in A2ZEJB_BrokerageSCAAPI project 6/11

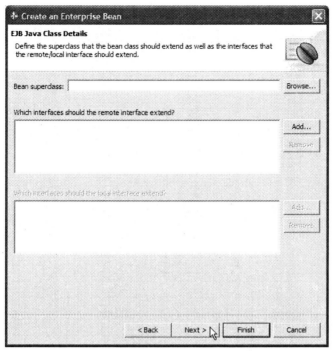

Figure 2-297   Create a facade session bean in A2ZEJB_BrokerageSCAAPI project 7/11

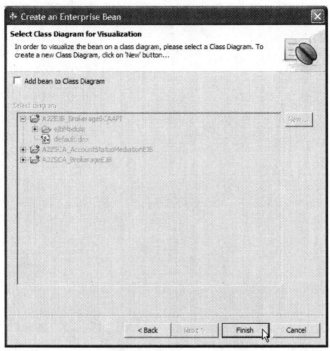

Figure 2-298   Create a facade session bean in A2ZEJB_BrokerageSCAAPI project 8/11

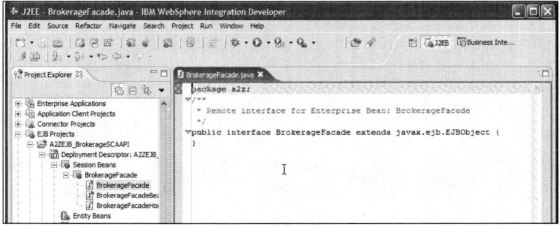

Figure 2-299   Create a facade session bean in A2ZEJB_BrokerageSCAAPI project 9/11

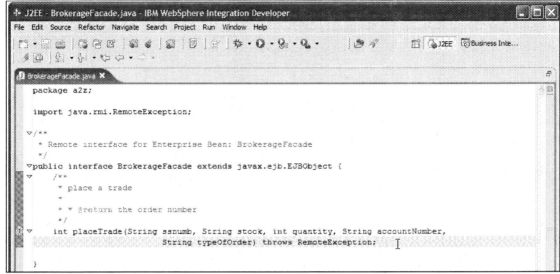

Figure 2-300   Create a facade session bean in A2ZEJB_BrokerageSCAAPI project 10/11

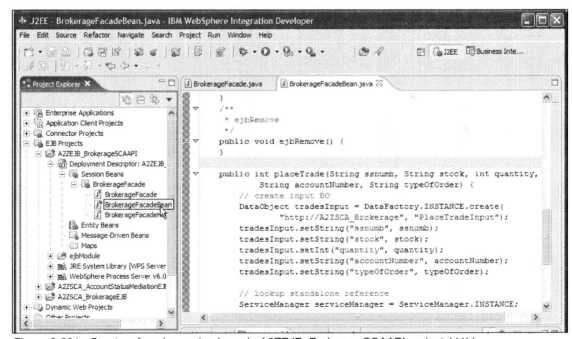

Figure 2-301   Create a facade session bean in A2ZEJB_BrokerageSCAAPI project 11/11

Example 2-10   BrokerageFacadeBean.java

```
package a2z;

import java.util.Date;

import com.ibm.websphere.sca.Service;
import com.ibm.websphere.sca.ServiceManager;
import com.ibm.websphere.sca.Ticket;
import com.ibm.websphere.sca.sdo.DataFactory;
import commonj.sdo.DataObject;

/**
 * Bean implementation class for Enterprise Bean: BrokerageFacade
 */
public class BrokerageFacadeBean implements javax.ejb.SessionBean {
    private javax.ejb.SessionContext mySessionCtx;
    /**
     * getSessionContext
     */
    public javax.ejb.SessionContext getSessionContext() {
        return mySessionCtx;
    }
    /**
     * setSessionContext
     */
    public void setSessionContext(javax.ejb.SessionContext ctx) {
        mySessionCtx = ctx;
    }
    /**
     * ejbCreate
     */
    public void ejbCreate() throws javax.ejb.CreateException {
    }
    /**
     * ejbActivate
     */
    public void ejbActivate() {
    }
    /**
     * ejbPassivate
     */
    public void ejbPassivate() {
    }
    /**
     * ejbRemove
     */
    public void ejbRemove() {
    }

    public int placeTrade(String ssnumb, String stock, int quantity,
            String accountNumber, String typeOfOrder) {
        // create input BO
        DataObject tradesInput = DataFactory.INSTANCE.create("http://A2ZSCA_Brokerage", "PlaceTradeInput");
```

```
        tradesInput.setString("ssnumb", ssnumb);
        tradesInput.setString("stock", stock);
        tradesInput.setInt("quantity", quantity);
        tradesInput.setString("accountNumber", accountNumber);
        tradesInput.setString("typeOfOrder", typeOfOrder);

        // lookup standalone reference
        ServiceManager serviceManager = ServiceManager.INSTANCE;
        Service tradesService = (Service) serviceManager.locateService("TradesInterfacePartner");
        DataObject operationResult = (DataObject) tradesService.invoke("placeTrade", tradesInput);

        // get value from result BO
        DataObject tradesOutput = operationResult.getDataObject("output");
        int result = tradesOutput.getInt("orderNumber");
        return result;
    }

}
```

Associate the EJB project with the WID module

The EJB project A2ZEJB_BrokerageSCAAPI must be associated with the
A2ZSCA_Brokerage WID module using WebSphere Integration Developer as
shown in Figure 2-302 through Figure 2-304 on page 298.

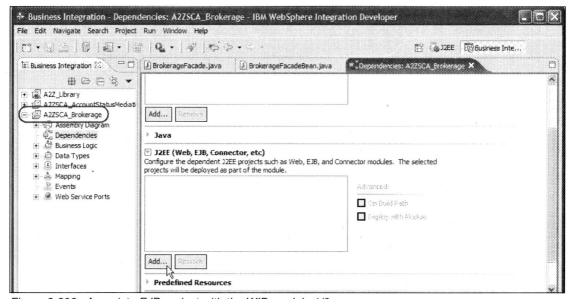

Figure 2-302   Associate EJB project with the WID module 1/3

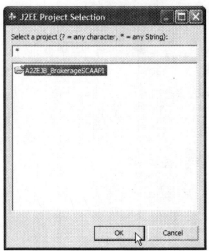

Figure 2-303   Associate EJB project with the WID module 2/3

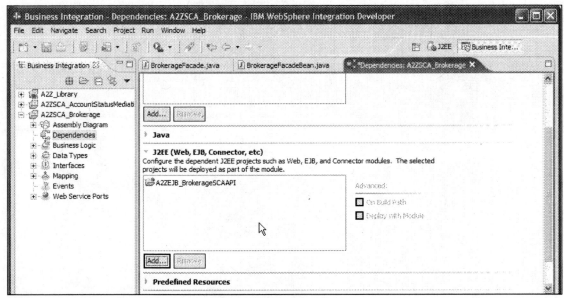

Figure 2-304   Associate EJB project with the WID module 3/3

Invoke the universal test client

Figure 2-305 on page 300 through Figure 2-315 on page 306 describe the steps involved in invoking the universal client to test an EJB.

Proceed as follows:

1. Select WebSphere Process v6.0 Server @lead, right-click in the right pane, and select **Restart universal test client** as shown in Figure 2-305 on page 300,

2. Click **OK** at the prompt in Figure 2-306 on page 300.

3. Next select **Run universal test client** in Figure 2-307 on page 301 and click JNDI Explorer in the Universal Test Client pane as shown in Figure 2-308 on page 302.

4. Click **BrokerageFacadeHome (a2z.BrokerageFacadeHome)** in Figure 2-309 on page 303 to view methods associated with it.

5. Click **BrokerageFacade create()** method in Figure 2-310 on page 304, and then click **Invoke** to instantiate the home as shown in Figure 2-311 on page 304.

6. Click **Work with Object** to view the methods associated with this bean as shown in Figure 2-312 on page 305.

7. Click the placeTrade method as shown in Figure 2-313 on page 305, supply the parameter values (such as "611-32-3978", "IBM", 10,"BA00010", and "B") for this method, and click **Invoke** as shown in Figure 2-314 on page 306.

8. The results of this invocation are shown in Figure 2-315 on page 306 indicating a returned value of 5022.

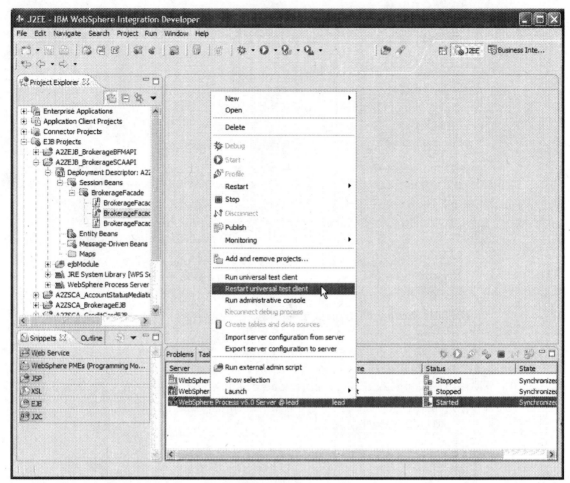

Figure 2-305   WID universal test client to test EJB 1/11

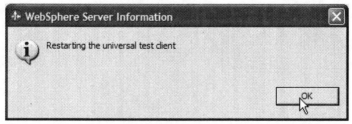

Figure 2-306   WID universal test client to test EJB 2/11

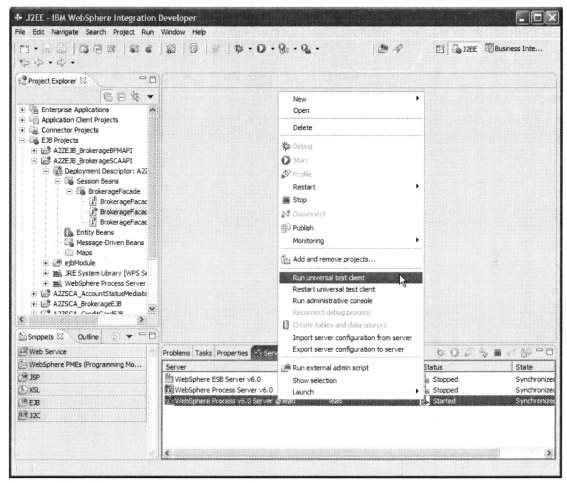

Figure 2-307   WID universal test client to test EJB 3/11

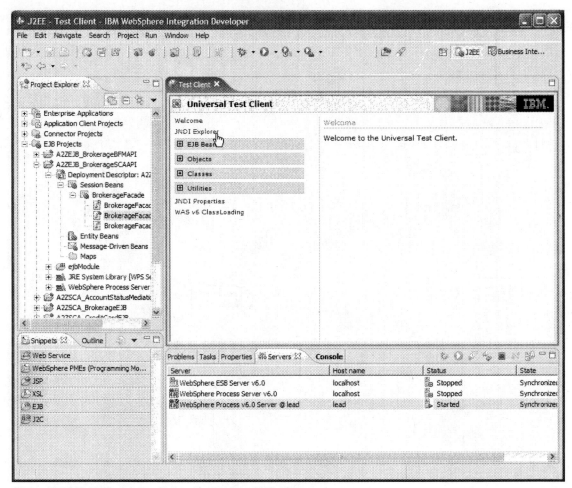

Figure 2-308   WID universal test client to test EJB 4/11

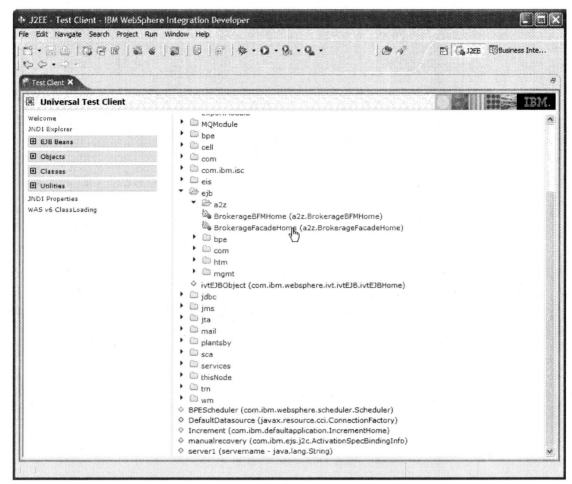

Figure 2-309   WID universal test client to test EJB 5/11

Chapter 2. Financial services business scenario   **303**

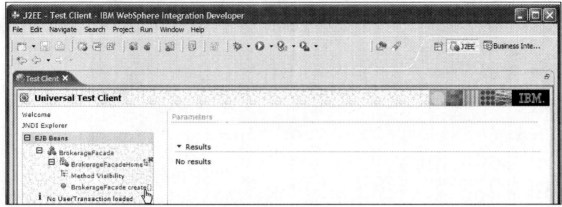

Figure 2-310   WID universal test client to test EJB 6/11

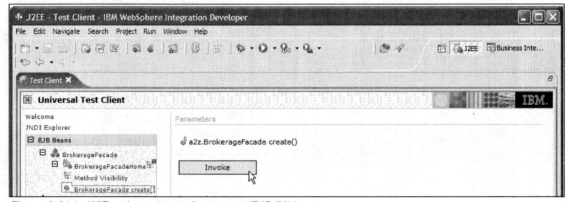

Figure 2-311   WID universal test client to test EJB 7/11

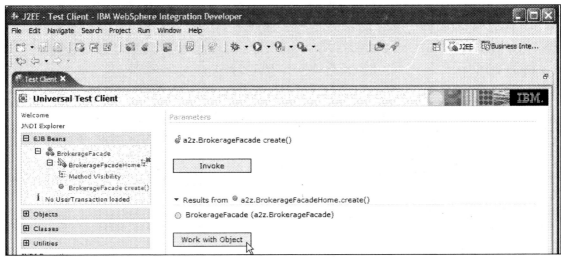

Figure 2-312   WID universal test client to test EJB 8/11

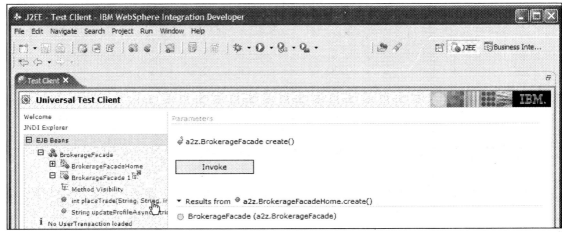

Figure 2-313   WID universal test client to test EJB 9/11

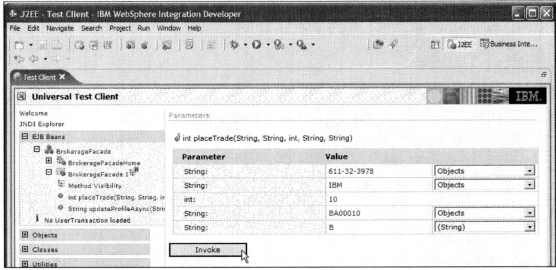

Figure 2-314   WID universal test client to test EJB 10/11

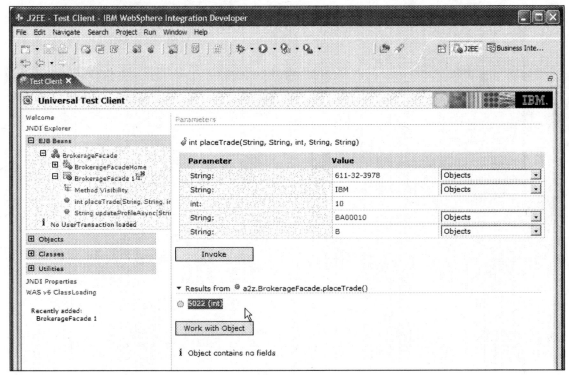

Figure 2-315   WID universal test client to test EJB 11/11

2.9 Step 5: Create "services" consumers

In this section, we describe how the IBM Information Server and WebSphere Integration Developer generated services (with a variety of bindings) are consumed by client applications. Our client development environments were chosen to demonstrate that IBM Information Server (and WID) generated services integrate seamlessly into typical integrated development environments such as:

► Rational Application Developer (RAD) to develop JSPs and portlets

► Microsoft Visual Studio® 2005 Professional Edition to develop ASPs using .NET as a fat client and thin client

► WebSphere Integration Developer to develop a JSP that invokes a WID generated service via an async API

Figure 2-316 on page 308 (Rational Application Developer), Figure 2-317 on page 308 (Visual Studio .NET Professional Edition with only SOAP over HTTP binding), and Figure 2-318 on page 308 (WebSphere Integration Developer with only SCA binding) provide an overview of some of the business functions and various "service consumer" examples implemented in the A2Z Financial Services' self service solution.

Also shown are certain business functions (such as Get Account balance) that are implemented exclusively using WID generated services, or exclusively using IBM Information Server generated services — the objective of this exercise was to demonstrate the impact on application development of using one approach over the other. Each of these examples is described in further detail in the following sections.

> **Important:** In all the examples, the focus is *not* on providing a tutorial on using a particular development tool such as RAD, Visual Studio and WID, but on the steps involved in invoking the IBM Information Server and WID generated services defined earlier. Therefore, little explanation is provided on the screen interaction of the particular development tool.

A2Z Financials Business Function (nile.itsosj.sanjose.ibm.com)	Information Server Services (radon.itsosj.sanjose.ibm.com)		WebSphere Integration Developer (lead.itsosj.sanjose.ibm.com)	
	Services	Binding	Services	Binding
Open brokerage account (JSP)			OpenAccountProcess	JMS
Perform a trade (JSP)	AuthorizationService placeTradesService AuditService	EJB SOAP over HTTP EJB		
Get Account balance for the brokerage accounts (Portlet)	AuthorizationService AccountStatusService AuditService	EJB SOAP over HTTP EJB	GetBalancesProcess	SOAP over HTTP
Perform a trade (portlet)	AuthorizationService placeTradesService AuditService	EJB EJB EJB	PlaceTradeProcess	SCA using Façade Session Bean

Figure 2-316   Client types, business functions, and service types developed using RAD .

A2Z Financials Business Function (laptop with VS .NET)	Information Server Services (radon.itsosj.sanjose.ibm.com)	WebSphere Integration Developer (lead.itsosj.sanjose.ibm.com)
	Services (SOAP over HTTP only)	Services (SOAP over HTTP only)
Update Credit Card customer (Thick client)		UpdateCustomer
Get Credit Card transactions (Thin client)		GetTransactions
Update Credit Card customer (Thin client)	CustomerIDLookupService AuthorizationService StandardizeAddressService CardMaintenanceService AuditService	UpdateCustomer

Figure 2-317   Client types, business functions, and service types developed using Visual Studio .NET

A2Z Financials Business Function (lead.itsosj.sanjose.ibm.com)	WebSphere Integration Developer (lead.itsosj.sanjose.ibm.com)	
	Services	Binding
Update Brokerage customer	UpdateBrokerageProfileProcess	Session Bean Façade to ASYNC SCA API

Figure 2-318   Client types, business functions, and service types developed using WID ASYNC

> **Attention:** A snippet of how a service is invoked from a client application with a particular binding is shown in Example 2-11 through Example 2-16 on page 312. These show the import of the relevant classes, libraries, and packages, as well as the lookup and invocation of the specific operation associated with a given service. This is explained in more detail in the relevant examples in the following sections.

Example 2-11   SOAP over HTTP binding client code

```
import A2Z_Library.GetAllBalances;
import A2Z_Library.GetAllBalancesOut;
........
protected GetAllBalances lookupGetAllBalances()
........

protected GetAllBalances lookupGetAllBalances() {
try {
Service locator = (Service)
ServiceLocatorManager.getServiceLookup(STATIC_GetAllBalances_REF_NAME,STATIC_GetAllBalances_CLASS);
GetAllBalances aGetAllBalances = (GetAllBalances) locator.getPort(STATIC_GetAllBalances_CLASS);
return aGetAllBalances;
}
.........
GetAllBalances aGetAllBalances = lookupGetAllBalances();
try {
    GetAllBalancesOut out = aGetAllBalances.getAllBalances(ssnumb);
```

Example 2-12   SOAP over HTTP binding .NET client code

```
Protected Sub invokeWIDServices()
        Dim service As New A2ZFinancialServices.UpdateCustomer.UpdateCustomer_UpdateCustomerInfoProcessHttpService
        Dim updateCustInfo As New A2ZFinancialServices.UpdateCustomer.updateCustomerInfo
        Dim custInfo As New A2ZFinancialServices.UpdateCustomer.CustomerInfo
        Dim response As A2ZFinancialServices.UpdateCustomer.updateCustomerInfoResponse
```

Example 2-13   JMS binding client code

```
import java.rmi.RemoteException;
import java.util.Date;
import java.util.HashMap;
import java.util.Iterator;
import java.util.Map;
import java.util.Properties;

import javax.ejb.CreateException;
import javax.jms.JMSException;
import javax.jms.MapMessage;
import javax.jms.Message;
import javax.jms.Queue;
import javax.jms.QueueConnection;
import javax.jms.QueueConnectionFactory;
import javax.jms.QueueReceiver;
import javax.jms.QueueSender;
import javax.jms.QueueSession;
import javax.jms.Session;
```

```
import javax.naming.Context;
import javax.naming.InitialContext;
import javax.naming.NamingException;
import javax.rmi.PortableRemoteObject;

import a2zselfserviceweb.forms.CustomerInfoForm;

import com.ibm.isd.CommonServicesApp.AuthorizationService.server.AuthorizationServiceHome;
import com.ibm.isd.CommonServicesApp.AuthorizationService.server.AuthorizationServiceRemote;
..................
static Context getContext() throws Exception
{
// create context for remote server where the JMS Queues are defined
Properties props = new Properties();
props.put(Context.INITIAL_CONTEXT_FACTORY,"com.ibm.websphere.naming.WsnInitialContextFactory");
props.put(Context.PROVIDER_URL, "iiop://lead:2809");
Context context = new InitialContext(props);
return context;
}


/**
* write the key-value pairs of the input as a JMS MapMessage
*/
public void writeOpenAccount(Map m) throws Exception
{
// lookup Queue
Context ctx = getContext();
Object o = ctx.lookup("jms/MQCFLead");
QueueConnectionFactory queueConnectionFactory = (QueueConnectionFactory) o;
o = ctx.lookup("jms/Q1lead");
Queue queue = (Queue) o;
// use standard JMS API to create message
QueueConnection queueConnection = queueConnectionFactory.createQueueConnection();
QueueSession session = queueConnection.createQueueSession(false,Session.AUTO_ACKNOWLEDGE);
QueueSender sender = session.createSender(queue);
MapMessage message = session.createMapMessage();
// use SSNumber as correlation ID
message.setJMSCorrelationID((String) m.get("ssnumb"));
// the "TargetFunctionName" property is used by the MQ JMS binding
//   use the name as indicated in the "native method" field
//   of the "Method binding" tab
message.setStringProperty("TargetFunctionName", "openAccount");

// prepare MapMessage
Iterator it = m.entrySet().iterator();
while (it.hasNext()) {
    Map.Entry entry = (Map.Entry) it.next();
    Object value = entry.getValue();
    message.setObject((String) entry.getKey(), value);
}
System.out.println("Write message: " + message);
sender.send(message);
queueConnection.close();
}


/**
* blocking read from the result queue
*/
public Map readOpenAccount() throws Exception
{
Map result = null;
Context ctx = getContext();
// lookup Queue
Object o = ctx.lookup("jms/MQCFLead");
QueueConnectionFactory queueConnectionFactory = (QueueConnectionFactory) o;
o = ctx.lookup("jms/Q2lead");
Queue outQ = (Queue) o;
```

```
QueueConnection outQConnection = queueConnectionFactory.createQueueConnection();
outQConnection.start();

// listen on queue
QueueSession outSession = outQConnection.createQueueSession(false,Session.AUTO_ACKNOWLEDGE);
QueueReceiver receiver = outSession.createReceiver(outQ);
Message receivedMessage = receiver.receive();
System.out.println("Received message: " + receivedMessage);

// create output
System.out.println("Message was delivered for SSnumber: " + receivedMessage.getJMSCorrelationID());
if (receivedMessage instanceof MapMessage)
{
    MapMessage mm = (MapMessage) receivedMessage;
    result = new HashMap();
    result.put("message", mm.getString("message"));
    result.put("newCustomerID", mm.getString("newCustomerID"));
    result.put("newAccountNumber", mm.getString("newAccountNumber"));
}
outQConnection.close();
return result;
}
```

Example 2-14   EJB binding client code

```
import com.ibm.isd.BrokerageApp.TradesService.server.TradesServiceHome;
import com.ibm.isd.BrokerageApp.TradesService.server.TradesServiceRemote;

................
............
private TradesServiceHome tradesServiceHome;
.............
.........
* Cache the home objects.
*/
protected Context lookupInformationServices() throws NamingException
{
Context isctx = super.lookupInformationServices();
Object o = isctx.lookup("ejb/BrokerageApp/TradesService");
tradesServiceHome = (TradesServiceHome) PortableRemoteObject.narrow(o, TradesServiceHome.class);
return isctx;
.........
.........
TradesServiceRemote tradesServiceRemote = tradesServiceHome.create();
result = tradesServiceRemote.placeTrade(symbol, new Integer(quantity), type, Calendar.getInstance(), accountNumber);
audit("Trade placed OrderNumber " , result.toString());
return result.intValue();
............
```

Example 2-15   SCA binding SYNC API client code

```
import com.ibm.websphere.sca.Service;
import com.ibm.websphere.sca.ServiceManager;
import com.ibm.websphere.sca.Ticket;
import com.ibm.websphere.sca.sdo.DataFactory;
import commonj.sdo.DataObject;
..................
// lookup standalone reference
ServiceManager serviceManager = ServiceManager.INSTANCE;
Service tradesService = (Service) serviceManager.locateService("TradesInterfacePartner");
DataObject operationResult = (DataObject) tradesService.invoke("placeTrade", tradesInput);
```

```
// get value from result BO
DataObject tradesOutput = operationResult.getDataObject("output");
int result = tradesOutput.getInt("orderNumber");
return result;
```

Example 2-16   SCA binding ASYNC API client code

```
import com.ibm.websphere.sca.Service;
import com.ibm.websphere.sca.ServiceManager;
import com.ibm.websphere.sca.Ticket;
import com.ibm.websphere.sca.sdo.DataFactory;
import commonj.sdo.DataObject;
......................
// lookup standalone reference
    ServiceManager serviceManager = ServiceManager.INSTANCE;
    Service updateProfileService = (Service) serviceManager.locateService("UpdateBrokerageProfilePartner");

// invoke the service asynchronously
Ticket ticket = updateProfileService.invokeAsync("updateProfile", customerInfo);

// wait for 5 seconds max
Object operationResult = updateProfileService.invokeResponse(ticket, 5000);

// get value from result BO
DataObject updateProfileOutput = (DataObject) operationResult;
String result = updateProfileOutput.getString("message");
return result;
```

2.9.1 Rational Application Developer (RAD)

We demonstrate the development and testing of client applications (JSPs and portlets) accessing IBM Information Server and WebSphere Integration Developer generated services using SOAP over HTTP, EJB, and JMS bindings in a J2EE environment.

As shown in Figure 2-316 on page 308 and Figure 2-317 on page 308, the following business function implementations using RAD are described here:

► Open a brokerage account (JSPs only)
► Perform a trade (JSPs and portlets)
► Get Account balance for the brokerage accounts (portlet only)

Note: The JSP implementation of these business functions uses the Struts framework.

"The Struts framework is based on the Model-View-Controller (MVC) design paradigm that clearly separates the three levels. The Model represents the business or database code, the View represents the page design code, and the Controller represents the navigational code. The Struts framework is designed to help developers create Web applications that utilize a MVC architecture."

The Struts framework fills the View and Controller layers, while the Model layer is left to the developer. The Struts framework stores application routing information and request mapping in a single file named struts-config.xml

For more details on the Struts framework, refer to the Web site:

`http://struts.apache.org/`

In the following figures we show some aspects of Struts usage:

► Figure 2-319 on page 313 through Figure 2-341 on page 329 show the development of a Struts framework application using RAD.

► Figure 2-319 on page 313 through Figure 2-327 on page 319 describe the creation of a project with Struts support.

► Figure 2-328 on page 320 through Figure 2-333 on page 323 describe the development of the Controller and View levels.

► Figure 2-334 on page 324 through Figure 2-341 on page 329 describe the development of the Model level.

The struts-config.xml file used here is shown in Example 2-17 on page 329.

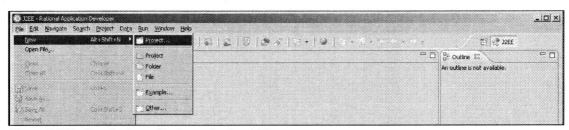

Figure 2-319   Developing a Struts application 1/23

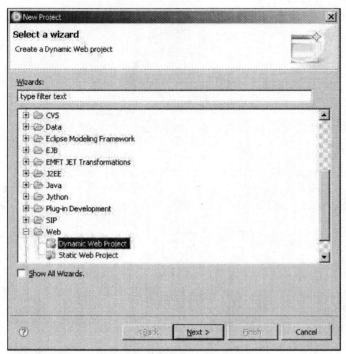

Figure 2-320   Developing a Struts application 2/23

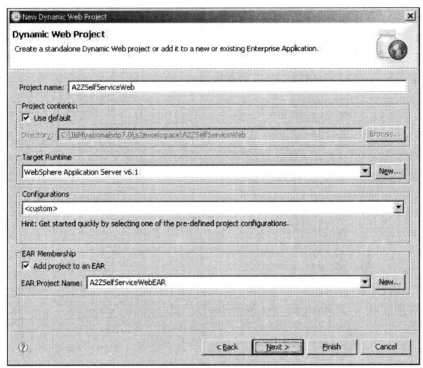

Figure 2-321   Developing a Struts application 3/23

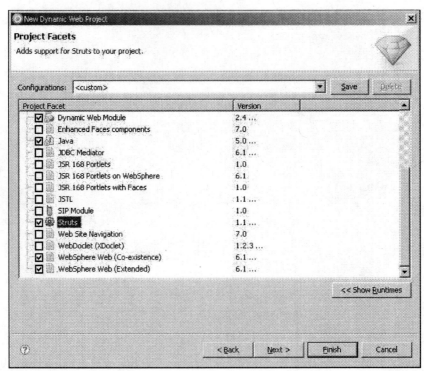

Figure 2-322   Developing a Struts application 4/23

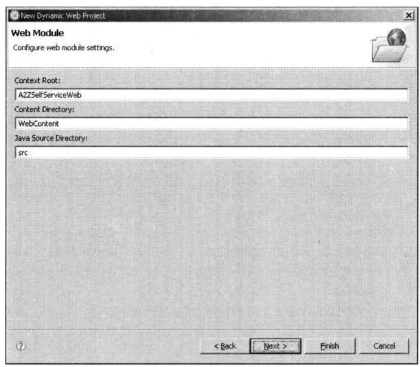

Figure 2-323   Developing a Struts application 5/23

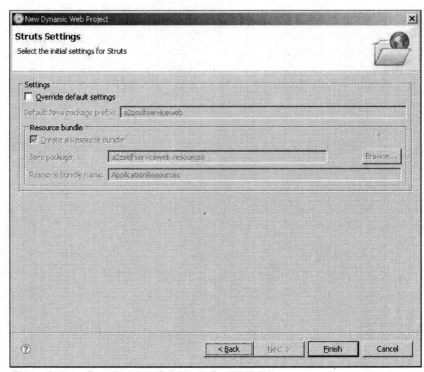

Figure 2-324   Developing a Struts application 6/23

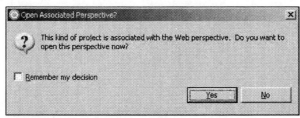

Figure 2-325   Developing a Struts application 7/23

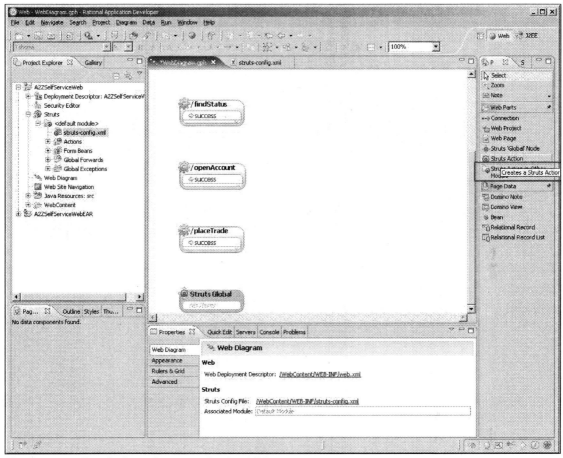

Figure 2-326   Developing a Struts application 8/23

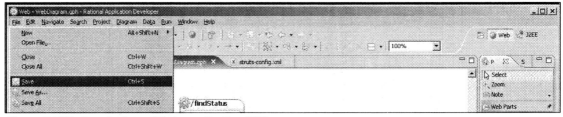

Figure 2-327   Developing a Struts application 9/23

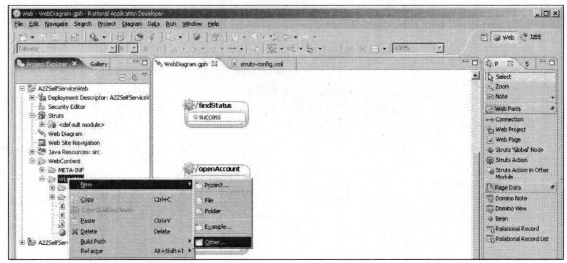

Figure 2-328   Developing a Struts application 10/23

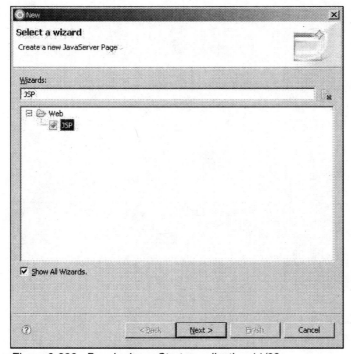

Figure 2-329   Developing a Struts application 11/23

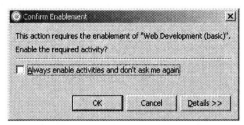

Figure 2-330 Developing a Struts application 12/23

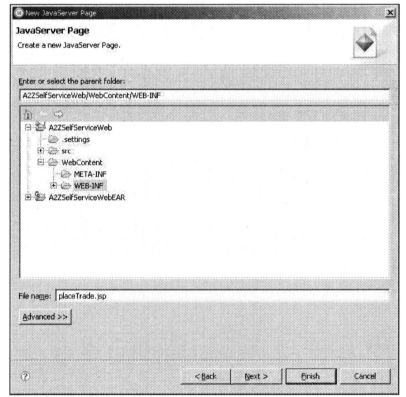

Figure 2-331 Developing a Struts application 13/23

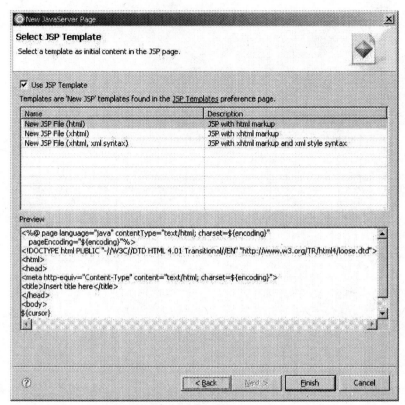

Figure 2-332   Developing a Struts application 14/23

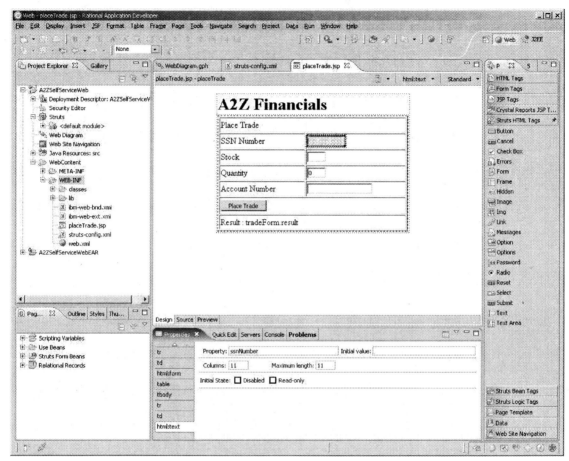

Figure 2-333   Developing a Struts application 15/23

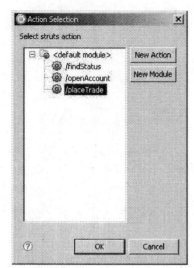

Figure 2-334   Developing a Struts application 16/23

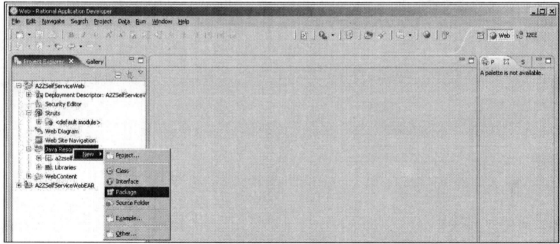

Figure 2-335   Developing a Struts application 17/23

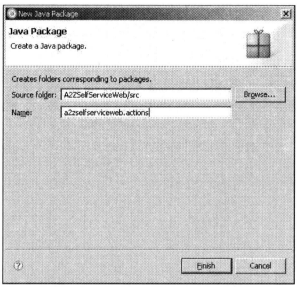

Figure 2-336   Developing a Struts application 18/23

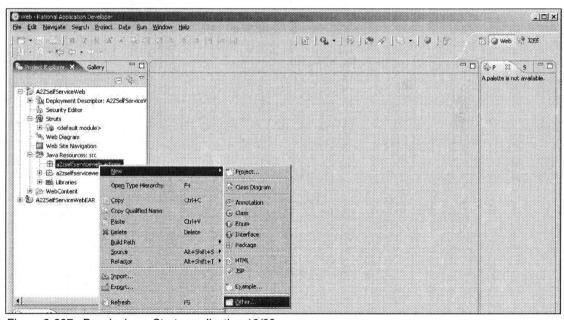

Figure 2-337   Developing a Struts application 19/23

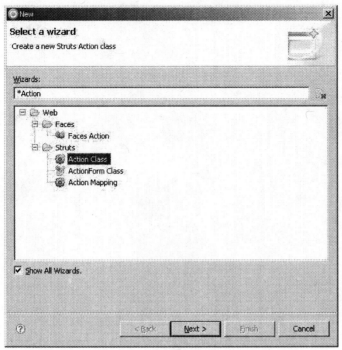

Figure 2-338   Developing a Struts application 20/23

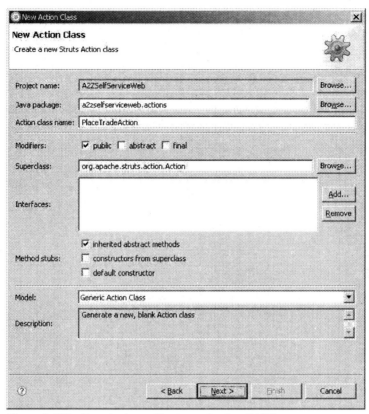

Figure 2-339   Developing a Struts application 21/23

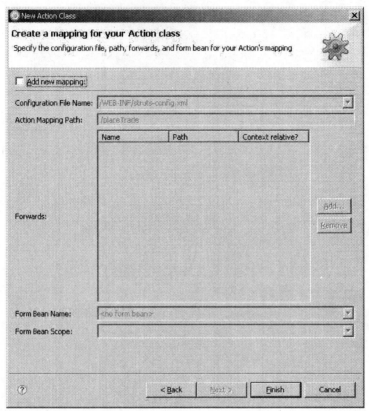

Figure 2-340   Developing a Struts application 22/23

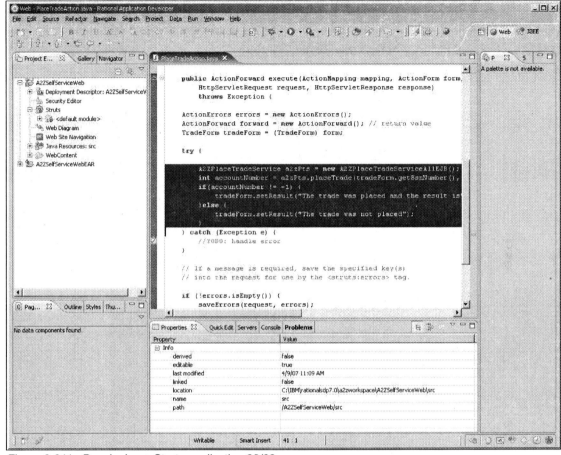

Figure 2-341   Developing a Struts application 23/23

Example 2-17   struts-config.xml

```xml
<?xml version="1.0" encoding="UTF-8" ?>
  <!DOCTYPE struts-config (View Source for full doctype...)>
- <struts-config>
- <!-- Data Sources
  -->
  <data-sources />
- <!-- Form Beans
  -->
- <form-beans>
  <form-bean name="tradeForm" type="a2zselfserviceweb.forms.TradeForm" />
  <form-bean name="customerInfoForm" type="a2zselfserviceweb.forms.CustomerInfoForm" />
  </form-beans>
- <!-- Global Exceptions
  -->
  <global-exceptions />
- <!-- Global Forwards
  -->
  <global-forwards />
- <!-- Action Mappings
```

```
    -->
-  <action-mappings>
-  <action name="tradeForm" path="/placeTrade" scope="session" type="a2zselfserviceweb.actions.PlaceTradeAction">
   <forward contextRelative="false" name="success" path="./placeTrade.jsp" />
   </action>
-  <action name="customerInfoForm" path="/openAccount" scope="session" type="a2zselfserviceweb.actions.OpenAccountAction">
   <forward contextRelative="false" name="success" path="./openAccount.jsp" />
   </action>
-  <action name="customerInfoForm" path="/findStatus" scope="session" type="a2zselfserviceweb.actions.FindAccountStatusAction">
   <forward contextRelative="false" name="success" path="./findAccount.jsp" />
   </action>
   </action-mappings>
-  <!-- Message Resources
    -->
   <message-resources parameter="a2zselfserviceweb.resources.ApplicationResources" />
   </struts-config>
```

Open a brokerage account (JSP)

The main aspects of this application are as follows:

► It was developed using the Struts framework.

► It executes on a server (nile.itsosj.sanjose.ibm.com) where WebSphere MQ Client is installed. It is distinct from WebSphere Process Server (lead.itsosj.sanjose.ibm.com).

► The WID generated service OpenAccountProcess was invoked using JMS binding, which executes on lead.itsosj.sanjose.ibm.com where WebSphere Process Server is installed. WebSphere MQ Server is installed on this server.

This is summarized in Figure 2-342. The WID generated service implementation of the *open a brokerage* business function is described here.

A2Z Financials Business Function (nile.itsosj.sanjose.ibm.com)	WebSphere Integration Developer (lead.itsosj.sanjose.ibm.com)	
	Services	Binding
Open brokerage account (JSP)	OpenAccountProcess	JMS

Figure 2-342   JSP invocation of the open brokerage account business function using RAD

Figure 2-343 on page 332 shows the aggregation service OpenAccountProcess that invokes IBM Information Server services (StandardizeAddressService, NewAccountService and AuditService) as well as RunCheck (human interaction task). The RunCheck task depends upon a human to declare the process complete and therefore the OpenAccountProcess is a "long running" process. The AuthorizationService is not included in this process, since we assume that a person can open an account in the A2Z Financial Services self service scenario.

The opening of an account involves:

1. Sending in a request to open an account using JMS binding by writing a message to a queue (jms/Q1lead)
2. Viewing the status of the request after some interval by reading a message from another queue (jms/Q2lead)

> **Note:** The OpenAccount.jsp (not shown here), OpenAccountAction class, and RemoteServiceGateway class all execute on nile.itsosj.sanjose.ibm.com, which is different from the server where the WebSphere Process Server executes.
>
> You need to declare the imports for the JMS[a] binding (corresponding to the WID OpenAccountAccess) in the RemoteServiceGateway helper class. You also need to declare the context factory and provider URL (iiop://9.43.86.68:2809) of the WebSphere Process Server

a. No EJB binding client equivalent jar file is available — you have to code this yourself.

The OpenAccountAction (Example 2-18 on page 332) class instantiates a RemoteServiceGateway (Example 2-19 on page 333) helper class object, and invokes its openNewAccountAsyncJMS method with customer details (CustomerInfoForm). This method writes a JMS message to the queue (jms/Q1lead) on the WebSphere Process Server (lead.itsosj.sanjose.ibm.com) using the writeOpenAccount method.

> **Note:** The A2ZOpenAccountDataBinding class handles the processing of the message in jms/Q1lead, the invoking of the WID OpenAccountProcess, and writing the response to the jms/Q2lead message queue.

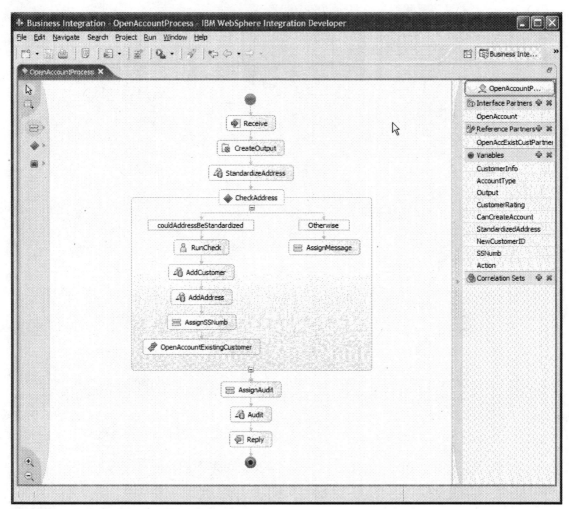

Figure 2-343   OpenAccountProcess

Example 2-18   OpenAccountAction.java

```
package a2zselfserviceweb.actions;

import javax.servlet.http.HttpServletRequest;
import javax.servlet.http.HttpServletResponse;

import org.apache.struts.action.Action;
import org.apache.struts.action.ActionErrors;
import org.apache.struts.action.ActionForm;
import org.apache.struts.action.ActionForward;
import org.apache.struts.action.ActionMapping;

import a2zselfserviceweb.common.RemoteServiceGateway;
import a2zselfserviceweb.forms.CustomerInfoForm;
```

```
/**
 * @version 1.0
 * @author
 */
public class OpenAccountAction extends Action

{

    public ActionForward execute(ActionMapping mapping, ActionForm form,
        HttpServletRequest request, HttpServletResponse response)
        throws Exception {

    ActionErrors errors = new ActionErrors();
    ActionForward forward = new ActionForward(); // return value
    CustomerInfoForm customerInfoForm = (CustomerInfoForm) form;

    try {

        RemoteServiceGateway.getInstance().openNewAccountAsyncJMS(customerInfoForm);

    } catch (Exception e) {
        //TODO : handle error
    }

    // If a message is required, save the specified key(s)
    // into the request for use by the <struts:errors> tag.

    if (!errors.isEmpty()) {
        saveErrors(request, errors);
    }
    // Write logic determining how the user should be forwarded.
    forward = mapping.findForward("success");

    // Finish with
    return (forward);

    }
}
```

Example 2-19   RemoteServiceGateway.java helper class

```
package a2zselfserviceweb.common;

import java.rmi.RemoteException;
import java.util.Date;
import java.util.HashMap;
import java.util.Iterator;
import java.util.Map;
import java.util.Properties;

import javax.ejb.CreateException;
import javax.jms.JMSException;
import javax.jms.MapMessage;
import javax.jms.Message;
import javax.jms.Queue;
import javax.jms.QueueConnection;
import javax.jms.QueueConnectionFactory;
import javax.jms.QueueReceiver;
import javax.jms.QueueSender;
import javax.jms.QueueSession;
import javax.jms.Session;
import javax.naming.Context;
import javax.naming.InitialContext;
import javax.naming.NamingException;
```

```java
import javax.rmi.PortableRemoteObject;

import a2zselfserviceweb.forms.CustomerInfoForm;

import com.ibm.isd.CommonServicesApp.AuthorizationService.server.AuthorizationServiceHome;
import com.ibm.isd.CommonServicesApp.AuthorizationService.server.AuthorizationServiceRemote;

public class RemoteServiceGateway {

    public static final String CORRELATION_KEY = "ssnumb";
    public static final String REMOTE_MQ_PUTQ_JNDI = "jms/Q1lead";
    public static final String REMOTE_MQ_GETQ_JNDI = "jms/Q2lead";

    public static final String CONTEXT_FACTORY = "com.ibm.websphere.naming.WsnInitialContextFactory";
    public static final String LEAD_URL = "iiop://9.43.86.68:2809";

    static class RemoteQCInfo {
        private QueueConnection queueConnection;
        private QueueSession queueSession;
        private Queue queue;
        public Queue getQueue() {
            return queue;
        }
        public void setQueue(Queue queue) {
            this.queue = queue;
        }
        public QueueConnection getQueueConnection() {
            return queueConnection;
        }
        public void setQueueConnection(QueueConnection queueConnection) {
            this.queueConnection = queueConnection;
        }
        public QueueSession getQueueSession() {
            return queueSession;
        }
        public void setQueueSession(QueueSession queueSession) {
            this.queueSession = queueSession;
        }

    }
    public static class AppCode {
        private String appCode;
        AppCode(String appCode) {
            this.appCode = appCode;
        }
    }
    public static final AppCode BROKERAGE = new AppCode("Brokerage");
    public static final AppCode CREDITCARD = new AppCode("CreditCard");

    private static final long DEFAULT_QUEUE_RECEIVE_WAIT_TIME = 5000;



    private static RemoteServiceGateway instance;

    private RemoteServiceGateway() {

    }
    public static RemoteServiceGateway getInstance() {
        if(instance == null ) {
            instance = new RemoteServiceGateway();
        }
        return instance;
    }
.............................

    private InitialContext createInitialContext(String url) throws NamingException {
```

```
        Properties props=new Properties();
        props.put(Context.INITIAL_CONTEXT_FACTORY,CONTEXT_FACTORY);
        props.put(Context.PROVIDER_URL,url);
        return new InitialContext(props);
}

public boolean openNewAccountAsyncJMS(CustomerInfoForm cib) {
    Map m = new HashMap();
    m.put("name", cib.getName());
    m.put("ssnumb", cib.getSsnNumber());
    m.put(CORRELATION_KEY , cib.getSsnNumber());
    m.put("telephone", cib.getTelephone());
    m.put("street", cib.getStreet());
    m.put("city", cib.getCity());
    m.put("state", cib.getState());
    m.put("zipcode", cib.getZipCode());
    m.put("dob", new Long(new Date().getTime()));
    m.put("accountType", "B");

    try {
        writeOpenAccount(m);
    } catch (Exception e) {
        return false;
    }

    return true;
}


protected void writeOpenAccount(Map m) throws Exception {

    RemoteQCInfo rqcInfo = null;
    try {
        rqcInfo = createRemoteQueueConnection(REMOTE_MQ_PUTQ_JNDI);
        QueueSender sender = rqcInfo.getQueueSession().createSender(rqcInfo.getQueue());
        MapMessage message = rqcInfo.getQueueSession().createMapMessage();
        message.setJMSCorrelationID((String)m.get(CORRELATION_KEY));
        message.setStringProperty("TargetFunctionName","openAccount");
        Iterator it = m.entrySet().iterator();
        while (it.hasNext()) {
            Map.Entry entry = (Map.Entry) it.next();
            Object value = entry.getValue();
            message.setObject((String) entry.getKey(), value);
        }
        sender.send(message);

    } finally {
        if (rqcInfo != null) {
            closeQueueConnection(rqcInfo.getQueueConnection());
        }
    }
}

public AccountInfo findNewAccountRequestStatus(String ssnNumber) {
    try {
        return readOpenAccount(ssnNumber);
    } catch (Exception e) {
        e.printStackTrace();
    }
    return null;
}

protected AccountInfo readOpenAccount(String correlationId) throws Exception {
    RemoteQCInfo rqcInfo= null;

    try {
        rqcInfo = createRemoteQueueConnection(REMOTE_MQ_GETQ_JNDI);
```

```
            QueueReceiver receiver = rqcInfo.getQueueSession().createReceiver(rqcInfo.getQueue() , "JMSCorrelationID = '"
+ correlationId.trim() +"'");
            Message receivedMessage = receiver.receive(DEFAULT_QUEUE_RECEIVE_WAIT_TIME);

            if (receivedMessage == null) {
                return null;
            }

            if (receivedMessage instanceof MapMessage) {
                MapMessage mm = (MapMessage) receivedMessage;
                AccountInfo aib = new AccountInfo();
                aib.setMessage(mm.getString("message"));
                aib.setAccountNumber(mm.getString("newAccountNumber"));
                aib.setCustomerId(mm.getString("newCustomerID"));
                return aib;
            }

            return null;
        } finally {
            if (rqcInfo != null) {
                closeQueueConnection(rqcInfo.getQueueConnection());
            }
        }
    }

    private void closeQueueConnection(QueueConnection queueConnection) {
        try {
            queueConnection.close();
        } catch (JMSException e1) {
            e1.printStackTrace();
        }
    }
    private RemoteQCInfo createRemoteQueueConnection(String queueName) throws JMSException, NamingException {
        Context ctx = createInitialContext(LEAD_URL);
        Object o = ctx.lookup(RemoteJNDIServices.REMOTE_MQ_QCF_JNDI);
        final QueueConnectionFactory queueConnectionFactory = (QueueConnectionFactory) o;
        o = ctx.lookup(queueName);
        Queue outQ = (Queue) o;
        QueueConnection outQConnection = queueConnectionFactory.createQueueConnection();
        outQConnection.start();
        QueueSession outSession = outQConnection.createQueueSession(false,Session.AUTO_ACKNOWLEDGE);

        RemoteQCInfo rqcInfo = new RemoteQCInfo();
        rqcInfo.setQueueConnection(outQConnection);
        rqcInfo.setQueue(outQ);
        rqcInfo.setQueueSession(outSession);
        return rqcInfo;
    }
}
```

Perform a trade (JSP)

The main aspects of this application are as follows:

► It was developed using the Struts framework.

► It executes on a server (nile.itsosj.sanjose.ibm.com) distinct from IBM
   Information Server (radon.itsosj.sanjose.ibm.com).

► The IBM Information Server services (AuthorizationService,
   placeTradesService, and AuditService) were invoked using a mix of SOAP
   over HTTP (placeTradesService) and EJB (AuthorizationService and
   AuditService) bindings.

This is summarized in Figure 2-344. The IBM Information Server services implementation of the *perform a trade* business function is described here.

A2Z Financials Business Function (nile.itsosj.sanjose.ibm.com)	Information Server Services (radon.itsosj.sanjose.ibm.com)	
	Services	Binding
Perform a trade (JSP)	AuthorizationService placeTradesService AuditService	EJB SOAP over HTTP EJB

Figure 2-344   JSP invocation of perform a trade business function using RAD

The placing of a trade involves:

1. Checking whether the requester is authorized to place a trade

2. Placing a trade if authorized

3. Writing an audit log record

Note: The placeTrade.jsp, PlaceTradeAction class, and A2ZPlaceTradeService class all execute on nile.itsosj.sanjose.ibm.com, which is different from the server where the IBM Information Server executes. The imports for EJB and SOAP with HTTP can be generated when the WSDL and EJB client.jar are imported into RAD, including the context factory and provider URL (iiop://radon.itsosj.sanjose.ibm.com:2809) of the IBM Information Server.

The placeTrade JSP (Example 2-20 on page 338) invokes the PlaceTradeAction (Example 2-21 on page 339) class. The PlaceTradeAction class then instantiates the A2ZPlaceTradeService (Example 2-22 on page 340) helper class object, and invokes its placeTrade method with order details (such as social security number, stock symbol, quantity etc.). This method invokes the AuthorizationService, placeTradeService, and AuditService IBM Information Server services that are accessed using a mix of EJB (AuthorizationService and AuditService) and SOAP over HTTP (placeTradeService).

The provider URL (iiop://radon.itsosj.sanjose.ibm.com:2809) is defined as a constant in the A2ZPlaceTradeService class. The EJB and SOAP over HTTP imports corresponding to the IBM Information Server services are also shown in the A2ZPlaceTradeService class.

Note: The various classes, libraries and packages need to be imported appropriately.

Example 2-20   placeTrade JSP

```
<!DOCTYPE HTML PUBLIC "-//W3C//DTD HTML 4.01 Transitional//EN" "http://www.w3.org/TR/html4/loose.dtd">
<%@page language="java" contentType="text/html; charset=ISO-8859-1"
    pageEncoding="ISO-8859-1"%>
<%@taglib uri="http://jakarta.apache.org/struts/tags-html" prefix="html"%>
<%@taglib uri="http://jakarta.apache.org/struts/tags-bean" prefix="bean"%>
<html:html>
<head>
<title>placeTrade</title>
<meta http-equiv="Content-Type" content="text/html; charset=ISO-8859-1">
<meta name="GENERATOR" content="Rational Application Developer">
<link rel="stylesheet" href="theme/Master.css" type="text/css">
</head>
<body>


<center><table border="0" class="Mtable">
    <tbody>
        <tr>
            <td><h1><span class="hRow">A2Z Financials</span></h1></td>
        </tr>
        <tr>
            <td><html:form action="/placeTrade" method="post">
    <table border="1" width="364" height="216">
        <tbody>
            <tr>
                <td colspan="2" class="hRow">Place Trade</td>
            </tr>
            <tr>
                <td>SSN Number</td>
                <td><html:text property="ssnNumber" size="11" maxlength="11"></html:text></td>
            </tr>
            <tr>
                <td>Stock</td>
                <td><html:text property="symbol" size="5" maxlength="5"></html:text></td>
            </tr>
            <tr>
                <td>Quantity</td>
                <td><html:text property="quantity" value="0" size="5" maxlength="5"></html:text></td>
            </tr>
            <tr>
                <td>Account Number</td>
                <td><html:text property="accountNumber"></html:text></td>
            </tr>
            <tr>
                <td colspan="2"><html:submit value="Place Trade"></html:submit></td>
            </tr>
            <tr>
                <td colspan="2">Result : <bean:write property="result" name="tradeForm" /></td>
            </tr>
        </tbody>
    </table>

</html:form></td>
        </tr>
    </tbody>
</table></center>
</body>
</html:html>
```

Example 2-21   PlaceTradeAction.java

```
package a2zselfserviceweb.actions;

import javax.servlet.http.HttpServletRequest;
import javax.servlet.http.HttpServletResponse;

import org.apache.struts.action.Action;
import org.apache.struts.action.ActionErrors;
import org.apache.struts.action.ActionForm;
import org.apache.struts.action.ActionForward;
import org.apache.struts.action.ActionMapping;

import a2z.web.services.A2ZPlaceTradeService;
import a2z.web.services.A2ZPlaceTradeServiceAllEJB;
import a2zselfserviceweb.forms.TradeForm;

/**
 * @version 1.0
 * @author
 */
public class PlaceTradeAction extends Action

{

    public ActionForward execute(ActionMapping mapping, ActionForm form,
        HttpServletRequest request, HttpServletResponse response)
        throws Exception {

    ActionErrors errors = new ActionErrors();
    ActionForward forward = new ActionForward(); // return value
    TradeForm tradeForm = (TradeForm) form;

    try {

        A2ZPlaceTradeService a2zPts = new A2ZPlaceTradeService();
        int accountNumber = a2zPts.placeTrade(tradeForm.getSsnNumber(), tradeForm.getSymbol(), tradeForm.getQuantity(),
tradeForm.getAccountNumber(), "B");
        if(accountNumber != -1) {
            tradeForm.setResult("The trade was placed and the result is" + accountNumber);
        }else {
            tradeForm.setResult("The trade was not placed");
        }
    } catch (Exception e) {
        //TODO: handle error
    }

    // If a message is required, save the specified key(s)
    // into the request for use by the <struts:errors> tag.

    if (!errors.isEmpty()) {
        saveErrors(request, errors);
    }
    // Write logic determining how the user should be forwarded.
    forward = mapping.findForward("success");
    // Finish with
    return (forward);

    }
}
```

Example 2-22   A2ZPlaceTradeService.java

```
package a2z.web.services;

import java.rmi.RemoteException;
import java.util.Calendar;
import java.util.Properties;

import javax.ejb.CreateException;
import javax.naming.Context;
import javax.naming.InitialContext;
import javax.naming.NamingException;
import javax.rmi.PortableRemoteObject;
import javax.xml.rpc.Service;
import javax.xml.rpc.ServiceException;

import com.ibm.etools.service.locator.ServiceLocatorManager;
import com.ibm.isd.BrokerageApp.TradesService.TradesService_PortType;
import com.ibm.isd.CommonServicesApp.AuditService.server.AuditServiceHome;
import com.ibm.isd.CommonServicesApp.AuditService.server.AuditServiceRemote;
import com.ibm.isd.CommonServicesApp.AuthorizationService.server.AuthorizationServiceHome;
import com.ibm.isd.CommonServicesApp.AuthorizationService.server.AuthorizationServiceRemote;

public class A2ZPlaceTradeService {

    private AuthorizationServiceHome authorizationHome;
    private AuditServiceHome auditServiceHome;

    private final static String STATIC_TradesService_PortType_REF_NAME = "service/TradesService";

    private final static Class STATIC_TradesService_PortType_CLASS = TradesService_PortType.class;

    //Constructor
    public A2ZPlaceTradeService() throws NamingException {
        lookupInformationServices();
    }

    //Generated
    protected TradesService_PortType lookupTradesService_PortType() throws ServiceException {
        Service locator = (Service) ServiceLocatorManager.getServiceLookup(
                STATIC_TradesService_PortType_REF_NAME,
                STATIC_TradesService_PortType_CLASS);

        TradesService_PortType aTradesService_PortType = (TradesService_PortType)
locator.getPort(STATIC_TradesService_PortType_CLASS);
        return aTradesService_PortType;
    }
    /**
     * Invoke the placetrade service and place trade for the given inputs.
     *
     * @param ssnNumber
     * @param symbol
     * @param quantity
     * @param accountNumber
     * @param type
     * @return
     * @throws RemoteException
     * @throws CreateException
     * @throws ServiceException
     */
    public int placeTrade(String ssnNumber, String symbol, int quantity,
            String accountNumber, String type) throws RemoteException, CreateException, ServiceException {
        boolean authorized = authorize(ssnNumber);
        if (!authorized)
            return 0;
        TradesService_PortType aTradesService_PortType = lookupTradesService_PortType();
        Integer result = new Integer(-1);
```

```
        if(aTradesService_PortType != null){
            result = aTradesService_PortType.placeTrade(symbol, new Integer(quantity),
                    type, Calendar.getInstance(), accountNumber);
            audit("Trade placed OrderNumber " , result.toString());
        }
        return result.intValue();
}
/**
 * Invoke the Audit service and audit the passed in message and result information.
 *
 * @param message
 * @param result
 * @throws RemoteException
 * @throws CreateException
 */
protected void audit(String message, String result) throws RemoteException, CreateException {
    AuditServiceRemote auditRemote = auditServiceHome.create();
    auditRemote.audit(message, result);
}
/**
 * Authorize the customer for the place trade action.
 *
 * @param ssnNumber
 * @return
 * @throws RemoteException
 * @throws CreateException
 */
protected boolean authorize(String ssnNumber) throws RemoteException, CreateException {
    AuthorizationServiceRemote authRemote = authorizationHome.create();
    Integer result = authRemote.isAuthorizedFor(ssnNumber, "Brokerage_PlaceTrade");
    return result != null && result.intValue() == 1;
}
/**
 * Cache the home objects.
 */
protected Context lookupInformationServices() throws NamingException {
    Properties props = new Properties();
    props.put(Context.PROVIDER_URL, "iiop://radon.itsosj.sanjose.ibm.com:2809");
    Context isctx = new InitialContext(props);
    Object o = isctx.lookup("ejb/CommonServicesApp/AuthorizationService");
    authorizationHome = (AuthorizationServiceHome) PortableRemoteObject.narrow(o, AuthorizationServiceHome.class);

    o = isctx.lookup("ejb/CommonServicesApp/AuditService");
    auditServiceHome = (AuditServiceHome) PortableRemoteObject.narrow(o, AuditServiceHome.class);

    return isctx;
}
}
```

Get Account balance (portlet)

The main aspects of this application are as follows:

► It executes on a portal server (swiss.itsosj.sanjose.ibm.com) distinct from IBM Information Server (radon.itsosj.sanjose.ibm.com) and WebSphere Process Server (lead.itsosj.sanjose.ibm.com).

► The IBM Information Server services (AuthorizationService, AccountStatusService, and AuditService) were invoked using a combination of SOAP over HTTP and EJB bindings.

► The WID GetBalancesProcess service is invoked using SOAP over HTTP binding.

This is summarized here in Figure 2-345. The IBM Information Server and WID generated services implementation of the *get account balance* business function are described here.

> **Attention:** This portlet code developed for IBM Information Server services (Example 2-24 on page 372), when compared with that developed for WID generated service (Example 2-25 on page 389), clearly shows the economy of application development code when invoking an aggregated (WID) service where only one invocation is required, as compared to invoking each individual (IBM Information Server) service to achieve the desired business function. The invocation process for a single service using the same binding is identical whether WID or an IBM Information Server service is invoked.

A2Z Financials Business Function (swiss.itsosj.sanjose.ibm.com)	Information Server Services (radon.itsosj.sanjose.ibm.com)		WebSphere Integration Developer (lead.itsosj.sanjose.ibm.com)	
	Services	Binding	Services	Binding
Get Account balance for the brokerage accounts	AuthorizationService AccountStatusService AuditService	EJB SOAP over HTTP EJB	GetBalancesProcess	SOAP over HTTP

Figure 2-345   *Portlet invocation of the get account balance business function using RAD*

Get Account balance using IBM Information Server services

In this section, we develop and test a portal application that directly invokes IBM Information Server services using SOAP over HTTP binding as described in Figure 2-346 on page 346 through Figure 2-383 on page 381.

Figure 2-346 on page 346 through Figure 2-349 on page 349 describe the import of the CommonServicesApp_client.jar file (corresponding to EJB bindings) into the A2ZPortlets project:

1. After launching RAD (not shown here), select **Import from the File menu** in Figure 2-346 on page 346.

2. Then select **File System** as the import source in Figure 2-347 on page 347, and click **Next**.

3. Specify the source directory (C:\Temp\isclient) and destination folder (A2ZPortletsEar), and click **Finish** as shown in Figure 2-348 on page 348.

4. Next add a jar dependency in the dependent project by double-clicking MANIFEST.MF under Web Content → META-INF in Project Explorer in Figure 2-349 on page 349. Check the box CommonServicesApp_client.jar to complete this action.

Figure 2-350 on page 350 through Figure 2-352 on page 351 describe the import of the a zipped file (A2ZSCA_BrokerageApp_WSDLFiles.zip) containing all WSDL files in the Brokerage application into the WSClients project (the creation is not shown here):

1. After launching RAD (not shown here), select **Import** from the File menu in Figure 2-350 on page 350.

2. Then select **Archive File** as the import source in Figure 2-351 on page 350, and click **Next**.

3. Specify the archive file (C:\Temp\A2ZSCA_BrokerageApp_WSDLFiles.zip) and destination folder (WSClient), and click **Finish** as shown in Figure 2-352 on page 351.

Figure 2-353 on page 352 through Figure 2-357 on page 356 describe the generation of a SOAP over HTTP client stub for the AccountStatusService. Proceed as follows:

1. Expand WSClients in Project Explorer, right-click **AccountStatusService.wsdl** and select **WebServices** and **Generate Client from this WSDL** as shown in Figure 2-353 on page 352.

2. Select Java Proxy from the Client type drop-down list, and click **Client project:A2ZPortal** in Figure 2-354 on page 353 to review and modify any options of interest.

3. Choose **A2ZPortlets** from the Client project drop-down list and click **OK** as shown in Figure 2-355 on page 354.

4. Click **Next** in Figure 2-356 on page 355 and **Finish** in Figure 2-357 on page 356 to complete the generation of a client stub for the AccountStatusService service.

> **Note:** Apart from the Java code, the tooling also generates a Web service reference in the Web module. This reference is used to select the service to call as shown in Figure 2-368 on page 366.

Figure 2-358 on page 356 through Figure 2-373 on page 371 describe the development of a portlet to access the IBM Information Server services.

First, let us consider the steps shown in Figure 2-358 on page 356 through Figure 2-364 on page 362:

1. From the File menu, select **New** and Portlet as shown in Figure 2-358 on page 356.

2. Choose a Portlet name (A2ZBrokBalancesISPortlet), A2ZPortlets from the Project drop-down list, Basic Portlet from the Portlet type drop-down list, and click **Next** as shown in Figure 2-359 on page 357.

3. Define the general settings of the portlet and click **Next** as shown in Figure 2-360 on page 358.

4. Check the boxes as shown in the Action and Preferences window in Figure 2-361 on page 359, and click **Next**.

5. Click **Finish** in Figure 2-362 on page 360. Modify the JSP form as shown in Figure 2-363 on page 361.

6. A sample java bean A2ZBrokBalancesISPortletSessionBean stores portlet instance data in a portlet session as shown in Figure 2-364 on page 362.

The A2ZBrokBalancesISPortletSessionBean class is shown in Example 2-23 on page 371.

The development of the A2ZBrokBalancesISPortlet class is shown in Figure 2-365 on page 363 through Figure 2-373 on page 371.

First let us consider the steps shown in Figure 2-365 on page 363 through Figure 2-366 on page 364:

1. The lookup of the IBM Information Services (AuthorizationService, CustomerIDLookupService, and AuditService, which are part of CommonServicesApp) is coded in the init() method of the portlet as shown in Figure 2-365 on page 363 — the imports corresponding to these classes are also coded manually (see Example 2-24 on page 372).

2. The processAction method of the portlet (Figure 2-366 on page 364) has code written to verify authorization as well as determine the customer id given the social security number. To get the balances, the AccountStatusService (which has SOAP over HTTP binding) has to be invoked.

RAD provides an easy way to include the necessary Web service method code as shown in Figure 2-367 on page 365 through Figure 2-371 on page 369:

1. Click **Call a WebService method** (which is found in the Snippets view) as shown in Figure 2-367 on page 365.

2. Then select the service reference **ServiceRef service/AccountStatusService**, and click **Next** as shown in Figure 2-368 on page 366.

3. Select **getBalances(String CustomerID)** method and click **Next** in Figure 2-369 on page 367.

4. Enter values for the String parameter (brokerageID) and click **Finish** as shown in Figure 2-370 on page 368.

5. The lookup of the service and the invocation code is added as shown in Figure 2-371 on page 369. The instantiation and invocation of the AuditService with EJB binding is coded manually.

> **Note:** RAD also supports the generation of instantiation and invocation code for services with EJB bindings, but we chose to write the code manually.

Example 2-24 on page 372 shows the entire A2ZBrokBalancesISPortlet code.

> **Note:** The various classes, libraries, and packages need to be imported appropriately.

Figure 2-372 on page 370 and Figure 2-373 on page 371 show the JSP code that invokes the A2ZBrokBalancesISPortlet portlet. Specifically, they show the highlighted code that iterates to display all the balances.

Figure 2-374 on page 376 through Figure 2-383 on page 381 describe the configuration of the portal on swiss.itsosj.sanjose.ibm.com, deployment of the portlet on it, and a test of the portlet.

1. Figure 2-374 on page 376 through Figure 2-379 on page 378 show the configuration of the portlet on the portal — a description of this is beyond the scope of this publication. Then you would proceed as follows:

2. Publish the A2ZBrokBalancesISPortlet to swiss.itsosj.sanjose.ibm.com (localhost in this case), by clicking the **Servers** tab, right-clicking **WebSphere Portal v6.0 Server @localhost** and selecting **Publish** as shown in Figure 2-380 on page 379.

3. Select **Open Portal** as shown in Figure 2-381 on page 380.

4. Navigate to the A2ZBrokBalancesISPortlet page and provide the social security number (611-32-3978) in Figure 2-382 on page 381.

5. View the results in Figure 2-383 on page 381.

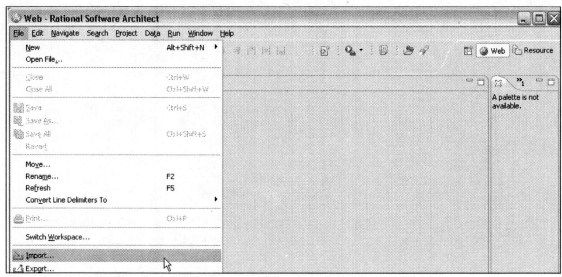

Figure 2-346   Import CommonServicesApp_client.jar into A2ZPortlets project 1/4

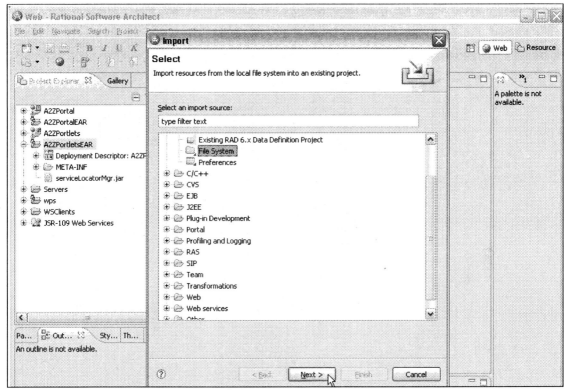

Figure 2-347 Import CommonServicesApp_client.jar into A2ZPortlets project 2/4

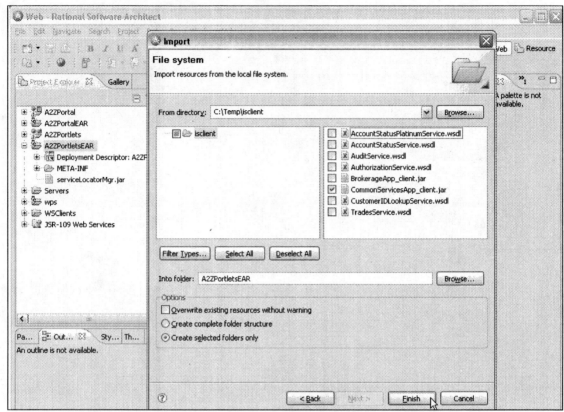

Figure 2-348   Import CommonServicesApp_client.jar into A2ZPortlets project 3/4

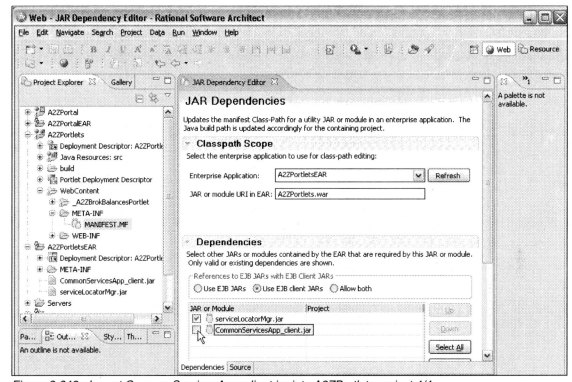

Figure 2-349   Import CommonServicesApp_client.jar into A2ZPortlets project 4/4

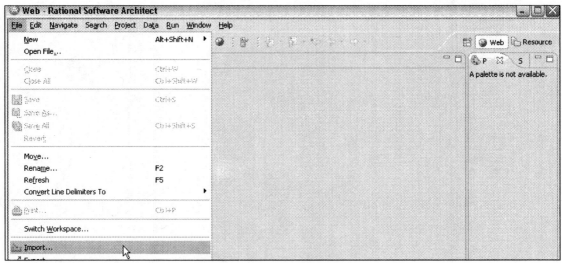

Figure 2-350   Import contents of archive files into WSClients project 1/3

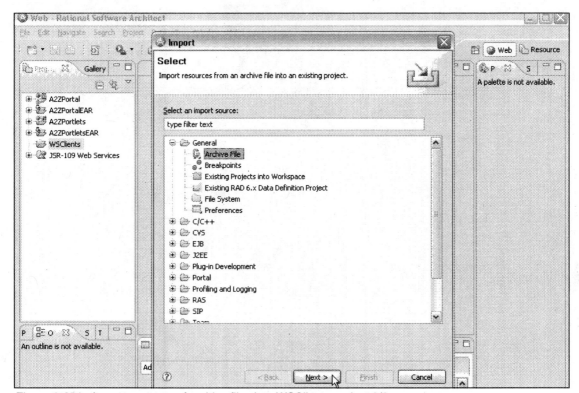

Figure 2-351   Import contents of archive files into WSClients project 2/3

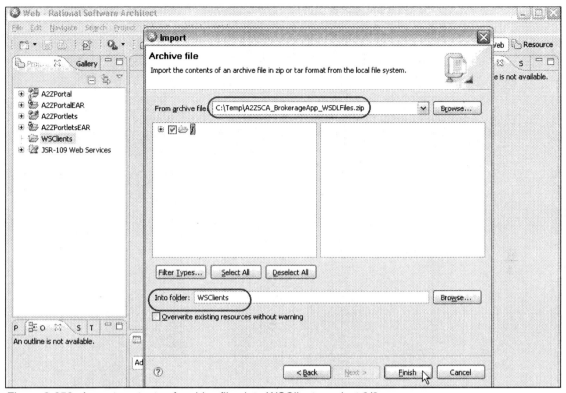

Figure 2-352   Import contents of archive files into WSClients project 3/3

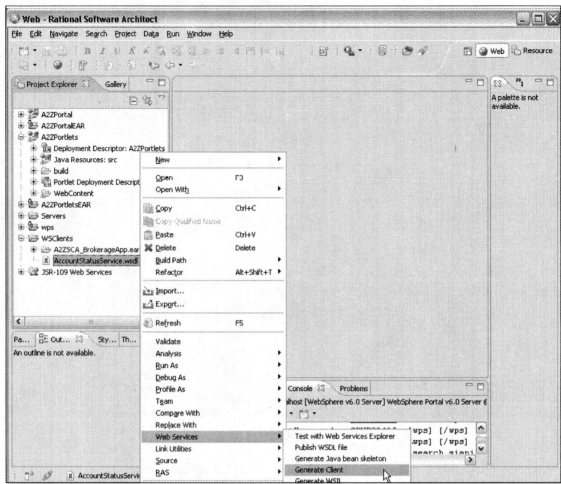

Figure 2-353   Generate AccountStatusService.wsdl client stub 1/5

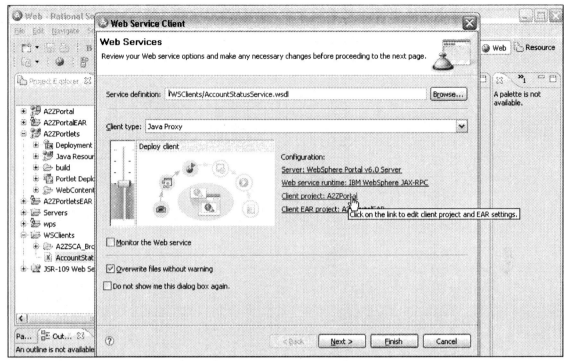

Figure 2-354   Generate AccountStatusService.wsdl client stub 2/5

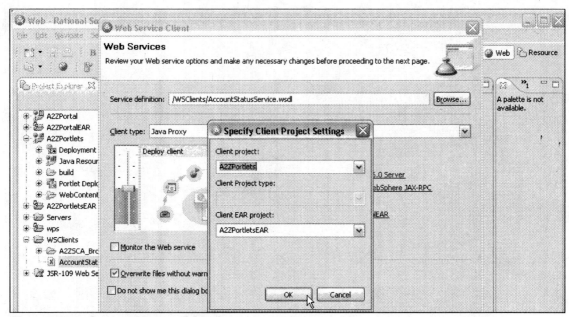

Figure 2-355   Generate AccountStatusService.wsdl client stub 3/5

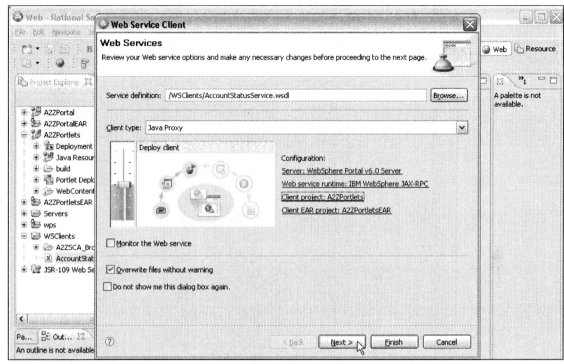

Figure 2-356   Generate AccountStatusService.wsdl client stub 4/5

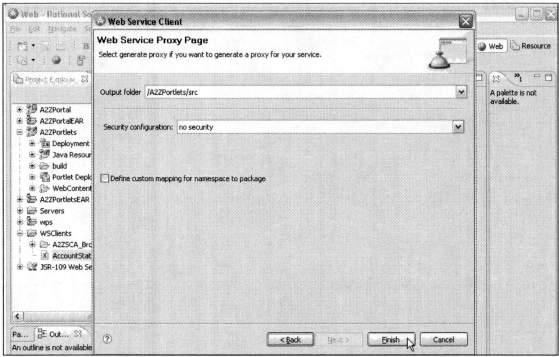

Figure 2-357 Generate AccountStatusService.wsdl client stub 5/5

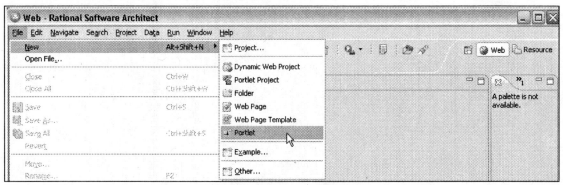

Figure 2-358 Create portlet A2ZBrokBalancesISPortlet in A2ZPortlets project 1/16

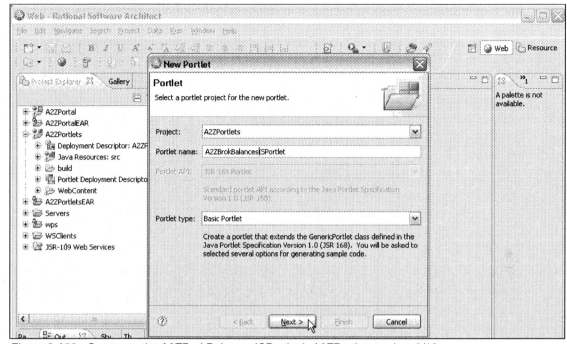

Figure 2-359   Create portlet A2ZBrokBalancesISPortlet in A2ZPortlets project 2/16

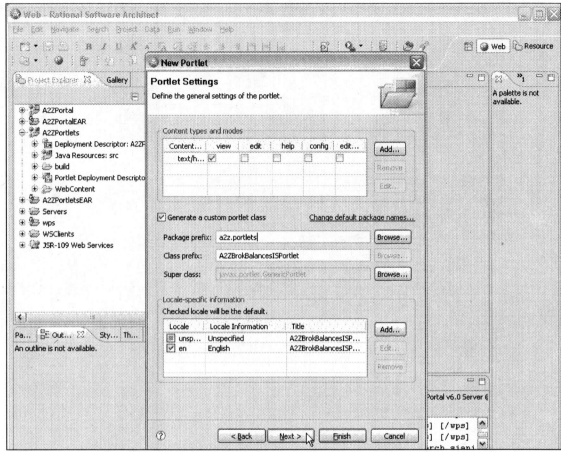

Figure 2-360   Create portlet A2ZBrokBalancesISPortlet in A2ZPortlets project 3/16

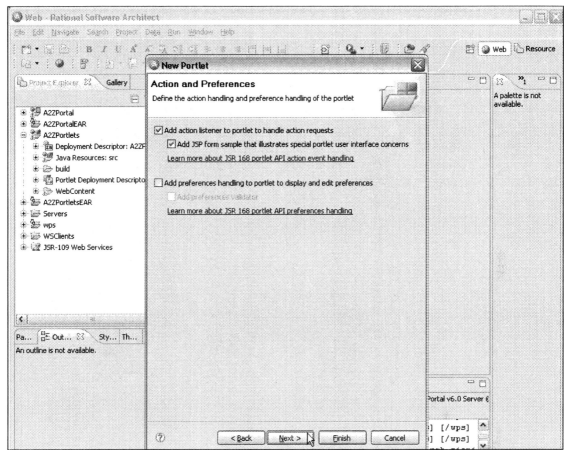

Figure 2-361   Create portlet A2ZBrokBalancesISPortlet in A2ZPortlets project 4/16

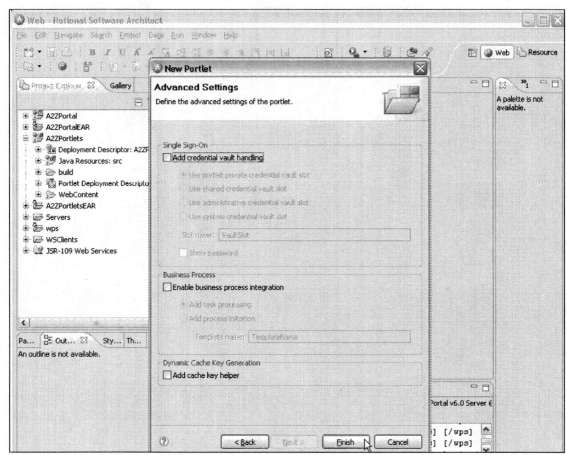

Figure 2-362   Create portlet A2ZBrokBalancesISPortlet in A2ZPortlets project 5/16

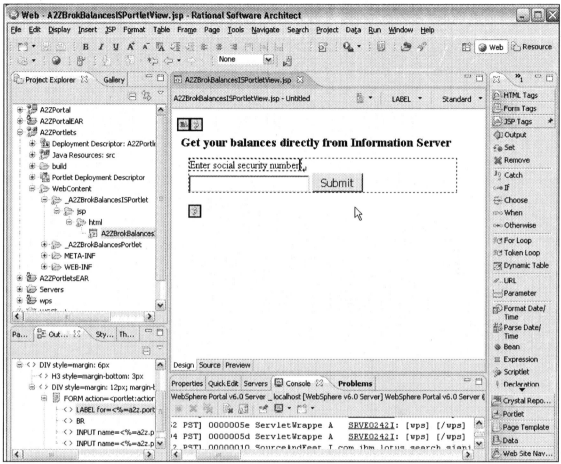

Figure 2-363   Create portlet A2ZBrokBalancesISPortlet in A2ZPortlets project 6/16

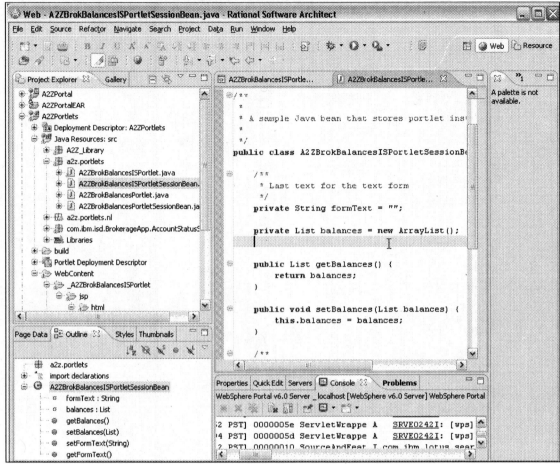

Figure 2-364   Create portlet A2ZBrokBalancesISPortlet in A2ZPortlets project 7/16

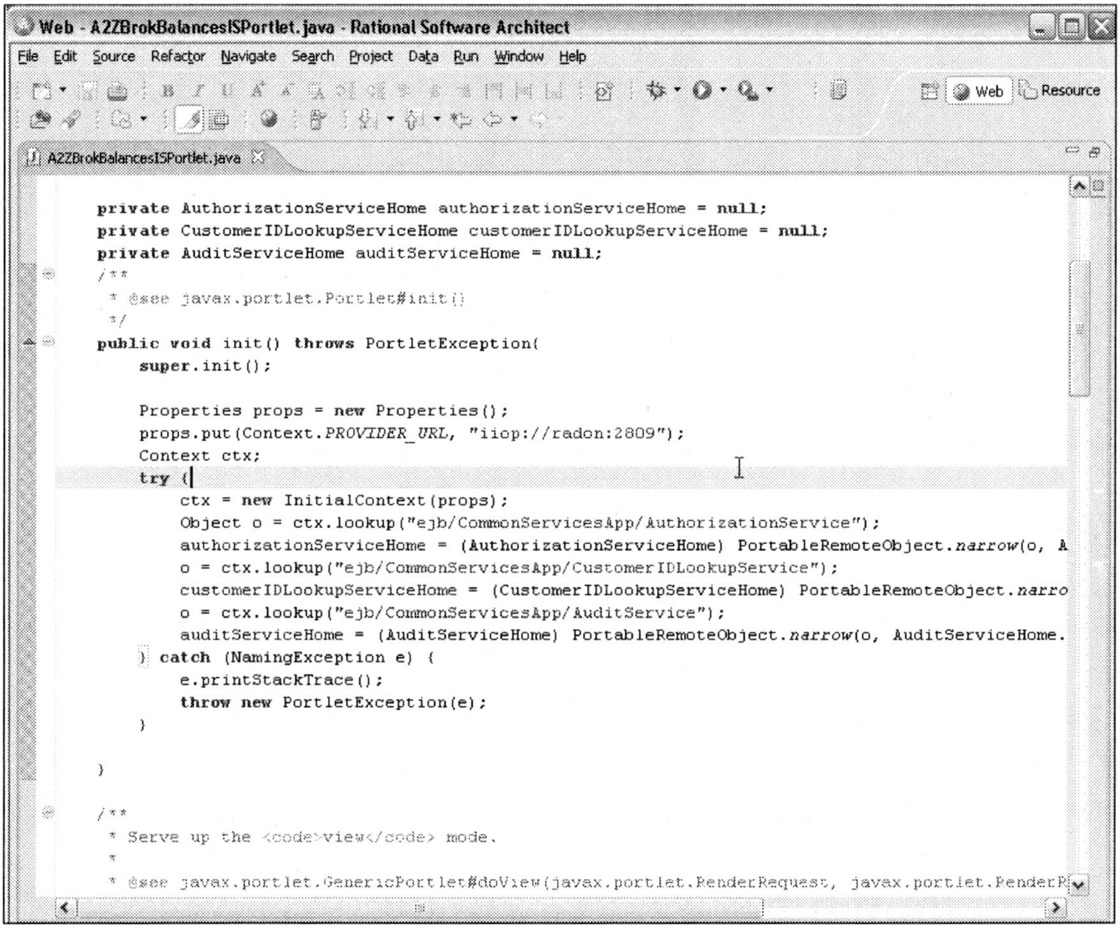

```
          private AuthorizationServiceHome authorizationServiceHome = null;
          private CustomerIDLookupServiceHome customerIDLookupServiceHome = null;
          private AuditServiceHome auditServiceHome = null;
          /**
           * @see javax.portlet.Portlet#init()
           */
          public void init() throws PortletException{
              super.init();

              Properties props = new Properties();
              props.put(Context.PROVIDER_URL, "iiop://radon:2809");
              Context ctx;
              try {
                  ctx = new InitialContext(props);
                  Object o = ctx.lookup("ejb/CommonServicesApp/AuthorizationService");
                  authorizationServiceHome = (AuthorizationServiceHome) PortableRemoteObject.narrow(o, A
                  o = ctx.lookup("ejb/CommonServicesApp/CustomerIDLookupService");
                  customerIDLookupServiceHome = (CustomerIDLookupServiceHome) PortableRemoteObject.narro
                  o = ctx.lookup("ejb/CommonServicesApp/AuditService");
                  auditServiceHome = (AuditServiceHome) PortableRemoteObject.narrow(o, AuditServiceHome.
              } catch (NamingException e) {
                  e.printStackTrace();
                  throw new PortletException(e);
              }

          }

          /**
           * Serve up the <code>view</code> mode.
           *
           * @see javax.portlet.GenericPortlet#doView(javax.portlet.RenderRequest, javax.portlet.RenderP
```

Figure 2-365   Create portlet A2ZBrokBalancesISPortlet in A2ZPortlets project 8/16

File Edit Source Refactor Navigate Search Project Data Run Window Help

A2ZBrokBalancesISPortlet.java

```java
    */
    public void processAction(ActionRequest request, ActionResponse response) throws PortletExcept
        if( request.getParameter(FORM_SUBMIT) != null ) {
            // Set form text in the session bean
            A2ZBrokBalancesISPortletSessionBean sessionBean = getSessionBean(request);
            if( sessionBean != null )
                sessionBean.setFormText(request.getParameter(FORM_TEXT));

            String ssnumb = sessionBean.getFormText();
            try {
                // do authorization
                String action = "Brokerage_GetAllBalances";
                AuthorizationServiceRemote authService = authorizationServiceHome.create();
                Integer isAuthorized = authService.isAuthorizedFor(ssnumb, action);
                String auditMessage = "NotAuthorized";
                if (isAuthorized.intValue() == 1) {
                    // get customer ID of brokerage app
                    CustomerIDLookupServiceRemote idLookupService = customerIDLookupServiceHome.crea
                    String brokerageID = idLookupService.lookupBrokerageCustomerID(ssnumb);

                    // get balances
                    |  I

                    auditMessage = "OK";
                }
                // write to audit
                AuditServiceRemote auditService = auditServiceHome.create();
                auditService.audit(action, auditMessage);
            } catch(CreateException e) {
                e.printStackTrace();
                throw new PortletException(e);
            }
```

Figure 2-366   Create portlet A2ZBrokBalancesISPortlet in A2ZPortlets project 9/16

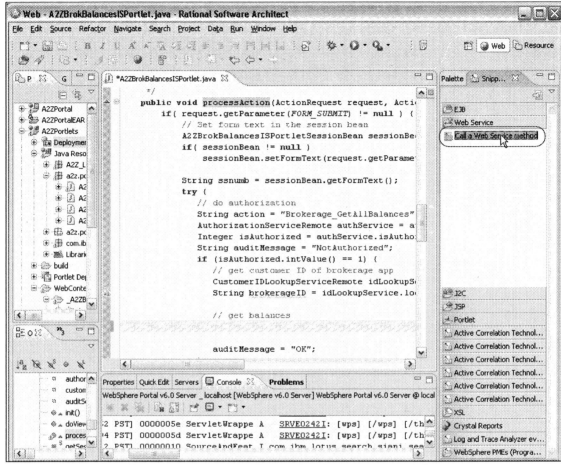

Figure 2-367   Create portlet A2ZBrokBalancesISPortlet in A2ZPortlets project 10/16

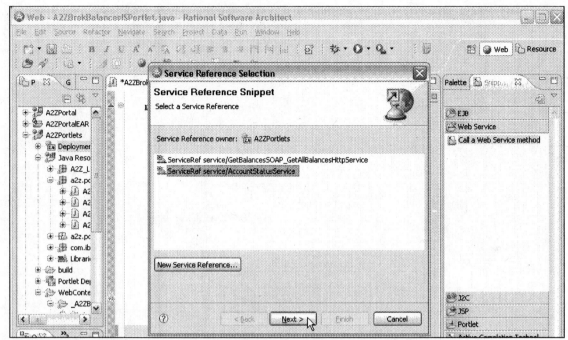

Figure 2-368   Create portlet A2ZBrokBalancesISPortlet in A2ZPortlets project 11/16

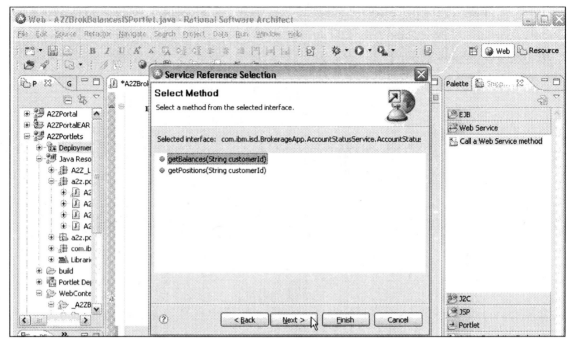

Figure 2-369   Create portlet A2ZBrokBalancesISPortlet in A2ZPortlets project 12/16

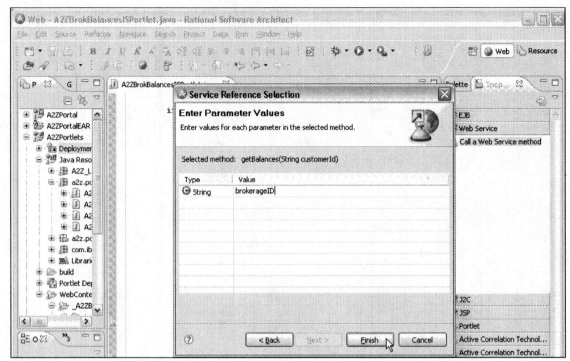

Figure 2-370   Create portlet A2ZBrokBalancesISPortlet in A2ZPortlets project 13/16

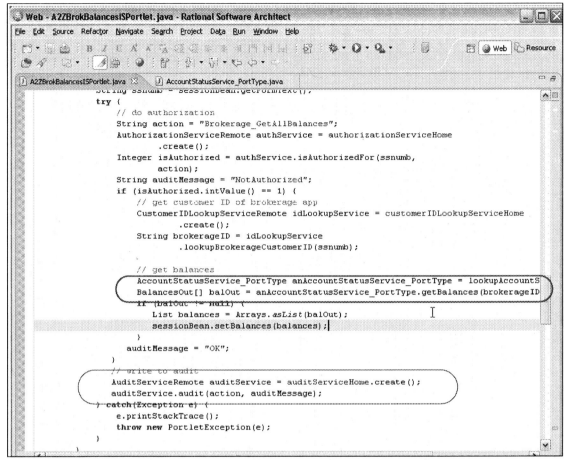

```
                    String ssnumb = sessionBean.getFormText();
    try {
        // do authorization
        String action = "Brokerage_GetAllBalances";
        AuthorizationServiceRemote authService = authorizationServiceHome
                .create();
        Integer isAuthorized = authService.isAuthorizedFor(ssnumb,
                action);
        String auditMessage = "NotAuthorized";
        if (isAuthorized.intValue() == 1) {
            // get customer ID of brokerage app
            CustomerIDLookupServiceRemote idLookupService = customerIDLookupServiceHome
                    .create();
            String brokerageID = idLookupService
                    .lookupBrokerageCustomerID(ssnumb);

            // get balances
            AccountStatusService_PortType anAccountStatusService_PortType = lookupAccountS
            BalancesOut[] balOut = anAccountStatusService_PortType.getBalances(brokerageID
            if (balOut != null) {
                List balances = Arrays.asList(balOut);
                sessionBean.setBalances(balances);
            }
            auditMessage = "OK";
        }
        // write to audit
        AuditServiceRemote auditService = auditServiceHome.create();
        auditService.audit(action, auditMessage);
    } catch(Exception e) {
        e.printStackTrace();
        throw new PortletException(e);
    }
}
```

Figure 2-371   Create portlet A2ZBrokBalancesISPortlet in A2ZPortlets project 14/16

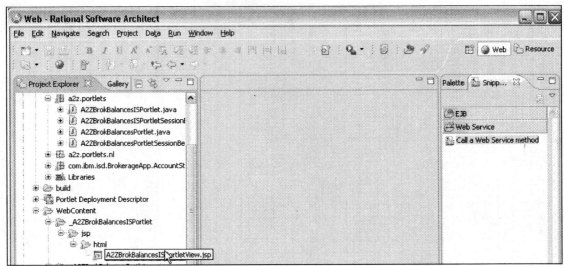

Figure 2-372   Create portlet A2ZBrokBalancesISPortlet in A2ZPortlets project 15/16

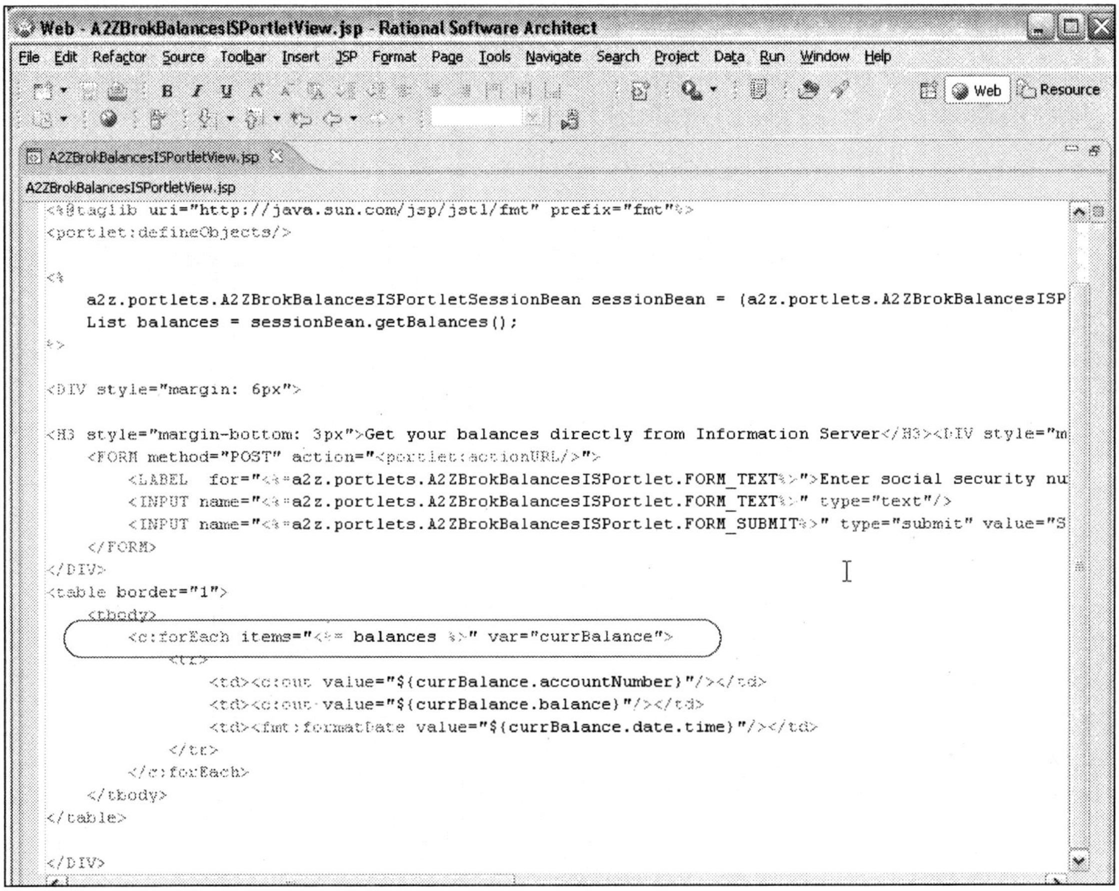

Figure 2-373   Create portlet A2ZBrokBalancesISPortlet in A2ZPortlets project 16/16

Example 2-23   A2ZBrokBalancesISPortletSessionBean

```java
package a2z.portlets;

import java.util.ArrayList;
import java.util.List;

/**
 *
 * A sample Java bean that stores portlet instance data in portlet session.
 *
 */
public class A2ZBrokBalancesISPortletSessionBean {

    /**
     * Last text for the text form
     */
    private String formText = "";

    private List balances = new ArrayList();
```

```java
    public List getBalances() {
        return balances;
    }

    public void setBalances(List balances) {
        this.balances = balances;
    }

    /**
     * Set last text for the text form.
     *
     * @param formText
     *              last text for the text form.
     */
    public void setFormText(String formText) {
        this.formText = formText;
    }

    /**
     * Get last text for the text form.
     *
     * @return last text for the text form
     */
    public String getFormText() {
        return this.formText;
    }

}
```

Example 2-24   A2ZBrokBalancesISPortlet.java portlet

```java
package a2z.portlets;

import java.io.IOException;
import java.util.Arrays;
import java.util.Properties;

import javax.naming.Context;
import javax.naming.InitialContext;
import javax.naming.NamingException;
import javax.portlet.ActionRequest;
import javax.portlet.ActionResponse;
import javax.portlet.GenericPortlet;
import javax.portlet.PortletException;
import javax.portlet.PortletRequest;
import javax.portlet.PortletRequestDispatcher;
import javax.portlet.PortletSession;
import javax.portlet.RenderRequest;
import javax.portlet.RenderResponse;
import javax.rmi.PortableRemoteObject;

import com.ibm.isd.CommonServicesApp.AuditService.server.AuditServiceHome;
import com.ibm.isd.CommonServicesApp.AuditService.server.AuditServiceRemote;
import com.ibm.isd.CommonServicesApp.AuthorizationService.server.AuthorizationServiceHome;
import com.ibm.isd.CommonServicesApp.AuthorizationService.server.AuthorizationServiceRemote;
import com.ibm.isd.CommonServicesApp.CustomerIDLookupService.server.CustomerIDLookupServiceHome;
import com.ibm.isd.CommonServicesApp.CustomerIDLookupService.server.CustomerIDLookupServiceRemote;
import com.ibm.etools.service.locator.ServiceLocatorManager;
import java.rmi.RemoteException;
import javax.xml.rpc.ServiceException;
import javax.xml.rpc.Service;
import com.ibm.isd.BrokerageApp.AccountStatusService.AccountStatusService_PortType;

/**
 * A sample portlet based on GenericPortlet
```

```
*/
public class A2ZBrokBalancesISPortlet extends GenericPortlet {

    public static final String JSP_FOLDER = "/_A2ZBrokBalancesISPortlet/jsp/"; // JSP folder name

    public static final String VIEW_JSP = "A2ZBrokBalancesISPortletView"; // JSP file name to be rendered on the view mode

    public static final String SESSION_BEAN = "A2ZBrokBalancesISPortletSessionBean"; // Bean name for the portlet session

    public static final String FORM_SUBMIT = "A2ZBrokBalancesISPortletFormSubmit"; // Action name for submit form

    public static final String FORM_TEXT = "A2ZBrokBalancesISPortletFormText"; // Parameter name for the text input

    private AuthorizationServiceHome authorizationServiceHome;

    private CustomerIDLookupServiceHome customerIDLookupServiceHome;

    private AuditServiceHome auditServiceHome;

    private final static String STATIC_AccountStatusService_PortType_REF_NAME = "service/AccountStatusService";

    private final static Class STATIC_AccountStatusService_PortType_CLASS = AccountStatusService_PortType.class;

    /**
     * @see javax.portlet.Portlet#init()
     */
    public void init() throws PortletException {
        super.init();
        Properties props = new Properties();
        props.put("java.naming.provider.url", "iiop://radon:2809");
        try {
            Context ctx = new InitialContext(props);
            Object o = ctx.lookup("ejb/CommonServicesApp/AuthorizationService");
            authorizationServiceHome = (AuthorizationServiceHome) PortableRemoteObject
                    .narrow(
                            o,
                            com.ibm.isd.CommonServicesApp.AuthorizationService.server.AuthorizationServiceHome.class);
            o = ctx.lookup("ejb/CommonServicesApp/CustomerIDLookupService");
            customerIDLookupServiceHome = (CustomerIDLookupServiceHome) PortableRemoteObject
                    .narrow(
                            o,
                            com.ibm.isd.CommonServicesApp.CustomerIDLookupService.server.CustomerIDLookupServiceHome.class);
            o = ctx.lookup("ejb/CommonServicesApp/AuditService");
            auditServiceHome = (AuditServiceHome) PortableRemoteObject
                    .narrow(
                            o,
                            com.ibm.isd.CommonServicesApp.AuditService.server.AuditServiceHome.class);
        } catch (NamingException e) {
            e.printStackTrace();
            throw new PortletException(e);
        }

    }

    /**
     * Serve up the <code>view</code> mode.
     *
     * @see javax.portlet.GenericPortlet#doView(javax.portlet.RenderRequest,
     *      javax.portlet.RenderResponse)
     */
    public void doView(RenderRequest request, RenderResponse response)
            throws PortletException, IOException {
        // Set the MIME type for the render response
        response.setContentType(request.getResponseContentType());

        // Check if portlet session exists
        A2ZBrokBalancesISPortletSessionBean sessionBean = getSessionBean(request);
        if (sessionBean == null) {
            response.getWriter().println("<b>NO PORTLET SESSION YET</b>");
            return;
        }
```

```
            // Invoke the JSP to render
            PortletRequestDispatcher rd = getPortletContext().getRequestDispatcher(
                    getJspFilePath(request, VIEW_JSP));
            rd.include(request, response);
    }

    /**
     * Process an action request.
     *
     * @see javax.portlet.Portlet#processAction(javax.portlet.ActionRequest,
     *      javax.portlet.ActionResponse)
     */
    public void processAction(ActionRequest request, ActionResponse response)
            throws PortletException, java.io.IOException {
        if (request.getParameter(FORM_SUBMIT) != null) {
            // Set form text in the session bean
            A2ZBrokBalancesISPortletSessionBean sessionBean = getSessionBean(request);
            if (sessionBean != null)
                sessionBean.setFormText(request.getParameter(FORM_TEXT));
            String ssnumb = sessionBean.getFormText();
            try {
                String action = "Brokerage_GetAllBalances";
                AuthorizationServiceRemote authService = authorizationServiceHome
                        .create();
                Integer isAuthorized = authService.isAuthorizedFor(ssnumb,
                        action);
                String auditMessage = "NotAuthorized";
                if (isAuthorized.intValue() == 1) {
                    CustomerIDLookupServiceRemote idLookupService = customerIDLookupServiceHome
                            .create();
                    String brokerageID = idLookupService
                            .lookupBrokerageCustomerID(ssnumb);

                    AccountStatusService_PortType anAccountStatusService_PortType = lookupAccountStatusService_PortType();
                    com.ibm.isd.BrokerageApp.AccountStatusService.BalancesOut balOut[] = anAccountStatusService_PortType
                            .getBalances(brokerageID);

                    if (balOut != null) {
                        java.util.List balances = Arrays.asList(balOut);
                        sessionBean.setBalances(balances);
                    }
                    auditMessage = "OK";
                }
                AuditServiceRemote auditService = auditServiceHome.create();
                auditService.audit(action, auditMessage);
            } catch (Exception e) {
                e.printStackTrace();
                throw new PortletException(e);
            }

        }
    }

    /**
     * Get SessionBean.
     *
     * @param request
     *            PortletRequest
     * @return A2ZBrokBalancesISPortletSessionBean
     */
    private static A2ZBrokBalancesISPortletSessionBean getSessionBean(
            PortletRequest request) {
        PortletSession session = request.getPortletSession();
        if (session == null)
            return null;
        A2ZBrokBalancesISPortletSessionBean sessionBean = (A2ZBrokBalancesISPortletSessionBean) session
                .getAttribute(SESSION_BEAN);
        if (sessionBean == null) {
            sessionBean = new A2ZBrokBalancesISPortletSessionBean();
            session.setAttribute(SESSION_BEAN, sessionBean);
        }
        return sessionBean;
```

```
    }

    /**
     * Returns JSP file path.
     *
     * @param request
     *            Render request
     * @param jspFile
     *            JSP file name
     * @return JSP file path
     */
    private static String getJspFilePath(RenderRequest request, String jspFile) {
        String markup = request.getProperty("wps.markup");
        if (markup == null)
            markup = getMarkup(request.getResponseContentType());
        return JSP_FOLDER + markup + "/" + jspFile + "."
                + getJspExtension(markup);
    }

    /**
     * Convert MIME type to markup name.
     *
     * @param contentType
     *            MIME type
     * @return Markup name
     */
    private static String getMarkup(String contentType) {
        if ("text/vnd.wap.wml".equals(contentType))
            return "wml";
        else
            return "html";
    }

    /**
     * Returns the file extension for the JSP file
     *
     * @param markupName
     *            Markup name
     * @return JSP extension
     */
    private static String getJspExtension(String markupName) {
        return "jsp";
    }

    protected AccountStatusService_PortType lookupAccountStatusService_PortType() {
        try {
            Service locator = (Service) ServiceLocatorManager.getServiceLookup(
                    STATIC_AccountStatusService_PortType_REF_NAME,
                    STATIC_AccountStatusService_PortType_CLASS);
            AccountStatusService_PortType anAccountStatusService_PortType = (AccountStatusService_PortType) locator
                    .getPort(STATIC_AccountStatusService_PortType_CLASS);
            return anAccountStatusService_PortType;
        } catch (ServiceException re) {
            // TODO Auto-generated catch block
            re.printStackTrace();
            return null;
        }
    }

}
```

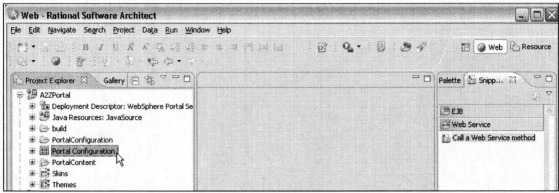

Figure 2-374   Configure portal and test portlet 1/10

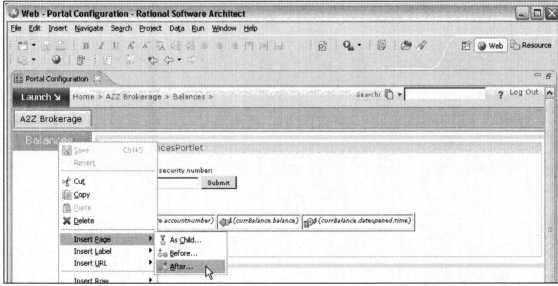

Figure 2-375   Configure portal and test portlet 2/10

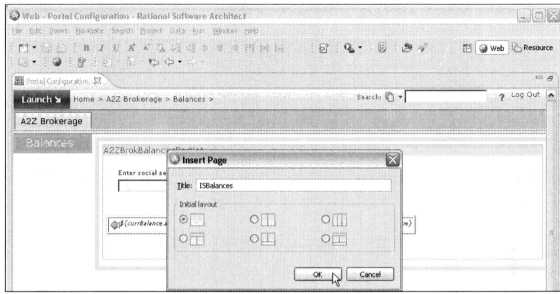

Figure 2-376   Configure portal and test portlet 3/10

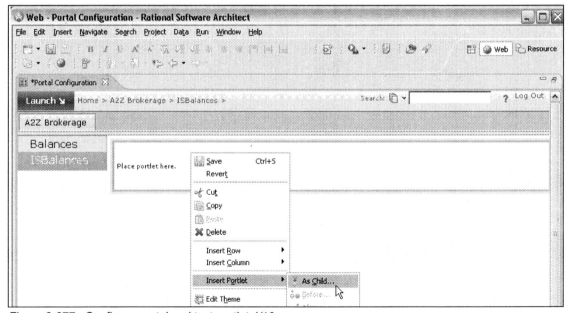

Figure 2-377   Configure portal and test portlet 4/10

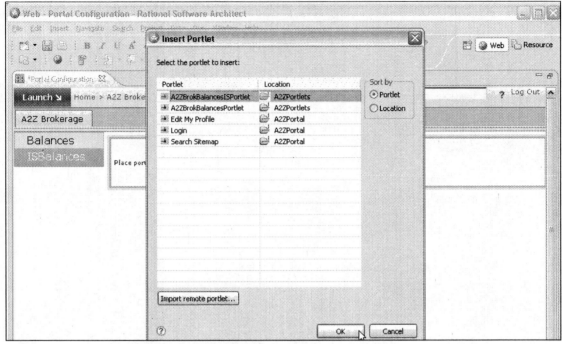

Figure 2-378   Configure portal and test portlet 5/10

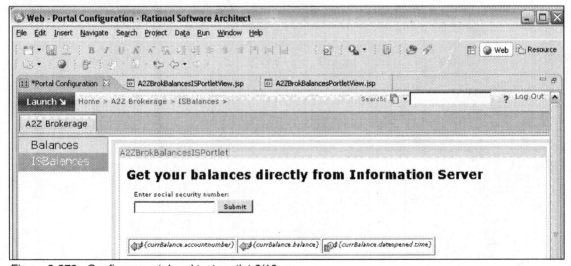

Figure 2-379   Configure portal and test portlet 6/10

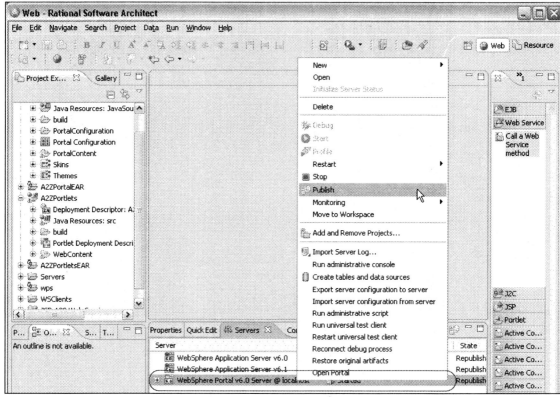

Figure 2-380   Configure portal and test portlet 7/10

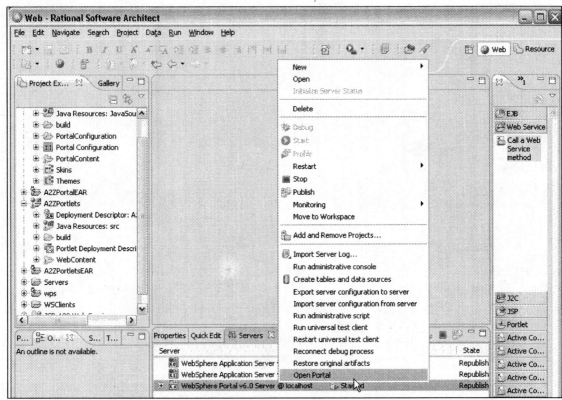

Figure 2-381   Configure portal and test portlet 8/10

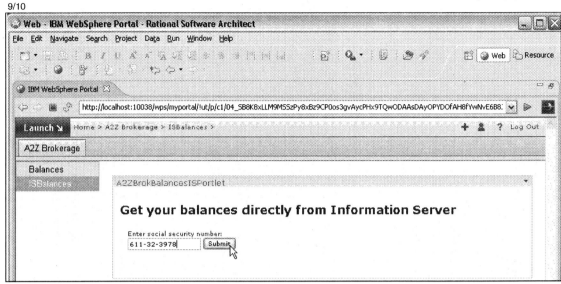

Figure 2-382   Configure portal and test portlet 9/10

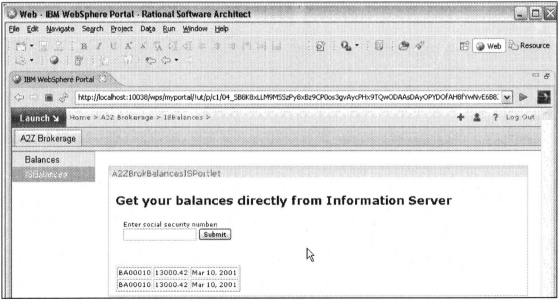

Figure 2-383   Configure portal and test portlet 10/10

Get Account balance using WID generated services

In this section, we develop and test the same portal application described in "Get Account balance using IBM Information Server services" on page 342 by invoking a corresponding WID generated service GetBalancesProcess that is exported with SOAP over HTTP binding. The WSDL is generated as GetBalancesSOAP_GetAllBalancesHttp_Service.wsdl.

> **Note:** The steps are identical to those described in "Get Account balance using IBM Information Server services" on page 342. Therefore, we will not be repeating the steps related to portlet development, portal configuration and testing. We will include the import of the WID generated service, and show the completed portlet code.

Figure 2-384 on page 383 shows the BPEL process that performs the get account balances function for brokerage, and it includes the AuthorizationService, AccountStatusService, and AuditService.

> **Note:** The generation of a SOAP over HTTP client stub from the GetBalancesSOAP_GetAllBalancesHttp_Service.wsdl (Figure 2-385 on page 384) is very similar to the one for AccountStatusService.wsdl described earlier, and is therefore not repeated here. The same applies to the creation of a new portlet (A2ZBrokBalancesPortlet) in the A2ZPortlets, defining the general settings of the Basic Portlet type, modifying the JSP form and the sample java bean A2ZBrokBalancesPortletSessionBean (similar to A2ZBrokBalancesISPortletSessionBean shown in Example 2-23 on page 371) that stores portlet instance data in a portlet session.

Figure 2-386 on page 384 through Figure 2-391 on page 389 describe the development of a portlet to access the WID GetBalancesProcess service. The processAction method of the portlet (Figure 2-386 on page 384) has to include code to invoke the WID GetBalancesProcess using SOAP over HTTP binding.

As in the case of the invocation of the AccountStatusService in "Get Account balance using IBM Information Server services" on page 342, Figure 2-386 on page 384 through Figure 2-391 on page 389 show the getAllBalances(String ssnumb) method included in the code by clicking **Call a WebService method** and following the prompts.

Example 2-25 on page 389 shows the entire A2ZBrokBalancesPortlet code.

> **Note:** The various classes, libraries and packages need to be imported appropriately.

Note: The JSP code that invokes the A2ZBrokBalancesPortlet portlet is identical to that invoking the A2ZBrokBalancesISPortlet, and is therefore not repeated here. Again, the deployment and test of the A2ZBrokBalancesPortlet is not repeated here, since it is identical to the testing of the A2ZBrokBalancesISPortlet.

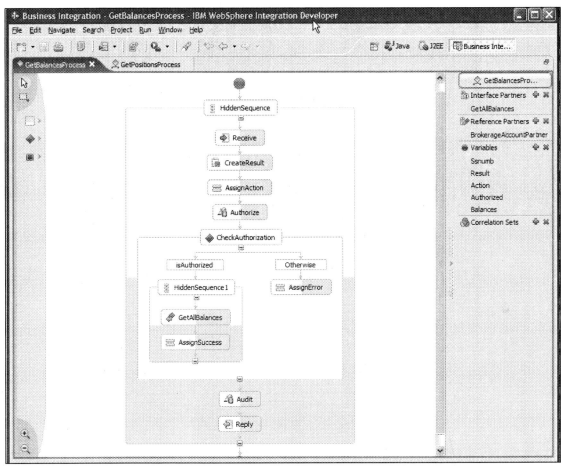

Figure 2-384   GetBalancesProcess BPEL process

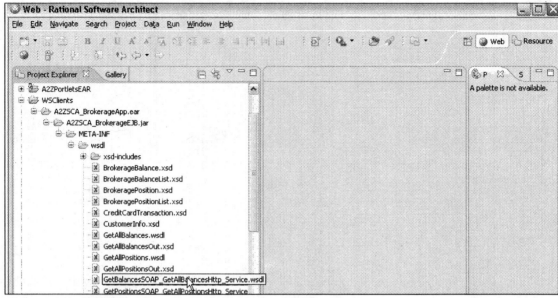

Figure 2-385   WSDL file of the GetBalancesProcess WID generated service

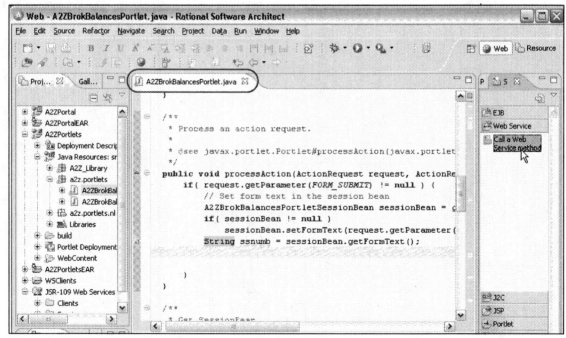

Figure 2-386   Create portlet A2ZBrokBalancesPortlet in A2ZPortlets project 1/6

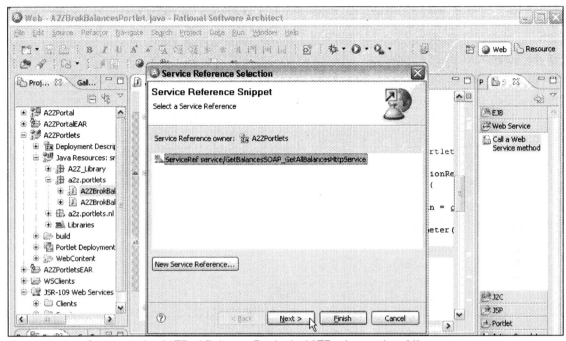

Figure 2-387   Create portlet A2ZBrokBalancesPortlet in A2ZPortlets project 2/6

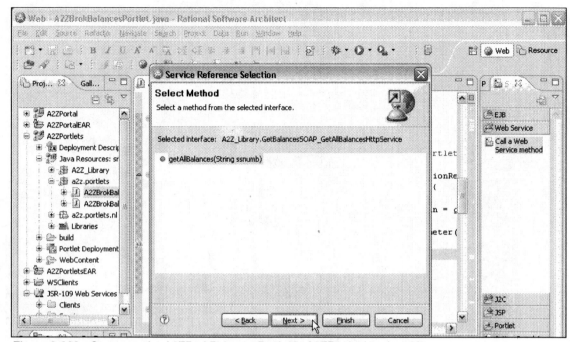

Figure 2-388   Create portlet A2ZBrokBalancesPortlet in A2ZPortlets project 3/6

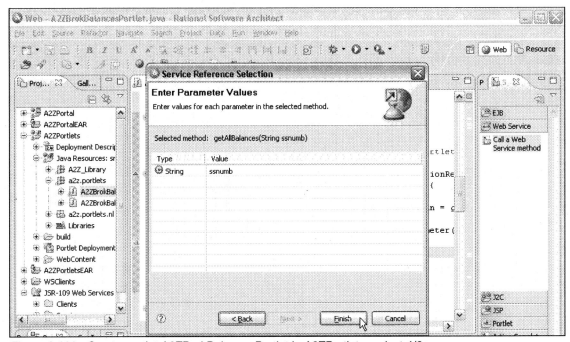

Figure 2-389   Create portlet A2ZBrokBalancesPortlet in A2ZPortlets project 4/6

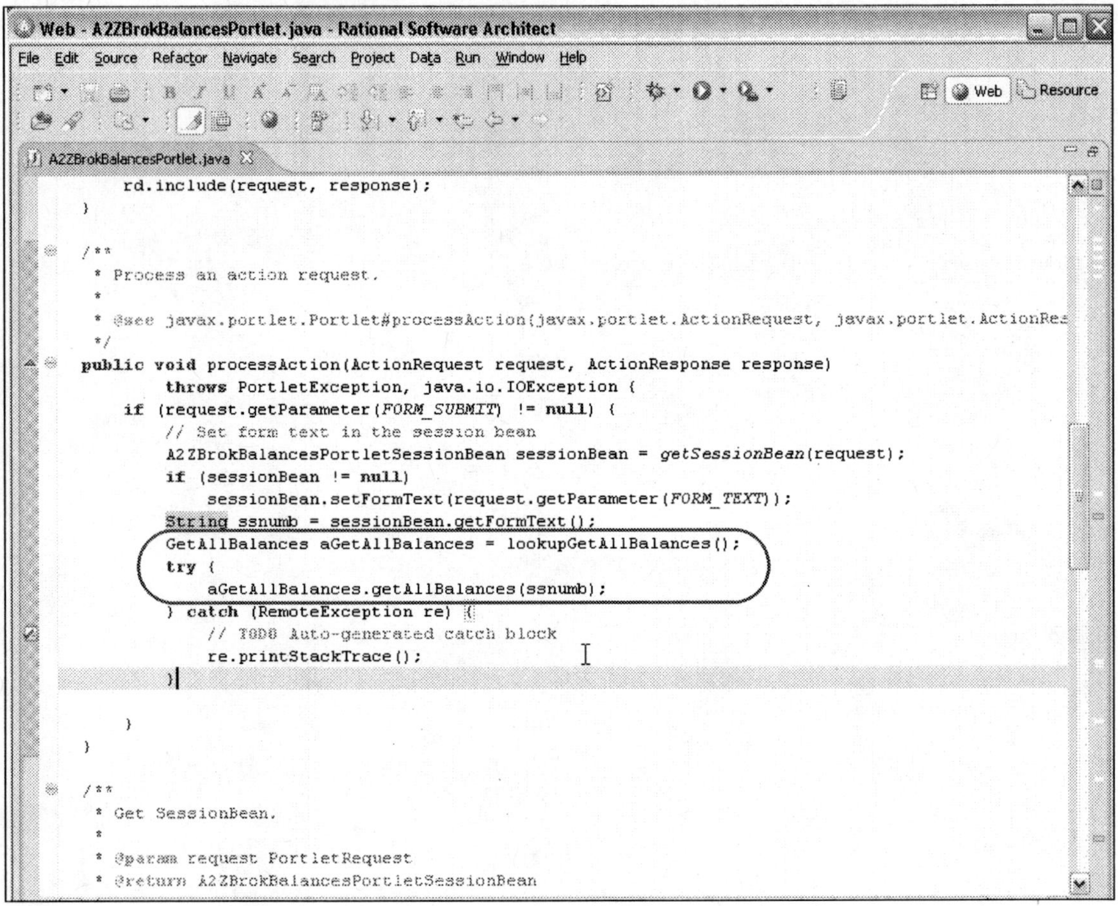
Web - A2ZBrokBalancesPortlet.java - Rational Software Architect
File Edit Source Refactor Navigate Search Project Data Run Window Help
Web
Resource
A2ZBrokBalancesPortlet.java
rd.include(request, response);
}
/**
* Process an action request.
*
* @see javax.portlet.Portlet#processAction(javax.portlet.ActionRequest, javax.portlet.ActionRes
*/
public void processAction(ActionRequest request, ActionResponse response)
throws PortletException, java.io.IOException {
if (request.getParameter(FORM_SUBMIT) != null) {
// Set form text in the session bean
A2ZBrokBalancesPortletSessionBean sessionBean = getSessionBean(request);
if (sessionBean != null)
sessionBean.setFormText(request.getParameter(FORM_TEXT));
String ssnumb = sessionBean.getFormText();
GetAllBalances aGetAllBalances = lookupGetAllBalances();
try {
aGetAllBalances.getAllBalances(ssnumb);
} catch (RemoteException re) {
// TODO Auto-generated catch block
re.printStackTrace();
}
}
}
/**
* Get SessionBean.
*
* @param request PortletRequest
* @return A2ZBrokBalancesPortletSessionBean

Figure 2-390 Create portlet A2ZBrokBalancesPortlet in A2ZPortlets project 5/6

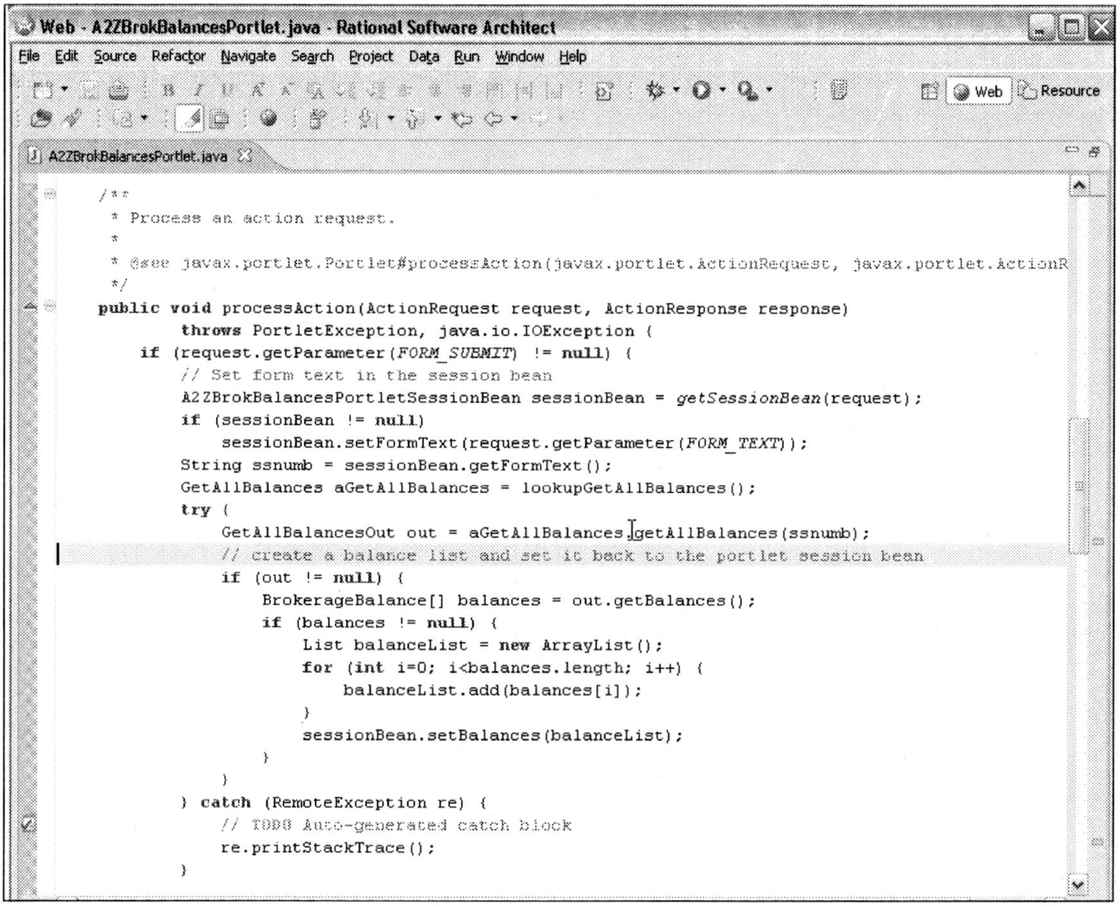

Figure 2-391   Create portlet A2ZBrokBalancesPortlet in A2ZPortlets project 6/6

Example 2-25   A2ZBrokBalancesPortlet portlet code

```java
package a2z.portlets;

import java.io.*;
import java.util.*;
import javax.portlet.*;
import com.ibm.etools.service.locator.ServiceLocatorManager;
import java.rmi.RemoteException;
import javax.xml.rpc.ServiceException;
import javax.xml.rpc.Service;
import A2Z_Library.GetAllBalances;
import A2Z_Library.GetAllBalancesOut;

/**
 * A sample portlet based on GenericPortlet
 */
public class A2ZBrokBalancesPortlet extends GenericPortlet {

    public static final String JSP_FOLDER = "/_A2ZBrokBalancesPortlet/jsp/"; // JSP folder name
```

```java
public static final String VIEW_JSP = "A2ZBrokBalancesPortletView"; // JSP file name to be rendered on the view mode

public static final String SESSION_BEAN = "A2ZBrokBalancesPortletSessionBean"; // Bean name for the portlet session

public static final String FORM_SUBMIT = "A2ZBrokBalancesPortletFormSubmit"; // Action name for submit form

public static final String FORM_TEXT = "A2ZBrokBalancesPortletFormText"; // Parameter name for the text input

private final static String STATIC_GetAllBalances_REF_NAME = "service/GetBalancesSOAP_GetAllBalancesHttpService";

private final static Class STATIC_GetAllBalances_CLASS = GetAllBalances.class;

/**
 * @see javax.portlet.Portlet#init()
 */
public void init() throws PortletException {
    super.init();
}

/**
 * Serve up the <code>view</code> mode.
 *
 * @see javax.portlet.GenericPortlet#doView(javax.portlet.RenderRequest,
 *      javax.portlet.RenderResponse)
 */
public void doView(RenderRequest request, RenderResponse response)
        throws PortletException, IOException {
    // Set the MIME type for the render response
    response.setContentType(request.getResponseContentType());

    // Check if portlet session exists
    A2ZBrokBalancesPortletSessionBean sessionBean = getSessionBean(request);
    if (sessionBean == null) {
        response.getWriter().println("<b>NO PORTLET SESSION YET</b>");
        return;
    }

    // Invoke the JSP to render
    PortletRequestDispatcher rd = getPortletContext().getRequestDispatcher(
            getJspFilePath(request, VIEW_JSP));
    rd.include(request, response);
}

/**
 * Process an action request.
 *
 * @see javax.portlet.Portlet#processAction(javax.portlet.ActionRequest,
 *      javax.portlet.ActionResponse)
 */
public void processAction(ActionRequest request, ActionResponse response)
        throws PortletException, java.io.IOException {
    if (request.getParameter(FORM_SUBMIT) != null) {
        // Set form text in the session bean
        A2ZBrokBalancesPortletSessionBean sessionBean = getSessionBean(request);
        if (sessionBean != null)
            sessionBean.setFormText(request.getParameter(FORM_TEXT));
        String ssnumb = sessionBean.getFormText();

        GetAllBalances aGetAllBalances = lookupGetAllBalances();
        try {
            GetAllBalancesOut out = aGetAllBalances.getAllBalances(ssnumb);
            if (out != null) {
                A2Z_Library.BrokerageBalance balances[] = out.getBalances();
                if (balances != null) {
                    List balanceList = new ArrayList();
                    for (int i = 0; i < balances.length; i++)
                        balanceList.add(balances[i]);

                    sessionBean.setBalances(balanceList);
                }
            }
        }
```

```java
            } catch (RemoteException re) {
                re.printStackTrace();
            }
        }
    }

    /**
     * Get SessionBean.
     *
     * @param request
     *            PortletRequest
     * @return A2ZBrokBalancesPortletSessionBean
     */
    private static A2ZBrokBalancesPortletSessionBean getSessionBean(
            PortletRequest request) {
        PortletSession session = request.getPortletSession();
        if (session == null)
            return null;
        A2ZBrokBalancesPortletSessionBean sessionBean = (A2ZBrokBalancesPortletSessionBean) session
                .getAttribute(SESSION_BEAN);
        if (sessionBean == null) {
            sessionBean = new A2ZBrokBalancesPortletSessionBean();
            session.setAttribute(SESSION_BEAN, sessionBean);
        }
        return sessionBean;
    }

    /**
     * Returns JSP file path.
     *
     * @param request
     *            Render request
     * @param jspFile
     *            JSP file name
     * @return JSP file path
     */
    private static String getJspFilePath(RenderRequest request, String jspFile) {
        String markup = request.getProperty("wps.markup");
        if (markup == null)
            markup = getMarkup(request.getResponseContentType());
        return JSP_FOLDER + markup + "/" + jspFile + "."
                + getJspExtension(markup);
    }

    /**
     * Convert MIME type to markup name.
     *
     * @param contentType
     *            MIME type
     * @return Markup name
     */
    private static String getMarkup(String contentType) {
        if ("text/vnd.wap.wml".equals(contentType))
            return "wml";
        else
            return "html";
    }

    /**
     * Returns the file extension for the JSP file
     *
     * @param markupName
     *            Markup name
     * @return JSP extension
     */
    private static String getJspExtension(String markupName) {
        return "jsp";
    }

    protected GetAllBalances lookupGetAllBalances() {
        try {
            Service locator = (Service) ServiceLocatorManager
```

```
                    .getServiceLookup(STATIC_GetAllBalances_REF_NAME,
                        STATIC_GetAllBalances_CLASS);
        GetAllBalances aGetAllBalances = (GetAllBalances) locator
                        .getPort(STATIC_GetAllBalances_CLASS);
        return aGetAllBalances;
    } catch (ServiceException re) {
        // TODO Auto-generated catch block
        re.printStackTrace();
        return null;
    }
}
}
```

Perform a trade (portlet)

The main aspects of this application are as follows:

▶ It executes on a portal server (swiss.itsosj.sanjose.ibm.com) distinct from IBM Information Server (radon.itsosj.sanjose.ibm.com) and WebSphere Process Server (lead.itsosj.sanjose.ibm.com).

▶ The IBM Information Server services (AuthorizationService, placeTradesService, and AuditService) were invoked using EJB bindings.

▶ The WID generated service PlaceTradeProcess aggregates these three IBM Information Server services, and is exposed with SCA binding.

> **Note:** RAD currently does not support access to services using SCA binding. Therefore, we created a session bean facade, which then invokes the PlaceTradeProcess WID generated service using the SCA API.

This is summarized here in Figure 2-392. The IBM Information Server and WID generated services implementation of the *perform a trade* business function are described here.

A2Z Financials Business Function (nile.itsosj.sanjose.ibm.com)	Information Server Services (radon.itsosj.sanjose.ibm.com)		WebSphere Integration Developer (lead.itsosj.sanjose.ibm.com)	
	Services	Binding	Services	Binding
Perform a trade (portlet)	AuthorizationService placeTradesService AuditService	EJB EJB EJB	PlaceTradeProcess	SCA using Façade Session Bean

Figure 2-392   Portlet invocation of perform a trade business function using RAD

The placing of a trade involves:

1. Checking whether the requester is authorized to place a trade
2. Placing a trade if authorized
3. Writing an audit log record

Perform a trade using IBM Information Server services

In this step, we develop and test a portal application that directly invokes IBM Information Server services using EJB binding.

The import of the CommonServicesApp_client.jar file (corresponding to EJB bindings) into the A2ZPortlets project has already been described in Figure 2-346 on page 346 through Figure 2-349 on page 349 along with adding a jar dependency in the dependent project. This is not repeated here.

The development of a new portlet (A2ZISPlaceTradePortlet) in the A2ZPortlets project, and the general settings are similar to those described in "Get Account balance using IBM Information Server services" on page 342. Therefore, it is not repeated here.

Example 2-26 on page 394 shows the JSP that invokes the A2ZISPlaceTradePortlet code (Example 2-27 on page 395) which in turn invokes a helper class A2ZISPlaceTradePortletAllEJB (Example 2-28 on page 397) which invokes the IBM Information Server services AuthorizationService, placeTradesService, and AuditService. All this code was manually written. We have highlighted the code in A2ZISPlaceTradePortlet that invokes the placeTrade method of the A2ZISPlaceTradePortletAllEJB helper class, and the invoking of the IBM Information Server services in the A2ZISPlaceTradePortletAllEJB helper class and import of the necessary classes.

Note: The process of deployment and test of the A2ZISPlaceTradePortlet is not repeated here, since it is identical to that described in "Get Account balance using IBM Information Server services" on page 342. Figure 2-394 on page 398 shows the user interface of the A2ZISPlaceTradePortlet portlet.

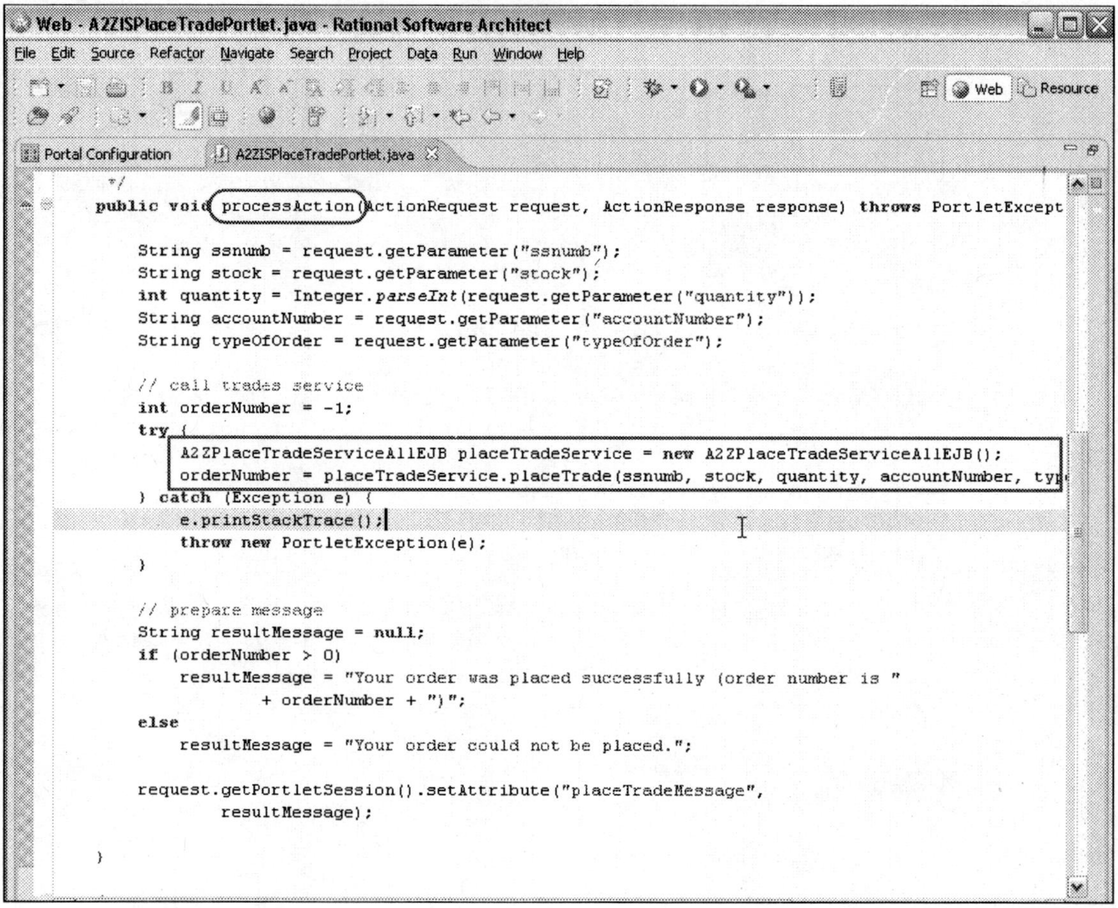

File Edit Source Refactor Navigate Search Project Data Run Window Help

Portal Configuration | A2ZISPlaceTradePortlet.java

```
public void processAction(ActionRequest request, ActionResponse response) throws PortletExcept

    String ssnumb = request.getParameter("ssnumb");
    String stock = request.getParameter("stock");
    int quantity = Integer.parseInt(request.getParameter("quantity"));
    String accountNumber = request.getParameter("accountNumber");
    String typeOfOrder = request.getParameter("typeOfOrder");

    // call trades service
    int orderNumber = -1;
    try {
        A2ZPlaceTradeServiceAllEJB placeTradeService = new A2ZPlaceTradeServiceAllEJB();
        orderNumber = placeTradeService.placeTrade(ssnumb, stock, quantity, accountNumber, typ
    } catch (Exception e) {
        e.printStackTrace();
        throw new PortletException(e);
    }

    // prepare message
    String resultMessage = null;
    if (orderNumber > 0)
        resultMessage = "Your order was placed successfully (order number is "
                + orderNumber + ")";
    else
        resultMessage = "Your order could not be placed.";

    request.getPortletSession().setAttribute("placeTradeMessage",
            resultMessage);

}
```

Figure 2-393   A2ZISPlaceTradePortlet

Example 2-26   A2ZISPlaceTradePortlet JSP

```
<%@page session="false" contentType="text/html" pageEncoding="ISO-8859-1" import="java.util.*,javax.portlet.*,a2z.portlets.*" %>
<%@taglib uri="http://java.sun.com/portlet" prefix="portlet" %>
<portlet:defineObjects/>

<%
    String resultMessage = (String) renderRequest.getPortletSession().getAttribute("placeTradeMessage");
%>

<DIV style="margin: 6px">

<H3 style="margin-bottom: 3px">Place a trade (Information Server)</H3><DIV style="margin: 12px; margin-bottom: 36px">
    <FORM method="POST" action="<portlet:actionURL/>">
    Your social security number: <INPUT name="ssnumb" type="text"/><br>
Your account number: <input type="text" name="accountNumber" size="20"><br>
Stock: <input type="text" name="stock" size="20"><br>
Quantity: <input type="text" name="quantity" size="20"><br>
TypeOfOrder: <select name="typeOfOrder">
    <option value="B" selected>Buy</option>
    <option value="S">Sell</option>
```

```
</select><br>
<br>
<br>
<INPUT name="<%=a2z.portlets.A2ZPlaceTradePortlet.FORM_SUBMIT%>" type="submit" value="Submit"/>
    </FORM>

<%= resultMessage != null ? "Result: " + resultMessage : ""   %>
</DIV>

</DIV>
```

Example 2-27   A2ZISPlaceTradePortlet portlet code

```java
package a2z.portlets;

import java.io.*;
import java.util.*;

import javax.ejb.CreateException;
import javax.portlet.*;
import javax.xml.rpc.ServiceException;

import a2z.web.services.A2ZPlaceTradeServiceAllEJB;

/**
 * A sample portlet based on GenericPortlet
 */
public class A2ZISPlaceTradePortlet extends GenericPortlet {

    public static final String JSP_FOLDER    = "/_A2ZISPlaceTradePortlet/jsp/";    // JSP folder name

    public static final String VIEW_JSP      = "A2ZISPlaceTradePortletView";        // JSP file name to be rendered on the view mode

    /**
     * @see javax.portlet.Portlet#init()
     */
    public void init() throws PortletException{
        super.init();
    }

    /**
     * Serve up the <code>view</code> mode.
     *
     * @see javax.portlet.GenericPortlet#doView(javax.portlet.RenderRequest, javax.portlet.RenderResponse)
     */
    public void doView(RenderRequest request, RenderResponse response) throws PortletException, IOException {
        // Set the MIME type for the render response
        response.setContentType(request.getResponseContentType());

        // Invoke the JSP to render
        PortletRequestDispatcher rd = getPortletContext().getRequestDispatcher(getJspFilePath(request, VIEW_JSP));
        rd.include(request,response);
    }

    /**
     * Process an action request.
     *
     * @see javax.portlet.Portlet#processAction(javax.portlet.ActionRequest, javax.portlet.ActionResponse)
     */
    public void processAction(ActionRequest request, ActionResponse response) throws PortletException, java.io.IOException {
        String ssnumb = request.getParameter("ssnumb");
        String stock = request.getParameter("stock");
        int quantity = Integer.parseInt(request.getParameter("quantity"));
        String accountNumber = request.getParameter("accountNumber");
        String typeOfOrder = request.getParameter("typeOfOrder");

        // call trades service
        int orderNumber = -1;
        try {
```

```java
            A2ZPlaceTradeServiceAllEJB placeTradeService = new A2ZPlaceTradeServiceAllEJB();
                orderNumber = placeTradeService.placeTrade(ssnumb, stock, quantity, accountNumber, typeOfOrder);
            } catch (Exception e) {
                e.printStackTrace();
                throw new PortletException(e);
            }

        // prepare message
        String resultMessage = null;
        if (orderNumber > 0)
            resultMessage = "Your order was placed successfully (order number is "
                    + orderNumber + ")";
        else
            resultMessage = "Your order could not be placed.";

        request.getPortletSession().setAttribute("placeTradeMessage",
                resultMessage);

    }

    /**
     * Returns JSP file path.
     *
     * @param request Render request
     * @param jspFile JSP file name
     * @return JSP file path
     */
    private static String getJspFilePath(RenderRequest request, String jspFile) {
        String markup = request.getProperty("wps.markup");
        if( markup == null )
            markup = getMarkup(request.getResponseContentType());
        return JSP_FOLDER + markup + "/" + jspFile + "." + getJspExtension(markup);
    }

    /**
     * Convert MIME type to markup name.
     *
     * @param contentType MIME type
     * @return Markup name
     */
    private static String getMarkup(String contentType) {
        if( "text/vnd.wap.wml".equals(contentType) )
            return "wml";
        else
            return "html";
    }

    /**
     * Returns the file extension for the JSP file
     *
     * @param markupName Markup name
     * @return JSP extension
     */
    private static String getJspExtension(String markupName) {
        return "jsp";
    }

}
```

Example 2-28   A2ZPlaceTradeServiceAllEJB helper class

```
package a2z.web.services;

import java.rmi.RemoteException;
import java.util.Calendar;

import javax.ejb.CreateException;
import javax.naming.Context;
import javax.naming.NamingException;
import javax.rmi.PortableRemoteObject;
import javax.xml.rpc.ServiceException;

import com.ibm.isd.BrokerageApp.TradesService.server.TradesServiceHome;
import com.ibm.isd.BrokerageApp.TradesService.server.TradesServiceRemote;

public class A2ZPlaceTradeServiceAllEJB extends A2ZPlaceTradeService {

    private TradesServiceHome tradesServiceHome;

    public A2ZPlaceTradeServiceAllEJB() throws NamingException {
        super();
    }
    /**
     * Invoke the placetrade service and place trade for the given inputs.
     *
     * @param ssnNumber
     * @param symbol
     * @param quantity
     * @param accountNumber
     * @param type
     * @return
     * @throws RemoteException
     * @throws CreateException
     * @throws ServiceException
     */
    public int placeTrade(String ssnNumber, String symbol, int quantity,
            String accountNumber, String type) throws RemoteException, CreateException, ServiceException {
        boolean authorized = authorize(ssnNumber);
        if (!authorized)
            return 0;

        Integer result = new Integer(-1);
        TradesServiceRemote tradesServiceRemote = tradesServiceHome.create();
        result = tradesServiceRemote.placeTrade(symbol, new Integer(quantity), type, Calendar.getInstance(), accountNumber);
        audit("Trade placed OrderNumber " , result.toString());
        return result.intValue();
    }
    /**
     * Cache the home objects.
     */
    protected Context lookupInformationServices() throws NamingException {
        Context isctx = super.lookupInformationServices();
        Object o = isctx.lookup("ejb/BrokerageApp/TradesService");
        tradesServiceHome = (TradesServiceHome) PortableRemoteObject.narrow(o, TradesServiceHome.class);
        return isctx;
    }
}
```

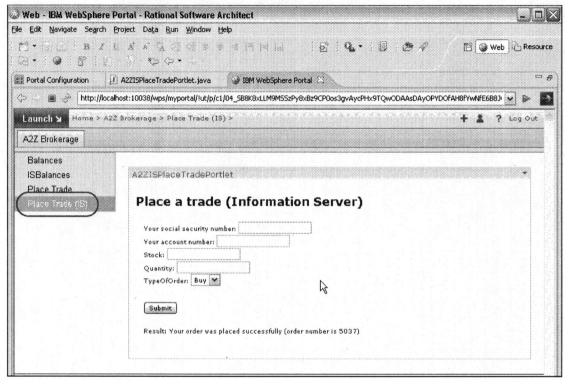

Figure 2-394   Test A2ZISPlaceTradePortlet

Perform a trade using WID generated services

In this step, we develop and test the same portal application described in "Perform a trade using IBM Information Server services" on page 393 by invoking a corresponding WID generated service PlaceTradeProcess that is exported with SCA binding. The portal application accesses the WID generated service using SCA binding via a session bean facade, since RAD currently does not support the SCA API.

> **Note:** Many of the steps are identical to those described in "Perform a trade using IBM Information Server services" on page 393. Therefore, we will not be repeating the steps related to portlet development, portal configuration and testing. We will include the import of the WID generated service, and show the completed portlet code.

We describe the following steps:

1. Figure 2-395 on page 400 shows the BPEL process that performs the perform a trade business function, and it includes the AuthorizationService, placeTradesService, and AuditService.

2. Figure 2-396 on page 400 through Figure 2-399 on page 403 describe the import of the A2ZEJB_BrokerageSCAAPIClient.jar file (corresponding to SCA bindings) into the A2ZPortletsEAR folder.

3. After launching RAD (not shown here), select **Import** from the File menu in Figure 2-396 on page 400.

4. Then select **File System** as the import source in Figure 2-397 on page 401, and click **Next**.

5. Specify the source directory (C:\Temp), select the **Temp** folder, check the box for A2ZEJB_BrokerageSCAAPIClient.jar, specify the destination folder (A2ZPortletsEar), and click **Finish** as shown in Figure 2-398 on page 402.

6. Next add a jar dependency in the dependent project by double-clicking MANIFEST.MF under Web Content → META-INF in Project Explorer in Figure 2-399 on page 403. Check the box A2ZEJB_BrokerageSCAAPIClient.jar to complete this action.

> **Note:** The creation of a new portlet (A2ZPlaceTradePortlet) in the A2ZPortlets, defining the general settings of the Basic Portlet type, modifying the JSP form is not repeated here since it is identical to that described in "Perform a trade using IBM Information Server services" on page 393.

7. Example 2-29 on page 403 shows the A2ZPlaceTradePortletSessionBean that stores portlet instance data in portlet session.

8. Example 2-31 on page 404 shows the A2ZPlaceTradePortlet portlet that invokes the BrokerageFacadeBean (Example 2-32 on page 407), which in turn invokes the WID PlaceTradeProcess service. All this code was manually written. We have highlighted the code particularly relevant to invoking the WID generated service, including the import of the necessary classes.

9. The JSP code that invokes the A2ZPlaceTradePortlet portlet is shown in Example 2-30 on page 404.

> **Note:** The deployment and test of the A2ZPlaceTradePortlet is not repeated here, since it is identical to the testing of the A2ZISPlaceTradePortlet.

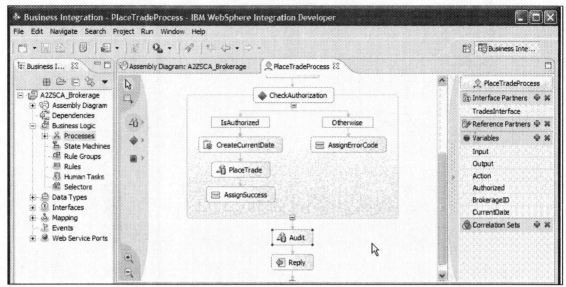

Figure 2-395   PlaceTradeProcess WID generated service

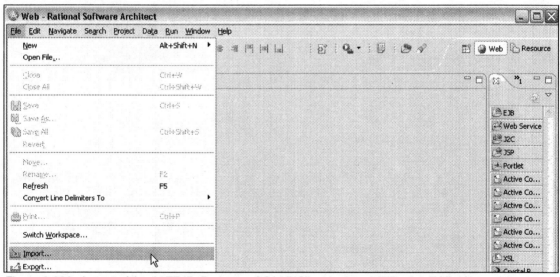

Figure 2-396   Import of the A2ZEJB_BrokerageSCAAPIClient.jar into A2ZPortletsEAR 1/4

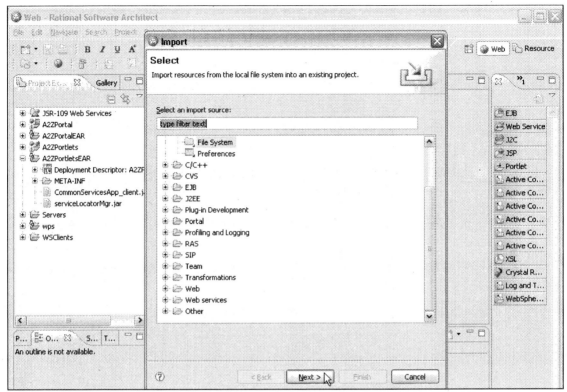

Figure 2-397   Import of the A2ZEJB_BrokerageSCAAPIClient.jar into A2ZPortletsEAR 2/4

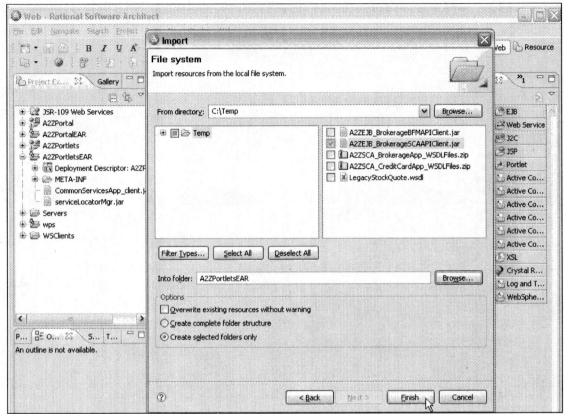

Figure 2-398   Import of the A2ZEJB_BrokerageSCAAPIClient.jar into A2ZPortletsEAR 3/4

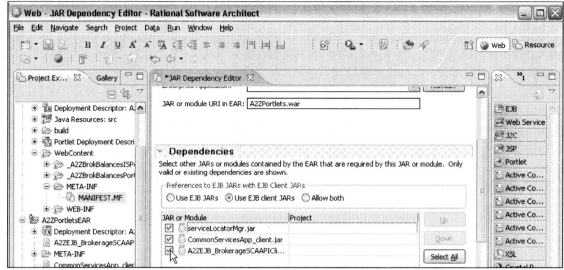

Figure 2-399   Import of the A2ZEJB_BrokerageSCAAPIClient.jar into A2ZPortletsEAR 4/4

Example 2-29   A2ZPlaceTradePortletSessionBean

```
package a2z.portlets;

/**
 *
 * A sample Java bean that stores portlet instance data in portlet session.
 *
 */
public class A2ZPlaceTradePortletSessionBean {

    /**
     * Last text for the text form
     */
    private String formText = "";

    /**
     * Set last text for the text form.
     *
     * @param formText last text for the text form.
     */
    public void setFormText(String formText) {
        this.formText = formText;
    }

    /**
     * Get last text for the text form.
     *
     * @return last text for the text form
     */
    public String getFormText() {
        return this.formText;
    }

}
```

Example 2-30   A2ZPlaceTradePortletView JSP

```
<%@page session="false" contentType="text/html" pageEncoding="ISO-8859-1" import="java.util.*,javax.portlet.*,a2z.portlets.*" %>
<%@taglib uri="http://java.sun.com/portlet" prefix="portlet" %>
<portlet:defineObjects/>

<%
    a2z.portlets.A2ZPlaceTradePortletSessionBean sessionBean =
(a2z.portlets.A2ZPlaceTradePortletSessionBean)renderRequest.getPortletSession().getAttribute(a2z.portlets.A2ZPlaceTradePortlet.SESS
ION_BEAN);
    String resultMessage = (String) renderRequest.getPortletSession().getAttribute("placeTradeMessage");
%>

<DIV style="margin: 6px">

<H3 style="margin-bottom: 3px">Place a trade (SCAFacadeAPI)</H3><DIV style="margin: 12px; margin-bottom: 36px">
    <FORM method="POST" action="<portlet:actionURL/>">
        <LABEL   for="<%=a2z.portlets.A2ZPlaceTradePortlet.FORM_TEXT%>">Your social security number:</LABEL> <INPUT
name="<%=a2z.portlets.A2ZPlaceTradePortlet.FORM_TEXT%>" type="text"/><br>
Your account number: <input type="text" name="accountNumber" size="20"><br>
Stock: <input type="text" name="stock" size="20"><br>
Quantity: <input type="text" name="quantity" size="20"><br>
TypeOfOrder: <select name="typeOfOrder">
    <option value="B" selected>Buy</option>
    <option value="S">Sell</option>
</select><br>
<br>
<br>
<INPUT name="<%=a2z.portlets.A2ZPlaceTradePortlet.FORM_SUBMIT%>" type="submit" value="Submit"/>
    </FORM>

<%= resultMessage != null ? "Result: " + resultMessage : ""   %>
</DIV>

</DIV>
```

Example 2-31   A2ZPlaceTradePortlet portlet

```
package a2z.portlets;

import java.io.IOException;
import java.util.Properties;

import javax.naming.Context;
import javax.naming.InitialContext;
import javax.naming.NamingException;
import javax.portlet.ActionRequest;
import javax.portlet.ActionResponse;
import javax.portlet.GenericPortlet;
import javax.portlet.PortletException;
import javax.portlet.PortletRequest;
import javax.portlet.PortletRequestDispatcher;
import javax.portlet.PortletSession;
import javax.portlet.RenderRequest;
import javax.portlet.RenderResponse;
import javax.rmi.PortableRemoteObject;

import a2z.BrokerageFacade;
import a2z.BrokerageFacadeHome;

/**
 * A sample portlet based on GenericPortlet
 */
public class A2ZPlaceTradePortlet extends GenericPortlet {

    public static final String JSP_FOLDER = "/_A2ZPlaceTradePortlet/jsp/"; // JSP folder name
    public static final String VIEW_JSP = "A2ZPlaceTradePortletView"; // JSP file name to be rendered on the view mode
    public static final String SESSION_BEAN = "A2ZPlaceTradePortletSessionBean"; // Bean name for the portlet session
    public static final String FORM_SUBMIT = "A2ZPlaceTradePortletFormSubmit"; // Action name for submit form
    public static final String FORM_TEXT = "A2ZPlaceTradePortletFormText"; // Parameter name for the text input
```

```java
private BrokerageFacadeHome brokerageFacadeHome;

/**
 * @see javax.portlet.Portlet#init()
 */
public void init() throws PortletException {
    super.init();
    Properties props = new Properties();
    props.put("java.naming.provider.url", "iiop://lead:2809");
    try {
        Context ctx = new InitialContext(props);
        Object o = ctx.lookup("ejb/a2z/BrokerageFacadeHome");
        brokerageFacadeHome = (BrokerageFacadeHome) PortableRemoteObject.narrow(o, a2z.BrokerageFacadeHome.class);
    } catch (NamingException e) {
        e.printStackTrace();
        throw new PortletException(e);
    }

}

/**
 * Serve up the <code>view</code> mode.
 *
 * @see javax.portlet.GenericPortlet#doView(javax.portlet.RenderRequest,
 *      javax.portlet.RenderResponse)
 */
public void doView(RenderRequest request, RenderResponse response)
        throws PortletException, IOException {
    // Set the MIME type for the render response
    response.setContentType(request.getResponseContentType());

    // Check if portlet session exists
    A2ZPlaceTradePortletSessionBean sessionBean = getSessionBean(request);
    if (sessionBean == null) {
        response.getWriter().println("<b>NO PORTLET SESSION YET</b>");
        return;
    }

    // Invoke the JSP to render
    PortletRequestDispatcher rd = getPortletContext().getRequestDispatcher(
            getJspFilePath(request, VIEW_JSP));
    rd.include(request, response);
}

/**
 * Process an action request.
 *
 * @see javax.portlet.Portlet#processAction(javax.portlet.ActionRequest,
 *      javax.portlet.ActionResponse)
 */
public void processAction(ActionRequest request, ActionResponse response)
        throws PortletException, java.io.IOException {
    if (request.getParameter(FORM_SUBMIT) != null) {
        // Set form text in the session bean
        A2ZPlaceTradePortletSessionBean sessionBean = getSessionBean(request);
        if (sessionBean != null)
            sessionBean.setFormText(request.getParameter(FORM_TEXT));
        // read parameters
        String ssnumb = sessionBean.getFormText();
        String stock = request.getParameter("stock");
        int quantity = Integer.parseInt(request.getParameter("quantity"));
        String accountNumber = request.getParameter("accountNumber");
        String typeOfOrder = request.getParameter("typeOfOrder");

        // lookup EJB and call ist
        int orderNumber = -1;
        try {
            BrokerageFacade brokerageFacade = brokerageFacadeHome.create();
            orderNumber = brokerageFacade.placeTrade(ssnumb, stock,quantity, accountNumber, typeOfOrder);
        } catch (Exception e) {
            e.printStackTrace();
```

```
        }

        // prepare message
        String resultMessage = null;
        if (orderNumber > 0)
            resultMessage = "Your order was placed successfully (order number is "+ orderNumber + ")";
        else
            resultMessage = "Your order could not be placed.";
        request.getPortletSession().setAttribute("placeTradeMessage",resultMessage);

    }
}

/**
 * Get SessionBean.
 *
 * @param request
 *            PortletRequest
 * @return A2ZPlaceTradePortletSessionBean
 */
private static A2ZPlaceTradePortletSessionBean getSessionBean(
        PortletRequest request) {
    PortletSession session = request.getPortletSession();
    if (session == null)
        return null;
    A2ZPlaceTradePortletSessionBean sessionBean = (A2ZPlaceTradePortletSessionBean) session
            .getAttribute(SESSION_BEAN);
    if (sessionBean == null) {
        sessionBean = new A2ZPlaceTradePortletSessionBean();
        session.setAttribute(SESSION_BEAN, sessionBean);
    }
    return sessionBean;
}

/**
 * Returns JSP file path.
 *
 * @param request
 *            Render request
 * @param jspFile
 *            JSP file name
 * @return JSP file path
 */
public static String getJspFilePath(RenderRequest request, String jspFile) {
    String markup = request.getProperty("wps.markup");
    if (markup == null)
        markup = getMarkup(request.getResponseContentType());
    return JSP_FOLDER + markup + "/" + jspFile + "."
            + getJspExtension(markup);
}

/**
 * Convert MIME type to markup name.
 *
 * @param contentType
 *            MIME type
 * @return Markup name
 */
private static String getMarkup(String contentType) {
    if ("text/vnd.wap.wml".equals(contentType))
        return "wml";
    else
        return "html";
}

/**
 * Returns the file extension for the JSP file
 *
 * @param markupName
 *            Markup name
 * @return JSP extension
 */
```

```
        private static String getJspExtension(String markupName) {
            return "jsp";
        }

}
```

Example 2-32   BrokerageFacadeBean session bean facade

```
package a2z;

import java.util.Date;

import com.ibm.websphere.sca.Service;
import com.ibm.websphere.sca.ServiceManager;
import com.ibm.websphere.sca.Ticket;
import com.ibm.websphere.sca.sdo.DataFactory;
import commonj.sdo.DataObject;

/**
 * Bean implementation class for Enterprise Bean: BrokerageFacade
 */
public class BrokerageFacadeBean implements javax.ejb.SessionBean {
    private javax.ejb.SessionContext mySessionCtx;
    /**
     * getSessionContext
     */
    public javax.ejb.SessionContext getSessionContext() {
        return mySessionCtx;
    }
    /**
     * setSessionContext
     */
    public void setSessionContext(javax.ejb.SessionContext ctx) {
        mySessionCtx = ctx;
    }
    /**
     * ejbCreate
     */
    public void ejbCreate() throws javax.ejb.CreateException {
    }
    /**
     * ejbActivate
     */
    public void ejbActivate() {
    }
    /**
     * ejbPassivate
     */
    public void ejbPassivate() {
    }
    /**
     * ejbRemove
     */
    public void ejbRemove() {
    }

    public int placeTrade(String ssnumb, String stock, int quantity,
            String accountNumber, String typeOfOrder) {
        // create input BO
        DataObject tradesInput = DataFactory.INSTANCE.create("http://A2ZSCA_Brokerage", "PlaceTradeInput");
        tradesInput.setString("ssnumb", ssnumb);
        tradesInput.setString("stock", stock);
        tradesInput.setInt("quantity", quantity);
        tradesInput.setString("accountNumber", accountNumber);
        tradesInput.setString("typeOfOrder", typeOfOrder);

        // lookup standalone reference
        ServiceManager serviceManager = ServiceManager.INSTANCE;
        Service tradesService = (Service) serviceManager.locateService("TradesInterfacePartner");
        DataObject operationResult = (DataObject) tradesService.invoke("placeTrade", tradesInput);
```

```
            // get value from result BO
            DataObject tradesOutput = operationResult.getDataObject("output");
            int result = tradesOutput.getInt("orderNumber");
            return result;  '
        }
.........................
}
```

2.9.2 Microsoft Visual Studio 2005 Professional Edition

Now we demonstrate the development and testing of a client application accessing IBM Information Server and WebSphere Integration Developer generated services using SOAP over HTTP in the .NET environment. A thick client environment, and a thin client environment are described here.

Thick client

In this environment, a visual basic client application invokes the Update Credit Card customer business function implemented using WebSphere Integration Developer services. Figure 2-400 on page 408 shows the aggregate WID generated service invoked by the visual basic application.

A2Z Financials Business Function	WebSphere Integration Developer
	Services (SOAP over HTTP only)
Update Credit Card customer (Thick client)	UpdateCustomer_UpdateCustomerInfoProcessHttpService

Figure 2-400   Thick client visual basic application using Visual Studio .NET

Figure 2-401 on page 409 through Figure 2-410 on page 414 describe the main steps in developing and testing the thick client application:

1. After launching Visual Studio (not shown here), create a project named A2ZCSR in location C:\Net Projects and Solution Name (A2ZCSR) for creating an application with a Windows user interface as shown in Figure 2-401 on page 409, and click **OK**.

2. Click **Add Web Reference** in the Solution Explorer for A2ZCSR in Figure 2-402 on page 410.

3. Then type in the URL where the Web services are to be found (http://lead.itsosj.sanjose.ibm.com:9080/A2ZSCA_CreditCardWeb/sca/UpdateCustomer?wsdl) and click **Go** as shown in Figure 2-403 on page 410.

4. One service is found, as shown in Figure 2-404 on page 411.

5. Modify the Web reference name (UpdateCustomer) from the default and click **Add Reference** which makes it available to this application. Next create the user interface form with controls as shown in Figure 2-405 on page 411.

6. Select the UpdateCustomer button and define the action to be taken when it is clicked as shown in Figure 2-406 on page 412 and Figure 2-407 on page 413. The UpdateButton_Click code defines the action to be taken when the UpdateCustomer button is clicked.

> **Note:** A portion of the code is shown in Example 2-33 on page 414, where the single WID generated service is initialized and invoked as highlighted (UpdateCustomer_UpdateCustomerInfoProcessHttpService).

7. To test the code, select Start Without Debugging from the Debug menu as shown in Figure 2-408 on page 413.

8. Provide details about a customer and click the **UpdateCustomer** button as shown in Figure 2-409 on page 414 to view the successful update message shown in Figure 2-410 on page 414.

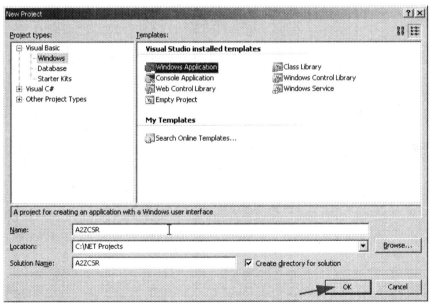

Figure 2-401   Thick client visual basic application 1/10

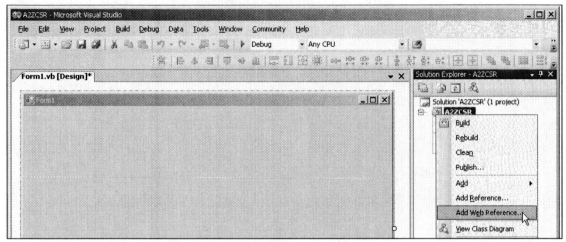

Figure 2-402   Thick client visual basic application 2/10

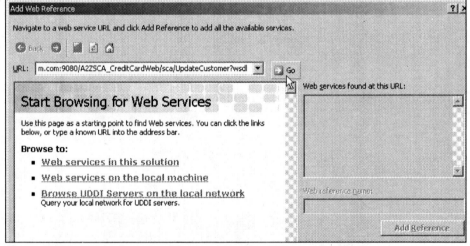

Figure 2-403   Thick client visual basic application 3/10

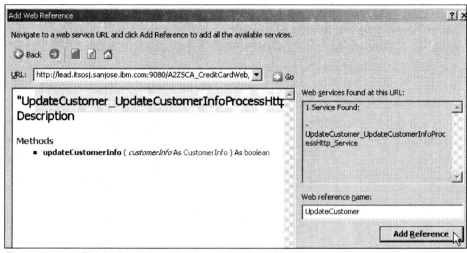

Figure 2-404   Thick client visual basic application 4/10

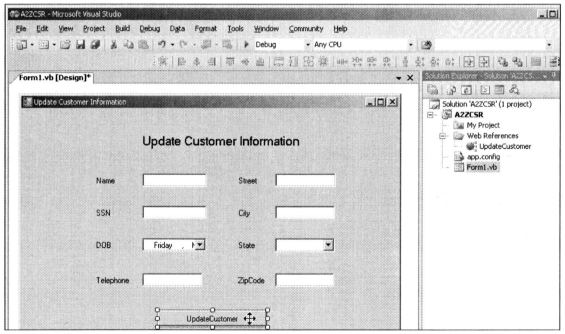

Figure 2-405   Thick client visual basic application 5/10

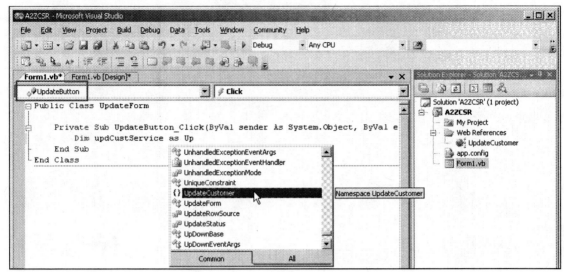

Figure 2-406   Thick client visual basic application 6/10

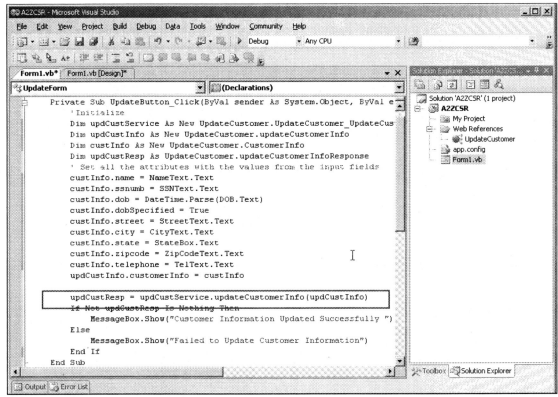

Figure 2-407   Thick client visual basic application 7/10

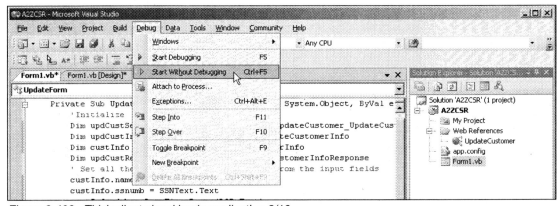

Figure 2-408   Thick client visual basic application 8/10

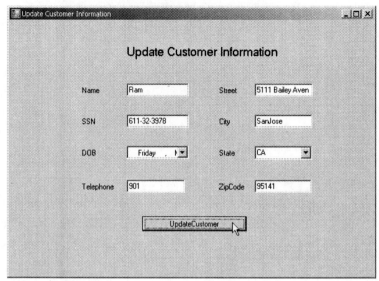

Figure 2-409   Thick client visual basic application 9/10

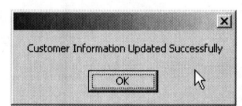

Figure 2-410   Thick client visual basic application 10/10

Example 2-33   Thick client visual basic application code

```
Public Class UpdateForm
    Private Sub UpdateButton_Click(ByVal sender As System.Object, ByVal e As System.EventArgs) Handles UpdateButton.Click
        invokeWIDServices()
    End Sub

    ' This method will invoke the BPEL process soap/http binding web service.
    Protected Sub invokeWIDServices()
        'Initialize
        Dim updCustService As New UpdateCustomer.UpdateCustomer_UpdateCustomerInfoProcessHttpService
        Dim updCustInfo As New UpdateCustomer.updateCustomerInfo
        Dim custInfo As New UpdateCustomer.CustomerInfo
        Dim updCustResp As UpdateCustomer.updateCustomerInfoResponse
        ' Set all the attributes with the values from the input fields
        custInfo.name = NameText.Text
        custInfo.ssnumb = SSNText.Text
        custInfo.dob = DateTime.Parse(DOB.Text)
        custInfo.dobSpecified = True
        custInfo.street = StreetText.Text
        custInfo.city = CityText.Text
        custInfo.state = StateBox.Text
        custInfo.zipcode = ZipCodeText.Text
```

```
        custInfo.telephone = TelText.Text
        updCustInfo.customerInfo = custInfo

        updCustResp = updCustService.updateCustomerInfo(updCustInfo)
        If Not updCustResp Is Nothing Then
            MessageBox.Show("Customer Information Updated Successfully ")
        Else
            MessageBox.Show("Failed to Update Customer Information")
        End If
    End Sub

    Protected Sub AlertError(ByVal message As String)
        MessageBox.Show(message, "Error", MessageBoxButtons.OK, MessageBoxIcon.Error)
    End Sub

    Protected Sub AlertInfo(ByVal message As String)
        MessageBox.Show(message, "Information", MessageBoxButtons.OK, MessageBoxIcon.Information)
    End Sub

End Class
```

Thin Client with create library (.dll)

In this environment an Active Server Pages (ASP) is developed that invokes the Get Credit Card transactions (WID generated service only) and Update Credit Card customer (IBM Information Server and WID generated services) business functions as shown in Figure 2-411 on page 415.

When multiple Web services may be invoked by multiple client applications, it is desirable to create a single library (.dll) of all these services which are reused by all the applications.

In this section, we describe the creation of a library (.dll) of Web services, and the development of an ASP that invokes WID generated or IBM Information Server services.

A2Z Financials Business Function	Information Server Services	WebSphere Integration Developer
	Services (SOAP over HTTP only)	Services (SOAP over HTTP only)
Get Credit Card transactions (Thin client)		GetTransactions_GetCreditCardTransactionsHttpService
Update Credit Card customer (Thin client)	CustomerIDLookupService AuthorizationService StandardizeAddressService CardMaintenanceService AuditService	UpdateCustomer_UpdateCustomerInfoProcessHttpService

Figure 2-411   Client types, business functions and service types developed using Visual Studio .NET

Create a library (.dll) of A2ZFinancialServices Web services

Figure 2-412 on page 416 through Figure 2-418 on page 419 show the main steps in creating a library (.dll) of Web Services references used in the A2Z Financial Services self service solution:

1. After launching Visual Studio (not shown here), select New and Project from the File menu as shown in Figure 2-412 on page 416.

2. Create a project for creating a VB class library (.dll) by selecting Windows and Class library as shown in Figure 2-413 on page 417.

3. Also provide details such as project Name (A2ZFinancialServices), Location (C:\NET Projects) and Solution Name (A2ZFinancialServices) and check the Create directory for solution box.

4. Click **OK**. After deleting the default class Class1.vb (not shown here), click **Add Web Reference** in the A2ZFinancialServices solution as shown in Figure 2-414 on page 417.

5. Then type in the URL where the Web services are to be found (http://lead.itsosj.sanjose.ibm.com:9080/A2ZSCA_CreditCardWeb/sca/GetTransactions?wsdl) and click **Go** as shown in Figure 2-415 on page 418.

6. One service is found as shown in Figure 2-416 on page 418.

7. Modify the Web reference name (CardTransactions) from the default and click **Add Reference**, which makes it available to this application. All the other Web references of interest to the A2ZFinancialServices self service solution need to be added as well (not shown here).

8. After that, select Build A2ZFinancialServices from the Build menu as shown in Figure 2-417 on page 418 — the results of this build (A2ZFinancialServices.dll) are shown in Figure 2-418 on page 419. Select **Close Solution** from the File menu.

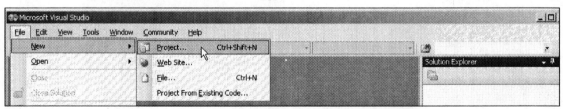

Figure 2-412   Create a library (.dll) of A2ZFinancialServices Web services 1/7

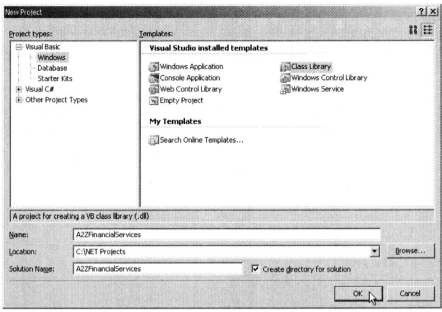

Figure 2-413   Create a library (.dll) of A2ZFinancialServices Web services 2/7

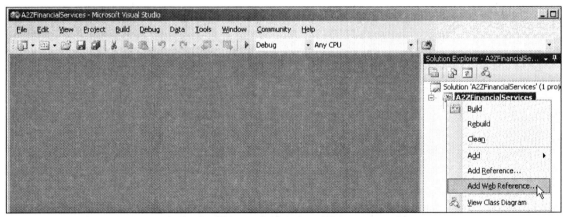

Figure 2-414   Create a library (.dll) of A2ZFinancialServices Web services 3/7

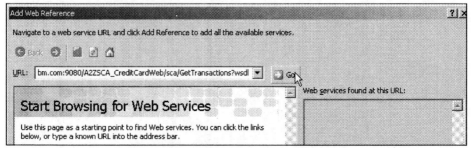

Figure 2-415   Create a library (.dll) of A2ZFinancialServices Web services 4/7

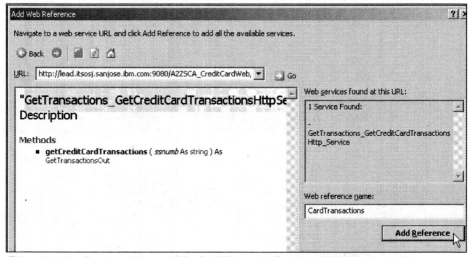

Figure 2-416   Create a library (.dll) of A2ZFinancialServices Web services 5/7

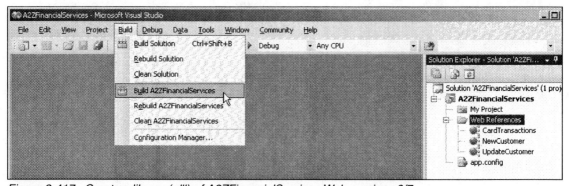

Figure 2-417   Create a library (.dll) of A2ZFinancialServices Web services 6/7

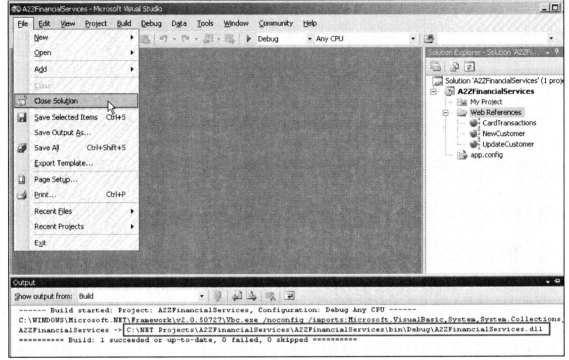

Figure 2-418   Create a library (.dll) of A2ZFinancialServices Web services 7/7

Develop and test an ASP

Next, we develop the ASP that will execute on a Microsoft IIS, and test it.

Figure 2-419 on page 420 through Figure 2-424 on page 424 show the development of an ASP (GetTrans) that will be invoked from a Web browser, while Figure 2-425 on page 427 through Figure 2-430 on page 429 show the testing of this ASP.

Develop an ASP as follows:

1. After launching Visual Studio .NET, select **New** and **Web Site** from the File menu as shown in Figure 2-419 on page 420.

2. Select the Visual Studio ASP.NET Web Site installed template, and provide details of its Location (File System and C:\Net Projects\A2ZWeb) and Language (Visual Basic®) in Figure 2-420 on page 421, and click **OK**.

3. In the Solution Explorer, select the Default.aspx in the newly created Web site, and select **Add Reference** from the Web site menu as shown in Figure 2-421 on page 421.

4. Click the **Browse** tab and select the **A2ZFinancialServices.dll** (defined earlier in "Thin Client with create library (.dll)" on page 415) as shown in Figure 2-422 on page 422.

5. Click **OK**. Build the user interface using controls for the ASP (GetTrans.aspx) as shown in Figure 2-423 on page 423.

6. The action to be taken on the form is developed in GetTrans.aspx.vb as shown in Figure 2-424 on page 424.

7. The entire code is shown in Example 2-34 on page 424. It includes code that either invokes IBM Information Server services (invokeISServices()) or WID generated services (invokeWIDServices()) depending upon whether the box, Use Information Server Directly, is checked in the form (see Figure 2-429 on page 429).

8. The highlighted code in Example 2-34 on page 424 shows the initialization and invocation of the IBM Information Server and WID generated services.

> **Attention:** This ASP code clearly shows the economy of application development code when invoking an aggregated (WID) service where only one invocation is required, as compared to invoking each individual (IBM Information Server) service to achieve the desired business function. The invocation process for a single service using the same binding is identical whether WID or an IBM Information Server service is invoked.

We can now test the GetTrans ASP we just developed.

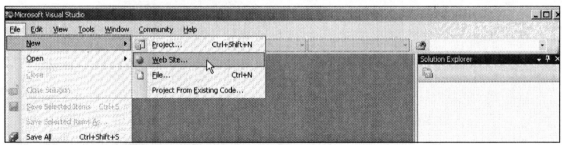

Figure 2-419   Develop thin client ASP 1/6

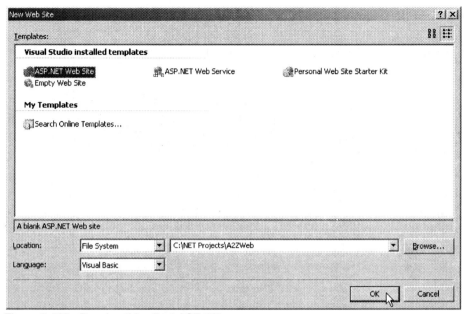

Figure 2-420   Develop thin client ASP 2/6

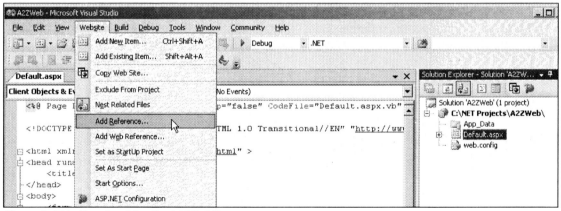

Figure 2-421   Develop thin client ASP 3/6

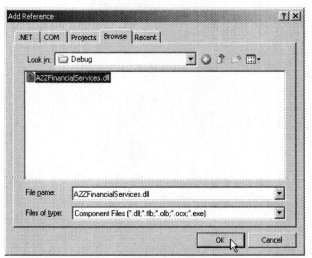

Figure 2-422   Develop thin client ASP 4/6

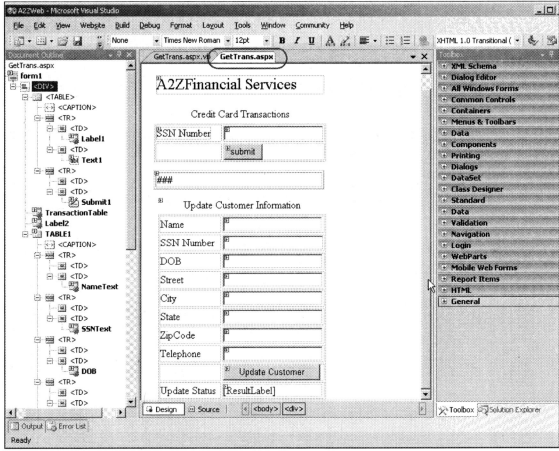

Figure 2-423   Develop thin client ASP 5/6

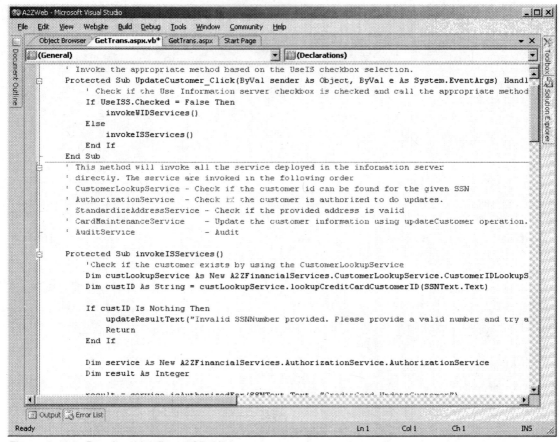

Figure 2-424 Develop thin client ASP 6/6

Example 2-34 Thin client ASP code

```
Partial Class GetTrans
    Inherits System.Web.UI.Page
    ' Invoke the appropriate method based on the UseIS checkbox selection.
    Protected Sub UpdateCustomer_Click(ByVal sender As Object, ByVal e As System.EventArgs) Handles UpdateCustomer.Click
        ' Check if the Use Information server checkbox is checked and call the appropriate method
        If UseISS.Checked = False Then
            invokeWIDServices()
        Else
            invokeISServices()
        End If
    End Sub
    ' This method will invoke all the service deployed in the information server
    ' directly. The service are invoked in the following order
    ' CustomerLookupService - Check if the customer id can be found for the given SSN
    ' AuthorizationService  - Check if the customer is authorized to do updates.
    ' StandardizeAddressService - Check if the provided address is valid
    ' CardMaintenanceService    - Update the customer information using updateCustomer operation.
    ' AuditService          - Audit

    Protected Sub invokeISServices()
```

```
    'Check if the customer exists by using the CustomerLookupService
    Dim custLookupService As New A2ZFinancialServices.CustomerLookupService.CustomerIDLookupService
    Dim custID As String = custLookupService.lookupCreditCardCustomerID(SSNText.Text)
    If custID Is Nothing Then
        updateResultText("Invalid SSNNumber provided. Please provide a valid number and try again")
        Return
    End If
    Dim service As New A2ZFinancialServices.AuthorizationService.AuthorizationService
    Dim result As Integer
    result = service.isAuthorizedFor(SSNText.Text, "CreditCard_UpdateCustomer")
    If result = 1 Then
        ' Call the Address Standardization service and check the address
        Dim stdAddressService As New A2ZFinancialServices.StandardizeAddressService.StandardizeAddressService
        Dim standardizedAddress As A2ZFinancialServices.StandardizeAddressService.StandardizedAddress
        standardizedAddress = stdAddressService.standardizeAddress(StreetText.Text, CityText.Text, State.Text,
ZipCodeText.Text)

        If Not standardizedAddress Is Nothing Then
            'Call the update customer service directly
            Dim updateService As New A2ZFinancialServices.CardMaintenanceService.CardMaintenanceService
            Dim DOBDate As Date
            DOBDate = DateTime.Parse(DOB.Text)
            updateService.updateCustomer(custID, NameText.Text, standardizedAddress.street, standardizedAddress.city,
standardizedAddress.state, standardizedAddress.zipcode, SSNText.Text, DOBDate, TelephoneText.Text)
            ' Audit the success information
            Dim auditService As New A2ZFinancialServices.AuditService.AuditService
            auditService.audit("CreditCard", "Customer information updated for customer with SSN " & SSNText.Text)
            'Update the result label with the success message
            updateResultText("The customer information was updated successfully")
        Else
            updateResultText("The address is incorrect. Please correct the errors and try again")
        End If
    Else
        updateResultText("You are not authorized to perform this operation")
    End If
End Sub
' This method will invoke the BPEL process soap/http binding web service.
Protected Sub invokeWIDServices()
    Dim service As New A2ZFinancialServices.UpdateCustomer.UpdateCustomer_UpdateCustomerInfoProcessHttpService
    Dim updateCustInfo As New A2ZFinancialServices.UpdateCustomer.updateCustomerInfo
    Dim custInfo As New A2ZFinancialServices.UpdateCustomer.CustomerInfo
    Dim response As A2ZFinancialServices.UpdateCustomer.updateCustomerInfoResponse

    custInfo.name = NameText.Text
    custInfo.ssnumb = SSNText.Text
    custInfo.dob = DateTime.Parse(DOB.Text)
    custInfo.dobSpecified = True
    custInfo.street = StreetText.Text
    custInfo.city = CityText.Text
    custInfo.state = State.Text
    custInfo.zipcode = ZipCodeText.Text
    custInfo.telephone = TelephoneText.Text
    updateCustInfo.customerInfo = custInfo
    response = service.updateCustomerInfo(updateCustInfo)
    If Not response Is Nothing Then
        ResultLabel.Text = response.response.Value
    End If
End Sub
Protected Sub PopulateTransactions(ByVal response As
A2ZFinancialServices.CardTransactions.getCreditCardTransactionsResponse)
    Dim row As TableRow
    Dim headerRow As New TableHeaderRow
    If response.result.transactions.Length <> 0 Then
        Dim columns() As String = {"Amount", "TransactionDate"}
        PopulateHeader(columns, headerRow)
        TransactionTable.Rows.Add(headerRow)
    End If
```

```
        ' Iterate through a collection
        For Each transaction As A2ZFinancialServices.CardTransactions.CreditCardTransaction In
response.result.transactions
            row = New TableRow()
            Dim col1, col2 As New TableCell()
            col1.Text = transaction.amount
            col2.Text = transaction.date
            row.Cells.Add(col1)
            row.Cells.Add(col2)
            TransactionTable.Rows.Add(row)
        Next

    End Sub
    Protected Sub PopulateHeader(ByVal cols As String(), ByVal TableRow As TableRow)
        Dim column As TableHeaderCell
        ' Iterate through a collection
        For Each col As String In cols
            column = New TableHeaderCell
            column.Text = col
            TableRow.Cells.Add(column)
        Next
    End Sub
    Protected Sub updateResultText(ByVal text As String)
        ResultLabel.Text = text
    End Sub
    Protected Sub Submit1_ServerClick(ByVal sender As Object, ByVal e As System.EventArgs) Handles Submit1.ServerClick
        Dim service As New A2ZFinancialServices.CardTransactions.GetTransactions_GetCreditCardTransactionsHttpService()
        Dim transactions As New A2ZFinancialServices.CardTransactions.getCreditCardTransactions()
        Dim response As A2ZFinancialServices.CardTransactions.getCreditCardTransactionsResponse

        transactions.ssnumb = Text1.Value
        response = service.getCreditCardTransactions(transactions)

        ' Process the response
        If Not response Is Nothing Then
            PopulateTransactions(response)
        End If
    End Sub
End Class
```

Test the GetTrans ASP as follows:

Figure 2-425 on page 427 through Figure 2-430 on page 429 show the test of the ASP:

1. Select **Build WebSite** from the Build menu as shown in Figure 2-425 on page 427.

2. Right-click the form for **GetTrans.apx** and select **View in Browser** as shown in Figure 2-426 on page 427.

3. Provide the SSN Number (611-32-3978) and click **Submit** in Figure 2-427 on page 428 to view credit card transactions as shown in Figure 2-428 on page 428.

4. Check the box, **Use Information server Directly**, provide customer information to update, and click the **Update Customer** button as shown in Figure 2-429 on page 429.

5. The successful update message is indicated in Figure 2-430 on page 429.

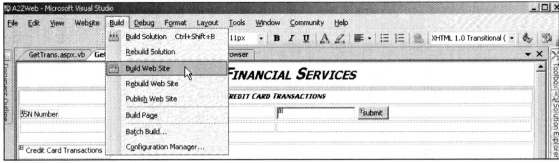
Figure 2-425   Test the thin client ASP 1/6

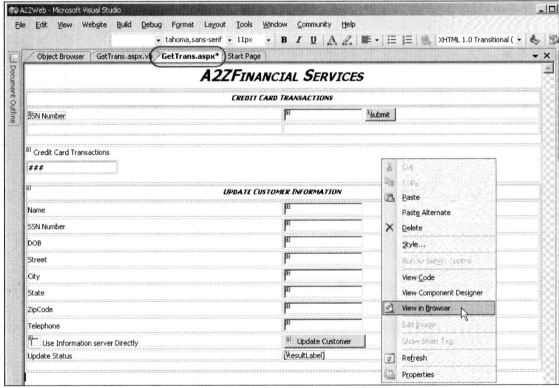
Figure 2-426   Test the thin client ASP 2/6

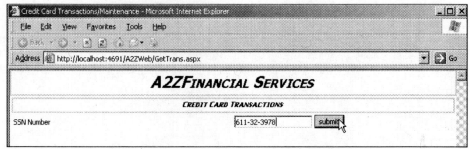

Figure 2-427   Test the thin client ASP 3/6

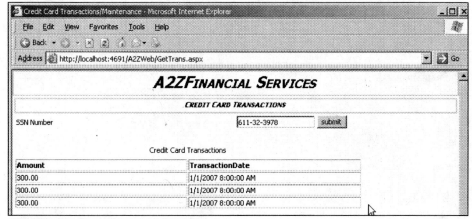

Figure 2-428   Test the thin client ASP 4/6

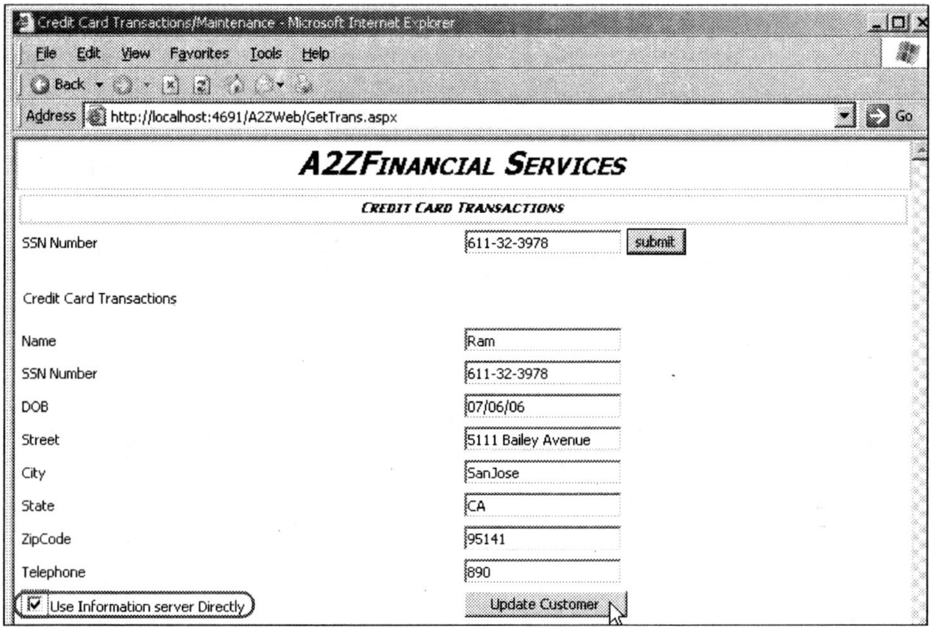

Figure 2-429   Test the thin client ASP 5/6

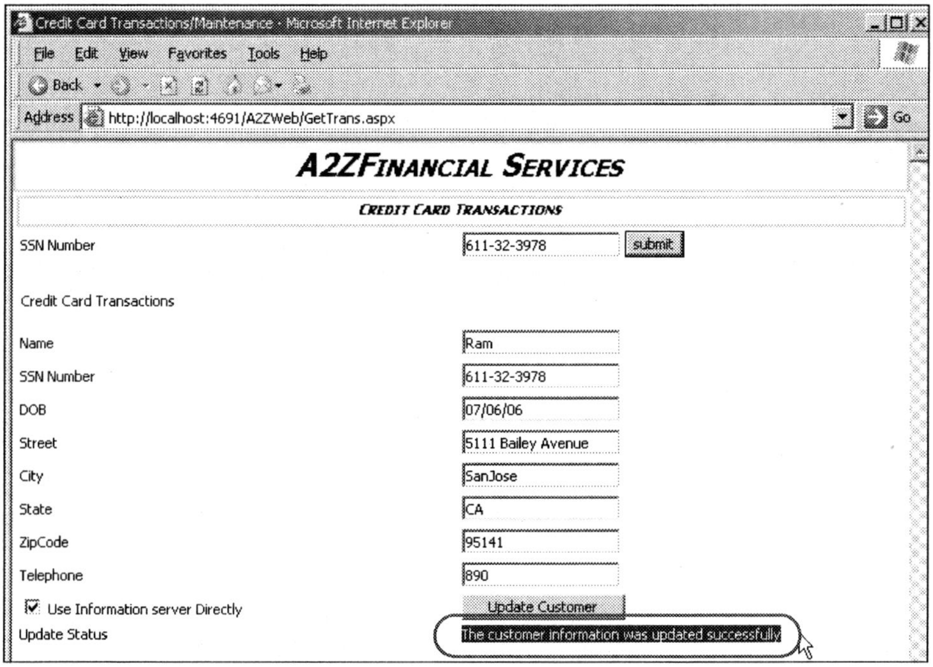

Figure 2-430   Test the thin client ASP 6/6

2.9.3 WebSphere Integration Developer

Besides the aggregation service capability, and JMS binding support, a WID generated service can be invoke asynchronously as well:

1. In this section we show the code in a session bean facade that asynchronously invokes the *Update brokerage customer* (WID generated service) business function, as shown in Figure 2-431 on page 430.

A2Z Financials Business Function	WebSphere Integration Developer	
	Services	Binding
Update Brokerage customer	UpdateBrokerageProfileProcess	Session Bean Façade to ASYNC SCA API

Figure 2-431   Client types, business functions and service types developed using WID ASYNC

2. Figure 2-432 on page 431 through Figure 2-433 on page 432 provide a very high level view of the process of creating a standalone reference to the UpdateBrokerageProfileProcess by an Add Wire connect as shown in Figure 2-432 on page 431. It shows the references associated with this Stand-alone Reference — specifically the one we just created named UpdateBrokerageProfilePartner.

3. A session bean facade BrokerageFacade is then created in EJB Projects for A2Z_BrokerageSCAAPI as shown in Figure 2-433 on page 432 which has to be modified appropriately.

4. The entire code is shown in Example 2-35 on page 433. The highlighted code shows the imported SCA classes, and the use of the locator to lookup the standalone reference, and the invocation of the *invokeasync* method.

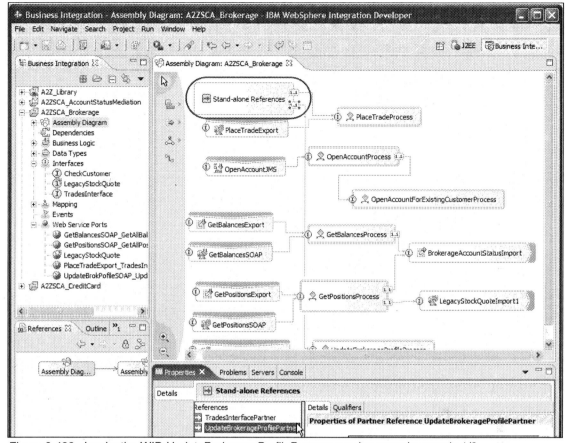

Figure 2-432   Invoke the WID UpdateBrokerageProfileProcess service asynchronously 1/2

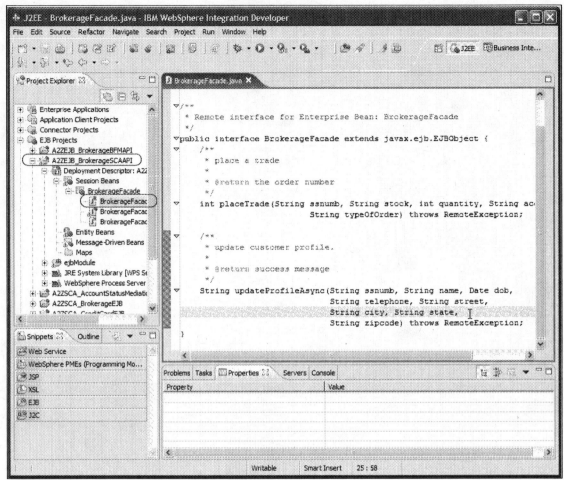

Figure 2-433   Invoke the WID UpdateBrokerageProfileProcess service asynchronously 2/2

```
package a2z;

import java.util.Date;
import com.ibm.websphere.sca.Service;
import com.ibm.websphere.sca.ServiceManager;
import com.ibm.websphere.sca.Ticket;
import com.ibm.websphere.sca.sdo.DataFactory;
import commonj.sdo.DataObject;

/**
 * Bean implementation class for Enterprise Bean: BrokerageFacade
 */
public class BrokerageFacadeBean implements javax.ejb.SessionBean {
    private javax.ejb.SessionContext mySessionCtx;
    /**
     * getSessionContext
     */
    public javax.ejb.SessionContext getSessionContext() {
        return mySessionCtx;
    }
    /**
     * setSessionContext
     */
    public void setSessionContext(javax.ejb.SessionContext ctx) {
        mySessionCtx = ctx;
    }
    /**
     * ejbCreate
     */
    public void ejbCreate() throws javax.ejb.CreateException {
    }
    /**
     * ejbActivate
     */
    public void ejbActivate() {
    }
    /**
     * ejbPassivate
     */
    public void ejbPassivate() {
    }
    /**
     * ejbRemove
     */
    public void ejbRemove() {
    }

    public int placeTrade(String ssnumb, String stock, int quantity,
            String accountNumber, String typeOfOrder) {
        // create input BO
        DataObject tradesInput = DataFactory.INSTANCE.create(
                "http://A2ZSCA_Brokerage", "PlaceTradeInput");
        tradesInput.setString("ssnumb", ssnumb);
        tradesInput.setString("stock", stock);
        tradesInput.setInt("quantity", quantity);
        tradesInput.setString("accountNumber", accountNumber);
        tradesInput.setString("typeOfOrder", typeOfOrder);

        // lookup standalone reference
        ServiceManager serviceManager = ServiceManager.INSTANCE;
        Service tradesService = (Service) serviceManager
                .locateService("TradesInterfacePartner");
        DataObject operationResult = (DataObject) tradesService.invoke(
                "placeTrade", tradesInput);
```

```
        // get value from result BO
        DataObject tradesOutput = operationResult.getDataObject("output");
        int result = tradesOutput.getInt("orderNumber");
        return result;
    }

    public String updateProfileAsync(String ssnumb, String name, Date dob,
                    String telephone, String street,
                    String city, String state,
                    String zipcode) {
        // create input customer info BO
        DataObject customerInfo = DataFactory.INSTANCE.create("http://A2Z_Library", "CustomerInfo");
        customerInfo.setString("name", name);
        customerInfo.setString("ssnumb", ssnumb);
        customerInfo.setDate("dob", dob);
        customerInfo.setString("telephone", telephone);
        customerInfo.setString("street", street);
        customerInfo.setString("city", city);
        customerInfo.setString("state", state);
        customerInfo.setString("zipcode", zipcode);

        // lookup standalone reference
        ServiceManager serviceManager = ServiceManager.INSTANCE;
        Service updateProfileService = (Service) serviceManager.locateService("UpdateBrokerageProfilePartner");
        Ticket ticket = updateProfileService.invokeAsync("updateProfile", customerInfo);

        // wait for 5 seconds max
        Object operationResult = updateProfileService.invokeResponse(ticket, 5000);

        // get value from result BO
        DataObject updateProfileOutput = (DataObject) operationResult;
        String result = updateProfileOutput.getString("message");
        return result;
    }

}
```

Service Oriented Architecture (SOA) overview

In this appendix, we provide an overview of Service Oriented Architecture (SOA) for an audience of Information Management specialists.

The topics covered include:

- ▶ Service-oriented architecture overview
- ▶ Web services architecture
- ▶ Web services and SOA
- ▶ Enterprise Service Bus

A.1 Service-oriented architecture overview

In this appendix, we briefly describe the evolution of service-oriented architecture (SOA). We then explore the relationship between component-based development and service-oriented architecture and show how components can be the cornerstones of the infrastructure for implementing services.

A.1.1 The business drivers for a new approach

While IT executives have been facing the challenge of cutting costs and maximizing the utilization of existing technology, they have to simultaneously strive to serve customers better, be more competitive, and be more responsive to their business' strategic priorities.

The two major challenges are heterogeneity and change, as follows:

► Heterogeneity:

 Most enterprises today contain a range of different systems, applications, and architectures of different vintage and technologies. Integrating products from multiple vendors and across different platforms are almost always challenging. But you usually cannot afford to take a single-vendor approach to IT, because application suite packages may not support your particular infrastructure, or you may inherit it as a result of mergers and acquisitions.

► Change:

 Globalization and e-business are accelerating the pace of change. Globalization leads to fierce competition, which leads to shortening product cycles, as companies look to gain advantage over their competition. Customer needs and requirements change more quickly driven by competitive offerings and wealth of product information available over the Internet. In response the cycle of competitive improvements in products and services further accelerates.

 Improvements in technology continue to accelerate, feeding the increased pace of changing customer requirements. Business must rapidly adapt to survive, let alone to succeed in today's dynamic competitive environment, and the IT infrastructure must enable businesses' ability to adapt.

As a result, business organizations are evolving from the vertical, isolated business divisions of the 1980's and earlier, to the horizontal business process focused structures of the 1980's and 1990's, towards the new ecosystem business paradigm. Business services now need to be componentized and distributed. There is a focus on the extended supply chain, enabling customer and partner access to business services.

The CBDI Forum Report *Business Integration - Drivers and Directions* illustrates this evolution of business as shown in Figure A-1. You can access this CBDI report and a related CBDI workshop titled *Service Based Approach* at:

`http://www.cbdiforum.com/`

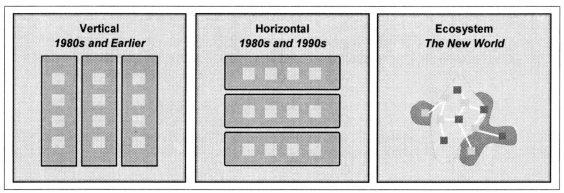

Figure A-1   The evolution of business

How do we make our IT environment more flexible and responsive to the ever changing business requirements? How can we make those heterogeneous systems and applications communicate as seamlessly as possible? How can we achieve the business objective without bankrupting the enterprise?

The issues of providing flexible and responsive IT environments to changing business requirements, and enabling seamless communication between the heterogeneous systems and applications in a cost-effective manner have been evolving in parallel with this evolution of business, as shown in Figure A-2. Many IT executives and professionals alike currently believe that the industry is close to providing a satisfactory solution with service-oriented architecture.

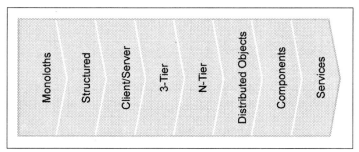

Figure A-2   The evolution of architecture

In order to alleviate the problems of heterogeneity, interoperability, and ever changing requirements, the architecture should provide a platform for building application services with the following characteristics:

▶ Loosely coupled
▶ Location transparent
▶ Protocol independent

Based on such a service-oriented architecture, a service consumer need not be aware of the particular service it is communicating with because the underlying infrastructure, or service "bus", will make an appropriate choice on behalf of the consumer. The infrastructure hides as many technical details as possible from a requestor. Particularly technical details from different implementation technologies such as J2EE or .NET should not affect the SOA users. We should also be able to reconsider and substitute a "better" service implementation if one is available, with better quality of service characteristics.

A.1.2 Service-oriented architecture as a solution

Since the beginnings of software engineering, the IT industry has been struggling to find solutions to solve the afore-mentioned problems. Throughout the years, the following documents the core technology advancements to date. We now briefly discuss those core technologies with a focus on how such technologies help resolve IT problems.

A.1.2.1 Object-oriented analysis and design

In *Applying UML and Patterns - An Introduction to Object-Oriented Analysis and Design,* Larman describes the essence of the object-oriented analysis and design as considering "a problem domain and logical solution from the perspective of objects (things, concepts, or entities)". In *Object-Oriented Software Engineering: A Use Case Driven Approach*, Jacobson, et al, define these objects as being "characterized by a number of operations and a state that remembers the effects of these operations".

In object-oriented analysis, such objects are identified and described in the problem domain, while in object-oriented design, they are transitioned into logical software objects that will ultimately be implemented in an object-oriented programming language.

With object-oriented analysis and design, certain aspects of the object (or group of objects) can be encapsulated to simplify the analysis of complex business scenarios. Certain characteristics of the object(s) can also be abstracted so that only the important or essential aspects are captured, in order to reduce complexity.

A.1.2.2 Component-based design

Component-based design is not a new technology. It evolved from the object paradigm. In the early days of object-oriented analysis and design, fine-grained objects were marked as a mechanism to provide "reuse", but those objects were at too fine a level of granularity and there were no standards in place to make their widespread reuse practical. Coarse-grained components have become more and more a target for reuse in application development and system integration. These coarse-grained components provide certain well defined functionality from a cohesive set of finer-grained objects. In this way, packaged solution suites can also be encapsulated as such "components".

Once the organization achieves a higher level of architectural maturity based on distinctly separate functional components, the applications that support the business can be partitioned into a set of increasingly larger grained components. Components can be seen as the mechanism to package, manage, and expose services. They can use a set of technologies in concert — coarse-grained enterprise components, which implement business-level use-cases, can be implemented using newer object-oriented software development in combination with legacy systems.

A.1.2.3 Service-oriented design

In *Component-Based Development for Enterprise Systems*, Allen includes the notion of services, describing a component as "an executable unit of code that provides physical black-box encapsulation of related services. Its service can only be accessed through a consistent, published interface that includes an interaction standard. A component must be capable of being connected to other components (through a communications interface) to a larger group".

A service is generally implemented as a course-grained, discoverable software entity that exists as a single instance and interacts with applications and other services through a loosely coupled, message-based communication model. Figure A-3 shows important service-oriented terminology:

► Services: Logical entities, the contracts defined by one or more published interfaces.

► Service provider: The software entity that implements a service specification.

► Service consumer (or requestor): The software entity that calls a service provider. Traditionally, this is termed a "client". A service consumer can be an end-user application or another service.

► Service locator: A specific kind of service provider that acts as a registry and allows for the lookup of service provider interfaces and service locations.

► Service broker: A specific kind of service provider that can pass on service requests to one or more additional service providers.

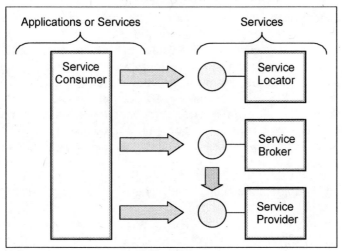

Figure A-3   Service-oriented terminology

A.1.2.4 Interface-based design

In both component and service development, the design of the interfaces is done such that a software entity implements and exposes a key part of its definition. Therefore, the notion and concept of "interface" is key to successful design in both component-based and service-oriented systems. Here are some key interface-related definitions:

► Interface: Defines a set of public method signatures, logically grouped but providing no implementation. An interface defines a contract between the requestor and provider of a service. Any implementation of an interface must provide *all* methods.

► Published interface: An interface that is uniquely identifiable and made available through a registry for clients to dynamically discover.

► Public interface: An interface that is available for clients to use but is not published, thus requiring static knowledge on the part of the client.

► Dual interface: Frequently interfaces are developed as pairs such that one interface depends on another; for example, a client must implement an interface to call a requestor because the client interface provides some callback mechanism.

Figure A-4 shows the UML definition of a customer relationship management (CRM) service, represented as a UML component, that implements the interfaces AccountManagement, ContactManagement, and SystemsManagement. Only the first two of these are published interfaces, although the latter is a public interface.

The SystemsManagement interface and ManagementService interface form a dual interface. The CRM service can implement any number of such interfaces, and it is this ability of a service (or component) to behave in multiple ways depending on the client that allows for great flexibility in the implementation of behavior. It is even possible to provide different or additional services to specific classes of clients.

In some run-time environments such a capability is also used to support different versions of the same interface on a single component or service.

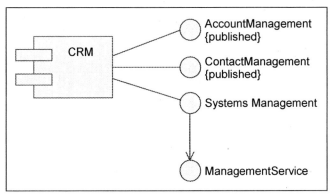

Figure A-4   Implemented services

A.1.2.5 Layered application architectures

As mentioned before, object-oriented technology and languages are great ways to implement components. While components are the best way to implement services, a good component-based application does not necessarily make an good service-oriented application. A great opportunity exists to leverage component developers and existing components, once the role played by services in application architecture is understood.

The key to making this transition is to realize that a service-oriented approach implies an additional application architecture layer. Figure A-5 demonstrates how technology layers can be applied to application architecture to provide more coarse-grained implementations as one gets closer to the consumers of the application.

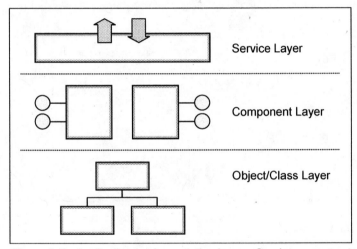

Figure A-5   Application implementation layers: Services, components, objects

A.1.3 A closer look at service-oriented architecture

Service-oriented architecture presents an approach to building distributed systems that deliver application functionality as services to either end-user applications or other services. It comprises elements that can be categorized as *functional* and *quality of service*. Figure A-6 shows the architectural stack and the elements that make up a service-oriented architecture.

> **Note:** Service-oriented architecture stacks have been evolving, with several different stacks being put forward by various proponents. The stack shown in Figure A-6 is not being positioned as definitive service stack. It is just being presented as a useful framework for structuring the SOA discussion in the rest of this publication.

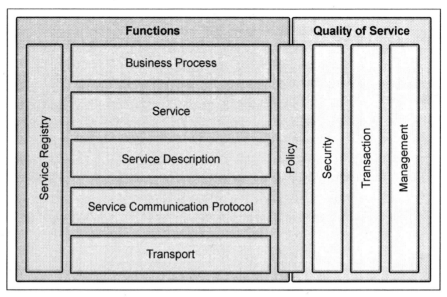

Figure A-6   Elements of a service-oriented architecture

The architectural stack is divided into two halves, with the left half addressing the functional aspects of the architecture and the right half addressing the quality of service aspects. These elements are described in detail as follows:

► Functional aspects include these:

  – *Transport* is the mechanism used to move service requests from the service consumer to the service provider, and service responses from the service provider to the service consumer.

  – *Service Communication Protocol* is an agreed mechanism that the service provider and the service consumer use to communicate what is being requested and what is being returned.

  – *Service Description* is an agreed schema for describing what the service is, how it should be invoked, and what data is required to invoke the service successfully.

  – *Service* describes an actual service that is made available for use.

  – *Business Process* is a collection of services, invoked in a particular sequence with a particular set of rules, to meet a business requirement.

> **Note:** A business process could be considered a service in its own right, which leads to the idea that business processes may be composed of services of different granularities.

- The *Service Registry* is a repository of service and data descriptions which may be used by service providers to publish their services, and service consumers to discover or find available services. The service registry may provide other functions to services that require a centralized repository.

► Quality of service aspects include these:

- *Policy* is a set of conditions or rules under which a service provider makes the service available to consumers. There are aspects of policy which are functional, and aspects which relate to quality of service; therefore we have the policy function in both functional and quality of service areas.

- *Security* is the set of rules that might be applied to the identification, authorization, and access control of service consumers invoking services.

- *Transaction* is the set of attributes that might be applied to a group of services to deliver a consistent result. For example, if a group of three services are to be used to complete a business function, all must complete or none must complete.

- *Management* is the set of attributes that might be applied to managing the services provided or consumed.

A.1.3.1 SOA collaborations

Figure A-7 shows the collaborations in a service-oriented architecture. The collaborations follow the "find, bind, and invoke" paradigm, where a service consumer performs dynamic service location by querying the service registry for a service that matches its criteria. If the service exists, the registry provides the consumer with the interface contract and the endpoint address for the service. The diagram illustrates the entities in a service-oriented architecture that collaborate to support the "find, bind, and invoke" paradigm.

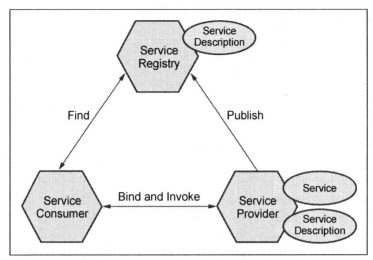

Figure A-7   Collaborations in a service-oriented architecture

These are the roles in a service-oriented architecture:

▶ Service consumer: The service consumer is an application, a software module, or another service that requires a service. It initiates the inquiry of the service in the registry, binds to the service over a transport, and executes the service function. The service consumer executes the service according to the interface contract.

▶ Service provider: The service provider is a *network-addressable entity* that accepts and executes requests from consumers. It publishes its services and interface contract to the service registry so that the service consumer can discover and access the service.

▶ Service registry: A service registry is the enabler for service discovery. It contains a repository of available services and allows for the lookup of service provider interfaces to interested service consumers.

Each entity in the service-oriented architecture can play one (or more) of the three roles of service provider, consumer, and registry.

The operations in a service-oriented architecture are:

▶ Publish: To be accessible, a service description must be published so that it can be discovered and invoked by a service consumer.

▶ Find: A service requestor locates a service by querying the service registry for a service that meets its criteria.

▶ Bind and invoke: After retrieving the service description, the service consumer proceeds to invoke the service according to the information in the service description.

The artifacts in a service-oriented architecture are:

▶ Service: A service that is made available for use through a published interface that allows it to be invoked by the service consumer.

▶ Service description: A service description specifies the way a service consumer will interact with the service provider. It specifies the format of the request and response from the service. This description may specify a set of preconditions, post conditions and/or quality of service (QoS) levels.

In addition to dynamic service discovery and definition of a service interface contract, a service-oriented architecture has the following characteristics:

▶ Services are self-contained and modular.
▶ Services support interoperability.
▶ Services are loosely coupled.
▶ Services are location-transparent.
▶ Services are composite modules, comprised of components.

Finally, service-oriented architecture is also an evolution of earlier technologies. Examples of technologies that are at least partly service-oriented, including CORBA, DCOM and J2EE, are shown in Figure A-8. Early adopters of the approach to service-oriented architecture have also successfully created their own service-oriented enterprise architectures based on messaging systems, such as IBM WebSphere MQ. Most recently, the SOA arena has expanded to include the World Wide Web (WWW) and Web Services.

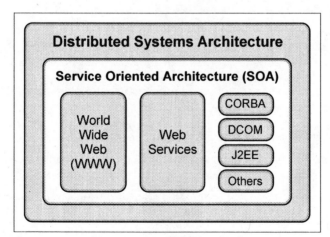

Figure A-8   Different implementations of service-oriented architecture

A.1.3.2 Services in the context of SOA

In service-oriented architecture, services map to the business functions that are identified during business process analysis. The services may be fine-grained or coarse-grained depending upon the business processes. Each service has a well-defined interface that allows it to be published, discovered and invoked. An enterprise can choose to publish its services externally to business partners or internally within the organization. A service can also be composed from other services.

A.1.3.3 Services versus components

A service is a coarse-grained processing unit that consumes and produces sets of objects passed-by-value. It is not the same as an object in programming language terms. Instead, it is perhaps closer to the concept of a business transaction such as a CICS® or IMS™ transaction than to a remote CORBA object.

A service consists of a collection of components that work in concert to deliver the business function that the service represents. Thus, in comparison, components are finer-grained than services. In addition, while a service maps to a business function, a component typically maps to business entities and the business rules that operate on them. As an example, let us look at the Purchase Order component model shown in Figure A-9.

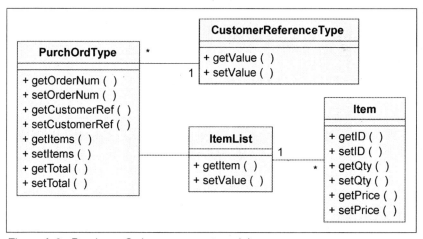

Figure A-9 Purchase Order component model

In a component-based design, components are created to closely match business entities (such as Customer, Purchase Order, Order Item) and encapsulate the behavior that matches the entities' expected behavior.

For example, the Purchase Order component provides functions to obtain information about the list of products ordered and the total amount of the order; the Item component provides functions to obtain information about the quantity and price of the product ordered. The implementation of each component is encapsulated behind the interface. So, a user of the Purchase Order component does not know the schema of the Purchase Order table and the algorithm for calculating tax, rebates and/or discounts on the total amount of the order.

In a service-oriented design, services are not designed based on business entities. Instead, each service is a holistic unit that manages operations across a set of business entities. For example, a customer service will respond to any request from any other system or service that needs to access customer information. The customer service can process a request to update customer information; add, update, delete investment portfolios; and enquire about the customer's order history. The customer service owns all the data related to the customers it is managing and is capable of making other service inquiries on behalf of the calling party in order to provide a unified customer service view. This means a service is a *manager* object that creates and manages its set components.

A.1.4 Service-oriented architecture benefits

As discussed earlier, businesses have to deal with adapting quickly and cost effectively to change. To remain competitive, businesses must adapt quickly to internal factors such as acquisitions and restructuring, or external factors like competitive forces and customer requirements. Cost-effective, flexible IT infrastructure is needed to support the business.

With a service-oriented architecture, you can realize several benefits to help your organization succeed in the dynamic business landscape of today:

► Leverage existing assets.

SOA provides a layer of abstraction that enables organizations to continue leveraging its investment in IT by wrapping these existing assets as services to provide business functions. Organizations potentially can continue getting value out of existing resources instead of having to rebuild from scratch.

► Easier to integrate and manage complexity.

The integration point in a service-oriented architecture is the service specification and not the implementation. This provides implementation transparency and minimizes the impact when infrastructure and implementation changes occur. By providing a service specification in front of existing resources and assets built on disparate systems, integration becomes more manageable since complexities are isolated. This is even more important as more businesses work together to provide the value chain.

- More responsive and faster time-to-market.

  The ability to compose new services out of existing ones provides a distinct advantage to an organization that has to be agile to respond to demanding business needs. Leveraging existing components and services reduces the time needed to go through the software development life cycle of gathering requirements, performing design, development and testing. This leads to rapid development of new business services and allows an organization to respond quickly to changes and reduce the time-to-market.

- Reduce cost and increase reuse.

  With core business services exposed in a loosely coupled manner, they can be more easily used and combined based on business needs. This means less duplication of resources, more potential for reuse, and lower costs.

- Be ready for what lies ahead.

  SOA prepares businesses for the future. Business processes which comprise of a series of business services can be more easily created, changed and managed to meet the needs of the time. SOA provides the flexibility and responsiveness that is critical to businesses to survive and thrive.

Like most technologies, SOA is not necessarily the answer to every business problem. Where SOA is appropriate, migration to it is non-trivial. Rather than migrating the entire enterprise to a service-oriented architecture overnight, the recommended approach is to migrate an appropriate subset of business functions as the business need arises or is anticipated.

A.2 Web services architecture

Web services is a relatively new technology that has received wide acceptance as an important implementation of SOA. This is because Web services provides a distributed computing approach for integrating extremely heterogeneous applications over the Internet. The Web services specification is completely independent of programming languages, operating systems, and hardware to promote loose coupling between the service consumer and provider. The technology is based on open technologies such as:

- eXtensible Markup Language (XML)
- Simple Object Access Protocol (SOAP)
- Universal Description, Discovery and Integration (UDDI)
- Web Services Description Language (WSDL)

Using open standards provides broad interoperability among different vendor solutions. These principles permit companies to implement Web services without having any knowledge of the service consumers, and vice versa. This facilitates just-in-time integration and allows businesses to establish new partnership easily and dynamically.

A.2.1 What Web services are

The W3C's Web Services Architecture Working Group has the following working definition of a Web service:

> "A Web service is a software application identified by a URI, whose interfaces and bindings are capable of being defined, described, and discovered as XML artifacts. A Web service supports direct interactions with other software agents using XML-based messages exchanged via Internet-based protocols."

Basic Web services combine the power of two ubiquitous technologies: XML, the universal data description language; and the HTTP transport protocol widely supported by browser and Web servers:

```
Web services = XML + transport protocol (such as HTTP)
```

Some of the key features of Web services are as follows:

► Web services are self-contained.

On the client side, no additional software is required. A programming language with XML and HTTP client support, for example, is enough to get you started. On the server side, a Web server and a servlet engine are required. It is possible to Web service enable an existing application without writing a single line of code.

► Web services are self-describing.

Neither the client nor the server knows or cares about anything besides the format and content of request and response messages (loosely coupled application integration).

The definition of the message format travels with the message. No external metadata repositories or code generation tools are required.

► Web services are modular.

Web services is a technology for deploying and providing access to business functions over the Web — J2EE, CORBA, and other standards are technologies for implementing these Web services.

► Web services can be published, located, and invoked across the Web.

The standards required to do so are:

  – Simple Object Access Protocol (SOAP), also known as service-oriented architecture protocol, an XML-based RPC and messaging protocol

  – Web Service Description Language (WSDL), a descriptive interface and protocol binding language

  – Universal Description, Discovery, and Integration (UDDI), a registry mechanism that can be used to look up Web service descriptions

► Web services are language independent and interoperable.

The interaction between a service provider and a service requester is designed to be completely platform and language independent. This interaction requires a WSDL document to define the interface and describe the service, along with a network protocol (usually HTTP). Because the service provider and the service requester have no idea what platforms or languages the other is using, interoperability is a given.

► Web services are inherently open and standards based.

XML and HTTP are the technical foundation for Web services. A large part of the Web service technology has been built using open source projects. Therefore, vendor independence and interoperability are realistic goals.

► Web services are dynamic.

Dynamic e-business can become a reality using Web services because, with UDDI and WSDL, the Web service description and discovery can be automated.

► Web services are composable.

Simple Web services can be aggregated to more complex ones, either using workflow techniques or by calling lower-layer Web services from a Web service implementation.

Figure A-10 shows a typical Web service collaboration that is based on the SOA model shown previously in Figure A-7 on page 445.

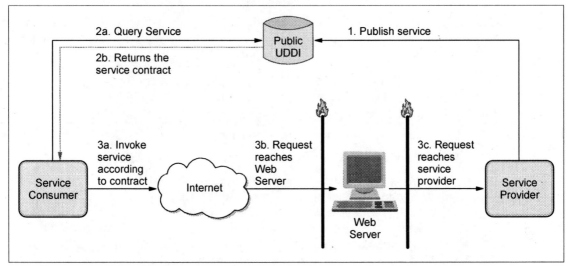

Figure A-10   Web service collaboration

A.3 Web services and service-oriented architecture

Web services is a technology that is well suited to implementing a service-oriented architecture. In essence, Web services are self-describing and modular applications that expose business logic as services that can be published, discovered, and invoked over the Internet. Based on XML standards, Web services can be developed as loosely coupled application components using any programming language, any protocol, or any platform. This facilitates the delivery of business applications as a service accessible to anyone, anytime, at any location, and using any platform.

It is important to point out that Web services are not the only technology that can be used to implement a service-oriented architecture. Many examples of organizations who have successfully implemented service-oriented architectures using other technologies can be found. Web services have also been used by others to implement architectures that are not service-oriented. In this publication, however, our focus is on using Web services to implement an SOA.

For more information on SOA and Web services, refer to:

`http://www.ibm.com/software/solutions/soa/`

This Web site provides a collection of IBM resources on this topic.

A.4 Enterprise Service Bus

Web services based technologies are becoming more widely used in enterprise application development and integration. One of the critical issues arising now is finding more efficient and effective ways of designing, developing and deploying Web services based business systems. More importantly, moving beyond the basic point-to-point Web services communications to broader application of these technologies to enterprise-level business processes. In this context, the Enterprise Service Bus (ESB) model is emerging as a major step forward in the evolution of Web services and service-oriented architecture.

A.4.1 Basic Web services

Basic (point-to-point SOAP/HTTP) Web services provide a solid foundation for implementing a service-oriented architecture, but there are important considerations that affect their flexibility and maintainability in enterprise-scale architectures, as follows:

▶ The point-to-point nature of basic Web services means that service consumers often need to be modified whenever the service provider interface changes. This is often not a problem on a small scale, but in large enterprises it could mean changes to many client applications. It can also become increasingly difficult to make such changes to legacy clients.

▶ You can end up with an architecture that is fragile and inflexible when large numbers of service consumers and providers communicate using point-to-point "spaghetti" style connections.

▶ Basic Web services require that each consumer has a suitable protocol adapter for each provider it needs to use. Having to deploy multiple protocol adapters across many client applications adds to cost and maintainability issues.

The following section describes how the Enterprise Service Bus approach addresses these issues.

A.4.2 What an Enterprise Service Bus is

The Enterprise Service Bus concept is not a product, but an architectural best practice for implementing a service-oriented architecture. As shown in Figure A-11, it establishes an enterprise-class messaging bus that combines messaging infrastructure with message transformation and content-based routing in a layer of integration logic between service consumers and providers.

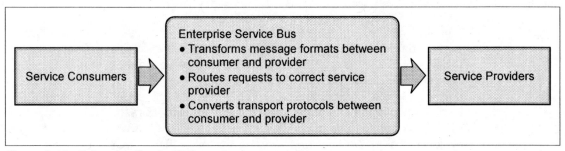

Figure A-11   Enterprise Service Bus

The main aim of the Enterprise Service Bus is to provide virtualization of the enterprise resources, allowing the business logic of the enterprise to be developed and managed independently of the infrastructure, network, and provision of those business services. Resources in the ESB are modelled as services that offer one or more business operations.

Implementing an Enterprise Service Bus requires an integrated set of middleware services that support the following architecture styles:

▶ *Services oriented architectures,* where distributed applications are composed of granular re-usable services with well-defined, published and standards-compliant interfaces

▶ *Message-driven architectures,* where applications send messages through the ESB to receiving applications

▶ *Event-driven architectures,* where applications generate and consume messages independently of one another

The middleware services provided by an Enterprise Service Bus need to include:

▶ Communication middleware supporting a variety of communication paradigms (such as synchronous, asynchronous, request/reply, one-way, call-back), qualities of service (such as security, guaranteed delivery, performance, transactional), APIs, platforms, and standard protocols

▶ A mechanism for injecting intelligent processing of in-flight service requests and responses within the network

▶ Standard-based tools for enabling rapid integration of services

▶ Management system for loosely-coupled applications and their interactions

A.4.3 The IBM vision

As shown in Figure A-12 on page 455, IBM is extending its Web services and service-oriented architecture vision with an Enterprise Service Bus architecture that provides a standards-based integration layer using the intermediary/mediator pattern.

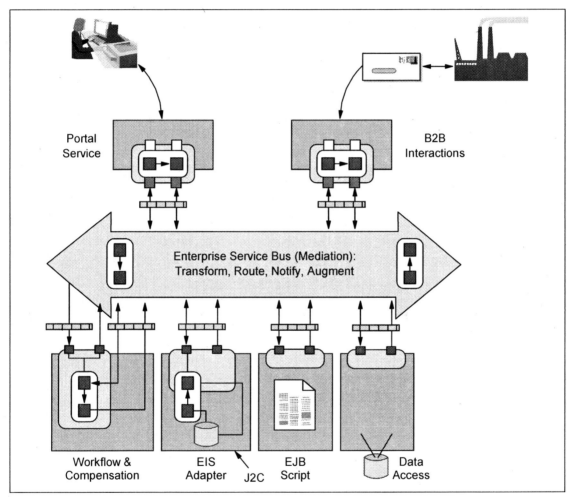

Figure A-12   Enterprise Service Bus conceptual model

Intelligent mediations are invoked between service consumer and provider that facilitate the selection of services, logging, usage metrics, and so on. These mediations can be configured by policies that define consumer and provider capabilities and requirements. For example, if a provider expects encrypted messages, the requester mediation should include such capability. If a requester only supports SOAP/HTTP, an intermediary should be added to convert to SOAP/JMS.

The other main components in this model include WSDL services that are generated using tools, or implemented by programmers. These include:

► A workflow and compensation system that executes business processes, or workflows. Activity nodes in a business process typically map to invoking an operation on a Web service. This component supports J2EE transactions and a compensation model for long duration business processes.

► Enterprise Information System (EIS) adaptors based on the J2EE Connector Architecture allow integration with legacy systems.

► XML database access through a WSDL interface.

► Custom-built WSDL services implemented by programmers using the J2EE programming model.

The Enterprise Service Bus supports multiple protocols for communication between services, including SOAP, HTTP, JMS, RMI/IIOP, and so on.

The Enterprise Service Bus can be implemented today using currently available IBM WebSphere products, for example:

► IBM WebSphere Application Server V5.1 provides a J2EE runtime environment for services using SOAP over HTTP or JMS, and J2EE Connectors for EIS integration.

► IBM WebSphere MQ provides the JMS messaging infrastructure.

► The Web Services Gateway with IBM WebSphere Application Server Network Deployment V5.1 provides SOAP message routing, transformation, and protocol conversion. The UDDI Registry provides dynamic service discovery.

► IBM WebSphere Application Server Enterprise V5.0 provides the Process Choreographer for service orchestration or workflow.

► IBM DB2 XML Extender enables database access via the ESB.

► IBM WebSphere Portal allows integrated, personalized end-user access to business services.

You can also expect a strong focus on Enterprise Service Bus capabilities in future releases of WebSphere family products.

Note: Implementation of an Enterprise Service Bus is beyond the scope of this publication. The intention here is just to provide an introduction to this important architectural best practice.

WebSphere Integration Developer overview

In this appendix, we provide a brief overview of WebSphere Integration Developer for an audience of Information Management specialists.

B.1 Introduction

Business integration means integrating applications, data and processes within an enterprise or among a set of enterprises. In the current merger, acquisitions, and globalization climate, business integration is critical to exploiting emerging business opportunities and achieving cost efficiencies. The challenge is essentially one of geography and heterogeneity. Integrated applications are usually quite complex. They can call applications on Enterprise Information Systems (EIS), involve business processes across departments or enterprises, and invoke applications locally or remotely written in a variety of languages and running on a variety of operating systems. When cross enterprise integration is involved, security issues become particularly significant.

The evolution of service-oriented architecture (SOA) with its concepts of loosely coupled integration (as described in Appendix A, "Service Oriented Architecture (SOA) overview" on page 435) has significantly eased the challenges of achieving cost-effective business integration.

WebSphere Integration Developer (WID) addresses the challenges of business integration within an enterprise or among enterprises. In the following sections, we briefly describe WID, and the Service Component Architecture (SCA) that WID implements.

For further details on WID (which is the tooling for WebSphere Process Server), visit the WebSphere Process Server information at the URL:

```
http://www.ibm.com/software/integration/wps/library/infocenter/
```

B.2 WebSphere Integration Developer

WID has been designed as a complete integration development environment for building integrated applications. WID uses visual tools to create integrated applications based on service-oriented architecture (SOA). WID is available on both Windows and Linux® platforms.

WID's tools present applications, including applications that exist remotely on EIS systems, and business processes as components. The components are created and assembled into other integrated applications (that is, applications created from a set of components) through visual editors. The visual editors present a layer of abstraction between the components and their implementations. An integration developer[1] using the tools can create an integrated application without detailed knowledge of the underlying implementation of each component.

WebSphere Integration Developer tools allow both a top-down design approach to building an integrated application, where the implementation for one or more components does not exist and is added later; or a bottom-up approach, where the components are already implemented and the developer assembles them by dragging and dropping them in a visual editor and then creates a logical flow among them by joining them with lines. A debugging and test environment means full testing before your applications are deployed to a production server. Setting monitoring points lets you see how an application is used in real time in order to fine tune it for optimal performance.

WebSphere Integration Developer's tools are based on a service-oriented architecture (SOA). Components are services and an integrated application involving many components is a service. The services created comply to the leading, industry-wide standards as follows:

► J2EE Connector Architecture standards are used for connectivity.

► For asynchronous messaging, often used in large applications requiring guaranteed delivery of data, the Java Message Service (JMS) standard is used.

► Integrates Web services based on Simple Object Access Protocol (SOAP). To describe a service, the well-established Web Services Description Language (WSDL) standard is used.

► Business Process Execution Language (BPEL) standard is employed to define a business process. Business processes become components.

These standards-based interfaces and components comprise an open-ended and pluggable architecture. Proprietary elements, however, are not excluded — they are accessed through the use of standardized interfaces, for example, applications created in WebSphere Integration Developer can interact with .NET applications as long as the binding is supported, such as SOAP over HTTP.

---

[1] The integration developer is the primary user of WebSphere Integration Developer. This person, through the use of visual tools, can build a complex integrated application without requiring extensive knowledge of the underlying implementation. WebSphere Integration Developer presents applications and business processes as components. The implementation of the components remains hidden and the components interoperate through interfaces. As a result, integration developers do not need to have extensive knowledge of the underlying implementation of the components to create an integrated application that uses them.

Integration developers, however, will likely have a broad technical knowledge in the integration field since they need some understanding of EIS systems, business processes, and applications coded in Java or other languages. For example, an architect has a broad understanding of how a system works without knowing what each component does in detail. Like an architect, an integration developer might be the person in an organization who designs the overall application, and then has others who code the implementation of the specific components.

WebSphere Integration Developer works in a multilingual environment, meaning that it can display and manipulate data represented in different languages. It also provides bidirectional language support for languages written from right to left.

B.3 Service Component Architecture (SCA)

SCA is based SOA and presents all business processes (such as Web services, Enterprise Information System (EIS) service assets, workflows, and databases) in a service-oriented way.

The goal of Service Component Architecture is to separate business integration logic from implementation so that an integration developer can focus on assembling an integrated application rather than on the implementation details. To achieve that end, service components that contain the implementation of individual services required by business processes are created. The result is an architecture of three layers comprising business integration logic, service components, and implementation as shown in Figure B-1.

Since the service components contain the implementation, they can be assembled graphically by the integration developer without the knowledge of low-level implementation details. Service components also provide the option of letting the integration developer, or someone who works for the integration developer, add the implementation later.

In WID, components are assembled together visually, in that you are not exposed to the code within the components. In the business integration logic level shown in Figure B-1, components are assembled independently of their implementation. The service-oriented architecture, then, lets you focus on solving your business problems by using and reusing components rather than diverting your attention to the technology that is implementing the services you are using.

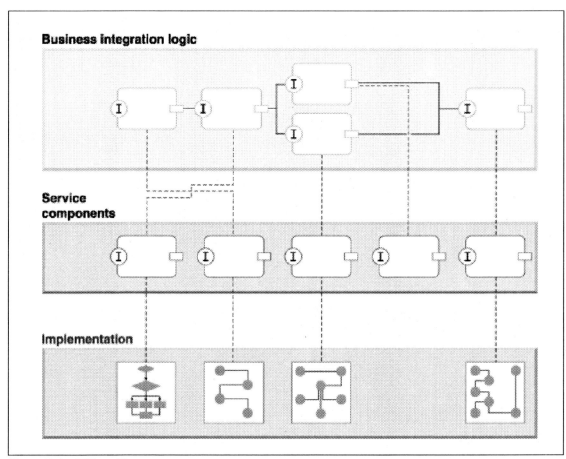

Figure B-1   SCA architecture

B.3.1 Service components

A service component configures a service implementation. A service component is presented in a standard block diagram as shown in Figure B-2.

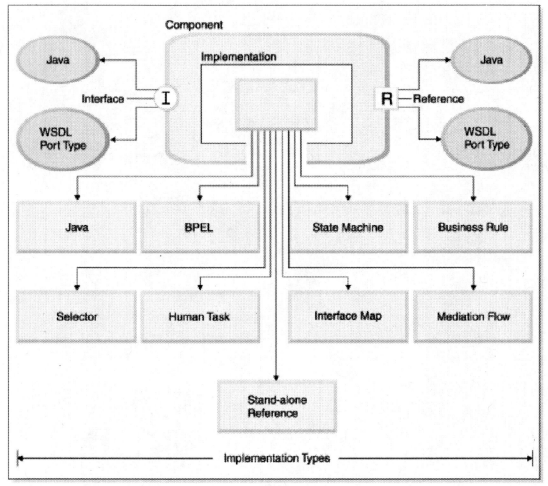

Figure B-2   Service component

As shown in Figure B-2, a component consists of:

► One or more interfaces that define its inputs, outputs, and faults:

  – An interface may be defined in one of two languages — a WSDL port type or Java.

  The recommended interface type is WSDL.

A Java interface, however, is used mostly in the case when a stateless session EJB is imported (described in "Imports and exports" on page 471). Should you develop a top-down[2] Java component, you should still use a WSDL interface.

You cannot mix WSDL-interface-based components with Java-interface-based components.

– An interface supports synchronous and asynchronous interaction styles.

► Zero or more references:

A reference identifies the interface of another service or component that this component requires or consumes.

► An implementation that is hidden when using WebSphere Integration Developer's tools. A component's implementation can be in various languages.

A service component implementation can be of different types as follows. They appear in services in the WID Assembly Editor and/or within BPEL processes:

– Java:

An implementation of a component in Java is referred to as a Java object or "plain old Java object" (POJO).

– BPEL:

A BPEL process component implements a business process. A BPEL process cannot be used in a mediation module. It can only be deployed to a WebSphere Process Server.

– State machines:

It is an alternative way of creating a business process.

– Business rules:

Business rules complement business processes and state machines.

– Selectors:

A selector is used to route an operation from a client application to one of several possible components for implementation.

– Human task:

A human task component implements a task done by a person. It represents the involvement of a person in a business process.

---

[2] You define a component and add the implementation later.

- Interface map:

  An interface map resolves differences between the interfaces of interacting components.

- Mediation flow:

  Mediation is a way of mediating or intervening dynamically between services. A mediation flow implements a mediation.

- Stand-alone references:

  Stand-alone references are references to applications that are not defined as SCA components (for example JSPs or servlets). Stand-alone references permit these applications to interact with SCA components.

Figure B-3 shows an example of a component service that is implemented in Java (MyValueImple.java) and has a Java interface (MyValue.java). It also has two references — another Java interface (CustomerInfo.java) and a WSDL interface (StockQuote.wsdl). A reference to this component from another component (MyValueInst1) is revealed visually by a line to its interface. A reference from this component would be revealed by a line from its reference point to the interface of other component.

A reference represents a service that this component consumes. By naming a reference and only specifying its interface, it allows the component implementation author to defer binding that reference to an actual service until later. At that later time, the integration specialist will do so by wiring from the reference to the interface of another component or import. This loose coupling, which allows for deferred binding and the re-use of implementations, is one of the strengths of WID's Service Component Architecture.

A component may also have properties and qualifiers. A qualifier is a quality of service (QoS) directive on interfaces and references for the run time. Qualifiers can be specified on service component references, interfaces, and implementations.

Since declaration of the QoS values are external to an implementation, you can change these values without changing the implementation, or set them differently when several instances of the same implementation are used in different contexts. Qualifier categories are as follows:

► Transaction which specify rules for the type of transaction

► Activity session which specify rules for joining the active session

► Security which specify rules for permission

► Asynchronous reliability which specify rules for asynchronous message delivery

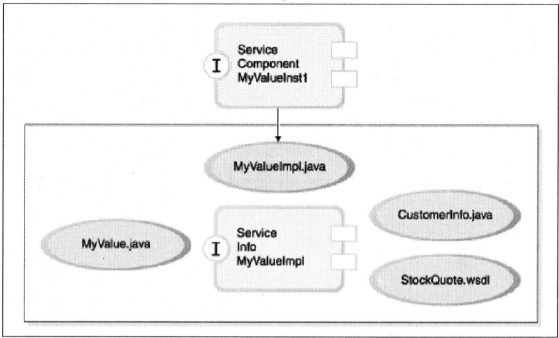

Figure B-3   Component example

B.3.2 Service data objects (SDOs)

Service data objects complement Service Component Architecture.

SCA defines the services as components and the connectivity between them. Service data objects define the data flowing between components. Each component passes information as input and output. When a service is invoked, data objects are passed as an XML document with document literal encoding when using a WSDL port type, or as a Java object when using a Java interface. Data objects are the preferred form for data and metadata in SCA services. Similar to components, SDOs separate the data object from its implementation. SDOs let the integration developer focus on working with business artifacts. In fact, SDOs are transparent to the integration developer. They are defined by a service data objects Java Specification Request (JSR).

Figure B-4 shows how SDOs are passed from an external service to an export, from an export to a component, from a component to a component, from a component to an import, and from an import to a service.

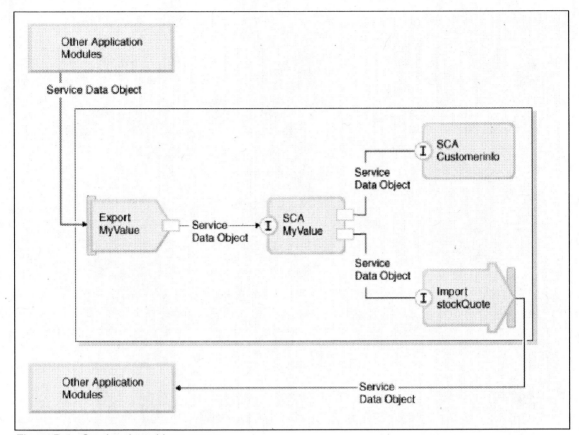

Figure B-4   Service data objects usage

B.3.3 Modules

A module is a unit of deployment that determines which artifacts are packaged together in an Enterprise Archive (EAR) file. Components within a module are collocated for performance, and can pass their data by reference.

A module can be seen as a scoping mechanism in that it sets an organizational boundary for artifacts. A module is a composite of service components, imports and exports as shown in Figure B-5. The service components, imports and exports reside in the same project and root folder, which also contain the wiring that links the components and the bindings needed for the imports and exports. A module may also contain the implementations and interfaces referenced by its components, imports and exports, or these may be placed in other projects, such as a library project.

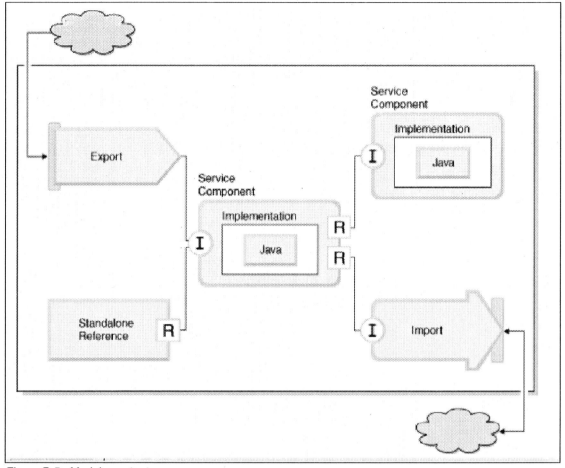

Figure B-5 Module contents

There are two types of modules, as follows:

► (Business Integration) module, which contains a choice of many component types, often used to support a business process.

► Mediation module, which contains up to one component, a mediation flow component, plus zero or more Java components that augment the mediation flow component. A mediation module is like a gateway to existing external services, which is common in enterprise service bus architectures. These external services or exports are accessed in a mediation module by imports or service providers.

By decoupling client service requesters from service providers by a mediation flow, your applications gain flexibility and resilience, a goal of service-oriented architecture. For example, your mediation flow can log incoming messages, route messages to a specific service determined at run time or transform data to make it suitable to pass to another service. These functions can be added and changed over time without modifying the requester or provider services.

Module and mediation module artifacts include these characteristics:

► Module definition defines the module.

► Service components define the services in the module. A service component name inside a module is unique. However, a service component can have an arbitrary display name, which is typically a name more useful to a user.

► Imports are calls to services external to this module. Imports have bindings, which are discussed in B.3.4, "Imports and exports" on page 471.

► Exports are used to expose components to callers that are external to this module.

► References define references from one component to another in the module.

► Stand-alone references reference applications that are not defined as Service Component Architecture components (such as JSPs), which enable these applications to interact with Service Component Architecture components. There can be only one stand-alone references artifact per module.

► Other artifacts such as WSDL files, Java classes, XSD files, and BPEL processes.

A module results in a service application tested and deployed to the WebSphere Process Server. A mediation module results in a service application tested and deployed to either the WebSphere Process Server or the WebSphere Enterprise Service Bus server. Both types of modules support imports and exports.

> **Note:** Implementations, interfaces, business objects, business object maps, roles, relationships, and other artifacts often need to be shared among modules. A library is a project used to store these shared resources.

Figure B-6 on page 471 shows an example of a module that contains an export (myvalue), two imports (customerInfo and stockQuote), and a service component (MyValueInst1) that uses them. Wiring is shown linking the interfaces and references.

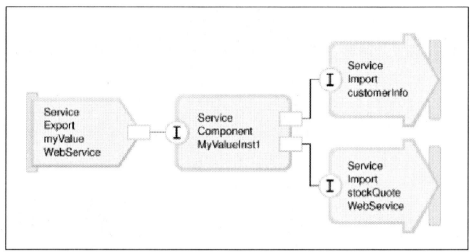

Figure B-6   Module example

B.3.4 Imports and exports

Imports and exports define a module's external interfaces or access points.

► Imports identify services outside of a module, so they can be called from within the module.

► Exports allow components to provide their services to external clients.

Imports and exports require binding information, which specifies the means of transporting the data from the modules.

► An import binding describes the specific way an external service is bound to an import component.

► An export binding describes the specific way a module's services are made available to clients.

Figure B-7 shows import and export usage, and bindings that can be associated with them as follows:

► The SCA or default binding lets your service communicate with other services in other modules. An import with an SCA binding lets you access a service in another module. An export with an SCA binding lets you offer a service to other modules.

► A Web service import binding allows you to bind an external Web service to an import. A Web service export binding allows you to provide a service to external clients as a Web service.

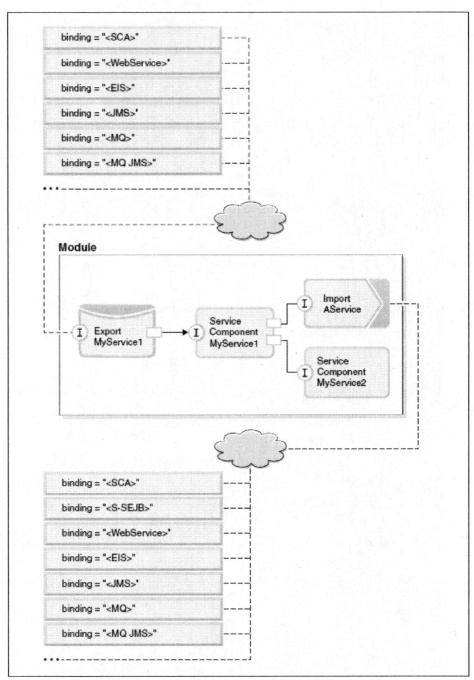

Figure B-7   Imports and exports and available bindings

- The enterprise service discovery wizard creates imports and exports representing a service on EIS and other systems such as IBM Information Server.

- Java Message Service (JMS), WebSphere MQSeries® (MQ), and WebSphere MQSeries JMS (MQ JMS) bindings are used for interactions with messaging systems, where asynchronous communication through message queues are critical for reliability.

- An import (though not an export) may also have a stateless session EJB binding.

The assembly editor lists the bindings supported and simplifies the creation of them when you want to create an import or export. A properties view in the assembly editor displays the binding information of any import or export.

Code and scripts used in the business scenario

In this appendix we document some of the code and scripts used in the A2Z Financial Services' legacy systems and self service scenario. All the code and scripts documented here are also available for download from the IBM Redbooks Web site:

`ftp://www.redbooks.ibm.com/redbooks/SG247402`

The topics covered include:

► Legacy systems tables and scripts
► Self service solution code

C.1 Legacy systems tables and SQL scripts

This section documents the tables, DDL used to create the tables, and the stored procedures defined to perform certain business functions in A2Z Financial Services' Brokerage, CreditCard, Operational Data Store, and Enterprise Data Warehouse systems, as follows:

- ► Brokerage system tables and scripts
- ► Credit Card system tables and scripts
- ► Operational Data Store tables and scripts
- ► Enterprise Data Warehouse tables and scripts

C.1.1 Brokerage system tables and scripts

Figure C-1 shows the DB2 tables and their relationships, while Example C-1 shows the DDL to create these tables. We have not included the DDL of the creation of the various indexes on these tables.

The following DB2 stored procedures are shown here:

- ► SQL stored procedure OPENBROKERAGEACCOUNT corresponding to the AddNewAccount federated stored procedure is shown in Example C-2 on page 478.

- ► SQL stored procedure ADDCUSTOMER corresponding to the AddNewCustomer federated stored procedure is shown in Example C-3 on page 478.

- ► SQL stored procedure PLACETRADE corresponding to the Trade federated stored procedure is shown in Example C-4 on page 478.

- ► Java stored procedure AddAddress corresponding to the AddAddress federated stored procedure is shown in Example C-5 on page 479.

- ► Java stored procedure UpdateCustomer corresponding to the UpdateCustomer federated stored procedure is shown in Example C-6 on page 479.

- ► Java stored procedure UpdateAddress corresponding to the UpdateAddress federated stored procedure is shown in Example C-7 on page 480.

- ► Java stored procedure UpdateAccount corresponding to the UpdateAccount federated stored procedure is shown in Example C-8 on page 480.

The LegacyStockQuoteService session bean was developed as a Web Service using Rational Application Developer as shown in Figure C-2 on page 481 through Figure C-8 on page 486.

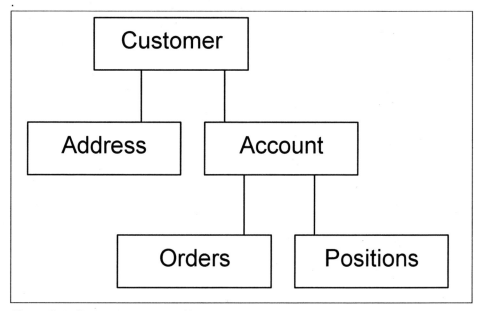

Figure C-1   Brokerage system tables

Example: C-1   Brokerage system DDL (indexes not shown)

```
CREATE TABLE BROKERAGE.CUSTOMER
    (
    CUSTID char(10) PRIMARY KEY NOT NULL,
    NAME VARCHAR(20) NOT NULL,
    SSNUMB CHAR(11) NOT NULL,
    DOB DATE NOT NULL,
    CUSTRATING CHAR(1),
    TELEPHONE CHAR(10) NOT NULL
    );

CREATE TABLE BROKERAGE.ADDRESS
    (
    STREET VARCHAR(20) NOT NULL,
    CITY VARCHAR(15) NOT NULL,
    STATE CHAR(2) NOT NULL,
    ZIPCODE CHAR(10),
    CUSTOMERFK CHAR(10),
    CONSTRAINT FK FOREIGN KEY (CUSTOMERFK) REFERENCES BROKERAGE.CUSTOMER (CUSTID)
    );

CREATE TABLE BROKERAGE.ACCOUNT
    (
    ACCOUNTNUMBER CHAR(15) PRIMARY KEY NOT NULL,
    ACCOUNTTYPE CHAR(1) NOT NULL,
    DATEOPENED DATE NOT NULL,
    BALANCE DECIMAL(11,2),
    CUSTOMERFK CHAR(10),
    constraint fk FOREIGN KEY (CUSTOMERFK) REFERENCES BROKERAGE.CUSTOMER(CUSTID)
    );

CREATE TABLE BROKERAGE.ORDERS
    (
    ORDERNUMB SMALLINT NOT NULL,
```

```
       SYMBOL CHAR(6) NOT NULL,
       QUANTITY SMALLINT NOT NULL,
       TYPEOFORDER CHAR(1) NOT NULL,
       ORDERDATE DATE NOT NULL,
       FILLEDON DATE,
       ACCOUNTFK CHAR(15),
       CONSTRAINT FK FOREIGN KEY (ACCOUNTFK) REFERENCES BROKERAGE.ACCOUNT(ACCOUNTNUMBER)
       );

CREATE TABLE BROKERAGE.POSITIONS
       (
       SYMBOL CHAR(6) NOT NULL,
       QUANTITY SMALLINT NOT NULL,
       PURCHASEPRICE DECIMAL(9,2),
       PURCHASEDATE DATE NOT NULL,
       CURRENTPRICE DECIMAL(9,2),
       ACCOUNTFK CHAR(15),
       CONSTRAINT FK FOREIGN KEY (ACCOUNTFK) REFERENCES BROKERAGE.ACCOUNT(ACCOUNTNUMBER)
       );
```

Example: C-2   SQL stored procedure OPENBROKERAGEACCOUNT

```
CREATE PROCEDURE BROKERAGE.OPENBROKERAGEACCOUNT(
          IN P_ACCOUNTTYPE CHAR(1), IN P_DATEOPENED DATE, IN P_CUSTOMERID CHAR(10),
          OUT P_ACCOUNTNUMBER VARCHAR(15))
          LANGUAGE SQL
BEGIN
   SET P_ACCOUNTNUMBER = 'BA' || CHAR(NEXTVAL FOR BROKERAGE.ACCOUNTSEQ );
   INSERT INTO BROKERAGE.ACCOUNT( ACCOUNTNUMBER, ACCOUNTTYPE, DATEOPENED, BALANCE, CUSTOMERFK)
      VALUES (P_ACCOUNTNUMBER, P_ACCOUNTTYPE, P_DATEOPENED, 0, P_CUSTOMERID);
END@
```

Example: C-3   SQL stored procedure ADDCUSTOMER

```
CREATE PROCEDURE BROKERAGE.ADDCUSTOMER(
                          IN NAME VARCHAR(20),
                          IN SSNUMB CHAR(11),
                          IN DOB DATE,
                          IN CUSTRATING CHAR(1),
                          IN TELEPHONE CHAR(10),  OUT P_CUSTID VARCHAR(10))
LANGUAGE SQL
BEGIN
   SET P_CUSTID = 'B' || CHAR(NEXTVAL FOR BROKERAGE.CUSTOMERSEQ);
   INSERT INTO BROKERAGE.CUSTOMER(CUSTID,NAME, SSNUMB, DOB, CUSTRATING,TELEPHONE) VALUES (P_CUSTID, NAME, SSNUMB, DOB,
CUSTRATING, TELEPHONE);
END@
```

Example: C-4   SQL stored procedure PLACETRADE

```
CREATE PROCEDURE BROKERAGE.PLACETRADE( IN P_SYMBOL VARCHAR(10), IN P_QUANTITY INTEGER,
                        IN P_TYPEOFORDER CHARACTER(1), IN P_ORDERDATE DATE, IN P_ACCOUNTNUM CHAR(15),
                        OUT OrderNumber SMALLINT)
LANGUAGE SQL
BEGIN
   SET ORDERNUMBER = NEXTVAL FOR BROKERAGE.ORDERSEQ;
   INSERT INTO BROKERAGE.ORDERS( ORDERNUMB, SYMBOL, QUANTITY, TYPEOFORDER, ORDERDATE, FILLEDON, ACCOUNTFK)
      VALUES (ORDERNUMBER, P_SYMBOL, P_QUANTITY, P_TYPEOFORDER, P_ORDERDATE, P_ORDERDATE, P_ACCOUNTNUM);
END@
```

Example: C-5   Java system stored procedure AddAddress

```
package brokerage;

import java.sql.*;                    // JDBC classes

public class AddAddress
{
    public static void addAddress (String street, String city, String state, String zipcode,String custid)
                                    throws SQLException, Exception
    {
        // Get connection to the database
        Connection con = DriverManager.getConnection("jdbc:default:connection");
        PreparedStatement stmt = null;

        String sql;

        sql = "INSERT INTO BROKERAGE.ADDRESS (STREET, CITY, STATE, ZIPCODE, CUSTOMERFK)"
            + "    VALUES (?, ?, ?, ?, ?)";
        stmt = con.prepareStatement( sql );
        stmt.setString(1, street);
        stmt.setString(2, city);
        stmt.setString(3, state);
        stmt.setString(4, zipcode);
        stmt.setString(5, custid);

        stmt.execute();
        stmt.close();
        con.close();
    }
}
```

Example: C-6   Java system stored procedure UpdateCustomer

```
package administrator;

import java.sql.*;                    // JDBC classes

public class UpdateCustomer
{
    public static void updateCustomer (String custid, String name, String ssnumb, Date dob, String custRating,
                                       String telephone  ) throws SQLException, Exception
    {
        // Get connection to the database
        Connection con = DriverManager.getConnection("jdbc:default:connection");
        PreparedStatement stmt = null;
        String sql;

        sql = "UPDATE BROKERAGE.CUSTOMER"
            + "    SET NAME = ?, SSNUMB = ?, DOB = ?,"
            + "        CUSTRATING = ?, TELEPHONE = ?"
            + "    WHERE CUSTID = ?";
        stmt = con.prepareStatement( sql );
        stmt.setString(6, custid);
        stmt.setString(1, name);
        stmt.setString(2, ssnumb);
        stmt.setDate(3,dob);
        stmt.setString(4, custRating);
        stmt.setString(5, telephone);

        stmt.execute();
        stmt.close();
        con.close();
    }
}
```

Example: C-7   Java system stored procedure UpdateAddress

```
package brokerage;

import java.sql.*;                    // JDBC classes

public class UpdateAddress
{
    public static void updateAddress (String custid, String street, String city, String state, String zipcode )
                                      throws SQLException, Exception
    {
        // Get connection to the database
        Connection con = DriverManager.getConnection("jdbc:default:connection");
        PreparedStatement stmt = null;
        String sql;

        sql = "UPDATE BROKERAGE.ADDRESS"
            + "    SET ZIPCODE = ?, STATE = ?,"
            + "        CITY = ?, STREET = ?"
            + "    WHERE CUSTOMERFK = ?";
        stmt = con.prepareStatement( sql );
        stmt.setString(4, street);
        stmt.setString(3, city);
        stmt.setString(2, state);
        stmt.setString(1, zipcode);
        stmt.setString(5, custid);

        stmt.execute();
    }
}
```

Example: C-8   Java system stored procedure UpdateAccount

```
package brokerage;

import java.sql.*;                    // JDBC classes
import java.math.*;
public class UpdateAccount
{
    public static void updateAccount (String accountNumber, String accountType, Date dateOpened, BigDecimal balance )
                                      throws SQLException, Exception
    {
        // Get connection to the database
        Connection con = DriverManager.getConnection("jdbc:default:connection");
        PreparedStatement stmt = null;
        String sql;

        sql = "UPDATE BROKERAGE.ACCOUNT"
            + "    SET BALANCE = ?, DATEOPENED = ?,"
            + "        ACCOUNTTYPE = ?"
            + "    WHERE ACCOUNTNUMBER = ?";
        stmt = con.prepareStatement( sql );
        stmt.setDate(2, dateOpened);
        stmt.setBigDecimal(1, balance);
        stmt.setString(4, accountNumber);
        stmt.setString(3, accountType);

        stmt.execute();
        stmt.close();
        con.close();
    }
}
```

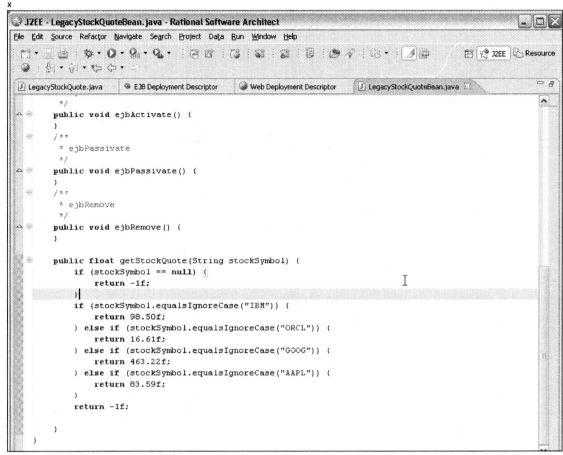

Figure C-2   LegacyQuoteStockService 1/7

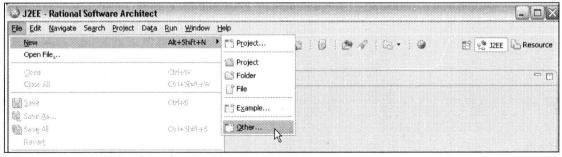

Figure C-3   LegacyQuoteStockService 2/7

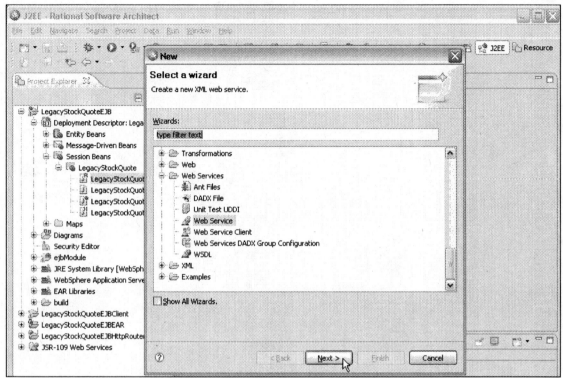

Figure C-4   LegacyQuoteStockService 3/7

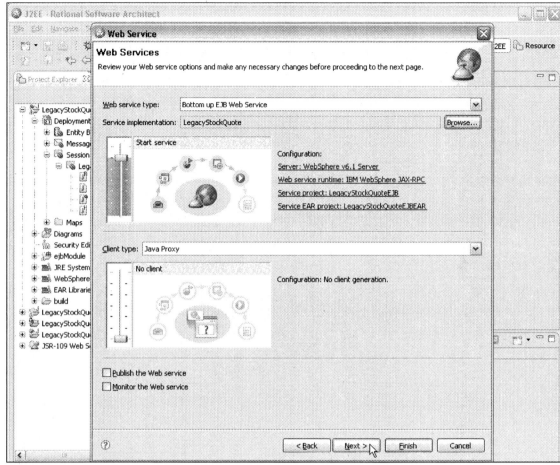

Figure C-5   LegacyQuoteStockService 4/7

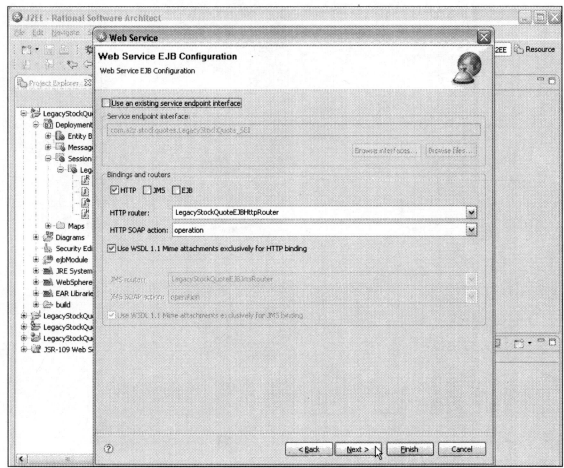

Figure C-6   LegacyQuoteStockService 5/7

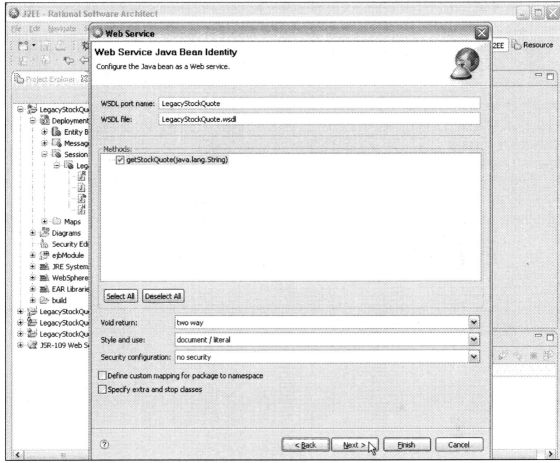

Figure C-7   LegacyQuoteStockService 6/7

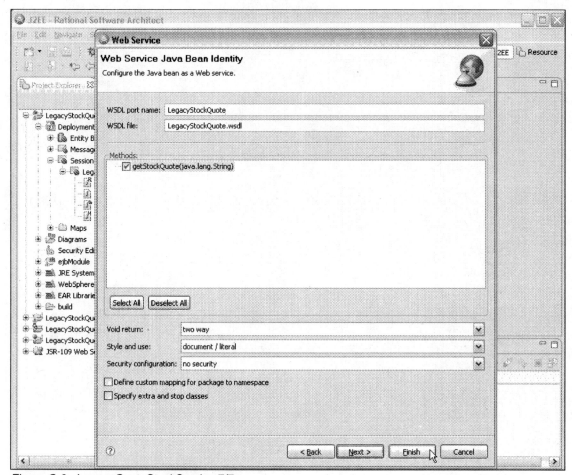

Figure C-8   LegacyQuoteStockService 7/7

C.1.2 Credit Card system tables and scripts

Figure C-9 shows the DB2 tables and their relationships, while Example C-9 shows the DDL to create these tables. We have not included the DDL of the creation of the various indexes on these tables.

The following DB2 stored procedures are shown here:

► SQL stored procedure ADDCUSTOMER corresponding to the AddNewCustomer federated stored procedure is shown in Example C-10 on page 488.

- ► SQL stored procedure ADDNEWCARD corresponding to the AddNewCardDetails federated stored procedure is shown in Example C-11 on page 488.
- ► Java stored procedure UpdateCustomer corresponding to the UpdateCustomer federated stored procedure is shown in Example C-12 on page 489.
- ► Java stored procedure UpdateCardDetails corresponding to the UpdateCardDetails federated stored procedure is shown in Example C-13 on page 489.

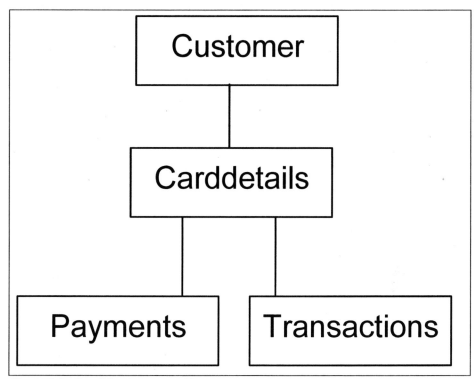

Figure C-9   CreditCard system tables

Example: C-9   CreditCard system DDL (indexes not shown)

```
CREATE TABLE CCA.CUSTOMER
    (
    CUSTID CHAR (10) NOT NULL PRIMARY KEY,
    NAME VARCHAR (35),
    STREET VARCHAR (30),
    CITY VARCHAR (25),
    STATE CHAR(2),
    ZIPCODE CHAR(10),
    SSNUMB CHAR(11),
    DOB DATE,
    TELEPHONE CHAR(10)
```

```
    );
CREATE TABLE CCA.CARDDETAILS
    (
    CARDNUMBER CHAR(16)NOT NULL PRIMARY KEY,
    CARDTYPE CHAR(2),
    DATEGIVEN DATE,
    VALIDUPTODATE DATE,
    LIMIT DECIMAL(9,2),
    OUTSTANDINGBALANCE DECIMAL(9,2),
    CUSTOMERFK CHAR(10) REFERENCES CUSTOMER
    );

CREATE TABLE CCA.TRANSACTIONS
    (
    TYP CHAR(2),
    AMOUNT DECIMAL(7,2),
    TRANDATE DATE,
    VENDOR CHAR (16),
    CARDDETAILSFK CHAR (16) REFERENCES CARDDETAILS
    );

CREATE TABLE CCA.PAYMENTS
    (
    AMOUNT DECIMAL(7,2),
    TRANDATE DATE,
    METHODOFPAY CHAR(2),
    CARDDETAILSFK CHAR (16) REFERENCES CARDDETAILS
    );
```

Example: C-10   SQL stored procedure ADDCUSTOMER

```
CREATE PROCEDURE CCA.ADDCUSTOMER(
                            IN NAME VARCHAR(35),
                            IN STREET VARCHAR(30),
                            IN CITY VARCHAR(25),
                            IN STATE CHAR(2),
                            IN ZIPCODE CHAR(10),
                            IN SSNUMB CHAR(11),
                            IN DOB DATE,
                            IN TELEPHONE CHAR(10), OUT P_CUSTID VARCHAR(10))
LANGUAGE SQL
BEGIN
    SET P_CUSTID = 'C' || CHAR(NEXTVAL FOR CCA.CUSTOMERSEQ);
    INSERT INTO CCA.CUSTOMER (CUSTID,NAME, STREET, CITY, STATE, ZIPCODE,SSNUMB, DOB, TELEPHONE) VALUES (P_CUSTID, NAME,
STREET, CITY,STATE,ZIPCODE,SSNUMB,DOB,TELEPHONE);
END@
```

Example: C-11   SQL stored procedure ADDNEWCARD

```
CREATE PROCEDURE CCA.ADDNEWCARD(
                            IN CUSTID VARCHAR(10),
                            IN CARDTYPE VARCHAR(2),
                            IN DATE_GIVEN DATE,
                            IN VALID_UPTO DATE,
                            IN LMT DECIMAL(9,2),
                            IN OB DECIMAL(9,2),
                            OUT CARD_NUMBER VARCHAR(16))
LANGUAGE SQL
BEGIN
    SET CARD_NUMBER = CHAR(NEXTVAL FOR CCA.CARDNUMBERSEQ);
    INSERT INTO CCA.CARDDETAILS (CARDNUMBER, CARDTYPE, DATEGIVEN, VALIDUPTODATE, LIMIT, OUTSTANDINGBALANCE,CUSTOMERFK)
                        VALUES (CARD_NUMBER , CARDTYPE , DATE_GIVEN , VALID_UPTO , LMT , OB , CUSTID);
END@
```

Example: C-12   Java stored procedure UpdateCustomer

```
package creditcard;

import java.sql.*;                    // JDBC classes

public class UpdateCustomer
{
    public static void updateCustomer ( String custid, String name, String street, String city, Strihng state,
                          String zipcode, String ssnumb,java.sql.Date dob, String telephone) throws SQLException, Exception
    {
        // Get connection to the database
        Connection con = DriverManager.getConnection("jdbc:default:connection");
        PreparedStatement stmt = null;
        String sql;

        sql = "UPDATE CCA.CUSTOMER"
            + "    SET NAME = ?, STREET = ?, CITY = ?, STATE = ?, ZIPCODE = ?,"
            + "        SSNUMB = ?, DOB = ?, TELEPHONE = ?"
            + "    WHERE CUSTID = ?";
        stmt = con.prepareStatement( sql );
        stmt.setString(1, name);
        stmt.setString(2, street);
        stmt.setString(3, city);
        stmt.setString(4, state);
        stmt.setString(5, zipcode);
        stmt.setString(6, ssnumb);
        stmt.setDate(7, dob);
        stmt.setString(8, telephone);
        stmt.setString(9, custid);
        stmt.execute();
        stmt.close();
        con.close();
    }
}
```

Example: C-13   Java stored procedure UpdateCardDetails

```
package creditcard;

import java.sql.*;                    // JDBC classes

public class UpdateCardDetails
{
    public static void updateCardDetails ( String cardNumber, String cardType, java.sql.Date dateGiven,
                          java.sql.Date validUpToDate, java.math.BigDecimal limit, java.math.BigDecimal outstandingBalance)
                          throws SQLException, Exception
    {
        // Get connection to the database
        Connection con = DriverManager.getConnection("jdbc:default:connection");
        PreparedStatement stmt = null;
        String sql;

        sql = "UPDATE CCA.CARDDETAILS"
            + "    SET CARDTYPE = ?, DATEGIVEN = ?, VALIDUPTODATE = ?, LIMIT = ?,"
            + "        OUTSTANDINGBALANCE = ?"
            + "    WHERE CARDNUMBER = ?";
        stmt = con.prepareStatement( sql );
        stmt.setString(1, cardType);
        stmt.setDate(2, dateGiven);
        stmt.setDate(3, validUpToDate);
        stmt.setBigDecimal(4, limit);
        stmt.setBigDecimal(5, outstandingBalance);
        stmt.setString(6, cardNumber);
        stmt.execute();
        stmt.close();
```

```
        con.close();
    }
}
```

C.1.3 Operation Data Store tables and scripts

Figure C-10 shows the DB2 tables and their relationships, while Example C-14
shows the DDL to create these tables. We have not included the DDL of the
creation of the various indexes on these tables.

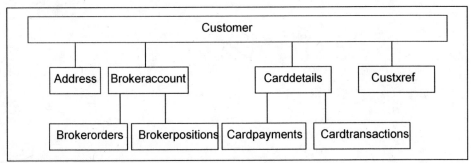

Figure C-10   Operational Data Store tables

Example: C-14   Operational Data Store DDL (indexes not shown here)

```
CREATE TABLE ODS.CUSTXREF
    (
    CUSTOMERID SMALLINT NOT NULL PRIMARY KEY,
    BROKCUSTID CHAR(10),
    CCCUSTID CHAR(10)
    );

CREATE TABLE ODS.CUSTOMER
    (
    CUSTOMERID SMALLINT NOT NULL PRIMARY KEY,
    NAME VARCHAR (50),
    SSNUMBER CHAR(11),
    DOB DATE,
    CUSTRATING CHAR(1),
    TELEPHONE CHAR(10),
    BROKERASSETS DECIMAL (11,2),
    CARDLIABILITIES DECIMAL(9,2)
    );

CREATE TABLE ODS.ADDRESS
    (
    STREET VARCHAR(50),
    CITY VARCHAR (25),
    STATE CHAR(2),
    ZIPCODE CHAR(10),
    CUSTOMERFK SMALLINT REFERENCES CUSTXREF
    );

CREATE TABLE ODS.BROKERACCOUNT
    (
    ACCOUNTNUMBER CHAR(15) NOT NULL PRIMARY KEY,
    ACCOUNTTYPE CHAR(1),
    DATEOPENED DATE,
```

```
            BALANCE DECIMAL(11,2),
            BROKERCUSTID CHAR(10),
            CUSTOMERFK SMALLINT REFERENCES CUSTOMER
            );

CREATE TABLE ODS.BROKERORDERS
            (
            ORDERNUMB SMALLINT,
            SYMBOL CHAR(6),
            QUANTITY SMALLINT,
            TYPEOFORDER CHAR(1),
            ORDERDATE DATE,
            FILLEDON DATE,
            BROKERACCOUNTFK CHAR(15) REFERENCES BROKERACCOUNT
            );

CREATE TABLE ODS.BROKERPOSITIONS
            (
            SYMBOL CHAR(6),
            QUANTITY SMALLINT,
            PURCHASEPRICE DEC(9,2),
            PURCHASEDATE DATE,
            CURRENTPRICE DEC(9,2),
            BROKERACCOUNTFK CHAR(15) REFERENCES BROKERACCOUNT
            );

CREATE TABLE ODS.CARDDETAILS
            (
            CARDNUMBER CHAR(16) NOT NULL PRIMARY KEY,
            CARDTYPE CHAR(2),
            DATEGIVEN DATE,
            VALIDUPTODATE DATE,
            LIMIT DECIMAL(9,2),
            OUSTANDINGBALANCE DECIMAL(9,2),
            CARDCUSTID CHAR(12),
            CUSTOMERFK SMALLINT REFERENCES CUSTOMER
            );

CREATE TABLE ODS.CARDTRANSACTIONS
            (
            TYPE CHAR(2),
            AMOUNT DECIMAL(7,2),
            TRANDATE DATE,
            VENDOR CHAR(16),
            CARDDETAILSFK CHAR(16) REFERENCES CARDDETAILS
            );

CREATE TABLE ODS.CARDPAYMENTS
            (
            AMOUNT DECIMAL(7,2),
            TRANDATE DATE,
            METHODOFPAY CHAR(2),
            CARDDETAILSFK  CHAR(16) REFERENCES CARDDETAILS
            );
```

C.1.4 Enterprise Data Warehouse tables and scripts

Figure C-11 show the DB2 tables and their relationships, while Example C-15 shows the DDL to create these tables. We have not included the DDL of the creation of the various indexes on these tables.

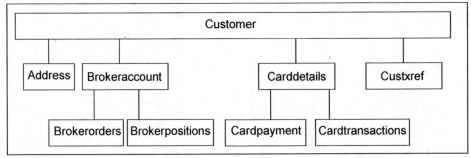

Figure C-11   Enterprise Data Warehouse tables

Example: C-15   Enterprise Data Warehouse DDL (indexes not shown here)

```
CREATE TABLE EDW.CUSTOMER
    (
    CUSTOMERID SMALLINT NOT NULL PRIMARY KEY,
    NAME VARCHAR(50),
    BROKERASSETS DECIMAL(11,2),
    CARDLIABILITIES DECIMAL(11,2)
    );

CREATE TABLE EDW.ADDRESS
    (
    STREET VARCHAR(50),
    CITY VARCHAR (25),
    STATE CHAR(2),
    ZIPCODE CHAR(10),
    CUSTOMERFK SMALLINT REFERENCES CUSTOMER
    );

CREATE TABLE EDW.BROKERACCOUNT
    (
    ACCOUNTNUMBER CHAR(15) NOT NULL PRIMARY KEY,
    ACCOUNTTYPE CHAR(1),
    DATEOPENED DATE,
    BALANCE DECIMAL(11,2),
    BROKERCUSTID CHAR(10),
    CUSTOMERFK SMALLINT REFERENCES CUSTOMER
    );

CREATE TABLE EDW.CUSTXREF
    (
    CUSTOMERID SMALLINT NOT NULL PRIMARY KEY,
    BROKCUSTID CHAR(10),
    CCCUSTID CHAR(1)
    );

CREATE TABLE EDW.BROKERORDERS
    (
    ORDERNUMB SMALLINT,
    SYMBOL CHAR(6),
    QUANTITY SMALLINT,
    TYPEOFORDER CHAR(1),
    ORDERDATE DATE,
    FILLEDON DATE,
    BROKERACCOUNTFK CHAR(15) REFERENCES BROKERACCOUNT
    );

CREATE TABLE EDW.BROKERPOSITIONS
    (
```

```
    SYMBOL CHAR(6),
    QUANTITY SMALLINT,
    PURCHASEPRICE DECIMAL(9,2),
    PURCHASEDATE DATE,
    CURRENTPRICE DECIMAL(9,2),
    BROKERACCOUNTFK CHAR(15) REFERENCES BROKERACCOUNT
    );

CREATE TABLE EDW.CARDDETAILS
    (
    CARDNUMBER CHAR(16) NOT NULL PRIMARY KEY,
    CARDTYPE CHAR(2),
    DATEGIVER DATE,
    VALIDUPTODATE DATE,
    LIMIT DECIMAL(9,2),
    OUSTANDINGBALANCE DECIMAL(9,2),
    CARDCUSTID CHAR(10),
    CUSTOMERFK SMALLINT REFERENCES CUSTOMER
    );

CREATE TABLE EDW.CARDTRANSACTIONS
    (
    TYPE CHAR(2),
    AMOUNT DECIMAL(7,2),
    TRANDATE DATE,
    VENDOR CHAR(16),
    CARDDETAILSFK CHAR(16) REFERENCES CARDDETAILS
    );

CREATE TABLE EDW.CARDPAYMENT
    (
    AMOUNT DECIMAL(7,2),
    TRANDATE DATE,
    METHODOFPAY CHAR(2),
    CARDDETAILSFK CHAR(16) REFERENCES CARDDETAILS
    );
```

C.2 Self service solution code

A2Z Financial Services' self service solution required the development of
DataStage jobs, QualityStage jobs, federated queries, stored procedures,
federated stored procedures, WebSphere Integration Developer services, JSPs
and portlets using Rational Application Developer, and .NET applications using
Microsoft Visual Studio .NET Professional Edition.

The DataStage jobs, QualityStage jobs, federated queries, stored procedures,
federated stored procedures developed are described in "Step 2: Identify and
create "core" information management processes" on page 44.

The client applications involving JSPs and portlets using Rational Application
Developer, and .NET applications using Microsoft Visual Studio .NET
Professional Edition are partially described in "Step 5: Create "services"
consumers" on page 307.

All this developed code can be downloaded from the IBM Redbooks Web site:

```
ftp://www.redbooks.ibm.com/redbooks/SG247402
```

Additional material

This Redbooks publication refers to additional material that can be downloaded from the Internet as described below.

Locating the Web material

The Web material associated with this Redbooks publication is available in softcopy on the Internet from the IBM Redbooks Web server. Point your Web browser at:

`ftp://www.redbooks.ibm.com/redbooks/SG247402`

Alternatively, you can go to the IBM Redbooks Web site at:

`ibm.com/redbooks`

Select the **Additional materials** and open the directory that corresponds with the Redbooks publication form number, SG24-7402.

Using the Web material

The additional Web material that accompanies this Redbooks publication includes the following files (all code samples on a Windows operating system):

File name	Hard disk space required
StockQuoteProjects.zip	26 KB
RADPortlets.zip	12 MB
MQClient.zip	4 KB
AllWIDProjects.zip	517 KB
A2ZNET_and_RAD_client.zip	2 MB

How to use the Web material

Create a subdirectory (folder) on your workstation, and unzip the contents of the Web material zip file into this folder.

Related publications

The publications listed in this section are considered particularly suitable for a more detailed discussion of the topics covered in this Redbooks publication.

IBM Redbooks

For information about ordering these publications, see "How to get IBM Redbooks" on page 498. Note that some of the documents referenced here may be available in softcopy only.

- ► *Technical Overview of WebSphere Process Server and WebSphere Integration Developer*, REDP-4041

- ► *Patterns: Service-Oriented Architecture and Web Services*, SG24-6303

Other publications

These publications are also relevant as further information sources:

- ► *IBM Information Server - Delivering information you can trust*, IBM United States Announcement 206-308 dated December 12, 2006

- ► *IBM Information Server Version 8.0 Planning, Installation, and Configuration Guide*, GC19-1048

- ► *IBM Information Server Version 8.0 Information Server Introduction*, SC19-1049

- ► *IBM Information Server Version 8.0 Reporting Guide*, SC19-1162

- ► *IBM Information Server Quick Start Guide*

- ► *WebSphere Integration Developer Version 6.0.1 Technical product overview*, SC10-4208-03

- ► *IBM WebSphere Developer Technical Journal: A guided tour of WebSphere Integration Developer -- Part 1*

- ► *Service-Oriented Architecture, IBM Systems Journal, Vol. 44, No. 4, 2005*, G321-0159-00

- ► Craig Larman, *Applying UML and Patterns: An Introduction to Object-Oriented Analysis and Design and the Unified Process*, 2nd Ed., Prentice Hall, 2001

- Ivar Jacobson, Magnus Christerson, Patrik Jonsson, Gunnar Overgaard, *Object-Oriented Software Engineering: A Use Case Driven Approach*, Addison-Wesley, 1992

- Paul Allen, *Component-Based Development for Enterprise Systems*, *Cambridge University Press*, 1998

Online resources

These Web sites are also relevant as further information sources:

- IBM SOA Web site:

  `http://www-306.ibm.com/software/solutions/soa/`

- IBM Information Server information center:

  `http://publib.boulder.ibm.com/infocenter/iisinfsv/v8r0/index.jsp`

- WebSphere Process Server Infocenter:

  `http://www.ibm.com/software/integration/wps/library/infocenter/`

- The following IBM developerWorks articles:

  - *First look at the WS-I Basic Profile 1.0*, available at:

    `http://www.ibm.com/developerworks/webservices/library/ws-basicprof.html`

  - *First look at the WS-I Usage Scenarios*, available at:

    `http://www.ibm.com/developerworks/webservices/library/ws-iuse/`

  - *Preview of WS-I sample application*, available at:

    `http://www.ibm.com/developerworks/webservices/library/ws-wsisamp/`

  - *Using Service-Oriented Architecture and Component-Based Development to Build Web Service Applications*, available at:

    `http://www.ibm.com/developerworks/rational/library/510.html`

- W3C Working Group Note, *Web Services Architecture*, available at:

  `http://www.w3.org/TR/2004/NOTE-ws-arch-20040211/`

How to get IBM Redbooks

You can search for, view, or download Redbooks, Redpapers, Hints and Tips, draft publications and Additional materials, as well as order hardcopy Redbooks or CD-ROMs, at this Web site:

`ibm.com/redbooks`

Help from IBM

IBM Support and downloads

ibm.com/support

IBM Global Services

ibm.com/services

Index

95
Thick client   408
Thin Client with create library (.dll)   415
topologies   20
Transaction   444
Transform your data into information and move   15
Transport   443

U
UDDI   24
UML   441
Understand your data   14
Unified metadata   17
Unified parallel processing   16
Unified service deployment   13
Unified user interface   6
UNIX®   10

V
visual basic client application   408

W
W3C   450
Web Admin interface   6
Web service export binding   471
Web service import binding   471
Web services
    Architecture   449
    Basic   453
    Service-oriented architecture   452
Web Services Description Language   13
Web Services Gateway   456
WebSphere Application Server   456
WebSphere Business Glossary   4, 11–12
WebSphere DataStage   3, 15, 21
WebSphere DataStage MVS™ Edition   4
WebSphere Federation Server   3
WebSphere Information Analyzer   4, 7, 15
WebSphere Information Services Director   3, 14, 39
WebSphere Integration Developer overview   460
WebSphere MetaBrokers   11–12
WebSphere Metadata Server   4, 11–12
WebSphere MQ   456
WebSphere Portal   456
WebSphere Process Server   34, 147, 205, 470
WebSphere QualityStage   3, 15, 21
WebSphere Service Registry and Repository   23

whitepaper   11, 35
WID   147, 460
WID generated service   415
WISD   27, 39
Workflow   456
Write "binding" code   206
WSDL   13, 96, 461
WSDL interface   466
WSDL Port Type   157
WSDL port type   464, 467
WSRR   23, 138, 226

X
XSD files   470